A Garland Series

British Philosophers and Theologians of the 17th & 18th Centuries

A Collection of 101 Volumes

Edited by
René Wellek

Thomas Woolston

SIX DISCOURSES
ON THE MIRACLES
OF OUR SAVIOUR
and
DEFENCES
OF HIS DISCOURSES
1727–1730

Garland Publishing, Inc., New York & London

1979

Bibliographical note:

The facsimile of the *First Discourse* has been made from
a copy in the Sterling Library of Yale University
except for pp. 25–32, which are from a copy in
the Bodleian Library of Oxford University;
all other facsimiles are from copies in
the Beinecke Library of Yale University.

The volumes in this series have been printed on
acid-free, 250-year-life paper.

Library of Congress Cataloging in Publication Data

Woolston, Thomas, 1670-1733.
    Six discourses on the miracles of Our Saviour
and defences of his discourses.

    (British philosophers and theologians of the
17th and 18th centuries)
    Reprint of works printed 1727-1730 for the
author, London.
    CONTENTS: A discourse on the miracles of Our
Saviour. --A second discourse on the miracles of
Our Saviour. --A third discourse on the miracles
of Our Saviour. (etc.)
    1. Jesus Christ--Miracles--Early works to 1800--
Addresses, essays, lectures. 2. Smalbroke, Richard,
Bp. of Lichfield and Coventry, 1672-1749--Addresses,
essays, lectures. 3. Gibson, Edmund, Bp. of London,
1669-1748--Addresses, essays, lectures. I. Title.
II. Series.
BT364.W68 1979   232.9'5   75-11268
ISBN 0-8240-1778-1

Printed in the United States of America

A
DISCOURSE
ON THE
MIRACLES
OF OUR
SAVIOUR,

In VIEW of the Present
Controverſy between INFIDELS
and APOSTATES.

——*Noſtrum eſt tantas componere Lites.*

The Fifth Edition.

By THO. WOOLSTON, B. D. ſometime
Fellow of *Sidney-College* in *Cambridge.*

LONDON:
Printed for the Author, and Sold by him
next door to the *Star,* in *Aldermanbury,*
and by the Bookſellers of *London,* and
Weſtminſter, 1728.
[Price One Shilling.]

TO THE

Right Reverend Father in God

EDMUND,

Lord BISHOP of *London*.

MY LORD,

 PON no other View do I make a Dedication of this Discourse to your *Lordship*, then to submit it to your acute Judgment, expecting soon to hear of your Approbation or Dislike of it. If it so happen, that you highly approve of it, I beg of you to be sparing of your Commendations, least I should be puff'd up with them.

A 2

In

In my *Moderator*, some Expreſſions dropt from my Pen about the Miracles of our Saviour, which, for want of Illuſtration then, gave your *Lordſhip* ſome Offence, and brought upon me more Trouble : But, having now fully and clearly explain'd my ſelf out of the Fathers, I hope you ll be reconciled to me ; and as you are a Lover of Truth, will, againſt Intereſt and Prejudice, yield to the Force of it.

Whether your Proſecution of me, for the *Moderator*, was juſt and reaſonable, I'll not diſpute here, having already expoſtulated that Matter with you in ſeveral Letters, to which you would not condeſcend to give me any Anſwer. For what Reaſon you was ſilent, is beſt known to your ſelf. But, in my own Vindication, I hope, I may publiſh without Offence, that your taking me for an *Infidel*, was ſuch a Miſtake,

take, as I thought no *Scholar* could have made ; and the Injury done to my Reputation and low Fortunes, by the Profecution, fo confiderable, that the leaft I expected from your *Lordſhip*, was a courteous Excuſe, if not an ample Compenſation, for it.

As to the Expediency of profecuting *Infidels* for their Writings (in whoſe Cauſe I am the fartheſt of any Man from being engaged) I will here ſay nothing. The Argument, *pro* and *con*, has already, by one or other, been copiouſly handled. And I don't know but I might be, with your *Lordſhip*, on the perſecuting ſide of the Queſtion ; but that it looks as if a Man was diſtruſtful of the Truth of Chriſtianity, and conſcious of his own Inability to defend it ; or he would leave that *good Cauſe* to God himſelf, and the Sword of the Spirit,

without

without calling upon the *Civil Magistrate* for his Aid and Assistance.

That scurvy *Writer* of the *Scheme of literal Prophecy*, &c. which your *Lordship* must have heard of, would insinuate, that they are only atheistical Priests, who, for fear of their Interests in the Church, set Persecutions on foot : But after your *Lordship* has publish'd a strenuous Defence of Christianity to the Purpose of our present Controversy, I'll have no such Suspicions of you.

Your *Lordship*'s persecuting (or, if you will, prosecuting) Humour, is reputedly all pure Zeal for God's Glory ; and, with all my Heart, let it be so accounted, whether it be according to Knowledge or not. Against Popery and Infidelity you are all Ardency ! Who does not commend you ? Who can question

the

the Sincerity of the Zeal of a Proteftant *Bifhop*, and of a Proteftant
Clergy, when they perfecute the
Enemies of their Church, that con-
fiders their own Steadinefs to Principles againft Intereft, under all
Changes, fince the Reformation ;
and their Abhorrence of Extortion
upon the People, for the Duties of
their Function, in and about this
City. Such Honefty and Conftancy
in their Profeffion, is a Proof of the
Integrity of their Hearts, or I know
not where to find one.

But that your *Lordfhip*'s Zeal for
Religion is very remarkable and
fuccefsful, I could prove by many
Inftances ; one is, *that* of your rout-
ing a turbulent Sect of *Peripateticks*
out of St. *Paul*'s Cathedral ; and if
you could as effectually clear *Chrift*'s
Church of *Infidels*, what a glorious
Bifhop would you be !

And

And what Pity is it, that *Infidels* likewife are not to be quell'd with your Threats and Terrors! which (without the Weapons of fharp Reafonings, and thumping Arguments, that others are for the Ufe of) would tranfmit your Fame to Pofterity, for a notable Champion for Chriftianity, as certainly as, that your judicious Profecution of the *Moderator* for Infidelity is here remember'd by,

My LORD,

The *Admirer* of

Your Zeal

London,
April 17,
1727.

Wifdom and

Conduct,

Thomas Woolfton.

A

DISCOURSE

ON THE

MIRACLES

OF OUR

SAVIOUR, &c.

 F ever there was an useful
Controversy started, or re-
vived in this Age of the
Church, it is *this* about
the *Messiahship* of the holy
Jesus, which the *Discourse
of the Grounds*, &c. has of late rais'd.
I believe this Controversy will end in
the absolute Demonstration of Jesus's
Messiahship from Prophecy, which is
the only way to prove him to be the

B   *Messiah*,

Messiah, that great Prophet expected by the *Jews*, and promised under the Old Testament. And tho this way of Proof from Prophecy seems to labour under many Difficulties at present; and tho some *Writers* against the *Grounds*, being distressed with those Difficulties, are for seeking Refuge in the Miracles of our Saviour; yet we must persist in it, till what I have no doubt of, his *Messiahship* shall be clearly made out by it.

And the way in Prophesy that I would take for the Proof of *Jesus's Messiahship*, should be by an allegorical Interpretation, and Application of the Law and the Prophets to him; the very same way, that all the Fathers of the Church have gone in; and the very same way, in which all the ancient *Jews* say their *Messiah* was to fulfil the Law and the Prophets : But this way does not please our ecclesiastical *Writers* in this Controversy, neither will they at present give any Ear to it.

The Way in Prophecy that they are for taking, is by a literal Interpretation and Application of some Prophecies of the Old Testament to our *Jesus*, but they are hitherto unsuccessful in this Way. The Authors of the *Grounds* and of the *Scheme*, grievously perplex them with their Objections against this way of Proof, so far as,

being

being senſible, I ſay, of almoſt inſuperable Difficulties in it, they are flying apace to the Miracles of our Saviour, as to their ſole and grand Refuge.

But to ſhow that there's no Sanctuary for them in the Miracles of our Saviour, I write this Diſcourſe : And this I do, not for the Service of Infidelity, which has no Place in my Heart, but for the Honour of the Holy *Jeſus*, and to reduce the *Clergy* to the good old way of interpreting Prophecies, which the Church has unhappily apoſtatis'd from, and which, upon the Teſtimony of the Fathers, will, one Day, be the Converſion of *Jews* and *Gentiles*.

For this Opinion, that there is no Sanctuary in the Miracles of our Saviour, I chanc'd to ſay in the *Moderator*, (1) *That Jeſus's Miracles, as they are now-a-days underſtood, make nothing for his Authority and Meſſiahſhip.* And again, (2) *That I believe, upon good Authority, ſome of the Miracles of Jeſus, as recorded by the Evangeliſts, were never wrought, but are only related as prophetical and parabolical Narratives of what will be myſteriouſly and more wonderfully done by him :* Which Expreſſions gave Offence to ſome of our *Clergy*, and brought upon me their

(1) Page 44.　　　(2) Page 53.

Indig-

Indignation and Difpleafure. I fee no Reafon to depart from the faid Expreffions, or fo much as to palliate and foften them, much lefs to retract them ; but in Maintenance of my Opinion, to the Honour of our *Meffiah*, and the Defence of Chriftianity, I write this Treatife on Jefus's Miracles, and take this Method following.

I. I will fhow, that the Miracles of healing all manner of bodily Difeafes, which *Jefus* was juftly famed for, are none of the proper Miracles of the *Meffiah*, neither are they fo much as a good Proof of his Divine Authority to found a Religion.

II. That the literal Hiftory of many of the Miracles of Jefus, as recorded by the Evangelifts, does imply Abfurdities, Improbabilities, and Incredibilities, confequently they, either in whole or in part, were never wrought, as they are commonly believed now-a-days, but are only related as prophetical and parabolical Narratives of what would be myfterioufly and more wonderfully done by him.

III. I fhall confider what Jefus means, when he appeals to his Miracles as to a Teftimony and Witnefs of his Divine Authority, and fhow, that he could not properly

perly and ultimately refer to thofe he then wrought in the *Flefh*, but to thofe myfti-cal ones, which he would do in the *Spirit* ; of which thofe wrought in the Flefh are but mere Types and Shadows.

In treating on thefe Heads, I fhall not confine my felf only to Reafon, but alfo to the exprefs Authority of the Fathers, thofe holy, venerable, and learned Preach-ers of the Gofpel in the firft Ages of the Church, who took our Religion from the Hands of the Apoftles, and of apoftolical Men, who dy'd, fome of them, and fuffer'd for the Doctrine they taught ; who pro-feffedly and confeffedly were endu'd with divine and extraordinary Gifts of the Spi-rit; who confequently can't be fuppofed to be Corrupters of Chriftianity, or Teach-ers of falfe Notions about the Miracles of our Saviour, or fo much as miftaken about the apoftolical and evangelical Senfe and Nature of them. I know not how it comes to pafs, but I am a profound Admirer, and an almoft implicit Believer of the Au-thority of the Fathers, whom I look upon as vaft Philofophers, very great Scholars, and moft orthodox Divines. Whatever they concurrently affert, I firmly believe. And tho they are, for the moft part, myf-terious Writers out of the Reach of the

Cepacities

Capacities of many, who flight them; yet I, who have had the Honour and Happiness of much of their Acquaintance, fancy my felf well apprifed of their Meanings. If at any time I read a Paffage in them which I don't prefently apprehend, I falute it with Veneration for all that, till my Underftanding is opened to receive the Senfe of it. If I meet with but a fingle Opinion in any one of them, I pay my Refpects to it; but where there is an Harmony and Agreement of Opinion amonft them, it is with me, and ought to be with all Chriftians, of fuch Weight, as to bear down all Prejudice, Oppofition, and Contradiction before it; or the Authority of no Man, whether ancient or modern, is to have any Regard paid to it; and of what ill Confequence to Religion fuch an utter Rejection of Authority will be, I need not fay.

This I thought fit to premife, concerning the Authority of the Fathers, to abate of the Prejudice beforehand, which fome may conceive againft the following Difcourfe about the Miracles of *Jefus*. I don't queftion, but fome may be ftartled at the foregoing Heads, as if, what is the fartheft of any thing from my Heart, the Service of Infidelity was in View; but craving the Temper and Patience of fuch Readers for
a while,

a while, and they shall find, that its no other than just Reasoning, clear Truth, and primitive Doctrine about *Jesus's* Miracles, that I advance : Or if it should so happen, that none besides my self should discern the Reasoning and Truth of the Argument; yet I hope it will not be thought a Crime to revive primitive Doctrine, which none will be able to deny it to be, whether they like it or not. If I err, I err upon Choice with the Fathers, of whose Faith I am. And if any are offended at what follows about the Miracles of *Christ*, let them turn their Displeasure and Indignation against the Fathers, for whose express or implicit Opinions I can be deserving of no Blame.

I am sorry for the Occasion of such a Preface against Offence, which the Apostacy of the Age, and its Unacquaintedness with the Fathers, has made necessary. So I enter upon the particular handling of the Heads foregoing. And,

I. I will show that the Miracles of healing all manner of bodily Diseases, which *Jesus* was justly famed for, are none of the proper Miracles of the Messiah, nor are they so much as a good Proof of *Jesus's* divine Authority to found and introduce a Religion into the World.

And

And to do this, let us confider, firft, in general, what was the Opinion of the Fathers about the Writings of the *Evangelifts*, in which the Life of *Chrift* is recorded. *Eucherius* fays, (3) *That the Scriptures of the New as well as Old Teftament, are to be interpreted in an allegorical Senfe.* And this his Opinion, is no other than the common one of the firft Ages of the Church, as might be proved by many the like Expreffions of other Fathers. As in fuch Expreffions, they do not except the Writings of the *Evangelifts* ; fo they muft include the Hiftory of *Chrift's* Miracles, which as well as other Parts of the Hiftory of his Life, is to be allegoriz'd for the fake of its true Meaning ; confequently the literal Story of Chrift's Miracles proves nothing.

But let's hear particularly their Opinion of the Actions and Miracles of our Saviour. *Origen* fays, that (4) *Whatfoever Jefus did in the Flefh, was but typical and fymbolical of what he would do in the*

(3) Univerfam porro Sacram Scripturam tam Novi quam Veteris Teftamenti ad allegoricum fenfum effe fumendam, admonet nos vel illud, Aperiam os meum in Parabolis. *In Prafat. ad Form. Spirit. Intell.*

(4) Si quidem Symbola quædam erant quæ tunc gerebantur eorum, quæ Jefu virtute femper perficiuntur. *In Mat.* C. xv.

Spirit ;

Spirit; and to our Purpofe, (5) that *the feveral bodily Difeafes which he healed, were no other than Figures of the fpiritual Infirmities of the Soul, that are to be cured by him.* St. *Hilary* is of the fame Mind with *Origen*, as any one may fee by the (6) Expreffions referr'd to, and his Commentary on St. *Matthew*. St. *Auguftin*, (7) and St. *John* (8) of *Jerufalem*, both fay, that the Works of *Jefus* import farther Myfteries; and with them, the reft of the Fathers agree, making the Miracles that *Jefus* did then, no more than the Shadow of fome more powerful and myftical Operations to be done by him, as I could fhow by more Citations out of them, if it was needful. But from the foregoing Citations out of the Fathers it is plain, in their Opinion, that our modern *Divines* are in the wrong of it, to lay much Strefs on any of the Operations of *Jefus*, which

(5) Omnis languor & omnis Infirmitas quam fanavit falvator tunc in Populo referuntur ad Infirmitates fpirituales Animarum, &c. *In* Mat. *C.* xvii.

(6) Chrifti Gefta aliud portendunt. *In* Mat. *C.* xii. Evangelicis geftis eft interior Senfus, *C.* xiv. Hæc licet in præfens gefta funt, quid tamen in futurum fignificent contuendum eft, *C.* x. Peragunt formam futuri gefta præfentia, *C.* xxi.

(7) Quæ a Jefu facta funt, alicujus fignificantia erant. *Serm.* 77.

(8) Omne quod fecit Jefus, Sacramenta funt, *Homil.* 31. *in* Marc. 9.

he did in the Flesh, for the Proof of his divine Authority and *Messiahship,* which is only to be proved by his more mysterious Works, of which those done in the Flesh are but Type and Figure.

But to come closer to the Purpose, let's see how indifferently, I had almost said contemptibly, the Fathers speak of the Miracles of *Jesus,* and particularly of his Power of healing all bodily Diseases, which by modern *Writers* is so much magnified and extoll'd. St. *Irenæus* says, (9) that if *we consider only the then temporal Use of Jesus's Power of Healing, he did nothing grand and wonderful* ; consequently *Irenæus* could not hold, that *Jesus*'s Miracles then wrought, were a sufficient Proof of his divine Authority, much less of his *Messiahship.* *Origen* says (10) that *tho many were brought to believe in Jesus upon the Fame of the Miracles which he did once among the* Jews, *yet* (what implies the Insufficiency of them for the Conversion of Men) *he intimates that his greater and mystical Works do prove his Authority.* St. *John* of *Jerusalem* says (11) that *Je-*

_____

(9) Si enim temporalis erat ab eo Utilitas, nihil grande præstitit iis, qui ab eo curati sunt, *L. V.* C. 12. *S.* 6.

(10) Contra Celsum, *L.* 11.

(11) Cœcum curavit, magnum quidem est, quod fecit, sed nisi quotidie fiat, quod olim factum, nobis quidem magnum esse cessavit. *Homil.* 30. *in* Marc. 9.

sus's

us's Cures *performed upon the Blind,* &c. *were indeed confiderable and great, but unlefs he do daily as mighty Works in his Church, we ought to forbear our Admiration of him.* St. *Auguflin* not only fays (12) that *if we examine into Jefus's Miracles by human Reafon, we fhall find he did nothing great, confidering his Almighty Power, and confidering his Goodnefs, what he did was but little*; but he tells us alfo, that (13) *fuch Works as Jefus did, might be imputed to, and effected by Magic Art.* And accordingly *Mofes* and our Saviour himfelf confefs, that falfe Prophets, and falfe Chrift's, will do Miracles; and *Anti-Chrift* himfelf, according to St. *Paul*, will do them to the Deception of Mankind. Nay, the Fathers (14) fay, what I believe, that *Anti-Chrift* will imitate and equal *Jefus* in all his Miracles which he wrought of old. How then can we diftinguifh the true Prophet from the falfe; the true *Chrift* from the *Anti-Chrift* by Miracles? our *Divines* will find it

(12) Si humano captu & ingenio confideremus Jefum facientem, & quod ad poteftatem non magnum aliquid fecit, & quod ad benignitatem, parvum fecit. *In* Johan. *Cap.* v. *Tract.* 17.

(13) Etfi atteftabantur Miracula, non defuiffent (ficut & nunc muffitant) qui magicæ potentiæ cuncta illa tribuerent. *Cont. Fauft. L.* XII. *C.* 45.

(14) *Vid.* Sanctum *Auguftinum* de *Anti-chrifto.*

C 2   hard

hard to do it, if what the Fathers say of
Anti-chrift be found true.   Moreover Hiftory affords us Inftances of Men, such as
of *Apollonius Tyanæus, Vefpafian*, and of
the *Irifh Stroaker, Greatrex*, who have
miraculoufly cured Difeafes to the Admiration of Mankind, as well as our *Jefus:*
But if any of them, or any other greater
Worker of Miracles than they were, fhould
withall affume to himfelf the Title of a
Prophet, and Author of a new Religion,
I humbly conceive, we ought not to give
heed to him.

Neither is there the leaft Reafon that
we fhould; for the Power of doing Miracles is no certain, nor rational Seal of the
Commiffion and Authority of a divine Law-
giver.   St. *Paul* fays (15) there is a *Di-
verfity of the Gifts of the Spirit, for to
one is given by the Spirit, the Word of
Wifdom ; to another the Word of Knowledge ; to another the Gift of Healing ;
to another the working of Miracles ; to
another Prophecy ; to another difcerning
of Spirits ; to another divers Kinds of
Tongues ; to another the Interpretation of
Tongues.*   Thefe Gifts may be given a-
part and feparately.   One of them may be
conferr'd on this Man, and another of them

(15) 1 *Cor.* C. xii.

of

on his Neighbour. There is no Necessity,
that any two or more of these Gifts should
meet in one Man. To argue then, that a
Man, who has one of these Gifts, must have
the other; that is, that he must needs have
the Gift of Wisdom, or of Prophecy, or
of discerning of Spirits, or of divers Kinds
of Tongues, because he has the Gift of
Healing and of working Miracles, is very
inconclusive, and false Reasoning: And yet
this is the Reasoning of our modern Writers who would prove *Jesus*'s Authority,
to found a Religion, from his Miracles. I
don't question but *Jesus* had all the foresaid Gifts and Powers of the Spirit in a
most superlative Degree; but then it is
unreasonably inferr'd, for all that, that a
Man, because he of Certainty has some of
them, must of consequence have the other.
St. *Augustin* (16) cautions us against being
deceived into a good Opinion of a Man's
Wisdom, because of his Power to do Miracles. And I think accordingly, that we
may as well say, that the strongest Man is
the wisest ; or that a good Physician must
needs be a good Casuist ; or that the best

(16) Atque illud ad Rem maxime pertineat, ne deci-
piamur tendentes ad Contemplationem Veritatis——Ar-
bitrantes ibi esse invisibilem sapientiam, ubi Miraculum
visibile viderimus. *In Serm. Dom. in monte, Lib. 2.*
§. 84.

Mathe-

Mathematician is the ableſt Stateſman, as
that *Jeſus*, becauſe he was a Worker of
Miracles, ſuch as his are, and a Healer of
all manner of Diſeaſes, ought to be received as the Guide of our Conſciencies, the
Director of our Underſtandings, the Ruler
of our Hearts, and the Author of a Religion.

What then will the Writers againſt
the *Grounds* do to prove *Jeſus*'s Authority and *Meſſiahſhip* from his Miracles ?
Or how by his Miracles will they be able
to diſtinguiſh him from an Impoſtor, a falſe
Prophet, and the *Anti-chriſt* ? Why, they
will ſay perhaps,

1. That beſides Greatneſs of Power, there
was nothing but Goodneſs, Kindneſs, and
Love to Mankind ſhewn in *Jeſus*'s Miracles. As to the Miracles of falſe Prophets
and Impoſtors, if they be, many of them,
of a kind and benevolent Aſpect, yet the
Devil's Foot, if we look well to it, will
diſcover it ſelf in ſome ludicrous and miſ-
chievous Pranks : But *Jeſus*'s Miracles were
all of a beneficent Nature ; He went about
doing good, healing all manner of Diſeaſes
among the People, and did no Wrong to
any one ; which is a good Argument, they
ſay, of his divine Authority, or God would
not have ſuffer'd, nor the *Devil* have
work'd ſuch a Teſtimony in behalf of it.
On

On this Head our *Divines* are copious and rhetorical, and many notable and florid Harangues have they made on it. But

In answer to them, they don't seem to have their Memories at Hand, when they declaim at this rate. The Fathers, upon whose Authority I write, will tell such Orators, that *Jesus*, if his Miracles are to be understood in the literal Sense, did not only as foolish Things as any Impostor could do, but very injurious ones to Mankind. I shall not here instance in the seemingly foolish and injurious Things which *Jesus* did for Miracles, intending under the next Head to speak to some of them : But they are such, if literally true, as our *Divines* do believe, as are enough to turn our Stomachs against such a Prophet; and enough to make us take him for a *Conjuror*, a *Sorcerer*, and a *Wizard*, rather than the *Messiah* and Prophet of the most High God. But

2. To prove the *Messiahship* of the Holy *Jesus* from his Miracles, our *Divines* urge the Prophecies of the Old Testament, such as that of *Isaiah*, *C*. xxxv. *V*. 5, 6. *Then the Eyes of the Blind shall he opened, and the Ears of the Deaf shall be unstopp'd; then shall the lame Man leap as the Hart, and the Tongue of the Dumb sing*; and say that these Prophecies were accurately fulfill'd

fill'd by our *Jesus* in the several specifical
Cures of Blindness, Deafness, Lameness,
and Dumbness, which he often perform'd
upon one or other ; and, inasmuch as our
Saviour seems to appeal to such Prophecies,
do conclude this his Accomplishment of
them, to be no less than a Demonstration,
that he was the true *Messiah*, that great
Prophet, who was to come into the World.
To which I answer,

First, That the Accomplishment of Prophecies that can neither be given forth by
human Foresight, nor fulfill'd in a Counterfeit, are good Proofs of *Jesus*'s *Messiahship* : But then, what shall we say if others
besides *Jesus* should do the like Cures and
Miracles ? It is said of *Anti-christ*, and I
believe it, that he will not only do all the
Miracles that *Jesus* did, but will appeal
to the like Prophecies too. How then we
are to distinguish the *true* Christ from the
false Christ by Miracles and Prophecies in
this Case, is the Question, which I leave
with our *Divines* to consider of an Answer to, against the Time that it is proved
that *Anti-christ* does all those Miracles,
which *Jesus* in the Flesh wrought. But

Secondly, The foresaid Prophecies and
others mentioned in *Isaiah*, neither were,
nor could be Prophecies of the miraculous
Cures of bodily Diseases which *Jesus then*
did.

did. And this may be made appear, not only from the Context of thofe Prophecies which received then no Accomplifhment from *Jefus*, who ought to have fulfill'd one Part of the Prophecy as well as the other, or is not to be taken for the Fulfiller of either; but from the Opinion of both *Jews* and *Fathers*, who adjourn the Accomplifhment of thofe Prophecies to Chrift's fpiritual Advent. But

Thirdly, The Prophet *Ifaiah*, in the Place above cited, fpeaks not of bodily Blindnefs, *&c.* which the *Meffiah* is to heal, but of the fpiritual Diftempers of the Soul, metaphorically fo called; as may be eafily proved, not only from the Prophecies themfelves, but from the old *Jews*, who were allegorical Interpreters of thofe Diftempers, and from the antient Fathers, (17) who fo underftood them. Confequently our *Jefus*'s healing of thofe bodily Difeafes, was no proper Accomplifhment of thofe Prophecies. It is true our Saviour, *Matt.* xi. 4, 5. feems to appeal

---

(17) Interim completur & Ifaiæ Prophetia non tantum in corporalibus, verum etiam in fpiritualibus, *Origen. In Matt. Cap.* xv. Aperientur igitur Oculi cæcorum, aures furdorum audient, nam qui quondam divinis fermonibus rejectis myfticam Sanctorum Inftitutionem recipere non ftuduerunt, libenter eam admittent. St. *Cyril in Loc. If. Vide & Sanctum Hieronymum in Loc. Ifai.*

to thofe Prophecies, and to make his Cure
of corporal Diftempers an Accomplifhment
of them : But he means not in the literal
Senfe, that our *Divines* take him in, as I
fhall fhow hereafter, when I come to confider what *Jefus* means, by appealing to
his Works and Miracles, as bearing Witnefs of him.

Our *Divines* then may admire and adore
Jefus as much as they pleafe for his Miracles of healing bodily Diftempers; but I am
for the fpiritual *Meffiah* that cures thofe
Diftempers of the Soul, that metaphorically
pafs under the Names of Blindnefs, Lamenefs, Deafnefs, *&c.* And the Cure of thefe
fpititual Difeafes, is the proper and miraculous Work of the true *Meffiah* ; for the fake
of which, fays (18) St. *Auguftin*, *Jefus*
condefcended to do thofe *little* Miracles
of healing bodily Diftempers, which were
but the Type and Shadow of his more ftupendous Miracles of curing fpiritual Difeafes. The Cure of fpiritual Infirmities
is a God-like (19) Work, above the Imitation of Man or of *Anti-chrift*, infinitely

(18) Et nunc majores fanitates operatur, propter quas
non eft dedignatus tunc exhibere illas minores. *In*
Serm. 88.

(19) In quibus Sipritualibus maxime Chrifti Perfona
eminet. *Auguft. Queft.* 2. *in Lucan.*

more miraculous than the healing any bodily Diſtempers can be.

Whether our *Jeſus* be at this Day ſuch a ſpiritual *Meſſiah*, I leave to our *Divines* to conſider, with thoſe ſpiritual Diſtempers of the Church, that ſeem to want his miraculous Hand and Touch. The Fathers of the Church ſaid, that *Jeſus* was *in part* ſuch a ſpiritual *Meſſiah* in their time, and argued (20) his *Meſſiahſhip*, not from bodily Cures, but from his moſt miraculous Cures of the Diſeaſes of the Soul : But there was another and future Time, in which he would be ſuch a ſpiritual and glorious *Meſſiah* to the greateſt Perfection. In the mean while, no healing of corporal Diſtempers can prove *Jeſus* to be the *Meſſiah*, nor any other of his miraculous Works recorded in the *Evangeliſts :* So far from it, that

II. I ſhall prove that the literal Story of many of *Jeſus*'s Miracles, as they are recorded in the *Evangeliſts*, and commonly believed by Chriſtians, does imply Improbabilities and Incredibilities, and the groſſeſt Abſurdities, very diſhonourable to the

(20) **Modo Caro cæca non aperit oculos miraculo** Domini, ſed cor cæcum aperit oculos Sermoni Domini. Modo non reſurgit mortale cadaver, ſed reſurgit anima quæ mortua jacebat in vivo Cadavere, &c. *Auguſt. Serm.* 88. *S.* 3.

Name

Name of Chrift ; confequently, they, in whole, or in part, were never wrought, but are only related as prophetical and parabolical Narratives of what would be myfterioufly and more wonderfully done by him.

The reading of this Head will, I doubt not, ftrike with Horror fome of our fqueamifh *Divines*, who, notwithftanding they will facrifice almoft any Principles to their Intereft, will not bear that our literal evangelical Hiftory of fuch renown'd Miracles fhould be thus called in Queftion, and contemptuoufly fpoken of. What does this *Author* mean, will fome fay, thus to do Service to Atheifm and Infidelity? Away with him! Our Indignation is moved againft him ! No Cenfure and Punifhment can be too fevere for fuch Impiety, Profanenefs, and Blafphemy, as is aim'd at, and imply'd in this Propofition.

To calm therefore the Spirits, and abate the Prejudices of fuch Accufers, I muft proceed with the greater Caution and with Reafon and Authority well fortify myfelf before and behind, or I fhall feel the Weight of the Difpleafure of our *Divines*, who are prepoffefs'd of the Belief of the literal Story of all *Jefus*'s Miracles.

Before then I enter upon theparticular Examination of any of his Miracles, I will
premife

premife two or three general Affertions of the Fathers about them. And firft *Origen* (21) fays, that in the hiftorical Part of the Scriptures, *There are fome Things inferted as Hiftory, which were never tranfacted, and which it was impoffible fhould be tranfacted; and other Things, again, that might poffibly be done, but were not.* This he afferts of the Writings of the *Evangelifts*, as well as of the Old Teftament, and gives many Inftances to this Purpofe. St. *Hilary* (22) fays, *There are many hiftorical Paffages of the New Teftament, that if they are taken literally, are contrary to Senfe and Reafon, and therefore there is a Neceffity of a myftical Interpretation.* And St. *Auguftin* (23) fays, that *there are hidden Myfteries in the Works and Miracles of onr Saviour, which if we incauti-*

(21) Hiftoria Scripturæ interdum interferit quædam vel minus gefta, vel quæ omnino geri non poffunt, interdum quæ poffunt geri, nec tamen gefta funt. *De Principiis*, Lib. 4.

(22) Multa funt, quæ non finunt nos fimplici fenfu dicta evangelica fufcipere. Interpofitis enim non nullis Rebus quæ ex Natura humani fenfus fibi contraria funt; Rationem quærere cæleftis Intelligentiæ admonemur. *In Matt. L.* xx. *S.* 2.

(23) Evangelica Sacramenta in Chrifti factis fignata omnibus non patent, & ea nonnulli minus diligenter interpretando afferunt plerumque pro falute Perniciem, & pro Cognitione Veritatis Errorem, &c. *De Quæft. Diverf. Queft.* 84.

oufly

ously and literally interpret, we shall run into Errors, and make grievous Blunders. Of the same Mind are the rest of the Fathers, as might be proved by express or implicit Citations; but, studying Brevity, I think the three Testimonies above, enough to cool the Rage, and assuage the Prejudices of my Adversaries against the Proposition before us, which I now come to a particular Consideration of; that is, to shew that the Story of many of *Jesus*'s Miracles is literally absurd, improbable, and incredible. And

1. To speak to that Miracle of *Jesus*'s *driving the Buyers and Sellers out of the Temple*, which all the (24) four Evangelists make mention of.

I have read in some modern Author whose Name does not occur to my Memory, that this was, in his Opinion, the most stupendous Miracle that *Jesus* wrought. And, in truth, it was a most astonishing one, if literally true, and *Jesus* must appear more than a Man, he must put on an awful and most majestick Countenance to effect it. It is hard to conceive, how any one in the Form of a Man, and of a des-

(24) *Matt.* xxi. *Mark* xi. *Luke* xix. *John* ii.

pised

pifed one too, (and we don't read that *Jefus* chang'd his human Shape) with a Whip in his Hand, could execute fuch a Work upon a great Multitude of People, who were none of his Difciples, nor had any regard for him. Suppofing he could, by his divine Power, infufe a *panick* Fear into the People; yet what was the Reafon that he was fo *eaten up* with Zeal againft the Profanation of that Houfe, which he himfelf came to deftroy, and which he permitted, I may fay commanded, to be filthily polluted not long after. But not to form by my felf an Invective againft the Letter of this Story, let's hear what the Fathers fay to it,

Origen makes the whole but a (25) Parable. His allegorical Expofitions of it, are frequent, and one time or other he gives us the myftical Meaning of every Part of it. By the *Temple*, he underftands the Church: By the *Sellers* in the Temple, he means fuch *Preachers* who make Merchandize of the Gofpel, whom the Spirit of Chrift, fome time or other, would rid his Church of. He is fo far from believing any thing of the

(25) In Comment. in *Matth.* xxi.

Letter

Letter of this Story, that he has form'd
a (26) large Argument againſt it : The
Subſtance of which is, that if *Jeſus* had
attempted any ſuch thing, the People
would have reſiſtcd, and executed their
Revenge on him ; if he had effected it, the
Merchants of the Temple might have reproach'd him with Damage done to their
Wares ; and would have juſtly accuſed
him of a Riot againſt Law and Authority. Whether there is not Reaſon in
this Argument of *Origen*, let any one
judge.

(26) Porro cui curæ eſt accuratior Inquiſitio conſiderabit, an juxta dignitatem præſentis Vitæ erat, ut Jeſus
rem talem auderet facere, extrudere videlicet Mercatorum Multitudinem, qui ad Diem feſtum aſcenderant, diſ-
tributuri boves ditioribus, & tanto populo oves mactan-
das per domos familiarium, quæ multorum millium com-
plerent numerum ; atque eos qui in rebus talibus gloriaň-
tes producturi erant in medio Columbas, quas multi emp-
turi erant, ceu in Conventu celeberrimo convivaturi.
Conſiderabit hic etiam, an Nummulariorum erat non ac-
cuſare Jeſum contumelioſe propter ſuas ipſorum effuſas pe-
cunias & menſas ſubverſas. Quis autem flagello e funi-
culis verberatus & expulſus ab eo, qui penes eos habeba-
tur vilis, hunc adortus non inclamaſſet totis viribus ſeſe
ulciſcens ? Cum præſertim haberet tantam multitudinem
eorum, qui ſibi æque contumeliam fieri credebant, faven-
tem ſibi adverſum Jeſum ? Inſuper conſideremus, Dei
filium funiculos ſumentem ; ſibique flagellum tenentem
ad extrudendum e templo, annon repræſentet Præter au-
daciam & temeritatem, inordinatum etiam quiddam ? In
Joban. Tom. XI.

St. *Hilary*

St. *Hilary* is of the fame Mind with *Origen*. He fays that this Story is only a (27) Præfiguration of what will be done in Chrift's Church upon another Occafion. And he admonifhes (28) us to fearch into the profound and myftical Import of every Part of it ; particularly he hints that (29) by *the Seats of thofe who fell Doves*, may be underftood the Pulpits of Preachers who make Sale of the Gifts of the Spirit, which is reprefented by a Dove. As to the Letter of the Story, he is plain enough, that there was no fuch (30) Market kept in the Temple of *Jerufalem:* And if any Hiftorians befides the *Evangelifts* had afferted it, I know of none, who would have been fo foolifh as to believe that Oxen and Sheep and Goats were there fold.

St. *Ambrofe* too is for the Myftery, and againft the Letter of this Story, faying, (31) what fhould be the Reafon that *Jefus*

E   fhould

(27) Præfiguratio futurorum dictis præfentibus continetur. *In Mat.* xxi.

(28) Admonemur altius Verborum Virtutes in iftius modi fignificationibus contuendas, *ibid.*

(29) In Cathedra eft facordotii fedes ; & eorum qui Spiritus fancti Donum venale habent, Cathedras evertet, *ibid.*

(30) Non habebant Judæi quod venire poffent, neque erat quod emere quis poffet, *ibid.*

(31) Cathedra autem Vendentium Columbas cur everterit ? Secundum Litteram non intelligo. Admonet

should overturn the Seats of those that sold
Doves? This must be, says he, a figurative Story, and signifies nothing less than
the future Ejection of Priests out of his
Church, who shall make Gain and Merchandize of the Gospel.

St. *Jerome*, as his manner is in other
Cases, gives us a literal Exposition of
this Miracle, as far as it will bear it: But
then corrects himself again, saying, there
are (32) Absurdities in the Letter; but,
according to its mystical Meaning, *Jesus*
will enter his Temple of the Church, and
cast out of it Bishops, Priests, and Deacons,
who make a Trade of Preaching. And in
another Place he tells us of the mystical
(33) Whip, that *Jesus* will make use of
to this Purpose.

St. *Augustin* also is against the Letter
of the Story of this Miracle, saying, (34)

monet Typo ejectorum de Templo hujusmodi
Mercatorum, in Ecclesia Dei Consortium eos habere non posse, qui sancti Spiritus Gratiam nundi-
nentur. *In Loc. Luc.*

(32) Juxta simplicem Intelligentiam—quod pe-
nitus absurdum—caeterum secundum Mysticos In-
tellectus Jesus ingreditur Templum Patris & ejicit
omnes Episcopos, Presbyteros, & Diaconos, &c. *In
Loc. Mat.*

(33) Faciet Dominus Flagellum de Scripturarum
Textuum Testimoniis. *In Zechar.* C. xiv.

(34) Non magnum Peccatum, si hoc vendebant
in Templo, quod emebatur, ut offerretur in Templo.
In Loc. Johan.

Where

Where could be the great Sin of selling and buying Things in the Temple, that were for the Use of it, and offer'd as Sacrifice in it? We must therefore, says he, look for the Mystery in this (35) figurative Story, and enquire what is meant by the Oxen, and Sheep, and Doves, and who are the Sellers of them in Christ's Church; and he is very positive that Ecclesiasticks, who are selfish, and make worldly Gain of the Gospel, are here meant. And as to the Expression of *turning the Temple into a Den of Thieves*, he says it has Respect to the (36) *Clergy* in Time to come, who would make such a Den of Christ's Church.

Lastly, with the foregoing Fathers agrees St. *Theophylact*, who is an Allegorist too upon this Miracle, saying, that those (37) who sell Doves, are the Priests who sell spiritual Gifts; and that Christ sometime or other would overturn their Seats, and clear his Church of them. In another Place

(35) Qui sunt tamen qui boves vendunt? ut in figura quæramus Mysterium facti, qui sunt qui Oves vendunt & Columbas? ipsi sunt qui sua quærunt in Ecclesia, non quæ Jesu Christi. *Ibid.*

(36) Vos enim fecistis Domum meum, Domum Negotiationis & speluncam Latronum, significat futuros in Ecclesia. *L.* II. *Evang. Quæst. Quæst.* 48.

(37) ΔιδύσκαλΘ ων, ου καταγγελλει λογον, ἡ μη κερδος εχει, και τουτου την τραπεζαν ανατρεπει ο ΚυριΘ. *In Johan.* C. ii.

he

he intimates what are meant by Oxen and Sheep, *viz.* the literal Senfe of the Scriptures. And if the literal Senfe be irrational and nonfenfical, the Metaphor we muft allow to be proper, inafmuch as now-a-days, dull and foolifh and abfurd ftuff we call Bulls, Tatlings, and Blunders.

Behold a wonderful Harmony among the Fathers in their Rejection of the literal, and Efpoufal of the myftical Senfe of this Miracle. It is faid of the Church in her firft Ages, that fhe was infpired; and fo fhe was, or before an Hire for the Prieft-hood was eftablifhed, and pleaded for, fhe could never have written in this Fafhion. If the Fathers had lived now, and written thus, we fhould have thought the Spirit of *Quakerifm* was gotten amongft them, or they would never have given fuch an Expofition of this Story to favour an Enmity to an *Hireling Priefthood*.

How and when Chrift's Power, according to the Figure and Parable before us, will enter his Church, and drive out of her thefe ecclefiaftical Merchants, is not the Queftion. But when ever it does fo effectually, it will be a ftupendous Miracle, much greater than the typical one is fuppofed to be; and not only a Proof of Chrift's divine Power and Prefence in his Church, but an abfolute Demonftration of

his

his *Meſſiahſhip*, from his Accomplishment both of the foreſaid Prophecies of the Fathers, and of other remarkable ones of the *Old Teſtament*, which will be then clearly underſtood, and which it is not my Buſineſs here to apply or mention.

Againſt the aforeſaid Expoſition of this Miracle, perhaps it may be objected, that (excepting a little Reaſoning againſt the Letter of it) this is only the chimerical and whimſical Dream of the Fathers, whoſe Notions are obſolete, and who (38) *have adulterated Chriſtianity with their Cant and Jargon*; and that none of our *Proteſtant* and Orthodox *Divines* have ever given into their Opinion.

I confeſs, that none of our Proteſtant *Divines*, whom I know, do embrace the foreſaid Expoſition of the Fathers, but it may be nothing the worſe for all that: And tho' their Expoſition may be very diſagreeable to the Prieſthood of this Age, yet I can tell them of the greateſt Man of theſe laſt Ages, and that was *Eraſmus*, who, cautiouſly expreſſing himſelf for fear of giving Offence to the *Clergy*, is of the ſame Mind with the Fathers; or he would

(38) *Chandler*'s Vindication, *&c.* p. 145.

not

not fay that (39) *that Work of* Jefus *did prefigure fomewhat elfe: For* Jefus *could not be zealous againſt the Prophanation of that Temple of the* Jews, *which was foon to be deſtroy'd, but meant to ſhew his* Diſlike *and Hatred of ecclefiaſtical Covetoufnefs, which, after the Way of the Type, he would take his Opportunity to rid the Church of.*

Before I difmifs this Miracle, I muft obferve, that if the Fathers are right above, then our *Latin* and *Engliſh* Tranflations of the Place in St. *Matthew* err in a main Point. Inftead of reading, *and Jefus caſt out them that fold and bought*, it fhould be, *thoſe who fold and preach'd*; that is, fold what they preach'd :. For the Word αγοραζειν, does more properly fignify to *preach* than to *buy*; and in this Senfe here, according to the Fathers, it fhould be conftrued.

Again, I muft obferve, that our Commentators are a little perplex'd to know

(39) Hoc facto longe aliud fignificabat Jefus, nec enim illum tantopere commovebat Templum illud mercimoniis Boum, Ovium, Hircorum & Columbarum profanatum ; fed oftendere voluit Avaritiam & Quæftium fore capitalem Peftem Ecclefiæ, quam Templum, cujus Religio mox erat abolenda, figurabat—In nullum Hominum Genus acrius fæviit Jefus, fed hos ipfe fibi fervavit ejiciendos, cum videbitur. *In Loc. Matt.* xxi.

who,

who, and what thofe Κολλυβιϛων, *Money-Changers*, were. The Greek (40) Word does import thofe who have a Knack to barter away little bafe and Brafs Money, with the Effigies of an Ox or Bull on it, in exchange for good Coin. How applicable the Word was to any Merchants of the old Temple at *Jerufalem*, is hard to conceive. But it is very agreeable to our ecclefiaftical *Collybifts*, who, as I may appeal to Freethinkers, vend their brafen-faced Bulls and Blunders at an extravagant and great Price. And if τραπεζας, which is tranflated *Tables*, does properly fignify (41) *Pulpits*, who can help it?

So much then on the Miracle of *Jefus*'s driving the *Sellers* and *Buyers* out of the Temple. And now I appeal to our *Divines*, whether it be not an abfurd, improbable, and incredible Story according to the Letter, and whether it be any other than, as the Fathers faid of it, a prophetical and parabolical Narrative of what would be myfterioufly and more wonderfully done by *Jefus*. And fo I come to fpeak to a

2. Second Miracle of Jefus, and that is,

(40) *Vid.* Suicerum in Κολλυβιϛης.
(41) Τϛαπεζα, apud Ariftophanem eft Pulpitum. *Vid.* Scapulam.

that

that of his (42) *casting the Devils out of the Madman or Madmen, and permitting them to enter into the Herd of Swine, which thereupon ran down a Precipice, and were all choaked in the Sea.*

To exorcife, or caft Devils out of the Poffefs'd, without confidering the Nature of fuch a Poffeffion, or the Nature and Power of the Devil, we'll allow to be not only a kind and beneficent Act, but a great Miracle. But then, be the Miracle as great as can be imagined, it is no more than what falfe Teachers, (43) *Workers of Iniquity*, and even fome Artifts amongft the *Jews*, have done before; confequently, fuch a Work of *Exorcifm* in our Saviour, could be no Proof of his divine Authority. And if there was no more to be faid againft this Miracle, this is enough to fet it afide, and to fpoil the Argument of *Jefus*'s divine Power from it. But there are many Circumftances in the Story literally confider'd, that would induce us to call the Truth of the whole into queftion. How came thofe Madmen to have their Dwelling amongft the Tombs of a Burying-Ground? Where was the Humanity of the People, that did not take Care of them, in Pity to them,

(42) *Matt.* viii. *Mark* v. *Luke* viii.
(43) *Luke* xiii. v. 27.

as well as for the Safety of others? Or if
no Chains, as the Text says, which is
hardly credible, could hold them, it was
possible surely, as well as lawful, to dis-
patch them, rather than their Neighbours
and Passengers should be in Danger from
them. Believe then this Part of the Story
who can? But what's worse, its not credible there was any Herd of *Swine* in that
Country. If any Historians but the *Evangelists* had said so, none would have believed it. The *Jews* are forbidden to eat
Swine's Flesh; what then should they do
with Swine (which are good for nothing
till they are dead) who eat neither *Pig*,
Pork, nor *Bacon?* Some may say that
they were kept there for the Use of Strangers: but this could not be; because that
after the Time of *Antiochus*, who polluted
the Temple with the Sacrifice of an Hog,
the *Jews* (44) forbad, under the Pain of
an *Anathema*, the keeping of any *Swine*
in their Country. Perhaps it may be said,
that the *Gadarens*, so call'd from the
Place of their Abode, were not *Jews*,
but neighbouring *Gentiles*, with whom it
was lawful to eat, and keep *Swine*. We
will suppose so, tho it is improbable; but
then its unlikely (without better Reason

(44) *Spencer* de Legibus Hebræ, *p.* 117.

F   than

than at prefent we are apprifed of) that
our Saviour would permit the Devils to
enter into a Herd of them to their Deftruction. Where was the Goodnefs and Juftice of his fo doing? Let our *Divines* account for it if they can. It is commonly
faid of our Saviour, and I believe it, that
his Life was entirely innocent, that his
Miracles were all ufeful and beneficial to
Mankind, and that he did no Wrong to
any one. But how can this be rightly faid
of him, if this Story be literally true? The
Proprietors of the Swine were great Lofers
and Sufferers; and we don't read that *Jefus* made them amends, or that they deferv'd fuch Ufage from him. The Proprietors of the Swine, it feems upon this
Damage done them by *Jefus*, defire him to
depart out of their Coafts, to prevent farther Mifchief; which was gentler Refentment, then we can imagine any others
would have made of the like Injury. I
know not what our *Divines* think of this
Part of the Story, nor wherefore *Jefus*
efcaped fo well; but if any *Exorcift* in this
our Age and Nation, had pretended to expel the Devil out of one poffefs'd, and permitted him to enter into a Flock of Sheep,
the People would have faid that he had
bewitch'd both; and our Laws aud Judges
too

too of the laſt Age, would have made him
to ſwing for it.

Without Offence, I hope, I have argued
againſt the Letter of this ſtrange Story of
the holy *Jeſus* ; I ſhould not have dared
to have ſaid ſo much againſt it, but upon
the Encouragement of *Origen* and other
Fathers, who ſay, we ought to expoſe the
Abſurdities of the Letter, as much as may
be, to turn Men's Heads to the myſtical
and true Meaning.

Let's hear then what the Fathers ſay to
this Miracle. *Origen*'s Commentaries on
this Part of St. *Matthew*, and St. *Luke*'s
Goſpel, are loſt ; otherwiſe unqueſtionably
he would not only have told us, that he
believed no more of the Letter of this Story, than he did of the Devil's (45) taking
our Saviour to the Top of a Mountain,
and ſhewing him all the Kingdoms of the
World ; but, as he is an admirable *Myſtiſt*,
would have given us curious Light into
the Allegory and Myſtery of it. But without *Origen*, we have enough in the other
Fathers againſt the Letter of this Story.

St. *Hilary* reckoning up all the Parts of
this Miracle together, ſays of it, that it is
(46) typical and parabolical, and written

(45) *Lib.* IV. De Principiis.
(46) Hanc habeant Cauſam, ut eſſet in rebus gerendis
futuri plena meditatio. *In Loc. Matt.* In hoc Typica
ratio ſervata eſt. *Ibid.*

for

for our Meditation of what would be done
hereafter by the holy *Jesus.* According
to him, and other Fathers, the *Madman*
is Mankind; or if they were two, they
were *Jew* and *Gentile* at Chrift's coming,
who may be faid to (47) be *poffefs'd with
Devils,* in as much as they were under
the Rule of diabolical Sins, and fubject to
the Worfhip of Δαιμονιων, falfe Deities, which
we tranflate *Devils.* They were *fo fierce*
(48) *as no Chains could hold them,* becaufe of their moft furious Rage and Enmity to the Church, whom no Bonds of
Reafon could reftrain from doing Violence
to the Chriftians. They are faid *to be* (49)
naked, becaufe they were deftitute of the
Clothing of the Spirit, and of Grace. And
may be faid to be *among the* (50) *Tombs* ;
becaufe they were dead in Trafpaffes and
Sins. After that *Jesus* had exorcis'd thefe
diabolical Spirits out of the *Gentiles,* and
brought them to their right Senfes, which

(47) Significatæ funt gentes quæ multis dæmonibus fer-
viebant *Auguftin in Luc. Queft.* 13.

(48) Humanum genus ad Adventum Domini vexabatur
furore dementi, rumpens vincula rationis. St. *Amb. in
Loc. Luc.*

(49) Nudus quicunque tegumentum Naturæ fuæ & Virtutis amifit. *Amb. Ibid.*

(50) In tumulis Sepulchrorum; quid enim aliud funt
Corpora perfidorum, nifi quædam defunctorum Sepulchra
in quibus Dei verbum non habitat. *Ibid.*

was upon their Conversion to the Faith ; then a *good Way off*, some Ages after, did the like *Devils*, by divine Permission, enter into a (51) *Herd of Swine*, i. e. into *Hereticks* of impure Lives, and furious Natures. What sort of *Hereticks* are meant, or whether they are not to be understood of Christians in general, let our *Divines* consider. But one would be apt to think that *Ministers of the Letter* are included, because the *Letter* of the Scripture is mystically call'd (52) *Swines* Food. I am not obliged to pursue the mystical Interpretation of this Parable (for so I will call it) thro' all its Parts, nor to say what is meant by the Sea, that the *Swine* are to be absorp't in ; but leave our *Divines* to chew upon this mystical Construction given them in part, and to consider, whether there's not a Necessity for such an Interpretation to make the Story credible.

And thus have I given you the Opinion and Exposition of the Fathers upon this Miracle, which they turn all into Mystery. If our *Divines* are still for adhering to the

(51) Videntes Dæmones non sibi jam locum in gentibus derelinqui, ut patiatur habitare se in Hæreticis deprecantur. *Hilar. in Loc. Matt.*

(52) Litera est Palea, & frequenter evenit, ut homines hujus sœculi mystica nescientes, simplici Scripturarum Lectione pascuntur. *Hieron. in* Isa. xi.

Letter.

Letter of this Story, let them account for
the Difficulties it is involv'd with. To cure
Men violently diftracted, and poffefs'd with
Devils, is, whether it be miraculous or not,
a good and great Work ; but to fend the
Devils, who without *Jefus*'s Permiffion
could not go into the *Herd of Swine*, was
an Injury done to the Proprietors, and unbecoming of the Goodnefs of the holy *Jefus*. Neither is there any other Way to
folve the Difficulty, than by looking upon
the whole, with the Fathers, as Type and
Figure.

If this miraculous Story had been recorded of *Mahomet*, and not of *Jefus*, our *Divines*, I dare fay, would have work'd it
up to a Confutation of *Mahometanifm.*
Mahomet fhould have been, with them,
nothing lefs than a *Wizard*, an *Enchanter*,
a *Dealer* with familiar Spirits, a fworn
Slave to the Devil ; and his *Muffulmen*
would have been hard put to it to write a
good Defence of him.

When our Saviour was brought before
Pilate to be arraign'd, try'd, and condem-
ned, *Pilate* put this Queftion to the *Jews*,
faying, *What Evil hath Jefus done ?* If
both, or either of the Stories above, had
been literally true of *Jefus*, there had been
no need of falfe Witneffes againft him. The
Merchants of the Temple were at hand,
who

who could have fworn " that he was the
" Author of an Uproar and Riot, the like
" was never feen on their Market-Day ;
" that they were great Sufferers, and Lo-
" fers in their Trades ; and, whether he
" or his Party had ftolen any of their
" Goods or not, yet fome were embez-
" zled, and others damaged ; and all thro'
" the outragious Violence of this unruly
" Fellow, againft Law and Authority."
If fuch Evidence as this was not enough
to convict him of a capital Crime, then
the *Swine-Herds* of the *Gadarenes* might
have depofed, " how they believed him to
" be a *Wizard*, and had loft two thou-
" fand Swine through his Fafcinations :
" That he bid the Devils to go into our
" Cattle, is not to be deny'd. And if he
" cured one or two of our Countrymen
" of a violent Poffeffion, yet in as much as
" he did us this Injury in our Swine, we
" juftly fufpect him of diabolical Practices
" upon both."

Upon fuch Evidence as this, *Pilate* asks the
Opinion of the *Jews*, faying, *What think
you ?* If they all had condemn'd him to be
guilty of Death, it is no wonder, fince
there is not a *Jury* in *England* would
have acquitted any one arraign'd and accufed in the like Cafe.

It is well for our literal *Doctors*, that such Accusations were not brought against *Jesus*; or their Heads would have been sadly puzzled to vindicate his Innocence, and to prove the Injustice and Undeservedness of his Death and Sufferings. But for this Reason, if no other, that no such Crimes were laid to his Charge, I believe little or nothing of either of the seemingly miraculous Stories before us, but look upon them both as prophetical and parabolical Narratives of what would mysteriously and more wonderfully, and consistently with the Wisdom and Goodness of *Jesus*, be done by him. And so I pass to a

3. Third Miracle of *Jesus*, and that is *his Transfiguration* (53) *on the Mount.* And this is the darkest and blindest Story of the whole Gospel, which a Man can make neither Head nor Foot of ; and I question whether the Conceptions of any two thinking *Doctors* do agree about it. To say there is nothing in the Letter of this Story, we Believers must not, because St. *Peter* (54) says he was an Eye-witness of *Jesus*'s Majesty, saw his Glory on the Mount, and heard the Voice out of the

(53) *Matt.* xvii. *Mark* ix. *Luke* ix.
(54) 2 *Pet. i.* 16, 17, 18.

Cloud.

Cloud. But as Infidels will be prying into the Conduct of *Jesus*'s Life, and forming their Exceptions to the Credibility or Probability of this or that part of it, so we Christians should be ready at an Answer, that might reasonably satisfy them ; and not forcibly bear down their Opposition, which will make no sincere Converts of them. And I believe they would easily distress us with Difficulties and Objections to the Letter of this Story.

St. *Augustin* himself (55) owns, that the whole of it might be perform'd by Magic Art ; and we know, in these our Days, that some Jugglers are strange Artists at the Imitation of a Voice, and to make it as if it came from a far off, when it is uttered close by us, and can cast themselves too into different Forms and Shapes, without a Miracle, to the Surprise and Admiration of Spectators.

But what, I trow, do our *Divines* mean by *Jesus*'s *Transfiguration*. We read that his Countenance did shine like the Sun, and his Raiment was made as white as Snow, and that's all. And is this enough can we think, to demonstrate that Transaction, a miraculous *Transfiguration?* Phi-

(55) Poſſunt Infideles iſtam Vocem delatam de Cælo, per conjecturas humanas & illicitas Curioſitates ad magicas Artes referre. *In Serm.* xliii. *Sect.* 5.

loſophers

lofophers will tell us, that the Reflections of the Light of the Sun will change the Appearance of Colours, and to none more than Whitenefs; and *Sceptics* will fay, that its no Wonder if the Countenance of *Jefus* look'd *Rubicund*, when the Sun might fhine on it.

The Word in the Original for *transfigured*, is μέταμορφωθη, that is, he was metamorphofed, transform'd, or, if you will, transfigured. And what is to be underftood by a *Metamorphofis*, we are to learn not only from the natural Import of the Word, but from the ancient Ufe of it. Accordingly, it fignifies nothing lefs than the Change or Transformation of a Perfon into the Forms, Shapes, and Effences of Creatures and Things of a quite different Species, Size, and Figure: But *Jefus*, it is conceived, was not fo *transfigured*. Our *Divines*, I fuppofe, would not have him thought fuch a *Pofture-Mafter* for the whole World. If I, or any one elfe, fhould affert, that *Jefus* upon the Mount tranfform'd himfelf into a Calf, a Lyon, a Bear, a Ram, a Goat, an Hydra, a Stone, a Tree, and into many other Things of the animate and inanimate World, I dare fay there would, among our orthodox *Divines*, be fuch Exclamations againft me for Blafphemy, as the like were never heard of. They,

to

to be sure, will not hear of such a Transfiguration; nor, like good plain believers, will bear any thing more than that *Jesus*'s *Countenance did shine* like the Sun, and the Colour of his Vestments was changed; which whether it comes up to the Import of a *Metamorphosis* or not, they don't care.

But to close with our *Divines*, and acknowledge that the glorious Change of *Jesus*'s Countenance, and of the Colour of his Vestments, was a true and proper Transfiguration, and that it was as real and wonderful a Miracle as could be wrought: But then we may, I hope, ask them, what was the particular Reason and Use of this Miracle? Was it a Miracle only for the sake of a Miracle? That's an Absurdity in the Opinion of (56) St. *Augustin*, who says, what is reasonable to think, that all and every one of *Jesus*'s Miracles had its particular End and Use; or he who is the Wisdom as well as Power of God, had never wrought them. And what, I pray, was the Use of this Miracle? Of that the evangelical History is silent, and our *Divines*, with all their reasoning Faculties, can say nothing to it.

---

(56) Neque enim Miracula propter Miracula faciebat, sed ut illa quæ faciebat, mira essent videntibus, vera essent intelligentibus. *In Serm.* xcviii. *Sect.* 3.

And

And what did *Moses* and *Elias* on the Mount with *Jesus*? Was it in their own proper Persons that they appear'd ? or were they only some Spectres and Apparitions in resemblance of them? It is said, that they were talking with *Jesus*; what then did they talk about? The three greatest Prophets and Philosophers of the Universe could not possibly meet and confer together, but on the most sublime, useful, and edifying Subject. Its strange that the Apostles, who over-heard their Confabulation, did not make a Report of it, and transmit it to Posterity for our Edification and Instruction. St. *Luke*, as our *English* Translation has it, seems to say that they talk'd together of *Jesus's Decease which he should accomplish at Jerusalem*; but this can't be the Meaning of St. *Luke's* (57) Words, which so interpreted, are no less than a *Barbarism*, and, I appeal to our Greek *Criticks*, an Improper Expression of such Signification. We must then look for a more proper Construction of the Phrase in St. *Luke*, or we must remain in the Dark, as to the Subject, that *Moses* and *Elias* talked with *Jesus* about.

But further, Why could not this Miracle have been wrought in the Valley as

(57) Ἔλεγον την εξοδον αυτου ην εμελλε πληρουν, C. ix. V. 31.

well as upon a Mountain, whither *Jesus* and his three Apoftles afcended for the Work of it? Naughty *Infidels* will fay, it was for the Advantage of a Cloud, which often moves and refts on the Tops of Mountains, to difplay his Pranks in. And why was it not done in the Prefence of the Multitude, as well as of his three Apoftles? The more Witneffes of a Miracle, the better it is attefted, and the more reafonably credited; and there could not furely be too many Witneffes of this, any more than of others of *Jesus*'s Miracles, if real ones. Ought not the unbelieving Multitude, for many Unbelievers unqueftionably were amongft them, to have had a Sight and Hearing of this Miracle, as well as the Apoftles? Who fhould rather fee the Miracle, than thofe who wanted Conviction? Were they to take the Report of the Miracle upon the Word of the Apoftles, who were Parties in the Caufe? Our *Divines* may poffibly fay they ought: But *Infidels* and *Free-Thinkers* would cry out againft them, for juggling Tricks, and pious Impoftures.

These are all Difficulties and hard Queftions about the Miracle of Chrift's Tranffiguration, which our *Clergy*, who are Admirers of the Letter of that Story, are obliged to account for; and I believe it will

will be long enough before they give a
proper and satisfactory Anſwer to many of
them.

Let's here then what the Fathers ſay to
this miraculous Story of *Jeſus*'s Transfiguration. And it is agreed amongſt them,
that the whole is but a Týpe, (58) Pre-
figuration, and (59) ænigmatical Reſemblance of a future and more glorious and
real Transfiguration. And whenever they
ſpeak of any Part of the Story, they never
explain to us how the Matter went upon
Mount *Tabor*, but tell us of what *this* or
that Part of it is figurative and emblematical ; and how it is to be underſtood, and
will be fulfill'd in future Time. As thus,
by *the* (60) *ſix Days*, they underſtood ſix
Ages of the World, after which a real and
myſterious Transfiguration will be exhibited to our intellectual Views. By *Moſes*

(58) Regni cœleſtis Honor preſiguratur. St. *Hilar. in
Loc. Matt.* In Transfiguratione futura Regni Præmedita-
tio & Gloria demonſtrata eſt. *St. Hierom. in Loc. Matt.*

(59) Ἀινιγματωδης παραδειξις της Βασιλειας, Anaſt.
in Transfig. Dom. Ὑποδειγμα της δοξης εκεινης. St.
Chryſoſt. in Loc. Matt.

(60) Sex millium ſcilicet Annorum Temporibus evolu-
tis. St. *Hilar. in Loc. Matt.* Sic poſt Sex ætates Dominus
a perfectis Famulis conſpicietur. *Dionyſ. Alex. apud Da-
maſcen. in Orat. de Transfig.*

and

and *Elias* (61) talking with *Jesus*, they mean the Law and the Prophets, upon an allegorical Interpretation, bearing Testimony unto Christ as the Fulfiller of them. By the (62) *Mountain* on which this future Transfiguration will be exhibited, they understand the sublime and anagogical Sense of the Law and the Prophets. By his *Transfiguration* it self, they mean his taking upon him, and passing through the Forms of all the Types of him under the Law, as of a Lamb, a Lion, a Serpent, a Calf, a Rock, a Stone, and of many others, which he is to fulfil, and which will then be clearly discern'd by us. By the black Cloud (63) that at present obstructs this Vision, they understand the Letter of the Old Testament. By the white (64) Vestments of *Jesus*, they mean the Words of the Scriptures, which will then shine

(61) Et Moses & Elias apparuerunt in Gloria, cùm Jesu colloquentes, in quo ostenditur Legem & Prophetas, cum Evangeliis confonare & in eadem Gloria spiritualis intelligentiæ refulgere. *Origen. in Epist. ad Rom.* c. 1.

(62) Montem afcendit ut te doceat, ne quæras eum nisi in Legis & Prophetarum montibus. *Origeu in Cantic. Cantic. Hom.* 3.

(63) Per nubem tetram intellige opacitatem Legis. *Damafcen. in Orat. de Transfigur.*

(64) Vestimenta candida Jesu funt Sermones & Scripta Evangeliorum. *Origen in Loc. Matt.*

clear

clear and bright. By the Voice out of the
Cloud, they mean, with St. *Peter*, the
Word of Prophecy, that will found in the
Ears of our Apprehenfions. And laftly,
they tell us, that the Way to attain to the
Sight of this glorious Vifion, is by afcend-
ing (not by local Motion, but by Reafon)
to the Tops of the Mountain of the myfterious and fublime Senfe of the Law and the
Prophets. If we continue in the Plains
and Vallies (65) of the Letter, like the
Multitude under the Mountain, we fhall
never fee *Jefus* in his fhining Veftments,
nor how he was transform'd into the Types
of the Law; nor *Mofes* and *Elias* talking
with him; nor the Law and the Prophets
agreeing harmonioufly in a Teftimony to
him.

After this fafhion do the Fathers, one or
other of them, copioufly treat on every
Part of this Transfiguration of *Jefus*. I
could colle&t an almoft infinite Number of
Paffages out of their Writings to this Pur-

(65) Si quis Litteram fequitur, & deorfum eft to-
tus, hic non poteft videre Jefum in vefte candida ; qui
autem fequitur Sermonem Dei & ad montana, id eft,
excelfa Legis confcendit, ifti Jefus commutatur——
Quamdiu Litteram fequimur occidentem, Mofes & Elias
cum Jefu non loquuntur ; fin fpiritualiter intelligimus,
ftatim Mofes & Elias veniunt, id eft Lex & Prophetæ
& colloquuntur cum Evangelio. *Johan. Hierof. Hom.*
32.

pofe : But from thefe few it is plain, they
look'd on the Story of Chrift's Transfiguration, but as a Figure and Parable ; and
they were certainly in the right on't, in as
much as this their Senfe of the Matter, and
no other, will folve the Difficulties before
ftarted againft the Letter, as any one may
difcern, if he attentively review and compare one with the other : As, for inftance,
this their Senfe and Interpretation lets us
into the Reafon of *Mofes* and *Elias*'s appearing on the Mount with *Jefus*; and
gives us to underftand what they talk'd
about, and that was, not on *Jefus*'s *De-
ceafe which he would accomplifh at* Jerufalem, as our Tranflation has it, but on the
Prophecy of the Old Teftament ; particularly, as St. *Luke* fays, on *Mofes*'s Book of
Exodus, and how he would fulfill it at the
New Jerufalem.

Whether any, befides my felf, does really apprehend, and is willing to underftand
this Story of Chrift's Transfiguration, as I
do, I neither know nor care. I am not
bound to find others Ears, Eyes, and Capacities. What I have faid is enough to
fhew the Senfe of the Fathers about this
Matter. If any diflike their concurrent
Opinion of *Jefus*'s Transfiguration's being
an Emblem, an Enigma, and figurative
Reprefentation of a future and moft glori-
H   ous

ous Transfiguration, such a one as they speak of; let him account for the Difficulties and Objections which I have before raised against the Letter of this Story. In the mean time I shall think it, literally, an absurd, improbable, and incredible one, and no other than a prophetical and parabolical Narrative of what will be mysteriously and more wonderfully done by *Jesus*.

And thus I have considered *three* of the Miracles of our Saviour, and shewn how they are Absurdities, according to the Letter, consequently do make nothing for his Authority and *Messiahship*. I can and will do as much by his other Miracles; for I would not have any one think I am gotten to the End of my Tedder, but for some Reasons best known to my self, I publish these Remarks on these three first. After the *Clergy* have chew'd upon these a while, I will take into Examination some others of *Jesus's* Miracles, which for their literal Story are admired by them. As for Instance,

I will take to task his Miracle (66) *of changing Water into Wine at a Marriage in Cana of Galilee*; which was the beginning of *Jesus's* Miracles, and should by right have been first spoken to; but I am

(66) *John* ii.

almost

almoft too grave to handle the Letter of
this Story as I ought; and if I had treated
it as ludicroufly as it deferves, I don't know
but at fetting out, I fhould have put the
Clergy quite out of all Temper. I would
not now for the World be fo impious and
profane, as to believe, with our D*ivines,*
what is contain'd and imply'd in the Letter
of this Story. If *Apollonius Tyanæus,* and
not *Jefus,* had been the Author of this
Miracle, we fhould often have reproached
his Memory with it. It is faid of *Apollonius Tyanæus,* that a Table was all on a
fudden, at his Command, miraculoufly
fpread with Variety of nice Difhes for the
Entertainment of himfelf and his Guefts;
which Miracle, our *Divines* can tell him,
makes not at all to his Credit, in as much
as it was done for the Service and Pleafure
of luxurious Appetites. But if *Apollonius*
had done, as our *Jefus* did at this Wedding, they would have faid much worfe
of him; and that, modeftly fpeaking, he
delighted to make his Friends thoroughly
merry, or he would not be at the Pains of
a Miracle to turn fo much Water into
Wine, after they had before *well drank.*
If the Fathers then don't help us out at the
myftical and true Meaning of this Miracle,
fuch farther Objections may be form'd a-

gainft

gainſt the Letter, as maymake our *Divines* aſham'd of it.

I will alſo take into Examination *Jeſus*'s Miracle (67) of *feeding many Thouſands in the Wilderneſs with a few Loaves and Fiſhes* ; which, according to the Letter, are moſt romantick Tales. I don't in the leaſt queſtion *Jeſus*'s Power to magnify or mul‑tiply the Loaves, and, if he pleaſs'd, to me‑liorate the Bread: But that many Thou‑ſands of Men, Women, and Children, ſhould follow him into the Wilderneſs, and ſtay with him three Days and Nights too, without eating, is a little againſt Senſe and Reaſon. Whether the Wilderneſs was near to, or far from the People's Habita‑tions, the Difficulties attending the Story are equally great. I wonder how *Jeſus* amuſed them all the while, that they had the Patience to ſtay with him without Food ; but I much more wonder, that no Victuallers beſides the *Lad* with his Loaves and Fiſhes, of whom, and his Occupation, whether it was that of a *Baker* or *Fiſh‑monger* ; and of his Neglect of his Maſter's Buſineſs here ; and of the Reaſon that he met with no hungry Chapmen for his Bread before, we ſhall make ſome En‑quiry ; but particularly why he alone, I

(67) *Matt.* C. xiv. and xv. &c.

ſay

fay, and no other Victuallers, no other Re-
talers of Cakes and Gingerbread followed
the Camp. In fhort, for all the imaginary
Greatnefs of the Miracle (which there is a
way to reduce and leffen) of *Jefus*'s feeding his Thoufands with a few Loaves, there
muft be fome Fafcination or Enchantment
(condemn'd by the Laws of the *Jews* as
well as of other Nations) in the Matter ;
or the People if they had ftay'd one Day,
would not two, much lefs three *to faint*,
but would, efpecially the Women and Children, have been for returning the firft
Night home. We muft then feek to the
Fathers (who fay the five Books of *Mufes*
are the *five Barley Loaves*, &c. and the
feptiform'd Spirit, the *feven Loaves*, &c.)
for a good Notion of this Miracle, and if
they don't make it a Parable; do what our
Divines can, it will turn to the Difhonour
of the holy Jefus.

I will alfo confider the Miracle of *Jefus*'s
(68) *curing the Man fick of the Palfy, for
whom the Roof of the Houfe was broken
up, to let him down into the Room where*
Jefus *was, becaufe his Bearers could not
enter in at the Door for the Prefs of the
People.* This literally is fuch a *Rodomon-
tado*, that were Men to ftretch for a Wa-

(68) *Mark* ii. *Luke* v.

ger,

ger, againſt Reaſon and Truth, none could
out-do it. Where was the Humanity of
the People, and wherefore did they ſo tumultuate againſt the Door of the Houſe ?
Its *ſtrange* they had not ſo much Compaſ-
ſion on the *Paralytick*, as to give way to
him : Its *more ſtrange* that his Bearers
could get to the Top of the Houſe with
him and his Bed too, when they could not
get to the Door, nor the Sides of it *:* Its
yet ſtranger, that the good Man of the
Houſe would ſuffer his Houſe to be broken
up, when it could not be long ere the
Tumult of the People would be appeas'd :
But moſt *ſtrange*, that *Jeſus*, who could
drive his Thouſands out of the Temple before him, and draw as many after him into the Wilderneſs, did not, by Force or
Perſuaſion, make the People to retreat, but
that ſuch needleſs Trouble and Pains muſt
be taken for the miraculous Cure of this
poor Man. Let's think of theſe Things
againſt the Time, that out of the Fathers I
prove this Story to be a Parable.

I will alſo take into Conſideration the
Miracle of *Jeſus's* curing *the* (69) *blind
Man, for whom Eye-Salve was made of
Clay and Spittle* ; which Eye-Salve, whe-
ther it was balſamick or not, does equally

(69) *John* ix.

affect

affect the Credit of the Miracle. If it was naturally medicinal, there's an End of the Miracle; and if it was not at all medicinal, it was foolishly and impertinently apply'd, and can be no otherwise accounted for, than by considering it, with the Fathers, as a figurative Act in *Jesus*.

I will also take into Consideration the several Stories of *Jesus*'s raising of the Dead; and, without questioning his actual bringing of the Dead to Life again, will prove from the Circumstances of those Stories, that they are parabolical, and are not literally to be apply'd to the Proof of *Jesus*'s divine Authority and Messiahship; or, for Instance, *Jesus*, when he raised *Jairus*'s (70) Daughter from the Dead, would never have turned the People out of the House, who should have been his best and properest Witnesses.

I will also consider the Mirale of *Jesus*'s (71) *cursing the Fig-Tree*, for its not bearing Fruit out of Season; which, upon the bare mention of it, appears to be a foolish, absurd, and ridiculous Act, if not figurative.

I will also consider the (72) Journey of the Wisemen out of the East, with their (li-

(70) *Mark* v.   (71) *Matt.* xxi.   *Mark.* xi.
(72) *Matt.* ii.

terally)

terally) fenfelefs and ridiculous Prefents of *Frankincense* and *Myrrhe*, to a new-born Babe. If with their *Gold*, which could be but little, they had brought their *Dozens* of Sugar, Soap, and Candles, which would have been of Ufe to the Child and his poor Mother in the Straw, they had acted like wife as well as good Men. But what, I pray, was the Meaning and Reafon of a Star, like a *Will-a-Whifp*, for their Guide to the Place, where the holy Infant lay. Could not God, by divine Impulfe, in a Vifion or in a Dream, as he ordered their Return home, have fent them on this important Errand; but that a Star muft be taken or made out of Courfe to this Purpofe? I wonder what Communication paffed between thefe Wifemen and the Star, or how they came to know one anothers Ufe and Intention. But the Fathers fhall fpeak hereafter farther to the Senfelefsnefs of this Story literally, and make out the Myftery and true Meaning of it.

I will alfo, by the Leave of our *Divines*, take again into Confideration the miraculous Conception of the Virgin *Mary*, and the Refurrection of *Jefus* from the Dead. I do believe, if it may fo pleafe our *Divines*, that *Jefus* was born of a pure Virgin, and that he arofe from the Dead: But fpeaking too briefly, in the

Moderator,

Moderator, to thefe two Miracles, they took Offence. I will therefore give them a Review, and fpeak home to them ; particularly to Chrift's Refurrection, the evangelical Story of which literally, is fuch a Complication of Abfurdities, Incoherences, and Contradictions, that unlefs the Fathers can help us to a better Underftanding of the *Evangelifts* than we have at prefent, we muft of Neceffity give up the Belief of it.

Thefe and many (73) other of the hiftorical and miraculous Parts of *Jefus's* Life, will I take into Examination, and fhew, that none of them literally do prove his divine Authority : fo far from it, that they are full of Abfurdities, Improbabilities, and Incredibilities; but that his whole Life in the Fleth, is but (74) Type, Figure, and Parable of his myfterious and fpiritual Life and Operations in Mankind.

In the End of this Head, it will be a curious and diverting Subject to examine the Miracles of *Jefus* as they are literally underftood, by the Notions which our

(73) Alia quam plurima his fimilia in Evangeliis inveniet, quicunque attentius legerit. *Origen. de Principiis*, lib. iv.
(74) Quæ Enarratio erit Evangelii fenfibilis, nifi accommodetur ad intelligible & fpirituale ? Nulla fane, *Origen. in Præfat ad Johan. Evang.*

Divines have advanced about Miracles ; and to fhew, that even their Notions compared with Chrift's Miracles, are deftructive of his Authority, and fubverfive of Chriftianity. This, I fay, would be a moft diverting Undertaking, and it will be ftrange, if fome *Free-Thinker*, that loves Pleafure of this kind, does not take the Hint, and fnatch the Work out of my Hands. If I do it my felf, I fhall have efpecial Regard to the Writers againft the *Grounds*, without paffing by Mr. *Chandler*'s *Effay on Miracles* ; on which the more Remarks will be made, if it be but to pay my Refpects to the *Archbifhop*'s Judgment, and to fhew my Admiration at thofe extravagant Praifes, which his *Grace* at *Lambeth* has beftowed on that Author. Among other his notable Notions of a Miracle (and the *Archbifhop* fays he has (75) *fet the Notion of a Miracle upon a clear and fure Foundation*) one is, (76) *That Miracles fhould be Things probable as well as poffible, that they do not carry along with them the Appearance of Romance and Fable, which would unavoidably prejudice Men againft believing them.* This

----

(75) *See Archbifhop* Wake's *Manufcript Letter to Mr.* Chandler, *which is handed about Town and Country.*

(76) Chandler's *Vindication*, &c. p. 81.

is certainly a good and right Notion of a divine Miracle; and I don't doubt, but according to it, Mr. *Chandler* and the *Archbishop* think, they can justify the literal Story of our Saviour's Miracles, against the Charge of *Fable* and *Romance*: But whether they are able to do it or not, I shall go on, in some Discourses hereafter to be publish'd, to prove that our *Divines*, by espousing the Letter of Christ's Miracles, have deceived themselves into the Belief of the most arrant *Quixotism* that can be devis'd and palm'd upon the Understandings of Mankind I say, they have deceived themselves; for neither the Fathers, nor the Apostles, nor even *Jesus* himself, meant that his Miracles, as recorded in the *Evangelists*, should be taken in a literal Sense, but in (77) a mystical, figurative, and parabolical one. And this should bring me to the

III. Head of my Discourse; that is, to consider what *Jesus* means, when he appeals to his Works and Miracles, as to a Witness and Testimony of his divine Authority; and to shew, that he could not properly and truly refer to those supposed

---

(77) Dominus noster ea quæ faciebat corporaliter, etiam spiritualiter volebat intelligi, &c. *August. Serm.* xcviii. Sect. 3.

to

to be wrought by him in the *Flesh*, but to
thofe myftical ones he would do in the
Spirit, of which thofe feemingly wrought
by him in the Flefh, are but Types and
Shadows.

But this Head can't be rightly fpoken
to, till I have more amply difcufs'd the
former, which, by God's Leave, I promife
to do: And if my *courteous Readers* will
be fo kind as to truft me till that Time, I
affure them to prove, that no Ignorance
and Stupidity can be greater, than the Imagination that *Jefus* really appeal'd to his
Miracles, fuppofed to have been wrought
by him in the Flefh, as to a Witnefs and
Teftimony of his divne Authority, and
Meffiahfhip.

In the mean Time our *Divines* may go
on in their own Way, if they think fit,
and admire *Jefus* of old, and celebrate his
Power and Praifes for healing of bodily
Difeafes, and doing other notable Feats
according to the Letter of the evangelical
Story ; but I am for the fpiritual *Jefus* and
Meffiah, who cures the worfe (78) Diftempers of the Soul, and does other myfterious and moft miraculous Works, of
which thofe recorded in the Evangelifts,

---

(78) **Quos** in corporibus morbos fanavit Chriftus, hi
in animabus exiftunt. & fupernam ejus opem requirunt.
Johan. Nepot. Hierof. Hom. LXI.

are

are but Figure and Parable. This is the primitive and concurrent Opinion about the true *Meſſiah*, which the Fathers univerſally adher'd to. Whether our *Jeſus*, at this Day, be ſuch a ſpiritual *Meſſiah* to his Church, or whether ſhe does not ſtand in need of ſuch a one, is the Queſtion that our *Divines* are to ſee to. But I will add here, what I believe, and ſhall have another Opportunity to prove, that God on purpoſe ſuffer'd or empower'd *falſe* as well as *true* Prophets, *bad* as well as *good* Men, ſuch as *Apollonius*, *Veſpaſian*, and many others to cure Diſeaſes, and to do other mighty Works, equal to what are literally reported of *Jeſus*, not only to defeat us of all diſtinction between true and falſe Miracles, which are the Object of our bodily Senſes, but to raiſe and keep up our Thoughts to the conſtant Contemplation of *Jeſus*'s ſpiritual, myſterious, and moſt miraculous Works, which are the Object of our Underſtandings, and loudly beſpeak the Power, Wiſdom, and Goodneſs of God ; and which are to be the abſolute Demonſtration of *Jeſus*'s divine Authority and *Meſſiahſhip* to the Converſion of *Jews* and *Infidels*,

I have no more to do at preſent, but, like a *Moderator*, to conclude with a ſhort Addreſs and Exhortation to *Infidels* and *Apoſtates*,

Apoſtates, the two contending Parties in the preſent Controverſy. And

Firſt, To *Apoſtates*, I mean the Writers againſt the *Grounds* and *Scheme*. Whether you, *grave Sirs*, who account your ſelves orthodox *Divines*, tho there is little but Contradiction and Inconſiſtency amongſt you, do like the Name of *Apoſtates* which is given you, I much queſtion: But it is the propereſt, I could think of, for your Deſertion of primitive Doctrine about Prophecy and Miracles. I could, not improperly have given you a worſe *Title*, but I was willing to compliment you, rather than reproach you with this.

But ſetting aſide the Title of *Apoſtates*, whether it be, in your Opinion, opprobrious or not; you may plainly perceive, that I am, *Sirs*, on your Side, as to the Truth of Chriſtianity; and if you'll accept of my Aſſiſtance for the Proof of *Jeſus*'s Meſſiahſhip from Prophecy, upon the Terms of the allegorical Scheme propoſed in my *Moderator*, you ſhall find me your hearty Abettor. Upon the allegorical Scheme, I don't doubt but we ſhall ſoundly drub and mawl *Infidels*, and beat them out of the Field of Battle. If you, being wedded to the literal Scheme, will not accept of my Aſſiſtance, you may go on in your own Way,

Way, and fee the Event of the Controverfy, which in the End will turn to your Difhonour.

You, *Sirs*, can't but be fenfible, how thofe two great Generals, Mr. *Grounds*, and Mr. *Scheme*, with their potent Armies of Reafons and Authorities againft your literal Prophecies, have grievoufly diftrefs'd and gall'd you ; and if you don't make an honourable Retreat in Time, and feek to *Allegorifts* for Help, will gain a compleat Victory and Triumph over you.

Inftead of the Help of *Allegorifts*, you, I find, under the Difappointment of your literal Scheme, chufe rather to have Recourfe to *Jefus*'s Miracles : But what little Dependence there is upon his Miracles, in your Senfe, I have in *part* proved in this Difcourfe; and this I have done (give me leave repeatedly to delare it) not for the Service of your unbelieving Adverfaries, but to reduce you to the good old Way of interpreting Oracles, which, upon the Teftimony of the Fathers, will, one Day, be the Converfion of the *Jews* and *Gentiles*.

Whether you, *Sirs*, will be pleas'd with this fhort Difcourfe on Chrift's Miracles, I much queftion. But before you put your felves into a Rage againft it, I beg of you to read St. *Theophilus* of *Antioch*, *Origen*, St. *Hilary*,.

St. *Hilary*, St. *Augustin*, St. *Ambrose*, St. *Jerome*, St. *Chrysostom*, St. *John* of *Jerusalem*, St. *Theophylact*, and other occasional ancient Pieces on one part or other of the *Evangelists* ; and you'll find how they countenance such a Discourse as this on Miracles, and will abundantly assist me in the Prosecution of it.

I expect, *Sirs*, that some of you will be ready to rave against me for this Discourse; but this is my Comfort, that if your Passion should arise to another Prosecution of me, you can't possibly separate any of mine from the Opinions of the Fathers to ground a Prosecution on : And what Dishonour in the End will redown to Protestant and pretendedly learned *Divines* of the Church of *England*, to persecute again the Fathers for primitive Doctrine, I desire you to think on.

But, as I suppose, you'll have more Wit, *Sirs*, than to prosecute me again for this Discourse ; so I hope you'll have more Ingenuity, than odiously (after your wonted manner) to represent me to the Populace, for Profaneness, Blasphemy, and Infidelity. If you dislike the whole, or any part of this Discourse, appear like **Men** and Scholars, from the *Press* against it. Use me as roughly in Print as you think fit, I'll not take it ill.

Veniam

Veniam petimus, dabimufq; viciffim.

I defire nothing more than to be furioufly attack'd from the *Prefs*, which, if I am not much miftaken, would give me a long'd for Opportunity to expofe your Ignorance to more Advantage.

Be not longer miftaken, *good Sirs.* The Hiftory of *Jefus*'s Life, as recorded in the *Evangelifts*, is an emblematical Reprefentation of his fpiritual Life in the Soul of Man ; and his Miracles are Figures of his myfterious Operations. The four Gofpels are in no Part a literal Story, but a Syftem of myftical Philofophy or Theology.

If you are refolved not to come into this Opinion, I beg of you again, before you break forth into a Paffion, to try to vindicate the literal Story of the three Miracles fpoken to in this Difcourfe, *viz.* thofe of *Jefus*'s *driving the Buyers and Sellers out of the Temple* ; *of his exorcifing the Devil out of the Madman* ; *and of his Transfiguration on the Mount* ; which if you are able to defend againft the Fathers, and my Objections, I'll give up the Caufe to you, and own my felf (what I am far enough from being) an impious Infidel and Blafphemer, and deferving of the worft Punifhment. In the mean time, I make bold again to affert, that the literal Story of Chrift's Life and

K   Miracles,

Miracles, is an abſurd and incredible Romance, full of Contradictions and Inconſiſtencies ; and that modern Paraphraſes
are not only a conſequential Reflection on
the Intellects of the *Evangeliſts*, and their
divine Gifts of the Spirit, as if they could
not write an intelligible and coherent Piece
of Biography without your Help at this
Diſtance of Time ; but have even darken'd
and obſcured the ſeemingly native Simplicity of the Story of the Life of *Jeſus*. So
leaving you to chew upon this, I turn

My Addreſs to *Infidels*, particularly to
the two moſt renown'd Writers of the Party, Mr. *Grounds*, and Mr. *Scheme*. I
ſhould, *Gentlemen*, by right, ſalute you
with the Title of *Free-Thinkers*, a proper
Name for your philoſophical Sect, who are
for the free Exerciſe of your Reaſon about
divine and ſpeculative Points in Theology.
And I had diſtinguiſh'd you by this Title
from your apoſtatical Adverſaries, but that
I had a mind to oblige my old Friends the
Clergy, in giving you a no more honourable Title than I do them. And I truſt you
will not be offended at the Title of *Infidels*, ſince not only your Writings ſeem to
have a Tendency to Infidelity ; but, if there
be any Fault in your Principles, you know
how to charge it on your Adverſaries, the
pretended Advocates for Chriſtianity, whoſe
Abſurdities,

Abfurdities. falfe Reafonings, Inconfiften-
cies, and foolifh Gloffes on the Scriptures,
have occafioned your Departure from the
Faith in Chrift.

I thank Mr. *Scheme* for the noble Prefent of his Book, which I received and read
with Pleafure. But inftead of one, he
fhould have fent me a *Dozen* for the Ufe
of Friends and Borrowers, who are very
curious and importunate for the Perufal of
it. For what Reafon he envies the *Bookfellers* the publick Sale of his Work, chu-
fing rather to give it away *gratis*, than that
they fhould reap any Profit by it, I know
not. Surely it is not to bring an *Odium*
on the *Clergy* for Perfecutors, as if fuch an
ufeful and philofophical Piece might not
appear publickly without Danger from
them : If fo, I hope the *Clergy* will re-
fent the Indignity, and invite him to a
Publication of his Book, with a Promife
of Impunity, which would wipe off the
Reproach, which this clandeftine Method
of difpofing of it has caft on them.

I once almoft defpair'd, *Sirs*, of feeing
fuch another Piece from your Quarter. I
was afraid the Profecution of the *Moderator*, would have deterr'd you from the
Prefs, whereby our excellent Controverfy
on Foot muft have been dropt : But the
fudden and unexpected Appearance of Mr.

Schema

Scheme, has revived me, and rejoiced the Cockles of my Heart. Go on then, *great Sirs,* in this Controverſy, which Mr. *Grounds* happily commenc'd ; and if you are deny'd the Liberty of the Preſs, and publick Sale of your Books, I hope you'll, for all that, as occaſion offers it ſelf, oblige the Learned and Curious with ſome more of your bright Lucubrations, tho you print them, and diſpoſe of them in this clancular and ſubtil Method.

It is not that I wiſh well to your Cauſe of Infidelity, that I thus encourage you. You have more Senſe and Reaſon than to ſuſpect me tainted with unbelieving Principles. Chriſtianity will ſtand its Ground againſt your battering Armour ; and the Church of Chriſt will be the more firmly eſtabliſh'd on a Rock of Wiſdom, for that Oppoſition you make to it. Tho' you will entirely vanquiſh the literal *Schemiſts,* and ride in Triumph over them, yet other Defenders of the Faith, call'd *Allegoriſts,* will ariſe to your Confutation and final Overthrow.

If I am not miſtaken, *Sirs,* your Adverſaries, the literal *Schemiſts,* whom I call *Apoſtates,* are about making a Retreat, and yielding the Field of Battle to you. The *Biſhop* of *Litchfield,* the greateſt General on their Side, will not only find it

hard

hard to levy any more Forces in Defence of his *twelve* literal Prophecies; but he knows that, if he draws his Sword any more against you, he must attack too the Authority of the Fathers for the allegorical Interpretation of some of those Prophecies, already urg'd in my *Supplements* to the *Moderator*; or, if the Fathers are neglected by him; they and I, keeping out of the Reach of his *Bug-Bear*, will treat him with such familiar Language, as never was given to one of his Order.

Mr. *Scheme* seems to promise us a Discourse on the Miracles in the Scriptures; I hope he'll be as good as his Word, and ere long publish it. This Discourse of mine can't possibly supersede his. As I question not but his Thoughts and Remarks on Miracles will be very considerable; so I shall be a little impatient till I see them. But be his Discourse on Miracles of what Kind soever, I believe it will hardly be an Obstruction to my Undertaking in Hand, which I intend, by God's Leave, to go on with, to the Honour of the holy *Jesus*, our spiritual *Messiah*, to whom be Glory and Praise for ever and ever. *Amen.*

F I N I S.

A SECOND

DISCOURSE

ON THE

MIRACLES

OF OUR

SAVIOUR,

In VIEW of the present Controversy between INFIDELS and APOSTATES.

Audendum est, ut illustrata Veritas pateat, multique ab Errore liberentur. Lactant.

By THOMAS WOOLSTON, sometime Fellow of *Sidney-College* in *Cambridge.*

LONDON:

Printed for the Author, Sold by him in *Bell-Alley, Coleman-Street,* and by the Booksellers of *London* and *Westminster.* 1727.

[Price One Shilling.]

TO THE

Right Reverend Father in God

E D W A R D,

Lord Bishop of *Lichfield.*

My Lord,

YOUR Fame for that celebrated Book, call'd the *Defence of Christianity,* is the Occasion of this Dedication. I need not tell you, what vast Reputation you have acquired by it: You have been not only often applauded from the Press, but have met with large Compliments and Thanks from your Clergy for it. And tho' Mr. *Scheme* has very untowardly written against you, yet this is *still* your Honour, that you are an *Author,* not unworthy of his Regard and Notice.

I am, in Opinion with the Fathers, against an establish'd Hire for the Priest=

Priesthood, thinking it of disservice to true Religion: But when I consider'd the Usefulness of your Lordship's Episcopal Riches and Honours to this Controversy, I almost chang'd my Mind. Your exalted Station in the Church, has given Credit and Authority to your Work, which, if it had came from the Hands of a poor Priest, had never been so much admir'd; neither would Mr. *Scheme*, I believe, nor my self, have paid so many Respects to it.

For this Reason, I wish some more of your *Order* would appear in this Controversy, that the World might see what famous Men are our *Bishops*, and of what Use their *Hundreds* and *Thousands* a Year are to the Defence of Christianity; which, if such able Hands were not amply hired to its Support, might be in Danger, as certainly as, that Men of low Fortunes must needs be Men of poor Parts, little Learning, and slender Capacities to write in Vindication of it.

Some have conceiv'd Hopes that the great *Bishop* of *London*, from his last

Charge

Charge to his *Clergy*, will second you in this Controversy; if so, there's no doubt on't, but his Performance will be commensurate to his State and Revenues. Of his Zeal in the Controversy, he has already given a notable Instance, when he prosecuted the *Moderator*; and I dare say, he'll vouchsafe us a more remarkable Specimen of his Knowledge in it, as soon as he can spare Time for't; and then (Oh my Fears!) he'll pay me off for my Objection against Christ's Resurrection, which he would have persuaded the Civil Magistrate to have done for him.

But whether the *Bishop* of *London* seconds you or not, it's Time, *my Lord*, to expect another Volume from you, in Answer to Mr. *Scheme*, which, for all the Reports that are spread of your intended Silence, I hope soon to see publish'd. What will the People say, if that *Philisthin* goes off, giving you the last Blow in the Controversy? Nothing less than that he has gotten the better of the Learned *Bishop* of *Lichfield*, and has re-

futed

futed Christianity to the Conviction of the Bishop himself, who would renounce it too, but for the temporal Advantages he enjoys by it.

Think, *my Lord*, on the Dishonour of such Reflections, and resume Courage against the Adversary. I look upon you as a more sturdy Gladiator than for one Cut on the Pate, to quit the Stage of Battle. Tho' Mr. *Scheme* has unluckily hit you on a soft Place, and weaken'd your Intellectuals for a while; yet he is a generous Combatant, and gives you Time to recover your wonted Strength of Reason. At him again then, *my Lord*, and fear not, in your Turn, to give him such a Home-Thrust, as will pierce his unbelieving Heart.

And when your *Lordship* engages him again from the *Press*, I hope you'll be more explicite for Liberty of Debate. Through godly Zeal for *Church*, you unhappily made a Slip, in your *Dedication* to the *King*, on the persecuting Side of the Question, which had lik'd to have sully'd the Glory of your whole Work. Such a

grand

grand Philofopher, as you are, fhould truft alone to the Goodnefs of your Caufe, and the Strength of your Reafonings, in Defence of it: Such a potent Champion for Chriftianity, as you are, fhould difdain the Affiftance of any, but of God, to fight for you. The Ufe of the Civil Sword on your Side, is not only a Difparagement to your Parts, but a Difgrace to our Religion.

I know not what your *Lordfhip* may think on't, but the Profecution of the *Moderator* was, in the Judgment of others, more than of my felf, fome Reproach to you : Becaufe of a few flender Animadverfions, I made on your renown'd Book, fome think I fuffer'd a Profecution, which you, in Honour, fhould have difcourag'd. I am willing to acquit you as much as may be; and would, if I could, impute it to your Forgetfulnefs, rather than your Malice, that you ftep'd not between me and Danger.

Whether this Difcourfe will be acceptable to your Lordfhip, is fomewhat uncertain; I am afraid it will be a little dis-

disgustful to your nice and delicate Taste in Theology, which relishes nothing better than the plain and ordinary Food of the Letter of *Christ's* Miracles: But however, you will readily interpret this *Dedication* to your Honour, and if you should make me a large present of Gold for it, I sincerely assure your *Lordship*, it will be more than I aim'd at; neither do I desire any other Return for it, than to be endulg'd the Liberty and Pleasure to pay my customary Respects to your Writings; and upon proper Occasions to testify to the World, how much I am,

MY LORD,

The Admirer of

Your Wit, Learning

London,
October 13th
1727.

and Orthodoxy,

Thomas Woolston.

A Second

DISCOURSE

ON THE

MIRACLES

OF OUR

SAVIOUR, &c.

I HERE publish another *Discourse* on our Saviour's Miracles, which I am not only oblig'd to, by the Promise I made in my former; but am encouraged to it by the Reception which *that* met with. If any of our *Clergy* were, and besides them, few or none could be offended at my former *Discourse,* they should have printed their Exceptions to it, and, if possible,

B

fible, their Confutation of it, which might perhaps have prevented me the giving them any more Trouble of this Kind.

In my former *Difcourfe* I fairly declar'd, that if the *Clergy* could difprove my Arguments againft the *Letter*, and for the *Spirit* of the Miracles I there took to task, I would not only defift from the Profecution of my Defign, but own my felf an impious *Infidel* and *Blafphemer*, and deferving of the worft Punifhment : But fince they are all mute and filent, even in this Caufe, which in Honour and Intereft they fhould have fpoken out to, they ought not to be angry, if I proceed in it. I have given them time enough to make a Reply, if they had been of Ability to do it : What muft I think then upon their Silence ? Nothing lefs than that my Caufe is impregnable, and my Arguments and Authorities in Defence of it irrefragable ; and though they don't profeffedly yield to the Force of them ; yet they have nothing to fay in Abatement of their Strength, or it had certainly feen the Light before now.

I go on then in my undertaking to write againft the literal Story of our Saviour's Miracles, and againft the Ufe that is commonly made of them to prove his divine Authority and Meffiafhip : And this I do, I folemnly again declare it, not for

the

the Service of Infidelity, but for the Honour of the Holy Jefus, and to reduce the
Clergy to the good *old Way*, and the *only
Way* of proving his Meffiafhip, and that
is, by the allegorical Interpretation of the
Law and the Prophets. Therefore, without any more Preamble, I refume again
the Confideration of the three Heads of
Difcourfe, before propofed to be treated
on to this Purpofe. And they are,

I. To fhew, That the Miracles of healing all manner of Bodily Difeafes, which
Jefus was juftly fam'd for, are none of
the proper Miracles of the *Meffiah*, neither are they fo much as a good Proof
of his divine Authority to found a Religion.

II. That the literal Hiftory of many of
the Miracles of *Jefus*, as recorded by the
Evangelifts, does imply Abfurdities, Improbabilities, and Incredibilities; confequently they, either in whole or in part,
were never wrought, as they are commonly believed now-a-days, but are only related as prophetical and parabolical Narratives of what would be myfterioufly, and
more wonderfully done by him.

III.

III. To confider, what *Jefus* means, when he appeals to his Miracles, as to a Teſtimony and Witneſs of his divine Authority; and to ſhew that he could not properly and ultimately refer to thoſe, he then wrought in the *Fleſh*, but to thoſe myſtical ones, which he would do in the *Spirit*, of which thoſe wrought in the Fleſh are but mere Types and Shadows.

I have already ſpoken, what I then thought ſufficient to the firſt of theſe Heads; and though I could now much enlarge my Reaſons, and multiply Authorities upon it to the ſame Purpoſe; yet I ſhall not do it; but only, by Way of Introduction to my following *Diſcourſe*, ſay, that if it had been intended by our Saviour, that any rational Argument for his divine Authority and *Meſſiaſhip* ſhould be urged from his miraculous healing Power; the Diſeaſes which he cured, would have been accurately deſcribed, and his Manner of Operation ſo cautiouſly expreſs'd, as that we might have been ſure the Work was ſupernatural, and out of the Power of Art and Nature to perform: But the *Evangeliſts* have taken no ſuch Care in their Narrations of Chriſt's Miracles. As for Inſtance, *Jefus* is ſuppoſed
often

often miraculously to cure *Lameness*; but there is no Account of the nature and degree of Lameness he cured; nor are we certain, whether the Skill of a *Surgeon*, or Nature it self, could not have done the Work without his Help. If the *Evangelists* had told us of Men, that wanted one or both their Legs, (and such miserable Objects of Christ's Power and Compassion, were undoubtedly in those Days as well as in ours) and how *Jesus* commanded Nature to extend itself to the entire Reparation of such Defects; here would have been stupendous Miracles indeed, which no Scepticism, nor Infidelity itself could have cavill'd at; nor could I, nor the Fathers themselves have told how to allegorize, and make Parables of them. But there is no *such* Miracle recorded of Christ, nor any thing equal to it; so far from it, that the best and greatest Miracles of *Jesus*, which must confessedly be those related at large, (for no Body can suppose he did greater than those more particularly specify'd) are liable to exception, being so blindly, and lamely, and imperfectly reported, as that, by Reasonings upon the Letter of the Stories of them, they may be dwindled away, and reduced to no Wonders, which brings me to treat again on the

II.

II. Second Head of my Difcourfe, and that is, to fhew, that the literal Hiftory of the Miracles of *Jefus*, as recorded in the *Evangelifts*, does imply Abfurdities, Improbabilities and Incredibilities; confequently they, in whole or in part, were never wrought, but are only related as parabolical Narratives of what would be myfterioufly, and more wonderfully done by him.

To this Purpofe I, in my former Difcourfe, took into Examination *three* of the Miracles of Jefus, *viz.* thofe, of *his driving the Buyers and Sellers out of the Temple* ; Of *his exorcifing the Devils out of the Madmen, and fending them into the Herd of Swine* ; and *Of his Transfiguration on the Mount*. How well I perform'd on thefe Miracles, which have been admired for their literal Story, let others judge and fay.

I now will take into Confideration three others of *Jefus*'s Miracles, *viz.* thofe, Of *his healing a Woman that was afflicted with an Iffue of Blood, twelve Years* ; Of *his curing the Woman that labour'd under a Spirit of Infirmity, eighteen Years* ; and Of *his telling the* Samaritan *Woman her Fortune of having had five Husbands, and living then in Adultery*

tery with another Man: Which are, all three, reputedly moſt miraculous and admired Stories. The two former, they ſay, are Arguments of *Jeſus*'s mighty Power ; and the latter, of his immenſe Knowledge : But how little of certain Power and Knowledge there is in any of them, according to the Letter, will be ſeen in the ſequel of this Diſcourſe. Infidels, I dare ſay, if they had not wanted Liberty, would e'er now have facetiouſly expoſed thoſe Stories. If I ſnatch that Work out of their Hands, our *Clergy* ought to be glad, becauſe what I do in it, is to the Honour of the Holy *Jeſus*, and to turn thoſe pretendedly miraculous Stories into divine Myſteries.

In my former Diſcourſe I gave my *Readers* ſome Reaſon to expect, that in *this* I would treat on ſome of *Jeſus*'s Miracles, which I there mentioned, *viz. On his turning Water into Wine at a Marriage in* Cana *of* Galilee; and *On his feeding of Thouſands with a few Loaves and Fiſhes in the Wilderneſs;* and *On his Cure of the Paralytick, for whom the Roof of the Houſe was broken up to let him down into the Room where* Jeſus *was,* &c. And I then really did deſign to ſpeak to theſe Miracles, but upon Conſideration, finding them moſt ludicrous Subjects according

to

to the Letter, I forbear it at prefent, having no Inclination to put the *Clergy* quite
out of all Temper. If any fhould fay,
this is Fear and Cowardice in me, I can't
help it: But, for all that, now I have the
Clergy in a tolerable good Humour for
Liberty, I'll endeavour to keep them in
it, and not difturb them by an hafty and
unneceffary Provocation of them. Who
knows not, that the *Clergy*, like an un-
tamed *Colt*, that I have a mind to ride, may
be apt to winch and kick, and may give
me a Fall before I come at the end of my
Journey, to the Difappointment of my
Readers? They fhall therefore be gently
handled and ftroak'd, till they are a little
more inur'd to the Bit and Saddle: And
for their Sakes will I poftpone fuch Miracles as are moft obnoxious to Ridicule,
and at prefent chufe the aforefaid *three*,
that of almoft any in the Gofpel may be
moft inoffenfively treated on. I begin
then,

1. To fpeak to that Miracle of *Jefus*'s
(1) healing a *Woman difeafed with an Iffue of Blood, twelve Years*. To pleafe
our *Divines*, I will allow as much of the
Truth of the Letter of this Story, as they

(1) *Matt. Ch. ix. Luke Ch. viii. Mark Ch. v.*

can

can defire. The Fathers themfelves, who are for turning the whole Hiftory of *Je-fus*'s Life into Allegory and Myftery, don't deny that a Woman was cured of an *Hæmorrhage*, after the Manner that is here defcribed by the Evangelifts. St. *Au-guftin* fays (2) of this Miracle, *that it was done, as it is related*; and I have a greater Veneration for his Authority, than to gainfay it. But for all that, *Infidels* may and will take into Examination the nature of this Miracle, and if poffible make little or nothing of it. And if I do this for them, it is not to do Service to Infidelity, but to turn Mens Heads to the myftical Ufe of it, for which it is recorded.

As there is a particular Narration of this Miracle, among the few others, that are fpecified; fo Reafon fhould tell us, that if the Letter of the Story of *Chrift*'s Miracles, as our *Divines* hold, is only to be regarded, this is one of the greateft that Jefus wrought, or it would not be related by itfelf, but thrown into the Lump of all manner of Difeafes, which He heal'd. And how then fhall we come to the Knowledge of the greatnefs

---

(2) Factum quidum eft, &, ita ut narratur, impletum. *In Serm.* lxxvii. *Sect.* 7.

of

of this Miracle? Why, there are but two Ways to it, and they are,

First, By considering the nature of the Disease, or the lamentable Condition of the Patient before Cure. And

Secondly, By considering the Manner or Means by which the Cure was performed. If one or both of these Considerations don't manifest the Certainty of a Miracle, *Infidels* may conclude there was none in it.

First, As to the nature of the Disease of this Woman, we are much in the Dark about it, and very uncertain of what Kind and Degree it was. St. *Matthew* writing of it, says the Woman was αιμορεγουσα, that is, *obnoxious to bleeding*; St. *Mark* and St. *Luke* say of her, that ουσα εν ρευματι αιματος, she was in an efflux or running of Blood. But neither one nor the other of the *Evangelists* signify of what Degree her *Hæmorrhage* was, nor from what part of her Body it proceeded, nor how often or seldom she was addicted to it. It might be, for ought we know, only a little bleeding at the Nose, that now and then she was subject to: Or it might be an obnoxious-
nefs

ness to an Evacuation of Blood by Siege
or Urine : Or it was, not improbably, of
the menstruous Kind. Any of these might
be the Case of this Woman for what's
written; and I don't find that any of our
Divines have determined of what sort it
was. But a great Miracle is wrought,
they think, in her Cure, without knowing the Disease; which *Infidels* will say
is asserted at Random and without Reason,
in as much as it is necessary to know the
nature of the Distemper, or none truly
and properly can say, there was a great,
much less a miraculous Cure wrought.

But supposing this *Hæmorrhage* proceeded from what Part of the Body our *Divines* think fit; How will they make a
grievous Distemper of it in order to a Miracle? The Woman subsisted too long under her Issue of Blood, and bore it too
well, for any to make her Case very grievous. *Beza* (3) will have it, that is was
a constant and incessant Effusion of Blood
that the Woman labour'd with. But this
could not be, nor was it possible, as I
suppose *Physicians* will agree, for Nature
to endure it so long, or the Woman to
live twelve Days, much less twelve Years
under it.

(3) *On Mat. Chap.* ix.

No

No more then, than some flight Indif-
position can reasonably and naturally be
made of this Woman's Distemper. And
it would be well, if Infidels would rest
here with their Objections against it. But
what if they should say, that this *Hæmorrhage* was rather of Advantage to the
Health of the Patient, than of Danger to
her, and that the Woman was more *nice*
than *wise*, or she would never have sought
so much for Help and Cure of it? Some
Hæmorrhages are better kept open than
stop'd and dry'd up; and if *Infidels* should
say, that *this* was a Preservative of the
Life of the Woman, like an *Issue*, at which
Nature discharges itself of bad Humours,
Who can contradict them? Nay, if they
should say that *Jesus*'s Cure of this Woman's *Hæmorrhage* was a Precipitation of
her Death, for she died some time after it,
rather than a Prolongation of her Life,
for she lived twelve Years under it, and
was of good Strength, when she applied
to our Saviour for Cure, or she could never have born the press of the People to
come at him; Who can gainsay them?
It is true she was very follicitous for a
Cure, and uneasy under her Distemper,
or she would never have spent all she had
on *Physicians*; which is a Sign, some
may say, that her Disease was grievous,
irksome,

irkſome, and dangerous, as well as incurable by Art. But *Infidels* will ſay,
not ſo; for there are ſome ſlight cutane-
ous Diſtempers, ſometimes iſſuing with
a little purulent and bloody Matter,
that nice Women will be at a great
Expence for Relief, and are always tam-
pering, and often adviſing about them,
though to no Purpoſe: And if they
ſhould ſay that this was the worſt of the
Caſe of this Woman, Who can diſprove
it ?

In ſhort then here is an uncertain Diſtemper both in Nature and Degree; how
then can there be any Certainty of a Miracle in the Cure of it ? Mr. *Moore*, the
Apothecary, accurately deſcribes the Diſeaſes he pretends to have cured; and he
is in the right on't ſo to do, or he could
not recommend his Art, and aggrandize
his own Fame. So the Bodily Diſeaſe of
this Woman ſhould have been clearly and
fully repreſented to our Underſtanding, or
we can form no Conception of Chriſt's
Power in the Cure of it. And I can't
but think that the *Evangeliſts*, eſpecially
St. *Luke* the *Phyſician*, had made a better
Story of this Woman's Caſe, if Chriſt's
Authority and Power had been to be urg'd
from the Letter of it. It's enough to make
us think, Chriſt cured no extraordinary and
grievous

grievous Maladies, or the *Evangelifts*
would never have inftanced in this, that
fo much Exception is to be made to. As
then, reafonably fpeaking, there was no
extraordinary Difeafe in this Woman cured,
and confequently no great Miracle wrought;
fo let us now,

Secondly, Confider the Manner of the
Cure, and whether any Miracle is to be
thence proved. *The Woman faid with-*
in her felf, (4) *that if fhe could but touch*
the Hem of Jefus's Garment, fhe fhould
be made whole. And I can't but commend her, at this diftance of Time, for
the Power of her Faith, Perfuafion, or
Imagination in the Cafe, which was a
good Preparative for Relief, and without
which, it's certain, fhe had continued
under her Difeafe. The Power of Imagination, it's well known, will work Wonders, fee Vifions, produce Monfters, and
heal Difeafes, as Experience and Hiftory
doth teftify. There being many Inftances to be given of Cures performed
by frivolous Applications, Charms, and
Spells, which are unaccountable any other
Way, than by the Imagination of the Patient. Againft the Reafon and Judgment

(4) *Matt. Ch.* ix. *v.* 2L.

of

of a *Physician*, sometimes the diseased will take his own Medicines and find Benefit. And I don't doubt, but Stories may be told of Cures wrought, the Imagination of the Patient helping, by as mean a Trifle, as the Touch of Christ's Garments, and no Miracle talk'd on for it. Even in the ordinary, natural, and rational Use of Physick, it is requisite, that the Patient have a good Opinion of his *Physician* and of his Medicines. A good Heart in the Sick, tends not only to his Support, but helps the Operation of Prescriptions. As despair and dejection of Mind sometimes kills, where otherwise reasonably speaking, proper Medicines would cure; so a good Conceit in the Patient at other times, whether the Medicines be pertinent or not, is almost all in all. And if Infidels should say that this was the Case of this Woman in the Gospel ; if they should say as St. *John* of *Jerusalem* (5) did, *that her own Imagination cured herself*; and should urge the Probability of it, because *Jesus* could do no Cures and (6) Miracles against Unbelief, Who can help it ? In this Case our *Divines* must prove, that this Woman's

(5) Non autem Fimbria Jesu, sed ejus Cogitatio eam salvam fecit. *In Loc. Marci.*

(6) *Matt. Ch.* xiii. *v.* 58.

Hamor-

Hæmorrhage was of that kind, that no Faith nor Fancy in herſelf could help her without the Divine Power; but this is impoſſible for them to do, unleſs there had been a more certain Deſcription of her Diſeaſe, than the *Evangeliſts* have given of it.

Our *Divines* will indeed tell us, what I believe, that it was the Divine Power co-operating with the Faith and Imagination of the Woman that cured her; becauſe Jeſus ſays *that Virtue had gone out of him* to the healing of her: And I wiſh *Infidels* would acquieſce here, and not ſay, that *Jeſus*'s Virtue hung very looſe on him, or the Woman's Faith, like a Faſcination, could never have extracted it againſt his Will and Knowledge: But what if they ſhould ſay, that *Jeſus*, being ſecretly appr z'd of the Woman's Faith, and Touch of him, took the Hint; and to comfort and confirm her in her Conceit, and to help the Cure forward, ſaid, *Virtue was gone out of him?* This would be an untoward Suggeſtion, which if Infidels ſhould make, our Divines muſt look for a Reply to it.

It is ſaid of the *Pope*, when he was laſt at *Benevento*, that he wrought three Miracles, which our Proteſtant *Clergy*, I dare ſay, believe nothing at all of. But, for all that, it is not improbable, but that
ſome

some diseased People, considering their superstitious Veneration for the *Pope*, and their Opinion of the Sanctity of the *Present*, might be persuaded of his Gift of Miracles, and desirous of his Exercise of it; and if they fancyfully or actually received Benefit by his Touch, I don't wonder, without a Miracle. And what if we had been told of the *Popes* curing an *Hæmorrhage* like this before us? What would *Protestants* have said to it? Why, " that a foolish,
" credulous, and superstitious Woman had
" fancy'd herself cured of some slight In-
" disposition; and the crafty *Pope* and his
" Adherents, aspiring after popular Ap-
" plause, magnified the presumed Cure
" into a Miracle. If they would have us
" *Protestants* to believe the Miracle, they
" should have given us an exacter Descrip-
" tion of her Disease, and then we could
" better have judg'd of it". The Application of such a supposed Story of a Miracle wrought by the *Pope*, is easy; and if *Infidels*, *Jews*, and *Mahometans*, who have no better Opinion of *Jesus*, than we have of the *Pope*, should make it, there's no Help for it.

And thus have I made my Descants on this supposed Miracle before us, and argued, as much as I could, against the Miraculousness of it, both from the *Nature*

of

of the Difeafe, and the *Manner* of the Cure of it. Whether any one fhall think I have faid any thing to the Purpofe or not, is all one to me. My Defign in what I have done, is not to do Service to Infidelity, but, upon the Command and Encouragement of the Fathers, to turn Mens Thoughts to the myftical Meaning of the faid Miracle, which I come now to give an Account of.

None of the Fathers (excepting St. *Chryfoftom* (7), who writes here more like an *Orator* than a *Phyfician*) ever trouble themfelves, when they fpeak of this Miracle, about the Nature of the Difeafe, literally, in this Woman, or the greatnefs of the Cure of it; but alone bend their Studies to the myftical Interpretation, for the fake of which, this Evangelical Story was written, and originally tranfacted.

Accordingly, they tell us that this Woman is a Type (8) of the Church of the *Gentiles* in after Times. And as to her *Hæmorrhage* or *Iffue of Blood*, they un-

(7) In Locum *Matt.*

(8) Illa vero Mulier quæ Fluxum Sanguinis patiebatur, Ecclefiam figurabat ex Gentibus. St. *Auguft. in Serm.* lxxvii. *Sect.* 8. Præparatur igitur Mulier, in cujus Typo univerfalis Ecclefia fub fpecie defignetur. *Pafchaf. Ratbert. in Loc. Matt.*

derftand

derftand it of the (9) Impurity and Corruption of the Church by ill Principles and bad Morals, that she would *flow with*. Some of the Fathers, as (10) *Gregory Nazianzen*, and (11) *Eufebius Gallicanus*, will have the *Iſſue of Blood* to be a Type of the ſcarlet Sin of Blood-guiltineſs in the Church: If ſo, we muſt underftand it of the Effuſion of Chriſtian Blood by War and Perſecution.

The *twelve Years* of the Woman's Affliction with her *Hæmorrhage* is a typical Number of the Church's impure State for above *twelve Hundred Years*. And whether ſome of the primitive Church did not, by the ſaid *twelve Years* of the Woman, underftand *twelve Ages*, I appeal to (12) *Irenæus*, to whom I refer my

---

(9) Hæc Mulier, i. e. Sancta Ecclefia de Gentibus congregata quæ lapſu Criminum deperibat Sancti *Ambroſii in Loc. Luc*. Ut Mulier, quæ fluxum ſanguinis patiebatur, &c. ita omnis Anima percuſſa incurabili Vulnere Peccati, habens fontem pravarum Cogitationum, &c. *Macarii Ægypt. in Hom* xx.

(10) Επιγαζες γαρ την φοινικην αμαρ]ιαι. *In Orat*. XL.

(11) Quæ eſt enim hæc Mulier niſi Eccleſia Gentium — Fluxum Sanguinis patiebatur, quia in ſuorum Peccatorum Sanguine verſabatur; quia Sanguinum Rapina & Occiſione nutriebatur. *In Dominic*. xxiv.

(12) Adverſus Hæreſes. *Lib*. I. *Cap*. iii.

Readers

Readers. Accordingly this typify'd Woman of the Church, fhould be the fame with the Woman (13) in the Wildernefs, that, as St. *John* fays, was twelve Hundred and fixty Days or Years there fuftained; and by whom many Proteftants, as well as the Fathers, underftand the Church univerfal. When the faid twelve Hundred and fixty Days or Years of the Church's being in the Wildernefs, did commence or will end, is none of my Bufinefs to enquire or afcertain. But as this Woman in the Gofpel is faid after *twelve Years* Affliction, to be cured of her Difeafe by *Jefus*; fo it is the Opinion of the Fathers, that the Church univerfal, after *twelve Hundred Years* of her Wildernefs State, will be purified and fanctified by the Gifts of the Spirit of Chrift, and enter upon a more holy, peaceable, and happy Condition, abfolutely freed from her *Iffue of Blood*, which, through Perfecution and War, fhe has for many Ages labour'd under. It is not my Concern to collect all the Authorities of the Fathers to this Purpofe; but only fay, that if at the End of twelve Hundred and fixty Days or Years, the Church, like the Woman, be not cur'd of her *Hæmorrhage* and myftical *Wounds* and *Sores*;

(13) *Revel. Chap.* xii. *v.* 6.

if

if her prefent impure and unfound State be not chang'd into an holy, healthy, and peaceable one; many good *Proteftants,* as well as the Fathers, are miftaken, and abundance of Prophecies of the Old and New Teftament, that have been hereunto urged, will lofe their Credit.

But who are meant by the *Phyficians* of the Woman, that have had the myfti-cal *Hæmorrhage* and Difeafes of the Church under Cure all this while? Who fhould, but pretended Minifters, of the Gofpel? Minifters of the Gofpel are not only by the Fathers call'd metaphorically (14) fpiritual *Phyficians;* but our *Divines* and Preachers of all Denominations like the Metaphor, and think themfelves able *Phyficians* at the Difeafes of the Church, which they are forward to pre-fcribe and apply Medicines to, whenever, in their Opinion, fhe ftands in need of them. Whether our *Divines* like to be accounted the *Phyficians* of the Text be-fore us, I much queftion; but it is certain that (15) *Eufebius Gallicanus* exprefly fays,

---

(14) Excellentes Verbi Prædicatores tanquam magni Medici. — *Sancti Auguft. in Pfal.* Lxxxvii. *Sect.* 10.

(15) Per hos enim Medicos, Ariolos & Philofo-phos intelligere poffumus, quorum perfuafionibus cæteri

says, that our *Divines* and pretended Philosophers are meant by them; and venerable *Bede* (16) upon the Place is of the same Mind too.

The Woman of the Gospel is said (17) to *suffer many Things of many Physicians, and was nothing better'd, but rather grew worse*; that is, she grew worse not in time only, but through the Use of her *Physicians*, who were her (18) Tormentors. So the Diseases of the Church in time have increased, for all the Use she has made of her spiritual Physicians, *the Clergy*. In every Age has the Church been degenerating in Morals and Principles, as any one knows, that is able to make an Estimate of Religion in times past; and all along have her ecclesiastical *Quack Doctors* contributed to her ill State of Health. As many Physicians with their different Applications tormented the poor Woman; so our many *Empericks* in Theology with their different *Schemes* of

cæteri credentes a fidei Veritate aberrantes ad Animæ Sanitatem attingere non valebant. *In Dominic.* xxiv.

(16) Per Medicos intellige falsos Theologos. *In Loc. Marci.*

(17) *Mark Ch.* v. v. 26.

(18) Medici Molestiam potius quam Sanitatem ægrotanti præbentes. *Ephræm. Syri.* p. 63.

Church

Church Government and various *Systems* of Divinity, like so many Prescriptions for Cure, have increased the Divisions, widen'd the Wounds, and inflamed the Sores of the Church. And if the Woman's *Issue of Blood* be, according to the Fathers, a particular Type of the Blood of the Church, that is shed in Persecution and War; our Theological Pretenders to Physick, have been so far from providing and prescribing a good *Stiptic* in this Case, that they have been the Occasion of the Effusion of much Christian Blood; there having been many a War and Persecution, that these *Incision* Doctors, who should be all *Balsam*, have been the Cause of.

The Woman *spent all her Living*, all her yearly Income, upon her Physicians, and as it seems to a bad Purpose; so very great and large Revenues of the Church, are expended on her ecclesiastical Doctors in spiritual Physick: And to what End and Purpose? Why, to open and widen the bleeding Wounds of the Church, which they should heal and salve up. It is now about *twelve Hundred Years*, like the *twelve Years* of the Woman, that the *Clergy*, our Practitioners in Theological Physick, have received of the Church vast Fees, Stipends and Gratuities (for before that time her *Doctors* prescrib'd freely) to take care of her Health and Welfare;

fare; but unlefs God provide in due time a Medicine of his own, fhe is likely to continue in a difeafed and forowful Condition for all them.

One would think that the Woman of the Gofpel might have had more Wit than to lay out all fhe was worth upon *Phyficians* to no good Purpofe; one would think that after fome Experience of their Infufficiency to cure her, fhe might have forborn feeing them, and referved the Remains of her Eftate for better Ufes: So the Fees and Revenues of the Church, after due Experience of the Inability of her fpiritual Doctors to heal her Sores, might have been in my Opinion better employ'd, and the Church of Chrift more out of Danger of Wounds and Sicknefs, by Sin and Error. Certain it is, that many an *Iffue of Blood*, through Perfecution and War, had been prevented; if fuch barbarous and blood thirfty Doctors of Ecclefiaftical Phyfick, had never been fo fee'd and hired to take care of the Welfare of the Church, which, for all their Spiritual Medicines, will continue in a languifhing Condition, till heal'd by the Virtue and Graces of the Spirit of Chrift in his forefaid appointed Time.

So much then to the myftical Interpretation of the Story of the Cure of the

Iffue

Iffue of Blood in this Woman. Every minute Circumſtance of it is thus to be allegorized, if need was. Whether the
Clergy will like this parabolical Explication of it, I neither know nor care. They
have their Liberty with *Atheiſts* and *Infidels* to believe as little of it as they think
fit; and I hope they'll give me leave with
the Fathers of the Church to believe as
much of it as I pleaſe. But whether they
approve of this allegorial Interpretation
of this ſuppoſed Miracle or not; they muſt
own, that if the Church, after the foreſaid *twelve Ages*, ſhould be purified and
ſanctified; if her Errors and Corruptions,
of which the Woman's *Uncleanneſs* is a
Type, ſhould be heal'd; if War and Perſecution, typified by her *Iſſue of Blood*,
ſhould then entirely ceaſe; if all Chriſtians ſhould then be united in Principle,
Heart and Affection, and made to walk in
a peaceable and quiet State, as the Woman was (19) *bid to go in Peace*; if the
Church ſhould then *come behind* Jeſus
(which (20) is a Figure of future Time)
and rightly touch by Faith, and appre-

(19) *Mark Ch.* v. *v.* 34.

(20) Dei Poſteriora ſunt noviſſima tempora.
Origen in Pſal. xxxvi.

E   hend

hend his (21) Garments or Words of Prophecy, about which Christians have hitherto been *pressing* and urgent ; and if the Gifts of the Spirit, like *Virtue on the Woman*, should then be poured forth upon the Church to the absolute Cure of her present Diseases, we must, I say, allow the Story of this Woman to be an admirable Emblem and typical Representation ; and the Accomplishment of it most miraculous and stupendous ; and not only an indisputable Proof of the Power and Presence of Christ with his Church, but a Demonstration of his *Messiaship*, in as much as an almost infinite Number of Prophecies of the Old Testament, will thereupon receive that Accomplishment, which hitherto, by no shadow of Reason, can be pretended to.

After such a mystical Healing of the *Hæmorrhage* of the Church, there's no doubt on't, but the Story of this Woman in the Gospel will be allow'd to be typical and emblematical. In the mean time, without making a Parable of the Story of her, I assert, there is little or nothing of a Miracle to be made of her Cure, unless we were at a greater Certainty about the

(21) Vestimenta Jesu sunt Sermones & Scripta Evangeliorum. *Origen in Matt. Ch.* xvii.

Nature

Nature of her Difeafe, and the Manner, rationally fpeaking, of *Jefus*'s healing of it. And fo I pafs to the Confideration of

2. Another Story of a miraculous Cure perform'd by *Jefus* on another Woman, and that is on her, who (22) *had a Spirit of Infirmity, eighteen Years, and was bow'd together, and could in no wife lift up herfelf —— being bound of Satan*, &c. This too, as I fuppofe, is with our *Divines* a great Miracle, and one of the greateft that *Jefus* wrought, or it had not been fpecify'd, but caft indifcriminately into the Number of all manner of Difeafes, which he heal'd. And for the fake of the Letter, and to pleafe our *Divines*, whom I would not offend wilfully, I will allow, that *Jefus* might lay his Hands on, and fpeak comfortably to fuch a drooping, ftooping, and vaporous Woman, full of Fancies of the *Devil*'s Temptation and Power over her ; and fhe might thereupon recover, and be afterwards of a more chearful Heart, and erect Countenance, freed from the whimfical Imagination of being *Satan-ridden* : And what of all that ? Where's the Mi-

(22) *Luke Ch.* xiii.

racle ?

racle ? If the Story of fuch a Miracle had been related of any *Impoſtor* in Religion, of an *Arch-Heretick*, or *Popiſh Exorciſt*, our *Divines* would have flouted at it; they would have told us, there was nothing ſupernatural and uncommon in the Event, nor any thing at all to be wonder'd at in it. Taking the *Devil* out of this Story, and there's no more in it, than what's common for a ſimple, melancholy, and drooping Woman, to be chear'd and elated upon the comfortable Advice and Admonition of a reputedly wife and good Man. And the putting the *Devil* into the Story, in another Caſe, our *Divines* would have ſaid was only the Fancy of the Woman, or the Device of the *Miracle-Monger*, to magnify his own Art and Power. And if *Infidels*, *Jews*, and *Mahometans*, ſhould ſay ſo of this Story of *Jeſus*, they would be no more unreaſonable in their Conjectures and Solutions of this Miracle, than we ſhould have been in another and parallel Caſe.

The *Pope*, when laſt at *Benevento*, is ſaid to have exorciz'd a *Dæmon* out of a young Maid, which our *Divines* no more believe than *Infidels* do. But it is not at all impoſſible or improbable, that a young Woman might be troubled with Vapours, and go droopingly upon it, whom the

holy

holy Father, of whose Prayers and Sanctity she had a good Opinion, might relieve with his Talk, and give another Turn
to her Thoughts and Temper: And if she
fancy'd herself before possess'd with a *Dæmon*, or rather, if the *Pope*'s Partizans persuaded her so, it's not unlikely to make a
Miracle on't. Just so may *Infidels*, with
their Descants on this Miracle before us,
reduce and lessen it: And what must we
Believers do then? Why, we must find
out a Way to ascertain the Truth and
Greatness of the Miracle, or give it up.
We must determine certainly what was the
Woman's Distemper, and how the Cure
of it by ordinary Means was impossible, or
make no more Words about it.

And how can we come at the Knowledge of this Woman's Disease, but by
the original Words of the *Evangelist*.
St. *Luke* says, she was one πνευμα εχουσα
αθενειας, *that had a Spirit of Weakness*,
that is, was poor-Spirited and pusilani-
mous; and if she was συνκυπ7ουσα, *bow'd
down* upon't, its no more than might be
expected of a disconsolate, melancholy and
dejected Person. Here then is the Disease
of the Woman: If it had been worse, St.
Luke, the Physician, if he was of Sufficiency in his Art, should better have express'd himself; so as to give us another
Con-

Conception of it. And if *Satan* had not been brought into the Tale, whom it is easy, by reasoning as above, to exorcise out of it, here is a no more grievous Distemper, than what upon the comfortable Exhortations of a wise Man may be cured. And do what our Divines can, they can make literally no more of this Story.

It is said, that for *eighteen Years* the Woman labour'd under this Disease. And she might be *hippish* and *drooping* for a longer time, and be no less easily at last cured. It's pity the *Evangelist* had not told us how old this Woman was, when the Distemper first seiz'd her; then we could have made better Conjectures about the Nature and Cure of it. If there was any room to suppose, either from the Words of Scripture or extra-scriptural History, that she was about *fifty* or *sixty*, when she first began to droop and the *Devil* got upon her Back; here had been Scope for a most stupendous Miracle; and our *Divines* might have asserted, what no Body could have contradicted, that *Jesus* had made an old Woman, who was *bow'd down*, not only under the Weight of *Satan*, but under the Burthen of seventy or eighty Years, young again; and had restored her to the Health, Vigor, and Beauty of one of fifteen. Here would have

have been a mighty Miracle indeed. And I don't doubt, but our *Divines* would willingly get into such a Notion of this Miracle, and would heartily espouse it, but for the Offence they must needs give to decrepid old Women, who may be out of Conceit with themselves upon it, as if they carried the *Devil* on their Shoulders, as the Cause of their Decripedness and Incurvity. And such an Offence would be of ill Consequence.

Reasonably then speaking, there was not much in the Disease and Cure of this Woman. Excepting that Part, which *Satan* bears, in the Story, there is nothing wonderful in it. And supposing *Jesus* might exorcise the *Devil* out of this Woman, or dismount him from off her Shoulders; yet even this makes nothing for his Divine Power and Authority, in as much as many *Exorcists* among the *Jews* and even among *Papists*, if Protestants had not more Wit than to believe it, could do as much. And after all, I don't believe the *Evangelist* intended, that our Saviour should be had in Admiration for the Letter of this Miracle, or St. *Luke* would accurately have described the Disease, so as to put it out of the Power of Nature and Art to heal it, and of the Wit of *Infidels* to cavil at the miraculous

Cure

Cure of it. Neither do I find that the Fathers of the Church ever trouble themselves about the Letter of this Story, which is some Argument, that no great Heed is to be given to it; but are only curious about the Mystery, for which this Miracle was related, and which I come now to give an Account of.

As the Fathers said of the Woman with her *Issue of Blood*, that she was a Type of the Church; so they say of this Woman with her *Spirit of Infirmity*, that she is a (23) Figure of the Church too.

As the Woman was *bow'd together*; so the Church, as the Fathers do interpret, may be said to be (24) *bow'd down* to the Earth, when she is *prone* and *bent* to, and *intent on* the literal or earthly Interpretations of the Scriptures; and *can in no*

(23) In Muliere infirma est Figura Ecclesiæ. *Theoph. Antioch. in Loc. Lucæ.* Unde intelligitur illa Mulier in Typo Ecclesiæ a Domino sanata & erecta, quam curvaverat Infirmitas, alligante Satana, *Sancti August. de Trinit. Lib.* iv. *Sect.* 7. In Typo Ecclesiæ fæminam salvat. *Sancti Ambros. in Loc. Lucæ.*

(24) Totum Genus humanum tanquam ista Mulier curvatum est ad terram, — Diabolus & Angeli ejus Animas hominum curvaverunt ad terras, id est, ut pronæ in ea quæ terrena, superna non quærerent. *Sancti. August. in Serm.* cccxcii. Qui occidentem sequuntur Literam terrena sapiunt. *Sancti Hieron. in Lib. Amos, Ch.* i.

wise

wife lift up her felf, like the Woman,
that is, can't raife her Thoughts to the
Contemplation of the cæleftial, fpiritual,
and fublime Senfe of them. Hence we
fee the Propriety of the Name of the Woman's Difeafe, call'd πνευμα αϑενειας, a *Spi-*
rit of Weaknefs, which is not properly
fignificative of any bodily Diftemper, but
fuccinctly is very expreffive of the Church's
Weaknefs at the *Spirit* of Prophecy, which
at this Day fhe labours under.

As it was *eighteen Years* that the Woman was griev'd with her *Spirit of Infir-*
mity, for fo long had her Diftemper been
growing on her; fo it is almoft eighteen
(hundred) Years, or the eighteenth Century of Years, that this *Infirmity* of the
Church at the *Spirit* of Prophecy has been
coming on her: And fhe is now fo *bent*
to the Earth of the Letter, that nothing
lefs than the Hand and Power of Jefus,
that erected the Woman, can raife her to
myftical, divine, and fublime Contemplations on the Law and Prophets. St. *Au-*
guftin (25) will have thefe eighteen *eigh-*
teen Years of the Woman's *Infirmity*, as

(25) Quid illa Mulier octo decem Annos habens
in Infirmitate. Sex Diebus Deus perfecit opera
fua. Ter feni decem & octo faciunt. Quod ergo
fignificavit triennium in Arbore, hoc octo decem
Anni in illa Muliere. *In. Serm.* cx.

fhe

she is a Type of the Church, to be synchronical with the (26) *three Years* of the
Fig-Tree's Unfruitfulness. I don't rightly
apprehend his mystical Arithmetic. But this
is certain, upon the Authority of the Fathers, that those two Numbers, with the
twelve Years of the Woman's *Issue of Blood*,
are all conterminous and will end together: Consequently at the same time, that
the Woman of the Church will be cured
of her *Issue of Blood*, she will be heal'd
of her *Infirmity* at the *Spirit* of Prophecy; *that is*, at the Conclusion of certain
grand Periods of Time, she will enter upon a blessed State of *Peace* and *Vision*;
which is the concurrent Doctrine of the
Fathers, as any one may discern, that has
dip'd into them, and is a good Confirmation of our present Exposition, and mystical Application of the miraculous Story
before us.

St. *Luke* says, that the Woman could
not lift up herself εἰς τὸ παντελὲς, *v.* 11. which,
without animadverting on our *English*
Translation, should be rendered, *until all
was perfected*, or until the *Perfection of
Time*, which, the Apostle (27) and the
Fathers agree, is the Time for the Church
to be cured of her *Weakness*, and to be

(26) *Luke Ch.* xiii. 7.
(27) 1 *Cor. Ch.* xiii. 9, 10.

endu'd

endu'd with *Power* at the Spirit of Prophecy.

As the Woman was heal'd by *Jesus* on the Sabbath-Day; so the Church, upon the ample Authorities of the Fathers, which Men of Reading will excuse me the Production of, is certainly to be heal'd of her *spiritual Infirmity*, at the Understanding of Prophecy against the mystical and (28) grand Sabbath, which, according to the Fathers, commences at the Expiration of her eighteen (hundred) Years *Weakness*.

But the *Ruler of the Synagogue is said to be moved with Indignation*, *v.* 14. at this charitable Work of *Jesus*, in healing of the Woman, because it was done on the Sabbath-Day; which in my Opi-

(28) Ut Deus sex Dies in tantis Rebus fabricandis laboravit; ita & Religio ejus & Veritas in his sex millibus Annorum laboret, necesse est, malitia dominante & prevalente. Et rursus, quoniam perfectis operibus requievit Die septimo, eumque benedixit; necesse est, ut in fine sexti millessimi Anni Malitia omnis aboleatur e terra & regnet per Annos mille justitia; sitq; tranquilitas & requies a Laboribus, quos Mundus jamdiu perpessus est. *In Lanctant. Instit. Lib.* VII. *Ch.* xiv. Dies septimus etiam nos ipsi erimus quando (Christi) Benedictione & sanctificatione fuerimus pleni & refecti; ibi vacantes videbimus, quoniam ipse est Deus. *Sancti August. de Civit. Dei. Lib.* XXII. *Ch.* xxx.

nion

nion, can't be literally true : Though I
am willing enough, to pleafe our *Divines*, to allow as much as may be of the
Letter of this Story, yet I except againft
this Part of it. *Origen* fays, there are
fome things of the Gofpel related as Facts,
which were not done ; and I believe this
of the Ruler of the Synagogue to be one
of them. Human Nature, I think, is not
capable of fuch bafe and unnatural Refentment. Works of Neceffity, and re-
quifite Offices of Kindnefs and Charity to
Man and Beaft, were allow'd by the Law,
and practifed by the *Jews* on the Sabbath:
And the Cure of this Woman, though on
the Sabbath-Day, was fuch an Act of Beneficence and Compaffion in the Holy *Jefus*,
that I can't but think *bad*, as well as *good*
Men, would rather glorify God, that had
given fuch Power unto Man, than find
fault with it. But in the Myftery of this
Part of the Story, there is clear Senfe
and Truth. Who then is this *Archifynagogus*, or Ruler of the Synagogue, that
will be full of Indignation at the healing of the Church of her forefaid *Infirmity* at the *Spirit* of Prophecy ? *Origen*
fays that the (29) right Interpretation of

(29) Contemnenda non eft accurata circa Nomina Diligentia ei qui voluerit prole intelligere fa-
cras Literas. *In Johan. Evang. Tom.* 8.

the

the Names of Perfons and Places in Scripture is of good Ufe to the myftical Application. Accordingly *Archifynagogus*
does fignify the *Chiefs of our Congregati-
ons :* And who fhould they be then but
the Clergy ? And if this ben't enough
to fix this Name and Character upon them,
then let *Theophanes Cerameus* fpeak here,
who fays, that the *Archifynagogus*, is a
(30) *Type of all Priefts*, who will be
againft the forefaid miraculous healing of
the Church. And why will the *Clergy*
be mov'd with Indignation at the curing
the Church of her *Infirm*, and reftoring
her to a *found* Spirit of Prophecy ? Becaufe
as St. *Auguftin* fays, (31) they are not
only *bow'd down* to the Letter themfelves ;
but becaufe this *Infirmity* of the Church
will be a Reproach to them, in as much
as it is a Proof of their Apoftacy and Infufficiency at Prophecy ; and the Cure of
it will be attended with fuch Confequences,
as affect their Reputation and Interefts.
Who can queftion but the *Clergy*, who
are the *Archifynagogus* of the Text, and
who are for the Church's *bending* and

(30) Jam Archi-Synagogus adumbrat omnes Sa-
cerdotes, &c. *In. Hom.* xii.

(31) Calumniabantur autem erigenti, qui, nifi
curvi ? *In Serm.* cccxcii.

ftooping

stooping to the low Senfe of the Letter of the Scripture, will be averfe to her being rais'd, *lifted up*, and erected to the Contemplation of the fublime, anagogical, and heavenly Senfe of it? Such an Healing and Erection of the Church will vex them at the Heart, as it will bring *Shame* and lofs of Intereft along with it ; and they will undoubtedly be *Adverfaries* to this good Work of *Chrift*, which, upon the Teftimony of all Antiquity, is to be done on or againft the Evangelical and great Sabbath.

Our Saviour is fuppofed to reprove the *Ruler* of the *Synagogue*, for his *Indignation* at the Cure of the Woman on the Sabbath-Day, faying, *v.* 15. *Thou Hypocrite, doth not each one of you on the Sabbath loofe his Ox or his Afs from the Stall, and lead him away to Watering? And ought not this Woman to be loos'd from this Bond on the Sabbath-Day?* There is Force in this Argument according to the Letter : And the *Ruler* of the *Synagogue*, and other *Jefus's* Adverfaries hereupon, might well be *afham'd* for finding Fault with fuch a merciful and beneficent Work done on the *Sabbath* ; when they themfelves did Works on the *Sabbath* of much lefs Confequence. But to

(32) the Myftery. What may be faid to our Minifters of the Letter, of whom the *Archifynagogus* is a Type, for their A- verfenefs to the healing of the Church in like manner? Why, that they are *Hypo- crites*, that is, fuperficial Criticks on the Scriptures, and don't confider that *the Law is fpiritual*, and how againft the Evangelical Sabbath every Man is to be releafed from his Bondage and Servility to irrational Principles (for which he has been like an *Ox* and an *Afs*) and to be conducted to drink of the Waters of Divine Wifdom: For this grand Sabbath will be a Day of abfolute Liberty, perfect *Reft*, immenfe Knowledge, real Vifion and Contempla- tion on God and his Providence, as the antient *Jews* and Fathers fo copioufly de- clare, that they who are ignorant herein, may be *afhamed* ; confequently they might know, that the Church is to be cured of her *Spirit of Weaknefs* at Pro- phecy on that Day.

But *Satan* is faid to have *v.* 16. *bound*, and, as is fuppofed, *bow'd down* this Wo- man ; the literal Truth of which I much

---

(32) Sed nefciebat Archi-Synagogus vel hoc vel illud multo excellentius facramentum, quod Sab- bato curando Dominus intimabat, quia fcilicet poft fex hujus feculi Ætates perpetuæ Vitæ immortalis erat gaudia daturus. *Venerab. Bed. in Loc.*

question :

queſtion: But how then has *Satan bound
and bow'd down* the Church? This, ſeemingly, is the great Difficulty in the myſtical
Application of this Story, and muſt be
the great Curioſity of my Readers to know
how I will account for it. If the Fathers
don't help me out at this dead Lift, and
that clearly and intelligibly too, I ſhall
abate of my Veneration for them. If they
don't tell me, and make me to apprehend,
what this *Satan* is, that for many Ages
has *bound* and oppreſs'd the Church after
the ſuppoſed Manner of the typical Woman, I had better have held my Peace,
and ſaid nothing to this parabolical Miracle.

The Writings of the *Evangeliſts* ſo a-
bound with Stories of *Satan*, *Belzebub*,
the *Devil*, and of greater and leſs Number of *Devils*, and of *Dæmons* and of
unclean Spirits, more than any Hiſtories
before, as one would think, if theſe Stories were literally to be underſtood, that
was the Age in which Chriſt came, that
Hell firſt broke looſe, and then prima-
rily infeſted Mankind; and that upon the
Deſtruction of *Judæa*, and Propagation
of the Goſpel, the *Devils* accompanied
the *Jews* in their Diſperſion, or the *Apoſtles* in their Travels, and have been the
Tempters,

Tempters, Seducers, and Tormentors of other Nations ever since.

Arnobius (33) says, *That before Chrift, Devils were things unknown to the World*; by which *Arnobius* muft mean, either that they were hardly talk'd of before, or that their Nature was not underftood, till Chrift inform'd us of it. In both thefe Senfes, I believe, *Arnobius* may be taken, *viz.* that there was not only little Talk of *Satan* and the *Devil*, but lefs of his Nature apprehended, before *Chrift* by his Parables and parabolical Miracles, rightly interpreted, inftructed us in it. And if after Ages have departed from the true and original Doctrine of *Devils*, making a literal Story of that, which is only myfti- cal and cabaliftical; and have formed to themfelves *Ideas* of hideous and horrible Fiends, *Mormos* and *Hobgoblins*, it fhall not difturb me.

As to the Place and State of *Hell*, ma- ny are the Notions of *Divines* of feveral Ages paft, as well as of the prefent. I fhall not recount them all here, much lefs refute any of them. But there is an anti- ent, rational, and cabaliftical Notion of Hell, which I have learned of the Fa- thers, who fignify, that the babylonifh

(33) Ante Chriftum in cogniti & a folo fciento detecti. *In Lib.* II. *adv. Gentes.*

and bewilder'd State of Chrift's Church may be call'd *Hell*, becaufe, as the Word ᾁδης does import, it is a State *without Vifion*. Hence *Origen* fays, (34) that whoever can form to himfelf an *Idea* of the Church in time to come, when fhe will be dignified with the Title of the *New Jerufalem*, for her Peace and Vifion, may underftand what is meant by *Hell*, and all that is written of it.

As then the Fathers had a cabaliftical Notion of *Hell*, which modern *Divines* are Strangers to; fo they had of *Satan*, and the *Devil* and his Angels. I own myfelf at a Lofs for an exprefs Teftimony out of the Fathers about *Satan* in the Text before us; but according to their Explications of *Satan* in other Places, nothing more is meant by him here than, " That furious Principle and Temper in " Man that is not only averfe to Liberty " in Religion, but for binding, reftraining, " and tying down the Church and Chrift- " ian People to certain Opinions and Ways " of Worfhip." In fuch a State of Bondage has the Woman of the Church been kept, by fuch a *Satan*, in one Order of Men

(34) Confequens autem eft ei, qui cognofcit quæ fit Hierufalem in divifione veræ Hæreditatis filiorum Ifrael, ut intelligat Sermonem de Gehenna. *In Matt. Ch.* xxiii.

or other, for all Ages paft. And that this is a
right and primitive Notion of *Satan*, I could
prove by Authorities enough. *Origen* tells us
(35) of the Names of Kings in prophetical
Scripture, which would be Enemies to
Chrift's Church; but fuch Kings never did,
nor would perfonally exift; their Names,
according to Interpretation, ftanding only
for fo many Sins and Vices, reigning in
Mankind. To the fame Purpofe he fays
(36) *human Vices are Devils:* And *Satan* himfelf, (as the Word fignifies *Adverfary*) is with him (37) and the antient
Jews too, no other than an *Averfnefs* in
Man to the Will of God. I could quote
other Fathers to this Purpofe; but being
fparing of my Pains at prefent, I refer

---

(35) Ego puto quod nomina hæc Scriptura divina
non pro Hiftoria narraverit fed pro Caufis & Rebus,
— non enim tam Regum quam Vitiorum Nomina, quæ regnant in hominibus referuntur. *In Nu-
mer. Ch.* xxxi.

(36) Quid ergo mirum videtur, fi per fingula
genera Peccatorum finguli Dæmones afcribuntur.
In Lib. Jofu. Ch. xi.

(37) Sed in alio quodam Libello, qui apellatur
Teftamentum duodecem Patriarcharum, talem
quendam fenfum invenimus, quod per fingulos
peccantes, finguli Satanæ intelligi debeant. Evi-
dentius autem & ipfa Nominis ejus interpretatio
hoc idem fignificare videtur; *Satanas* namq; Ad-
verfarius dicitur. Omnes ergo qui adverfantur
dei voluntati, Satanæ poffunt dici. *Ibid.*

(38) On Miracles, *p.* 36.

my

my Readers to my former (38) *Discourse*,
in which they will see the Opinion of the
Fathers about the *Devils* in the Madman,
and afterwards in the Herd of Swine ; from
which let them judge, whether the Fathers
could have any other Notion of *Satan*
here, than what I have reprefented. It
is certain, and may be eafily prov'd, that
by *Satan*, the *Dragon* and the *Devil*,
mentioned in the *Revelations*, nothing
more is to be underftood, than a furious,
perfecuting, fatanical, and diabolical Temper in Man; and if what St. *John* writes
of *Satan* be cabaliftical and allegorical ;
the other Affertions of the Evangelifts and
Apoftles about *him* will of Courfe come
under that Denomination ; or the primitive
Rule of Interpretation of Scripture according to the natural Signification of the Names
of Perfons and Places is not good.

As then the *Woman* of the Gofpel was,
as is fuppofed, *v.* 16. *bound by Satan*,
loe, for eighteen Years: So the forefaid
furious Principle in Man, which is a myftical *Satan*, an *Adverfary* to Liberty, has
bound the Church, *loe*, to the *eighteenth*
Century of Years: But fhe is to be entirely releafed from this fpiritual Bondage,
and

(39) Quamdiu vera Pax veniat, & Sabbatifmus,
& Septem decadarum Numerus. — Ecclefia non
plenam

and set at (39) *perfect Liberty* against the
acceptable and Evangelical Sabbath. And
here it is to be noted out of St. *Augustin,*
and most worthy of Observation it is, that
at the (40) same time, in which the Church
will be loosed from her Bondage ; *Satan*
himself will (41) be *bound* and *chain'd* for
a (42) *thousand Years,* the time of the evangelical Sabbath, that is, says *Ephræm Syrus*
(43) for ever. And how will our mystical
Satan or the *Dragon* be bound and chain'd?
Not with Chains or Links of Iron or other
Metal ; but *Vinculis Rationis,* with the
Chains of Reasons and Arguments for
Christian Liberty, which will restrain the
Adversary, Satan, from any more Impo-
sitions and Persecutions of the Church.
And I can't here but applaud the great
Mr. *Grounds* and Mr. *Scheme,* for their
Work and Labour of Love to Mankind,

plenam recipiat Libertatem. *Sancti. Hieron. in
Zechar. Ch.* i.

   (40) Illa Mulier curvata intelligitur figurare Ec-
clesiam, quam *in Sexta Mundi Ætate* a Captivi-
tate Diaboli Jesus liberabit. *In Quæst.* 25. *Dialog.* LXV *Quæst.*

   (41) Vidi Angelum habentem Clarem & Cate-
nam ad ligandum draconem. — *In Sexto Annorum Millenario* hæc Res agitur. *De Civit. Dei.
L.* XX. *Ch.* vii.

   (42) *Revel. Ch.* xx. *v.* 2.

   (43) Propter Infinitatem Annorum Mille Annos
dixit. *In Serm de Pænitentia.*

in making *Chains* of Argumentations for
Liberty, which I hope will prove of sufficient Strength to bind *Satan* and reſtrain
him (in Dr. *Rogers*, Biſhop *G — bſ — n*,
and others his Angels) from giving any
more Moleſtation to Chriſtian Philoſophers
in their Enquiries after, and Lucubrations
on Divine Truth. All the Honour that I
aim at in that Work is, by the Help of
the Fathers, to point out that anti-Chri-
ſtian Principle or Temper in the *Clergy*
(44) which, for its *Averſeneſs* to Liberty,
is called *Satan*; for its *Calumnies*, is called the *Devil*; for its *Furiouſneſs*, is called the *Dragon*; and for its *Unreaſona-
bleneſs*, is called the *Beaſt*, to the intellectual Views of Mankind, and to direct
them how to apprehend and lay hold on
it.

Our Saviour, according to *Origen*, had
never call'd *Peter*, (45) *Satan*, if *Satan*
had been any Thing elſe than *Man-averſe*
to the Will of God.

And thus have I ſpoken to the Miracle
of *Jeſus*'s healing the *Woman of her Spirit of Infirmity, whom Satan had bound*

(44) Diaboli Forman aſſumimus — Leonis Per-
ſonam induimus & Draconis, — **quando crudeles**
& callidi ſumus. *Origen. in Luc. Hom.* viii.

(45) *Mark Ch.* viii. *v.* 33.

and

and bow'd down, which, according to the Letter, is no Miracle at all; and some Parts of the Story are improbable and incredible; but the mystical Completion of it will be most prodigious, and a Demonstration not only of Christ's Power and Presence in his Church, but of his *Messiaship*, in as much as a vast Number of Prophecies of the *Old Testament*, more than can soon be collected to this Purpose, will thereupon receive their Accomplishment. And so I come to a

3. *Third* miraculous Story of *Jesus's*, that is of his telling (*John* iv.) the Woman of *Samaria* her Fortune, *of having had five Husbands, and being then an Adulteress*, &c. in which there is a notable Miracle display'd, in the Opinion of our *Divines*, that proves *Jesus's* Omniscience, or he could not so have search'd into the Heart of this Woman, and told her such Occurrences, that concern'd her Life past. I thought once of transcribing here entirely this Story; and so I would, but that it is a long one, and might have set some Readers, who are by this time awaken'd to pry into the Absurdities of the Letter, a laughing, before I had time my self regularly to animadvert on it.

Whether

Whether there was any Truth at all in the Letter of this Story, I fhould much have queftioned, but that fome Fathers write of it, as if they believed it literally, tho' they make a myftical and allegorical Explication of the whole and every part of it. And I, having a fincere Veneration for the Fathers, will not contradict them, (and I hope this Conceffion will pleafe the *Clergy*) but, for all that, can't like any part of this Story literally, but could al-moft wifh, that the Fathers, for the Ho-nour of *Jefus*, had made the whole no other than a Parable.

It's ftrange, that no *Jews* or *Infidels* have as yet ludicroufly treated this Story to the, almoft, Confutation of our Reli-gion. If their Tongues had not been ty'd by the aforefaid *Satan* or *Adverfary* to Liberty, I can't think but they muft have made fome pleafant Animadverfions upon it before now. If fuch a broken, ellip-tical, and abfurd Tale had been told of any other Impoftor in Religion; the Wits of our *Clergy* had been at Work to expofe it plentifully; and indeed there's no need of much Wit to make this Tale naufeous and ridiculous to vulgar Underftandings.

I fhall not myfelf here make all the Re-marks I can to the Difadvantage of this Story: I am not as yet fo difpofed to make

Scoffers

Scoffers and *Infidels* laugh at the *Clergy* for their Adherence to the Letter of it. All I shall do now, is to make my Observations on the two Uses, that the Clergy very seriously put this Story to, and they are,

First, to prove the Expectation that there was amongst the *Samaritans*, of a *Messiah* to come ; And

Secondly, to prove *Jesus*'s Omniscience, or he could not have entered into the Heart of the Woman, and told her, that she had had five Husbands, and was then an Adulteress. To these two Purposes, I find this Story urged by our *Divines*, and I must needs say, as to the

First of them ; it is rightly from hence asserted by the (46) *Bishop* of *Lichfield* and others, that the *Samaritans* had an Expectation of a *Messiah* : But why then did not the *Bishop* and others, who are now in Quest after Arguments of *Jesus*'s Messiahship, prove him hence to be the *Messiah*, because he told the *Samaritan* Woman her Fortune ? If this was a real and substantial Argument to her of *Jesus*'s *Messiahship*, it ought to be urg'd by the Clergy at this Day. The Controversy about *Jesus*'s Messiahship is now on foot ;

(46) Defence of Christianity, *p.* 8.

H   why

Why do the Advocates for it overlook this Proof of it? Why, becaufe, as I fuppofe, they are aware, that *Infidels* would make fport with it. But if *Jefus*'s telling the Woman her Fortune was no real and concluſive Argument of his being the *Meſſiah*; St. *John* has told us an impertinent Tale of a ſimple Woman, upon whofe Credulity and faife Notions *Jefus* palm'd himſelf as the true *Meſſiah*; and whether he did not ill thus to banter and deceive the Woman, let any one judge.

But let us here behold the Difference amongſt the *Jews* and *Samaritans*, as to the Expectation of a *Meſſiah*. Some of the old *Jews*, like the Apoſtles, expected the *Meſſiah* would be a temporal Prince, a great Warriour and Conqueror of the World. Others (47) of them, like the Fathers, expected he would be a Prophet

(47) Doctioribus inter Judæos notiſſimum eſt, — quod Mofes qui primus fuit Salvator Iſraelis etiam in omni Vita & Operibus fuis fuerit Typus & Figura ultimi Redemptoris. *Chriſtian. Meyer de Gen. Chriſti*, p. 145. Judæi Veteres expecta-bant fimilem Ægyptiacæ Liberationem, ut ſcilicet Pharaoh & omnis ejus Exercitus qui per 430 An-nos Populum Dei Captivum tenuit, in Mari Ru-bro fubmerfus eſt; fic etiam Romani qui eodem Annorum Numero Judæos poſſeſſuri, Ultione Do-mini deleantur. *San-cti Hieron. in Joel. Ch.* v.

like

like *Moses* in all Things, and deliver his
People out of another *Egypt* : But here
the *Samaritans* expected he would be a
Conjurer and *Fortune-Teller*; or there is
no Senfe in what the Woman faid to the
Men of the City, *v.* 29. *Come and fee a
Man that has told me all that I have
done*, particularly my Fortune of having
had five Husbands, and being now an
Adulterefs, *Is not this the Chrift?* What
could fhe mean, but that the *Meffiah*
would be a ftroling *Fortune-Teller*, to inform People of the Events of their Lives
paft and to come? And *Jefus* to humour
the Woman in her Conception of himfelf
and of the *Meffiah*, fays to her, *v.* 26.
I that fpeak unto thee, am He. Whether our *Divines* like *Jefus* the better for
this Story of him literally, I can't tell;
but I am fure they diflike the Fortune-
telling Trade at this Day in others, and
believe it to be all Fraud, and are for pu-
nifhing ftroling *Gypfys* for Cheats, who
practice it; and in the laft Age were intent on the (49) Profecution of judicial A-
ftrologers, who pretended to it : And if
antient Hiftory had furnifh'd us with an Inftance of the Punifhment of a pretended
Fortune-Teller in the Reign of *Tiberius*,
they could not have found Fault with it.
Whether any Accufations were laid againft

Jesus for such his Delusions of the People, we know not. Evangelical History is silent, or the *Evangelists* have prudently suppressed it. But I much wonder, that our *Gypsys*, from this Story, don't account themselves the genuine Disciples of *Jesus*, being endu'd with the like Gifts, and exercising no worse Arts, than he himself practised.

If the *Samaritans* did not expect the *Messiah* would be a *Fortune-Teller*; how came the Thought into the Woman's Head, that *Jesus* was the *Messiah*, because he had told her, her Fortune? What can our *Divines* say to it? Why, they must either say, that his telling the Woman her Fortune was a real Proof of his *Messiahship*; or that the Woman was foolish and credulous, and drew a false Conclusion; and if she had not been an impudent and graceless Whore, would have gone away blushing, and never have divulg'd, as the Text supposes she did, her Shame to the Men of *Sychar*, who too had but little Wit, or they had never stir'd from their Homes, to see such a Fortune-Teller upon the Report of a poor Whore.

But the Men of the City had their Fortunes too told them by *Jesus*, and they concluded him to be the *Messiah* upon it; or there is no Sense in what they *v.* 42. *said*

to

to the Woman, Now we believe not becaufe of thy Saying, for we have heard him ourfelves, and know that this is indeed the Chrift: What could they hear, but their Fortunes, as the Woman had before? And if *Jefus,* whofe Ability at all fair Queftions in the magic Art I don't queftion, did tell them their Fortunes; I hope he had more Prudenee than to talk to them in common of their Fornications and Adulteries, which might occafion domeftick Jarrs, and the Breach of good Neighbourhood amongft them; but if he directed any of them to find their loft Cattle, and help'd them again to their ftolen Goods, he did well, and they alone did amifs, to conclude thereupon, *that he was indeed the Chrift.* Let our *Divines* now judge whether I have not made a natural and excellent Comment on this part of the Story, which relates to the Expectation and Opinion, which the *Samaritans* had of a *Mefliah* to come. But,

Secondly, From this Story literally our *Divines* prove *Jefus's* (50) Omnifcience; and *Cardiognoftick* Power to tell what was in the Hearts and Thoughts of Man. But how fo? Is it becaufe he told a Woman, that fhe was an Adulterefs, and had had

(50) See Dr. *Hammond* on the Place.

five

five Husbands? Where's the Confequence?
Duncan Campbel, and other *Moorfields*-
judicial-Aftrologers have done greater Feats
at Conjuration than *this*, and never were
thought to be Omnifcient. And for any
Thing appears in this Story of our Saviour, it might be all Cheat and Fraud in
him. If *Infidels* fhould affert it, our *Divines* could not difprove it. If they
fhould fay, it was poffible for *Jefus* to
get Intimations of thefe and other Circumftances of the Woman's Life, before he
attempted to tell her, her Fortune; we
can't fay, that this is an impious and un-
reafonable Suggeftion, fince it is the common Subtilty of delufive Fortune-Tellers,
to get what Intelligence they can by Infinuations and Informations, before they utter their Oracles, and ambiguous Refpon-
fes to fimple poor Folks. And there is one
Circumftance in this Story, that looks very
ill upon *Jefus*, and is enough to make
him fufpected for a Cheat in his pretended
Art, and that is, he feems to draw the
Woman in by a (51) *Wile* to hear her Fortune, faying to her, *v.* 16. *Woman go,
call thy Husband*; upon whofe denying
fhe had any Husband, Jefus was forward,

---

(51) Percontando de Viro, Occafionem cepit
occulta revelandi. *Sancti Cyril. Alex. in Loc.*

very forward to furprize her with his Knowledge of her having had five Huf-bands, and living then in Adultery; which raifing the filly Woman's Admiration of his prophetick and foothfaying Talent, he clofes with her Conceptions, and what upon other Occafions, before wifer People, he was (25) backward to own, fays to her, *that he was the Meffiah*; and fo he pafs'd for the *Meffiah* with her and the Men of *Sychar*, who had no more Wit than to receive him for fuch, upon fuch Proof, and gave him Entertainment for no lefs than *v.* 40. *two Days*. I am glad we hear of no Money, he fqueez'd out of them for the exercife of his prophe-tick Art, which our *Divines* would have made an Argument of their Divine Right to Tythes, Fees, and Stipends for their Divinations.

But no more of this filly Story accord-ing to the Letter. To point at it is enough to expofe it to the confiderate and unprejudiced. I could not help faying fo much as I have; becaufe it is neceffary to form fome Invective againft the Letter, to make way for the Reception of the myfti-cal and allegorical Interpretation of it, which I am now to fpeak to.

(52) *John Ch.* x. *v.* 24.

Tho'

Tho' the Fathers, against whose Authority I dare not write, or I should be tempted to it in this Case, acknowledge the Letter of this Story, suspecting only some (53) particular Passages of it; yet they look upon the whole, for all that, as a (54) typical Narration, and endeavour at the mystical Construction of all and every part of it. St. *Augustin*, as if he was afraid some Christians of after Times should espouse, as our Divines do, only the Letter, prefaces his Exposition of this Story with these Words, saying, (55) *There are Mysteries in all the Sayings and Actions of our Saviour, particularly in the Story of the Woman of* Samaria, *and whoever carelesly and imprudently* (meaning lite-

---

(53) Fortasse verum non erat, *Judæos cum Samaritanis Commercium non habere,* — ac ne illud quidem verum, *neque Haustorium habes, & Puteus altius est,* — fortasse etiam neque illud, *quod Jacob ex Puteo biberit, & filii ejus, & Pecora ejus. Origen. in Loc.*

(54) Plena Mysteriis & gravida Sacramentis. *Sancti August. in Johan. Ch.* iv.

(55) Evangelica Sacramenta in Domini nostri Jesu Christi dictis factisque signata non omnibus patent, & ea nonnulli minus diligenter, minusque sobrie interpretando, afferunt plerumque pro salute Perniciem, & pro Cognitione Veritatis Errorem, inter quæ illud est Sacramentum quod Scriptum est de hac Samaritana, *&c. In Quæst.* 63, *de* Lxxxiii. *Quæst.*

rally)

rally) *interprets it*, *will advance erro-neous and pernicious Doctrine*; which, if modern Commentators had any Regard for the Authority of St. *Augustin*, is enough to deter them from their literal Expositions. The most literal Interpreter among the Fathers, whom I know of, is St. *Cyril*, and he says (56) there is a Type and Parable in this Story. But to descend to Particulars.

By the *Woman of Samaria* is to be understood an (57) Heretical and Adulterous Church, which Jesus, *being wearied* with her (58) corrupt State, will meet with in *the sixth Hour*, that is in (59) the *sixth grand Age* of the World. So, by the By, according to the Fathers, *Jesus* will come to, and meet with the *Samaritan* Church to her Edification, at the same time, that he cures the Church of her *Issue of Blood* and *Spirit of Infirmity*.

(56) Ὡς εν τυτω παλιν ημιν και δι αινιγματος υπο-δεικνυς. *In Loc. Johan.*

(57) Illa Mulier Typum gerebat Ecclesiæ, quæ ventura erat ex Gentibus — Ecclesiæ non justificatæ, sed justificandæ. *Sancti. August .in Loc. Johan.*

(58) Tunc fatigatur Christus, quando nullam Virtutem in Populo suo recognoscit. *Sancti August. in Serm.* xciii. *Appen.*

(59) Hora sexta id est, sexta Ætate Generis Humani. *Sancti August. in Quæst.* 64. lxxxiii. *Quæst.*

I   And

And where did *Jesus* meet with the Woman of *Samaria?* At *Jacob's Well*, where she was for Water to quench Thirst: So at the (60) *Well* of the Holy Scriptures, whose Sense 1 es deep as in a Well, and flows with Knowledge as with Water, will Christ then find his Church, drawing and drinking of the (61) Waters of the Letter, which could not quench the Thirst of the Soul hitherto: But in the Perfection of Time, signified by the *sixth Hour*, will Christ, according to the Fathers, enable her to draw out of this *Well* of the Profundity of the Scriptures, spiritual Waters of Divine Knowledge, which will daily more and more, like the Fountains of the Waters of Life, arise and flow in upon the Soul, and constantly recreate and refresh her with Wisdom, to her Delight and Satisfaction; so as she

(60) Puteus est Divina Scriptura, scientia scatens, ut aqua, Cujus putei Profunditas sunt plena Mysteriis Symbola. *In Theoph. Ceram Homil.* xxxviii. *de Samaritana.*

(61) Lex secundum Literam est aqua amara. *Hieronym. in Ezekiel. Ch.* xlvii. Qui bibit ex hac aqua sitiet rursus, id est, qui participat profunditatem humanæ sapientiæ, prudentesque Rationes, receptis Intelligentiis judicio suo inventis, tamen rursus secundo cogitans, denuo dubitabit de his in quibus requieverat. *Origen. in Loc. Johan.*

may

may be said never to thirst more, after the Manner she does now.

And Jesus *then* told the Woman of *Samaria, all that she had done:* So will Christ in the *sixth Hour*, that is, towards the latter End of the *sixth Age* of the World, give the Woman of the Church to understand *all that she has done*, according to the Writings of *Moses* and the Prophets, who, upon the Testimony of the Fathers, have written a prophetical History of her, in Types, Symbols and Parables; which Understanding of the Things that have been prophecy'd of her, will enable her, of Consequence, to prove and declare to the World, with Joy and Pleasure, that *Jesus* is the true Messiah, the Christ, and Fulfiller of the Law and the Prophets.

But particularly, as *Jesus* then told the Woman that *she had had five Husbands, and was then an Adulteress* with one who was not her true Husband: So the Church will be made to apprehend, according to (62) *Origen* and (63) St. *Augustin*, and others, how she

I 2   has

---

(62) *In Locum Johan. Evang.*

(63) Quinque enim Viros habuisti, & nunc quem habes *non est Vir tuus.* Sed non sunt hæc carnaliter accipienda, ne huic ipsi Mulieri Samaritanæ similes

has had five Husbands of the five bodily Senses, that is, metaphorically speaking, has been *wedded* not only to sensual Pleasures, but to the sensible Things of the Letter of the five Books of *Moses* ; and that at present, consequently, she lives in Adultery (64) with Anti-Christ, whom the Fathers call the Devil, instead of the Spirit of Christ, the Spirit of the Law, who should be her true Spouse, whom she should *call* for, and believe in.

And not only the Woman of *Samaria*, but the Men of the City, *Sychar*, believ'd *Jesus* to be the Messiah, *v.* 42, upon what he said to themselves as well as to her : So the Ministers of the Letter, who are *Sycharites*, according to *Origen* and *Theophanes Cerameus*, will be clearly convinced, and be able to convince others, that *Jesus is the Christ or Messiah*, when

---

similes videamur, — Per quinque Viros, quinque Libros Mosis Nonnulli accipiunt — sed quinque Viri intelliguntur quinque Corporis sensus. Et quia naturales sunt ipsi Sensus, qui ætatem primam regunt, recte dicuntur Mariti. *In Quæst.* 64. *de* lxxxiii. *Quæst.*

(64) *Et nunc quem habes non est Vir tuus*; Quia non est in te (Ecclesia) Spiritus qui intelligat Deum, cum quo legitimum potes habere conjugium ; sed Error Diaboli potius dominatur, qui te adulterina Contaminatione corrumpit. *Venerab. Bedæ in Locum.*

they

they shall hear, learn and apprehend from the Spirit of the Law and the Prophets, that the Church and all she has been doing, was foretold and prophecy'd of.

Lastly, *Jesus*'s Disciples, *v.* 27. are said *to Marvel that he talk'd with the Woman.* What in the Name of Wonder, literally, could be the Meaning of this? Did they *Marvel* at *Jesus*'s Condescention to speak to a Woman, as if the Sex was beneath his Care? Or did they *Marvel* that he who was very bashful, had Courage to speak to one? Or did they *Marvel* at his Conversation with a Whore, for fear of his being tempted by her? Some one or other of these must be the *Marvel* of the Disciples; but how absurd and ridiculous they all are, according to the Letter, let a reasonable Man judge. But mystically, the true Disciples of our Lord, who understand the Mysteries of the Kingdom of Heaven, will, when they are apprized of *Jesus*'s spiritual Conversation with his Church, and of all the Things that she has done according to Prophecy, *Marvel* with rapturous Astonishment at the Wisdom and Power of God in the Accomplishment of the Scriptures.

After such a Mystical and Allegorical Manner, is every minute Circumstance of this Story of the *Samaritan* Woman to be
apply'd.

apply'd. St. *Auguſtin* (65) ſays there are
ſo many great Myſteries contain'd in it,
that they require much Time to go through
them all. I find it ſo, and that no leſs
than a Volume might be written of them,
out of the Fathers. But what I have
briefly here touch'd on, is enough to convince any one of the Abſurdities of the
Letter of this Miracle, which conſiſted in
the telling a Woman her Fortune, and ſuch
a Fortune, as *Jeſus* by Craft might come
to the Knowledge of. Therefore, for the
Honour of *Jeſus*, let us look upon the
whole Story as a typical and parabolical
Repreſentation of what would be myſteriouſly and more wonderfully done by him.

And thus I have ſpoken to the three
Miracles, propoſed to be treated on in this
Diſcourſe. Before I enter upon my third
general Head, which is, *to conſider what
Jeſus means when he appeals to his Miracles as to a Witneſs of his Divine Authority*; I muſt take to Task ſome more
of his pretended Miracles, even till I have
not left him a good, credible and ſubſtan-
tial Miracle, according to the Letter, to
appeal to. The Conſequence of which
will be, that his myſterious Operations

(65) Magna quidem acta ſunt Sacramenta, ſed
anguſtum Tempus eſt, ut omnia pertractentur.
In Serm. xci. *Sect.* 2.

are

are to prove his Authority and Meffiafhip, or we muft give up him and his Religion for a Piece of Fraud and Impofture.

What Miracles will be the Subject of my next Difcourfe, I can't certainly foretell, but there are many Hiftorical as well as miraculous Parts of *Jefus*'s Life, that according to the Letter, are to be call'd into Queftion; fuch as

The Hiftory of his riding on an Afs to *Jerufalem*. I have given fome Offence on this Point already in my *Moderator*, and ought to excufe or juftify my felf, by calling the Fathers to Account for laughing at the Letter of that Story. It was an untoward Saying of St. *Jerome*, that I there cited, and fuffered a Profecution for: But it is a worfe Intimation of St. *John* of *Jerufalem*, who, if there was any literal Truth in the Peoples pulling off their Garments, and Branches of Trees, and ftrewing them in the Way of *Jefus*, will needs have it not refpectfully but mifchievoufly done, to make the Colt ftumble, and fo difmount his Rider. And according to him it may be queftioned, whether the *Hofannahs* of the People were of any more Refpect to *Jefus*, than the *Huzzahs* of a *Mob* would be to the Bifhop of *L———n*, if to fhew his Meeknefs and Lowlynefs, he fhould ride upon an Afs, in his *Pontificalibus* through
this

this City.   But I have here a momentous
Controverfy to decide about the Beaft *Jefus* rode on.   St. *Matthew* feems to fay,
he rode upon both *Afs* and *Colt* together.
St. *Mark* and St. *Luke* fay, he rode upon
the *Colt, on which Man never before fat.*
The Bifhop of *Lichfeild* fays, he rode
upon the *Afs* (on which Man had before
fat) and the *Colt* ambled after.   St. *Cyril*
and St. *Chryfoftom* fay, he rode upon the
Colt, and the *She-Afs* trotted after.   St.
John the *Evangelift* fays, he rode upon
a *Mule*, or an ονασιον Afs-like Creature of
the neuter Gender.   The *Jewifh Cabalifts*
fay, their *Meffiah* was to ride on a great
huge *Afs*, big enough to carry him and
all true Ifraelites, and that the Minifters
of *Antichrift* would then hang an *A-fs*.
So do the great Doctors of the World
differ! To whom I fhall decree the Prize
of Orthodoxy, I fhan't foretel ; but am
inclined to favour the Opinion of the *Cabalifts*.   However, I fhall be very grave
as well as learned on this Head: And if I
can, I will, to oblige Dr. *Sherlock*, hook
in a Digreffion about *Shilo*'s *binding his
Fole to the Vine, and his Affes Colt
to the choice Vine :* The Accomplifhment
of which *literal* Prophecy feems to have
been drop'd in the Providence of God, or
the

the *Dean* of *Chichester* (67) had never stopt at it. I will endeavour to look it up, in some Corner of History, if it be but to merit the Praises of the *Master* of the *Temple*.

I must also sometime take into Consideration the Story of *Jesus*'s Abode in the Wilderness, forty Days, in Company of the *Devil*, who tempted him. This literally, as our *Divines* understand it, is a Scandalous Story. The *Jews*, in our Saviour's Time, said, that through *Belzebub*, he cast out *Devils*; and their Posterity have asserted, that he learn'd the Magick Art of a *Dæmon*. This Story gives too much Grounds for such a Suspicion. Our *Divines*, who should know best, talk of abundance of Mischief, the *Devil* has been permitted to do in the World ever since; I hope it was not by Compact and Agreement between them; but it would have been of some Satisfaction to the Contrary, if the *Evangelist* had told us expresly upon what Terms they mett and parted. As Fables go, it is said to the Honour of St. *Dunstan*, that he took the *Devil* by the Nose, when he tempted him; and if *Jesus* had taken him by the *Collar*, and thrust him into his

---

(67) *In his Dissertation on the Blessing of* Judah.

K   *Dungeon,*

Dungeon, and there chain'd him, and shut *Hell-Gates* upon him; I appeal to honest plain Christians, whether such an *Herculean* Labour would not have pleased them well. Ever since I read of *Martin Luther*'s Conversation with the *Devil*, I have had but indifferent Thoughts of his *Protestantism*; and unless the Fathers turn this Story before us into Mystery, Allegory and Cabalism, I shall think ill of Christianity.

I should also take into Examination the Story of an Angel's appearing to the Shepherds, and saying to them; *Behold I bring you Tidings of great Joy*, &c. If there was any Truth literally in *this* Story, and in *that* of a Star's appearing to the wise Men, there must be a great Mistake in the Report of both of them. St. *Matthew* and St. *Luke* have both blunder'd. It was the Star that appear'd to the Shepherds by Night; and the Angel (I speak upon Reason and Authority) that was sent to the wise Men. What then to do with these two Stories, and to salve the Credit of the *Evangelists*, I knew not, till the Fathers directed me to the Use of a mythological *Metamorphosis*: And then I presently learn'd the Trick on't, to transform Stars into Angels, and Shepherds too, or Pastors of Christ's Flock
(which

(which was the Difficulty) into wife Men; and fo I made one Moral or Miftery of the two Fables.

I muft alfo fome Time take to task the Story of the *many dead Bodies of the Saints, that upon Chrift's Refurrection, came out of their Graves, and appear'd unto many*; which is too imperfectly related to merit Credit. The *Evangelift*, if he would have a reafonable Man believe his Story, fhould have told us, who thofe Saints were, and what Numbers of them; and whether they appear'd to the converted or unconverted *Jews*; whether they were fome of the Patriarchs and Prophets of old, or fome lately departed Difciples, who, for all *Jefus's* healing Power, died in the Time of his Miniftry; and whether there were any Women among thofe Saints; and whether they appear'd naked (as *Jefus* modeftly did to *Mary Magdalen*, unlefs he flip'd himfelf by *Stealth* into the Cloths of the Gardener, which might be the Reafon of her Miftake, for fhe fuppos'd fhe faw the Gardener) and whether they return'd again to Corruption, or afcended into Heaven. For want of thefe fpecifical Circumftances, the *Evangelift* has told us a Tale, that has neither Head nor Foot to it: and unlefs the Fathers myftically anfwer, to Satisfaction, every one of the aforefaid

Que-

Queries, I'll reject this Story for mere Romance and Imposture.

These and many other historical and seemingly miraculous Stories of the Gospel, are some time to be taken into Consideration ; for I will not give this Work over, till I have demonstrated beyond all Contradiction, that the evangelical Writings are but the Shadow of Divine Mysteries ; and that literal Interpreters, whom (68) *Origen* calls *vulgar Capacities*, are under a Mistake, if they think, they understand any Thing, as they ought, of the four Gospels.

I should conclude now, as it becomes a *Moderator*, with an Address to *Infidels* and *Apostates*, the great Combatants in this Controversy. But I have not Room to be as large, as I would, in my Exhortations to them distinctly, so I can only desire them to continue the Controversy with Zeal and Vigour, not doubting but it will end to the Honour of Jesus, the Good of his Church, and the Happiness of Mankind. The blessed Fruits of this Controversy are already seen and felt in

---

(68) Ut Lex Umbram continet futurorum bonorum, quæ declarantur ab ea Lege ; sic etiam Evangelium, quod vel a quibusque vulgaribus intelligi existimatur, Umbram docet Mysteriorum Christi. *In Præfat. ad Johan. Evang.*

the

the almoſt Cure of a moſt malignant Diſtemper, call'd *Bigottry*, which has been the Bane of human Society, and in Times paſt more deſtructive of the World than either War or Peſtilence. Go on then, *Great* and *Good Sirs*, till the Cure is perfected. And as you merit Praiſes and Rewards for your ſeveral Labours; So I hope you'll meet with them. The *Nobility* and *Gentry* of the Kingdom, as I learn, are ſenſibly touch'd with the Uſefulneſs of this Controverſy; whereupon it is to be hoped the *Legiſlative Authority* will ſoon give Thanks to the great Mr. *Grounds* and Mr. *Scheme* for their Pains in it; and not forget to do Juſtice to the *Biſhops* and *Clergy* according to their Merits. But I can't ſtay here to talk more on this Head, being obliged to make an Epiſtolary

P. S. To Mr. *T. Ray*, the Author of a *Diſcourſe*, call'd *Our Saviour's Miracles vindicated*, &c. As I, *Sir*, enter'd the *Preſs*, you came forth, or I might poſſibly have paid more of my Reſpects to you another Way. But upon mature Conſideration, I found a properer Reply could not be made to you, than is the foregoing Diſcourſe; which, if you are not ſick of your former Performance, will find you ſome more Work. And that you may write

write more pertinently againſt this Diſcourſe, than you did againſt my other,
I'll give you ſome Inſtruĉtions, *viz.* if you
think of writing to the Purpoſe, you muſt
prove theſe two Things; *Firſt*, that the
Fathers did not hold the Stories of *Jeſus*'s
Miracles to be typical and figurative; and
Secondly, that *Jeſus*'s Miracles neither
will nor can receive a myſterious and more
wonderful Accompliſhment. But you have
not ſaid one Syllable to either of theſe
Points; conſequently have written nothing
to the Purpoſe againſt me. As for Inſtance; In the Miracle of *Jeſus*'s *driving*
the Buyers and Sellers out of the Temple:
You ſhould prove, *Firſt*, that the Fathers
don't hold that Miracle to be typical of
the future Ejeĉtion of *Biſhops*, *Prieſts*,
and *Deacons* out of the Church, that
make Merchandize of the Goſpel: And *Se-*
condly, that it was impoſſible that the Miracle ſhould receive ſuch an Accompliſhment. But you have done nothing of this.
So, if you ſhould attempt again to write
againſt this Diſcourſe, as for Inſtance, a-
gainſt my Explication of the Miracle of
Jeſus's healing the Woman, that *had an*
Iſſue of Blood; you muſt prove that *that*
Story neither was in the Opinion of the
Fathers Typical, nor could receive a myſtical Accompliſhment; or you may as
well

well hold your Peace. And after all, whether your Reafonings for the Letter of Chrift's Miracles, are equal to mine againft it, let our Readers judge, who will eafily difcern, that you jump over my choiceft Invectives againft the Letter, as if you was afraid of being touch'd by them.

As to your charging me falfly in one or two Places, with Mifreprefentations of the Fathers, I'll expoftulate that Matter with you, when I hear that the *Bifhop* of *London* gives your Performance, the Reputation of a folid, and fubftantial one, by a Change of your *Cloak* into a *Gown*, which you feem to aim at; or you had never fo befmear'd the *Bifhop* with your Compliments, nor had been fo mealy-mouth'd as to the Point of Liberty.

But what need you, *Sir*, have told the World, that you take me for an *Unbeliever of the Scriptures.* If the *Bifhop's* wife Profecution of me for an *Infidel* had not given you the Hint, you could never of your felf have made that Difcovery. And why did you not join the Fathers with me in Unbelief? I thought I had been of the fame Faith with them. A Man of your Penetration into another's Principles, will, I fuppofe, from this prefent going Difcourfe, conclude me to be

a

a downright *Atheist*. And what muſt I do then to clear my ſelf!

If you write any more, *Sir*, I deſire you, without making more Haſte than good Speed, to be as expeditious as you can; or you will not prevent my Publication of another Diſcourſe, like theſe two, to the Honour of *Jeſus*, to whom be Glory for ever and ever. *Amen.*

F I N I S.

A THIRD

DISCOURSE

ON THE

MIRACLES

OF OUR

SAVIOUR,

In VIEW of the Present
Controversy between INFIDELS
and APOSTATES.

Litteratos gravissimo Somno stertere con-
vincam, HIERON.

The Third Edition.

By THO. WOOLSTON, B. D. sometime
Fellow of *Sidney-College* in *Cambridge.*

LONDON:

Printed for the Author, and Sold by him
next door to the *Star,* in *Aldermanbury,*
and by the Booksellers of *London,* and
Westminster. 1728.
[Price One Shilling.]

TO THE

Right Reverend Father in GOD

RICHARD,

Lord Bishop of St. DAVID's.

MY LORD,

N your Sermon *before the* Societies *for* Reformation *of* Manners, *you are pleased to give a* Character *of my former* Discourses on Christ's Miracles; *which, tho I don't at all like, yet I thank you for the Favour of taking Notice of them; a* Favour *that I have long'd for from a* considerable

A 2 Clergy-

Clergyman; *but could not flatter my-*
self with the Hopes of receiving it from
so great a Prelate.

Some of the inferior Clergy, *whom*
I despise for their Ignorance and
Malice, have before in their Conver-
sation represented me as an impious
and blasphemous Infidel ; *and I have*
met with Affronts for it : But I never
imagin'd that any, much less your Lordship, *would have ventur'd such a*
Character of me from the Press, *for*
fear of a Resentment, which would not
be agreeable. Surely your Lordship
has not read my Discourses, *but has*
taken a Report of them upon Trust,
from some Ecclesiastical Noodle ; *or*
you could never have been so much mis-
taken about my Design in them.

I took myself to be a Christian *of*
the same Faith with the Fathers of
the Church ; and, without Vanity,
think, I have publish'd some Tracts,
in

in Defence of Christianity, equal, if
not superior to any Thing this Age has
produced. I repeatedly also in my Dif-
courses on Miracles, to obviate the
Prejudices of an ignorant Clergy, made
solemn Protestations of the Sincerity of
my Design, not to do Service to Infidelity, but to make Way for the Demonstration of Jesus's Messiahship from
Prophecy: But all these Asseverations
of the Integrity of my Heart, it seems,
stand for nothing (and I don't wonder
at it) with the Clergy, who in their
Principles, their Oaths, and Subscriptions are so accustom'd to prevaricate
with God and Man. I shall make no
more serious Protestations of my Faith,
but expect your Lordship should soon
publish a Defence of your foul Charge
against me, that I may see what Skill
you have in the impious and blasphemous
Writings of an Infidel.

And if your railing Accusation be
not soon followed with a Dissertation
of

of more Reason, I shall insist on a publick Reparation of the Injury done to my Reputation by your vile *and* slanderous *Sermon ; and appeal to the* worshipful Societies *for* Reformation *of Manners, whether it be not just and reasonable, you should do one or the other.*

Now I have laid hold on your Lordship, *than whom I could not have wish'd for an* Adversary, *that will do me more Honour to overcome, I will hold you fast ; and you must expect to be teaz'd and insulted from the* Press, *if you enter not the Lists against me.*

A clear Stage, *my Lord, and no* Favour. *If you have the* Sword *of the* Spirit *in your Hand, cut as sharply as you can with it. I had conceiv,d a great Opinion of your Learning, and should have been a little apprehensive of the* Power *of it ; if you had not in your* Sermon *betray'd as great Weakness and Ignorance,*

Ignorance, as could be in a poor Curat; *or you had never asserted that the* Greek Commentators *adher'd more strictly to the litteral Sense of the Holy Scriptures; as if you knew not, that* St. Theophilus *of* Antioch, *and even* Origen *himself and others, the greatest* Allegorists, *if a Comparison may be made, were* Commentators *of the* Greek Church.

The sooner your Lordship *appears from the* Press, *the better, in as much as you may possibly prevent my* Publication *of more* Discourses *of this* Kind. *And that it may not be long first, I will accept of a* Dissertation *from you, on any two or three of the* Miracles, *I have handled, as sufficient for all.* Take your Choice *of them: but don't I beseech you, touch the* Miracle *of* Jesus's *driving the* Buyers *and* Sellers *out of the* Temple, *because it is a* hot *one, and may possibly burn your* Fingers. *The* Miracles, *that I* have

have moſt ludicrouſly and, of conſequence, moſt offenſively handled, are the two of this preſent Diſcourſe. If you pleaſe, my Lord, let them be the eaſy and ſhort Task impoſed on you. If you can defend the Letter of the Stories of theſe two Miracles, I'll quietly give up the Reſt to you.

So heartily thanking your Lordſhip for the Favour done me, in taking Notice of my Diſcourſes on Miracles, which ſhall be turn'd to good Uſe and Advantage, I ſubſcribe myſelf,

My LORD,

Feb. 26.
1738

Your moſt obliged

Humble Servant,

Tho. Woolſton.

A THIRD
DISCOURSE
ON THE
MIRACLES
OF OUR
SAVIOUR, &c.

Y two former Diſcourſes
having met with a favoura-
ble Reception, I am encou-
rag'd to go on and publiſh
another; which, without
any more Preface, I enter
upon, by a Repetition of three general
Heads, at firſt propoſed to be ſpoken to,
and they were,

B I

I. To show that the Miracles of healing all Manner of bodily Diseases, which
Jesus was justly famed for, are none of the
proper Miracles of the *Messiah*, neither are
they so much as a good Proof of his divine
Authority, to found a Religion.

II. To prove, that the literal History of
many of the Miracles of *Jesus*, as recorded by the *Evangelists*, does imply Absurdities, Improbabilities, and Incredibilities;
consequently they, either in whole or in
part, were never wrought, as they are
commonly believed now-a-days, but are
only related as prophetical and Parabolical
Narratives of what would be mysteriously
and more wonderfully done by him.

III. To consider, what *Jesus* means,
when he appeals to his Miracles, as to
a Testimony and a Witness of his divine
Authority; and to show that he could not
properly and ultimately refer to those he
then wrought in the *Flesh*, but to those
Mystical ones, that he would do in the
Spirit, of which those wrought in the Flesh
are but mere Types and Shadows.

Tho I have already, spoken what may
be thought sufficient, to the first of these
Heads; yet I have several Things still, both
from

from Reaſon and Authority, to add to it; but having not here a convenient Place for that purpoſe, I defer it to a better Opportunity; and ſo paſs immediately to the Reſumption of my

II. Second general Head, and that is, to prove, that the literal Hiſtory of many of the Miracles of *Jeſus*, as recorded by the *Evangeliſts*, does imply Abſurdities, Improbabilities and Incredibilities; conſequently they, either in whole or in part were never wrought, as it is commonly believed now-a-days, but are only related, as Prophetical and parabolical Narratives of what would be myſteriouſly and more wonderfully done by him.

To this Purpoſe I have taken into Examination ſix of the Miracles of *Jeſus, viz.* thoſe.

1. Of his driving the Buyers and Sellers out of the Temple.

2. Of his exorciſing the *Devils* out of the Mad-men, and ſending them into the Herd of Swine.

3. Of his Transfiguration on the Mount.

4. Of his healing a Woman, that had an Iſſue of Blood, twelve Years.

5. Of his curing a Woman that had a Spirit of Infirmity, eighteen Years, and

6. Of

6. Of his telling the *Samaritan* Woman her Fortune of having had five Husbands, and being then an Adulteress with another Man.

Whether I have not prov'd the Storys of these Miracles, either in whole or in part, to consist of Absurdities, Improbabilities, and Incredibilities, according to the Proposition before us, I leave my *Readers* to judge; and now will take in Hand

7. A Seventh Miracle of *Jesus*; *viz.* that (1) *of his cursing the Figtree, for not bearing Fruit out of Season*; which Miracle, upon the bare mention of it, appears to be such an absurd, foolish, and ridiculous, if not malicious and ill-natured Act in *Jesus*, that I question, whether, for Folly and Absurdity, it can be equalled in any Instance of the Life of a reputed wise Man. The Fathers, such as *Origen*, St. *Augustin*, St. *John of Jerusalem*, and others, have all said as smart Things, as the wittiest Infidels can, against the Letter of this Story. St. *Augustin* (2) very plainly says, that *this Fact in Jesus*, upon Supposition that it was done, was *a foolish one*. If therefore I treat

---

(1) *Matt.* Chap. xxi. *Mark*, Cap. xi. (2) Hoc factum, nisi figuratum, stultum invenitur. *In Serm.* lxxvii.

this

this Story a little more ludicrously than ordinary, and expose the Folly of the Fact as well as of the modern Belief of it, I hope their Authority and Example will plead my Excuse for it.

Jesus was hungry, it seems, and being disappointed of Figs, to the Satisfaction of his Appetite, cursed the Figtree. Why so peevish and impatient? Our *Divines*, when they please, make *Jesus* the most patient, resign'd and easy under Sufferings, Troubles and Disappointments, of any Man. If he really was so, he could hardly have been so much out of Humour, for want of a few Figs, to the Allay of his Hunger. But to curse the Figtree upon it, was as foolishly and passionately done, as for another Man to throw the Chairs and Stools about the House; because his Dinner is not ready at a critical Time, or before it could be got ready for him.

But *Jesus* was hungry, some will say, and the Disappointment provoked him. What if he was hungry? He should, as he knew the Return of his Appetite, have made a better and more certain Provision for it. Where was *Judas* his Steward and Caterer with his Bag of Victuals as well as Money? Poor Fore-
cast

caſt, and Management amongſt them, or
Jeſus had never truſted to the uncertain
Fruits of a Figtree, which he eſpy'd at a
Diſtance, for his Breakfaſt.

And if *Jeſus* was fruſtrated of a long'd-
for Meal of Figs, what need he have ſo
reveng'd the Diſappointment on the (3)
ſenſleſs and faultleſs Tree? Was it, becauſe he was forc'd to faſt longer than uſual
and expedient? not ſo, I hope neither :
Could not Angels, if he was in a deſert
Place, have adminiſtred unto him? Or
could not he miraculouſly have created
Bread for himſelf and his Company, as
he multiplied or increaſed the Loaves for
his Thouſands in the Wilderneſs? What
Occaſion then for his being out of Humour for want of Food? If he was of
Power to provide Bread for others on a ſud-
den, he might ſure have ſupply'd his own
Neceſſities, and ſo have kept his Temper,
without breaking into a violent Fit of
Paſſion, upon preſent Want and Diſappointment.

But what is yet worſe, *the Time of
Figs was not yet*, when Jeſus look'd and
long'd for them. Did ever any one hear

---

(3) Nulla eſſet Ligni Culpa, quia Lignum ſine
ſenſu non habebat Culpam. Auguſtin *in Serm.* lxxxix.

or

or read of any thing more (4) unreasonable than for a Man to expect Fruit out of Seaſon? *Jeſus* could not but know this before he came to the Tree, and if he had had any Conſideration, he would not have expected Figs on it, much leſs, if he had regarded his own Reputation, as a wiſe Man, would he have ſo reſented the Want of them. What, if a *Yeoman* of *Kent* ſhould go to look for *Pipins* in his Orchard at *Eaſter*, (the ſuppoſed Time (5) that *Jeſus* ſought for theſe Figs) and, becauſe of a Diſappointment, cut down all his Trees; What then would his Neighbours make of him; Nothing leſs, than a *Laughing-ſtock*; and if the Story got into our publick News, he would be the Jeſt and Ridicule of Mankind. How *Jeſus* ſalv'd his Credit upon this his wild Prank; and prevented the Laughter of the *Scribes* and *Phariſees* upon it, I know not; but I cannot think of this Part of the Letter of this Story, without ſmiling at it at this Day; and wonder our *Divinss* are not laugh'd

---

(4) Quærit poma; neceſciebat tempus nondum eſſe? quod Cultor Arboris ſciebat, Creator Arboris neſciebat? *Auguſtini in Serm.* lxxxix.

(5) Hoc ideo probamus, quia Paſſionis Domini Dies propinquabat, et ſcimus quo tempore paſſus ſit. *Ibid.*

out

out of Countenance for reading it gravely, and having *Jesus* in Admiration for it.

Again, I would gladly know, whose Fig-tree this was, and whether *Jesus* had any legal Right to the Fruit, if haply he had found any on it, or any Leave or Authority to smite it with a Curse for its Unfruitful-ness? As to the Tree's being *Jesus*'s Property, that could not be. For he was so far from being either Landlord or Tenant, that it's said he had not where to lay his Head. During the Time of his Ministry, he was but a Wanderer, like a Mendicant Fryar, or an itenerant Preacher, and before that Time was no better than a Journey-man Carpenter (of whose Workmanship, I wonder, the Church of *Rome* has no holy Relicks, not so much as a Three-footed-stool, or a Pair of Nutcrackers ;) conse-quently he had no House nor Land of his own by Law, much less any Figtree, and least of all *this* which he espy'd at a di-stance in his Travels. How then had he any Right to the Figs, if he had met with any ? I hope he ask'd Leave beforehand of the Proprietor, or *Infidels* will say of him, that if he had had an Opportunity he would have been a *Rob-Orchard.* And if he had no Right to the Fruit, much less to smite the Tree with a Curse ; where was
his

his Honour, (6) *his Juftice*, his Goodnefs, and his Honefty in this Act ? The *Evangelifts*, if they would have us to think, *Jefus* did no wrong to any Man, fhould have left us fomewhat upon Record, to Satisfaction, in this Cafe ; or *Infidels*, who have here Scope for it, will think worfe of *Jefus*, than poffibly he may deferve. Whether *Jefus*, modeftly fpeaking, met with any Blame or Reprimand from the Proprietor, for his Act of Execration, none can affirm or deny. But if any one fo fpitefully and malicioufly fhould deftroy almoft any other Tree, whether fruitful or not, of another Man's, in this Country, he would have good Luck, if he efcaped the Houfe of Correction for it.

And what now have our *Divines* to fay, to all this Reafoning againft the Letter of this Story ? Nothing more than " That " the Act of curfing the Figtree, whether " it be at this Diftance of Time recon- " cileable to Reafon, Juftice and Pru- " dence or not, was a fupernatural Work, " above the Power of Nature or Art to " imitate, confequently it was a Miracle, " and they will admire and adore *Jefus*

(6) Arbor non eft jufté ficcata. *Joban. Hierofol in Loc. Marci.*

C   " for

" for it." And to agree with them at
prefent, that it was a real Miracle, and
a fupernatural Event, yet I hope, they'll
acknowledge, that if *Jefus*, as St. *Auguftin* (7) fays, had, inftead of curfing the
Figtree, made a dry, dead and withered
one, immediately to bud, flourifh and revive, and in an Inftant to bring forth
ripe Fruits, out of Seafon, it would have
pleafed them much better. Such an Inftance of his Power had been an indifputable Miracle: Such an Inftance of his
divine Power had carry'd Goodnefs along
with it, and none of the forefaid Exceptions could have been made to it: Such
an Inftance of his Almighty Power, had
been a Demonftration of his being Lord
of the Creation, and Author of the Fruits
of the Earth for the Ufe of Man, in
their Seafon, or he could not have produced them out of Seafon: In fuch

(7) Si miraculum fuerat tantummodo commendandum,
et non alquid prophetice figurandum, multo clementiùs
dominus et fua mifericordia digniùs fecerat, Si quam aridam invenerat, viridem redderet, ficut languentes fanavit. Tunc vero e contrario, quafi adverfus Regulam
Clementiæ fuæ invenit Arborem virentem, præter tempus fructus nondum habentem, non tamen fructum agri-
colæ negantem, et aridam fecit. *In Serm.* lxxxix.
Sect. 3.

an

an Inftance of Power, his Divine Care and Providence againft Hunger and Want would have been vifible ; and it would have been an Admonition to us, to depend daily upon him for the Comforts and Neceffaries of Life : Such an Inftance of his Power would have been, as St. *Auguftin* fays above, like his Miracles of healing Difeafes, of making the Languid, *Sound* ; and the Feeble, *Strong* ; and we might more certainly have inferr'd from one with the other, that both were the Operations of a good God. But this Inftance of his curfing the Figtree in this Fashion fpoils the Credit, and fullies the Glory of his other Miracles. It is in its own Nature of fuch a malevolent Afpect, that its enough to make us fufpect the Beneficence of *Chrift* in his other Works, and to queftion whether there might not be fome latent Poyfon and diabolical Defign under the Colour of his fairer Pretences to Almighty Power. It is fo like the malignant Practices of *Witches*, who, as Stories go, upon Envy, Grudge, or Diftafte, fmite their Neighbours Cattle with languifhing Diftempers, till they die, that it's hard, if not impoffible, to diftinguifh one from the other, in Spite and Malice. If *Mahomet*, and not *Jefus*, had been the Author

C 2

of

of this Miracle, our *Divines* would prefently have difcover'd the *Devil*'s Foot
in it, and have faid that *Satan* drew him
into a Scrape, in the Execution of this
mad and foolifh Frolick, on purpofe to expofe *him* for a *Wizard* and *his* Muffel-
men of all Ages fince for *Fools* in believing on him. The Spirit of *Chriſt*,
who is all Love and Mercy, fhould, one
would think, breath forth nothing but
Goodnefs and Kindnefs to Mankind ; but
that fuch a peftilential Blaft, like a morti-
ferous North-Eaft Wind in fome Seafons,
fhould proceed from his Mouth, to the
Deftruction of another Man's harmlefs and
inoffenfive Tree, is what none upon Earth
can account for.

Our *Divines*, one or other of them,
have publifh'd feveral notable Notions a-
bout Miracles, and have laid down good
Rules to diftinguifh *true* from *falſe* ones ;
but none of them, as far as I perceive,
have taken any Pains to fhew the Con-
fiftence of *Jeſus*'s Miracles to their own
Rules and Notions. Mr. *Chandler*, (who
as the *Archbiſhop* (8) fays, has rightly
ftated the Notion of a Miracle) among

(8) See Arch-Bifhop *Wake*'s Letter to Mr. *Chandler*,
which is handed about Town and Country.

his

his Rules of judging by whom Miracles are perform'd, fays, (9) *That the Things pretended to be done, are to be fuch, as that it is confiftent with the Perfections of God to intereft himfelf in* ; and again, *they muft be fuch as anfwer to the Character of God as a good and gracious Being* ; and again, *It feems reafonable to believe, that whenever the firft and beft of Beings is pleafed to fend an extraordinary Meffenger with a Revelation of his Will, he will furnifh him with fuch Proofs of his Miffion, as may argue, not only the Power of him in whofe Name he comes, but his Love to Mankind, and his Inclination to do them good.* I have no Diflike to thefe Notions of Mr. *Chandler*; but as it is not to be queftioned, that he (and the *Archbifhop* too) had this Miracle of *Jefus*'s curfing the Figtree, and fome others, as of *his boifterous driving the Buyers and Sellers out of the Temple* ; of *his fending the Devils into the Herd of Swine* ; of *his turning Water into Wine for the Ufe of Men, who had before well drank,* &c. in his View, when he gave forth the forefaid Rules ; (for acute and learned Writers in Theology are fuppofed to have their Wits about them ;) fo it is

(9) *Vindication of the Chriftian Religion,* p. 82.

to be hop'd that he or the *Archbishop* will
soon publish somewhat to reconcile these
Miracles of *Jesus* to their own Notions;
tho I don't expect it before *latter Lammas.*

But after all, it may be questioned, if
Infidels should go about it, whether this
Work of *Jesus* was miraculous; and whether there was not more of the Craft of
Man, than of the Power of God in it;
or to use Mr. *Chandler's* (10) Words,
whether it don't *look like the little Tricks
and cunning Deceits of Impostors.* St. *Matthew* says, *presently the Figtree withered
away*; but this *presently* is an indetermi-
nate Time, and may be understood of a
Day, or a Week or two, as well as of the
Moment in which the Words were spoken,
*Let no Fruit grow on thee henceforward for
ever.* St. *Mark* says, *that in the Morning
as the Disciples passed by; they saw the
Figtree dry'd up from the Roots,* which
was at least the Day (11) after the Curse
was utter'd, so that there was certainly
four and twenty Hours for its withering;
and if it is said that the *Tree dry'd up from
the Roots,* it does not imply that the
Trunk of it perish'd, or was reduc'd to

---

(10) *Ibid.* (11) Quod sequenti die viderint exaruisse
ficum. *Theophylact. in Locum Marci.*

nothing

nothing; but only that the green Leaves of the Whole, and of every Part of it, were in a withering Condition: And might not all this be done without a Miracle? What if *Jews* and *Infidels* should say, that *Jesus*, being minded to impose on his Disciples and Followers, took a secret Opportunity beforehand to lay his Carpenter's Ax to the Root of this Tree, and so imperceptibly circumcised it, as that the Leaves did, what they will do, wither in a Night and a Day's Time. God forbid, that I should think, *Jesus* did so; but as to the Possibility of such a Fraud in an Impostor, none can doubt of it.

I am so far from thinking there was any such Fraud in this supposed Miracle of *Jesus*, that I don't believe it was at all done by him according to the Letter: And for this I have not only a clear and intrinsick Proof from the Story itself; but the Authority of the Fathers. St. *Ambrose*, treating on the Parable of the Figtree in (12) St. *Luke*, intimates, that what St. *Matthew* and St. *Mark* write of *Jesus*'s cursing the Figtree, is but (13) Part of the same Pa-

(12) Chap. xiii.
(13) Quid sibi vult, quod in Evangelio suo Dominus Fici Parabolam *frequenter* inducit: Habes enim alibi, quod jussu Domini Viriditas omnis hujus Ligni frondentis aruerit. *In Loc. Lucæ.*

rable.

rable. And St. *John* of *Jerusalem* (14) says exprefly enough, that the three *Evangelifts* write of one and the fame Figtree, confequently parabolically, and that, what St. *Matthew* and St. *Mark* write of it, was no more a literal Tranfaction, than the Parable in St. *Luke*. Thanks to thefe holy Fathers for their ridding us of the Belief of the Letter of this Story, which otherwife might have perplex'd us with its Abfurdities before urg'd. And to their Opinion I defire it may be added and confidered, whether it be not as reafonable in itfelf to take what the three *Evangelifts* write of this Figtree as Part of one Story, as well as, what they write of the *Woman with her Iffue of Blood*, and of *Jefus's cafting the Devils out of the Madmen*, and of other Miracles which are but feveral Relations of the fame Story, Parable or Miracle. Neither is it any Argument for a literal Tranfaction of this Miracle, that the *Evangelifts* fpeak of it, as a Thing done : For, as *Origen* fays, there are fome Things fpoken of in the *Evangelifts*, as Facts, which were never tranfacted ; fo it is of the Nature of Prophecy (and our

(14) Videamus, ubi alibi fcriptum de ifta ficu ; in Evangelio fecundum Lucam legimus, &c. *In Loc. Marci. Hom.* xii.

Saviour

Saviour in his whole Life prophefied) to
fpeak of Things to come, as if they were
already paft ; becaufe fuch Prophecies are
not to be underftood till after their Accomplifhment, and then the Reafon of
the Ufe of the *præter*, inftead of the *future* Tenfe, in Prophecy, will be vifible.
But what, in my Opinion, is an abfolute Demonftration, that there's no Truth
in the Letter of this Story, is, what our
Saviour adds, upon the Difciples wonder-
ing at the fudden withering of the Figtree,
faying, (15) *that if they had Faith they
fhould not only do what was done to the
Figtree ; but fhould fay to this Mountain,*
(that was near him, I fuppofe) *be thou
removed and caft into the Sea, and it fhall
be done.* But thefe Things were never litterally done by them, confequently *Jefus*
himfelf did not litterally curfe the Figtree ;
or the Difciples wanted Faith for the
doing the faid Miracles, which is an Abfurdity to fuppofe ; or *Jefus* talked idely
of a Promife to inveft them with a Power,
they were never to be poffefs'd of. But of
what ill Confequence to Religion, either
of thefe Suppofitions is, let the old Ob-

(15) *Matth.* Chap. xxi. 21.

D   jection

jection in *Paſchaſius Rathertus* (16) ſpeak;
which I ſhall not ſtay here to urge and
revive; but only ſay at preſent, that if
Jeſus actually curſed a Figtree, his Diſciples ought to have done ſo too, and to remove Mountains. If we adhere to the
Letter in one Caſe, we muſt in the other
alſo; but we are only to look to the
Myſtery in both, or St. *Auguſtin* (17) will
tell us, that *Jeſus* utter'd vain, empty and
inſignificant Words and Promiſes.

St. *Auguſtin*, who believes no more of
the Letter of this Story, than I do, ſays,
that the Works of *Jeſus* are all figurative
and of a ſpiritual Signification, which is ſo
manifeſt from his Act of curſing the Figtree,
as Men muſt, (18) *whether they will or
not* acknowledge it. But he is miſtaken:
Tho there might be none in his Time

---

(16) Quanquam igitur juxta Literam Hæc facta non
legantur ab Apoſtolis, ſicut quidam Paganorum calumniati
ſunt, et garriunt contra nos, etiam in ſuis ſcriptis aſſerentes
Apoſtolos non habuiſſe fidem, quia montes non tranſtulerunt
neque Ficulneas verbo exſiccarunt. *In Loc. Matth.*

(17) Legimus Apoſtolorum miracula, nuſquam autem,
legimus arborem ab his arefactam, aut montem in mare
tranſlatum; quæramus ergo in myſterio ubi factum ſit, non
enim Verba Domini vacare potuerant. *In Serm.* lxxxix.

(18) Sed futurum aliquid Miraculo commendaſſe, multa ſunt quæ nos admoneant, nobiſq; perſuadeant, imo ab
invitis extorqueant. *Ibid.*

who

who would queſtion, that this ſuppoſed
Fact of *Jeſus* had a myſtical Signification; yet if he had liv'd in our Days, he
would have met with *Divines*, who, for all
the foreſaid Abſurdities and their Cogen-
cy to drive us to Allegory, do adhere to
the Letter only, whether the Truth, Credibility and Reaſonableneſs of it be defen-
ſible or not. But then to do Juſtice to
St. *Auguſtin*'s Aſſertion, he would have
met with others, who *againſt their Wills*,
interpret this Miracle figuratively, ſuch
as Dr. *Hammond* and Dr. *Whitby*, who
ſay, *Jeſus* curſed the Figtree by way of
Type of the Deſtruction of the *Jewiſh*
State, which declined and waſted away
after the Similitude of this withering Tree.
But why then don't theſe *Commentators* allegorically interpret and apply other Miracles of our Saviour? Becauſe they think
the Letter will ſtand good and abide the
Teſt without an Allegory. And why do
they allegoriſe this Miracle only? Becauſe of the Difficulties and Abſurdities of
the Letter, which they can't account for.
And are theſe Reaſons good? No, certainly: The *Evangeliſts* ſhould have made the
Diſtinction for them. They ſhould have
told us, which Miracles are to be allegoris'd
and myſtically applied, and which are not;

or

or we are to allegorife all or none at all.
And how came thefe modern Allegorifts
of this Miracle to apply it as they do,
and to make it a myftical Reprefentation of the Ruin of the *Jewifh* State?
Did they take up this Notion of their
own Heads, or did they borrow it of
the Fathers? Why in all Probability they
took the Hint from the Fathers; wherefore then don't they, what none of them
do, cite and acknowledge their Authors
for it? Becaufe, like Men of Subtilty,
they would be thought to devife it of
themfelves; for if they had quoted the
Fathers for it, the Fathers would have
oblig'd them, upon their Authority, to
allegorife the reft of *Jefus*'s Miracles,
in the way that I have interpreted fome of
them; but this would not have agreed with
their Stomachs for many Reafons. No
Thanks then to the aforfaid *Commentators*
for their allegorical Application of this
Miracle, which they are again to defert,
or abide the Confequence of allegorifing
others alfo, which for their Interefts and
Reputations they will not do. Therefore
let them return again to the Letter of
this Miracle, and fay for it, what is all
that is to be faid for it, with *Victor An-
tiochenus*, an Apoftatical Writer of the
fifth

fifth Century, (19) *that when we read this Paſſage of Scripture concerning the Fig-tree,* Jeſus *curſed, we ought not curi-ouſly to enquire whether it was wiſely or juſtly done of* Jeſus, *or not ; but we ought to contemplate and admire this Miracle, as well as that of* Jeſus's *drowning the Swine, notwithſtanding ſome think it void of the Face of Juſtice.* Ay, ay, our *Divines* muſt allegoriſe all *Jeſus's* Miracles, or betake themſelves to this Opinion of *Victor* ; which this *Free-thinking* Age will hardly let them quietly reſt in. So, ſuppoſing our *Di-vines* to be, what they generally are, ſtill Miniſters of the Abſurdity of the Letter, I paſs to the Conſideration of the Autho-rity of the Fathers, and to ſee, whether we can't learn of them this Parable of the Figtree.

Who or what is meant by the Figtree ſeems not to be agreed among the Fathers ; or, more properly ſpeaking, they are not agreed, all of them to apply it always to

---

(19) **Porro quando in** hunc locum incidimus, nemo curioſè inquirat, aut anxie diſputet, juſtene an ſecus factum ſit ; ſed Miraculum editum contempletur et ad-miretur. Nam de ſubmerſis Porcis quoq ; nonnulli hanc quæſtionem moverant, factumq ; juſtitiæ colore deſtitutum prædicare veriti non ſunt. *In Loc. Merſi.*

one and the same Thing. Some, as (20) *Gregory* the *Great*, say Human Nature or Mankind is typified by the Figtree. Others, as (21) St. *Hilary*, say the *Jewish* Church or State is meant by it. Others, as (22) *Origen* say, it is a Type of the Church of Christ. So do the Fathers seem to be divided in their Opinions; but it is without any Difference or Inconsistency with each other. For as there is, according to the Fathers, Mystery upon Mystery in all the Actions of *Jesus*; so I believe the Figtree here, as a Type, may be properly enough apply'd to the foresaid three Purposes. And if the Fathers had been ask'd their Opinion in this Case, I dare say, they would have said so too. This is certain that *Origen* (23) understands it as applicable to the *Jewish* as well as the *Christian* Church. And St. *Augustin*, as Occasion offers itself, takes it in the foresaid three Senses. When they understand it as a Type of all Mankind, they say that the *three Years* of its Un-

(20) Quid Arbor fici, nisi humanam naturam designet? *In Homil.* xxxi.

(21) In Ficu, Synogogæ positum Exemplum est. *In Loc. Matt.*

(22) Absit a nobis, ut, Jesu veniente ad nos et volente manducare de ficu (*Ecclesiæ*) non inveniatur Fructus in eâ. *In Matth. Tract.* xxx.

(23) Potest autem ficus illa intelligi populus Circumcisionis. *Ibid.*

fruitfulness

fruitfulnefs are to be interpreted of the
(24) *three grand Periods* of the World;
the *one* before the Law of *Mofes*; *another*
under the Law; and the *third* under the
Gofpel; at the Conclufion of which *third*
Period, as it was an ancient and common
Opinion, *Jefus* in Spirit would come to
his Figtree of Mankind, and animadvert
on them for their Unfruitfulnefs, not by
any Deftruction of human Nature, but by
a Ceffation of its Unfruitful State, which
then will wither away, and be turn'd into a
fruitful one againft the grand Sabbath, or
acceptable Year, which is the Year fignified in the Parable, *that it is to be let alone
to bring forth Fruit in.* They that underftand the Figtree as a Type of the *Jewifh*
State, mean by the *three Years Jefus* came
to it, the *three Years* of his preaching a-
mong the *Jews*; at the End of which, after *Chrift*'s Paffion and Refurrection, the
Jewifh State, like the Figtree, withered a-
way, and, for its Unfruitfulnefs, was root-
ed up. They, that underftand the Figtree
as a Figure of the Church of *Chrift*, by
the *three Years*, mean the apocalyptical

---

(24) Arbor ficulnea Genus humanum eft —— Triennium autem tria funt Tempora, unum ante Legem,
alterum fub Lege, tertium fub gratia. St. *Auguftin in
Serm.* cx.

twelve

twelve hundred and sixty Days (that is,
three Years and a half) of the Church's
barren and unfruitful State in the Wilderness, at the Conclusion of which, the Fathers say, *Jesus* will come again to his
Church or Figtree, seeking Fruit on it.

Some perhaps may be ready here to
interpose with a Question, and say, how
will *Jesus* then come to his Church? I
have carefully perused the Fathers upon
this Question, and can't find that they
mean any more by *Christ's* second or spiritual Advent, than that clear *Truth*, right
Reason and divine *Wisdom* (which are the
mystical Names of *Jesus*) will descend upon the Church, on the Clouds of the
Law and the Prophets, to the Removal
of her unfruitful and unprofitable Errors,
and to enable her to bring forth the Fruits
of the Spirit, against the grand Sabbath.
Neither can any reasonable Man conceive how otherwise (25) *the Lord should
come*, (not *with ten thousand of his Saints,*
as our Translation has it, but) *εν μυριασιν
αγιαις αυτου*, that is, as *Origen* interprets, *in
his holy thousands of* Allegorists *ποιησαι κρι-
σιν, to criticise upon all* the Scripture, and
to convince *Ministers of the Letter* of their

(25) *Jude,* ver. 14,

abominable

abominable Errors, and of their horrid
Blasphemies spoken, preach'd and printed against the Holy, (Ghost or) Spirit
of the Law and Prophets. As to that
literal and common Pulpit-Story (with
all its Appendages) of *Jesus*'s second Coming on ætherial Clouds, as on a Wool-
sack, in his human, tho' glorious and majestick Appearance, for the Resurrection
of Mens Bodies, by the Sound of a Trumpet,
in the Audience of the Dead, *&c.* it is the
most absurd, nonsensical and unphilosophi-
cal, (such groundless and worthless Stuff
have the *Clergy* sold and preach'd to God's
People!) that ever was told against Reason,
against prophetick and evangelical Scripture, and against other antient and good
Authority. It is no Place here to multiply
Testimonies and Arguments to either of
these Purposes which my Readers, if they
do but attend, will see no Occasion for.
But if our *Divines* should think I have
put a false Gloss on the Text of St. *Jude*
above, I have a Bundle of Arguments and
Testimonies to produce in Defence of it,
at their Service.

In the Parable of St. *Luke*, it is said,
*Lo, these three Years come I seeking Fruit on
this Figtree*; as if *Jesus* came annually and
successively for *three Years* together: but
according to the Original, it ought to be

E   read

read, *Lo, it is three Years and I now come*, or, *Lo, the three Years are now paſt, and I come*. And here it is to be noted, that whether we underſtand the Figtree, as a Figure of the Church in particular, or of Mankind in general ; the myſtical Number of *three Years* will terminate about the ſame Time, againſt the Evangelical Sab-bath, on which the Unfruitfulneſs of the Church, or of Mankind, according to the Fathers, is to have an End put to it.

And *Jeſus*, when he came to the Fig-tree, *found nothing thereon but Leaves on-ly:* So *Jeſus*, when he comes to his Church, will find nothing in her but Leaves only. And what is here meant by Leaves? Let the Fathers, ſuch as (26) St. *Hilary*, St. *John* (27) of *Jeruſalem*, and (28) St. *Theo-phylaƈt* tell us, who by Leaves underſtand a vain and empty Appearance of Wiſ-dom and good Works, or the Words and Letter of the Scriptures, which are the Leaves of the Oracle, without any Figs of

(26) Inveniet infœcundam, foliis tantummodo veſtitam, id eſt Verbis inanibus gloriantem, ſed fruƈtibus vacuam, Operibus quippe bonis ſterilem. *In Loc. Matt.*

(27) Habentem folia et non fruƈtus ; Verba, non Senſus ; Scripturas, non intelligentiam Scripturarum. *In Loc. Marci.*

(28) Folia ſola habentem, hoc eſt, apparentem Litte-ram, non Fruƈtus Spiritus. *In Loc. Matt.*

spiritual Interpretations of them. And whether this ben't the Case of the Church at present, our *Divines* are to consider. The Figs that *Jesus* may be supposed to look for at his Coming, are not only the Fruits of the Spirit mention'd by St. *Paul*, but (29) *spiritual Interpretations* of the Scriptures, which St. *Jerome* (30) says are *mystical Figs*; because, as ripe Figs are sweet to the Palate of our Mouths, so are they no less delicious to the Soul of Man.

But *Jesus* is said to be *hungry* after Figs: so will *Jesus* in Spirit *hunger* for the mystical Figs of his Church, that is, as *Origen* (31) rightly interprets, he will earnestly desire, like a Man that is hungry, the Fruits of the Spirit in his Church, which will be as grateful to him as Figs can be to a Man naturally. To understand this Expression of *Jesus*'s *Hunger* literally, is such a mean Circumstance of Life, that unless it be, what's next to impossible, necessarily introductory to some noble Trans-

(29) Quærens non Sensiles Fructus sed intellectilem ex Lege et Prophetis dulcemq, Fæcunditatem. *Cæsarii in Dialog.* 40.

(30) Ficus sunt dona dulcissima Spiritus Sancti, Spiritualia dogmata et Scientia Scripturarum. *In Agga*; *Cap.* ii.

(31) Esuriit autem Jesus semper in justis, volens manducare Fructum Spiritus Sancti i neis. *In Matt. Tract.* xxx.

action

action, its unfit to be remember'd of a *Saint* in History. *Diogenes Laertius* would have difdain'd to mention fuch a frivolous Circumftance in the Life of a Philofopher as *this* of *Jefus*. But if we underftand this *Hunger* in *Jefus* myftically, and figuratively of his Defires of the Fruits of the Spirit in his Church, it is fublime and noble; and the Emblem confeffedly proper and inftructive.

But *Jefus* is faid to come to the Figtree at an unfeafonable Time; *For the Time of Figs was not yet*; which Expreffion has been the Perplexity of *Commentators*, who with all their Wit and Sagacity can't get well over it. I fhall not mention here all or any of their pretended Solutions of this Difficulty; but let us fee whether we can't eafily and at once unlofe it St. *Mark*'s Words are ου γαρ ην καιρος συκων, which are and have been commonly tranflated, *for the Time of Figs is not yet*. But if we change the *Point* into an *Interrogation*, and read thus, *for was it not the Time of Figs?* the Difficulty vanifhes as certainly, as that it is abfurd to fuppofe *Chrift* fhould come to his Figtree and look for Fruit, when he could not reafonably expect any. This my Solution of this Difficulty certainly ferves the Purpofe of the myftical Interpretation;

on ; and if it does not the litteral, I answer, we are not to heed the Letter, which
seldom or never has any Sense or Truth in
it. But, by the by, it does the litteral
too, since there are no Grounds from the
Text to think, what has been the common Opinion, that it was about the
Jewish Passover that *Jesus* came to the
Figtree. If this my Solution of the Difficulty don't please, I must say with (32)
Heinsius, that it must be left as a Knot
for *Elias* to untie, who, according to the
(33) ancient *Jews*, is first to gather Fruits
off this mystical Figtree, and present them
to the intellectual Taste of Mankind. But,
that my Solution is good, will appear by
what follows.

And *Jesus* finding Leaves only says,
in St. *Matthew*, to the Figtree, *Let no
Fruit grow on thee henceforward for e-
ver* ; which (with its parallel Place in St.
Mark) is in my Opinion a false Translation : The Original is, Μηκέτι εκ σου καρ-
πος γενηται εις τον αιωνα, and ought to be

_____

(32) Ad quem (Locum) intelligendum, ut oportet,
expectandum esse Eliæ, ut nonnunquam loquuntur Veteres
de Locis obscurissimis Adventum. *In Excercitat. Sac. Lib.*
ii. *cap.* 6.

(33) Fructus dulces omne genus de arbore Vitæ come-
dendum præbebit Elias. *Apud Buxtorf. Synag.* p. 738.

english'd

englifhed, *not as yet*, or *not until now*, (that I come) *againſt the* (grand) *Age* (of the Sabbath) has Fruit grown on thee. So that the Miracle of *Jeſus* was to make the Figtree of the Church fruitful; and if her preceding unfruitful State, which (in St. *Mark*) *Jeſus* is ſaid to curſe, or rather to devote to Ruin, waſted away, it was by Conſequence.

But what Time of Day was it that *Jeſus* came to the Figtree? It was in the *Morning*. And of what Day? That is uncertain as to the Letter, but accotding to the myſtical Extent of the *Three Years*, whether we underſtand the Figtree as a Type of the Church, or of all Mankind of all Ages, it will be on the *Morning* of the great Sabbath, when, upon the Appearance of the Light of Chriſt, like the Riſing of the Sun, an unfruitful and erroneous Church muſt needs wither away. And the Diſciples on the ſaid *Morning* will, as *Origen* (34) ſays, with their intellectual Eyes behold her waſte with Admiration. And then too, they under Chriſt *will do what is done to the Figtree*, of the Church, and *remove Mountains* of Antichriſtian Power, that exalt themſelves a-

(34) Oculis Spiritalibus viderunt Myſterium fici ficcatz, *Matt. Traſ.* xvi.

gainſt

gainſt him; as the Fathers interpret, and
I need not explain.

And what is meant by the Means, which
St. *Luke* ſpeaks of, to make the Figtree
of the Church fruitful on the Sabbatical
Year ; *the Year it is to be let alone to
bear Fruit in?* There muſt be *digging a-
bout it,* that is (35) into the Earth of the
Letter of the Scriptures, and *dunging* of
it, that is calling (36) to Remembrance her
Sins and Errors of the Time paſt, which
rationally ſpeaking will make the Church
to bring forth good Fruit.

After this Faſhion is the reſt of the Parable of the Figtree to be allegorized out
of the Fathers. St. *Gregory* (37) the *Great*
and St. *Auguſtin,* make theſe two Stories
or Parables, *viz.* of the Figtree, and of
the Woman with her *Spirit of Infirmity,*
as they are blended together in St. *Luke,*
to be Figures of the ſame Myſtery. The

(35) Effodientes Literam Legis. *Cyril. Glaphyr.* L. 1c
P. 1.

(36) Mittitur ergo Cophinus Stercoris ad Radi-
cem Arboris, quando pravitatis ſuæ Conſcientia tan-
gitur memoria Cogitationis. *Gregor. M. in Hom.*
xxxi.

(37) Sed hoc ſignificat Ficulnea infructuoſa, quod Mulier inclinata ; et hoc Ficulnea reſervata, quod Mulier
erecta. Hoc autem & octodecem Annorum Numero ſig-
natur, quod tertio die Dominus Vineæ Ficulneam ve-
niſſe perhibetur. *In Homil.* xxxi.

eighteen Years of the Woman's Infirmity and the *three Years* of the Figtree's Unfruitfulness, they will have to be myftically fynchromical. And the Woman's *Incurvity* to the Earth is, they fay, fignificative of the fame Thing with the *Unfruitfulnefs* of the Figtree. And the *Erection* of the Woman on the Sabbath is of the fame Import with the *Refervation* of the Tree for Fruitfulnefs on that Day. And let any one fee, if they don't admirally agree, as I have interpreted thefe two Parables.

Before I difmifs this Story of the Figtree, I can't but adore the Providence of God, that the Miracle has been hitherto placed in the withering away of the Tree. If the Miracle had been a plain Story of a dead and wither'd Tree's being made to bring forth Leaves and Fruit on a fudden ; this would have been fuch a manifeftly fupernatural Work, and fo agreeable to modern Notionifts about Miracles, that Mens Thoughts would have been fo abforpt in the Confideration of the Letter, as they would never have extended them to the Contemplation of the Myftery. And our Divines would have made fuch a Noife, in our Ears of the Excellency and Marvelloufnefs of fuch a Miracle, as that there would be no bearing of it. But

as

But as the *Evangelists* have in a good Measure suppress'd all mention of the after Fruitfulness of the Tree; and the Story, by Misconstruction, is clog'd with the foresaid Difficulties and Absurdities, we are of Necessity driven to the search after Mystery for good Sense and Truth in it.

And thus have I spoken enough to the Miracle of *Jesus*'s cursing the Figtree, which according to the Letter is a foolish and absurd Story : But the mystical Operation, of which the Letter is a Shadow, will be ravishing, marvellous and stupendous ; and not only a Proof of *Christ*'s Power, and Presence in his Church, but a Demonstration of his *Messiahship*, in as much as an infinite Number of Prophecys upon Prophecys, will thereupon be discern'd to be accomplish'd, or the Church can't bring forth the Fruits of the Spirit, that is Spiritual Interpretations of the Scriptures, like ripe Figs. And so I pass to an

8. *Eighth* Miracle of *Jesus*, and that is, (38) " of his healing a Man of an " Infirmity, of thirty eight Years Dura-" tion, at the Pool of *Bethesda*, that had " five Porches, in which lay a great Mul-" titude of impotent Folk, blind, halt, " withered, waiting the troubling of the

(38) *John*, Chap. v.

F   Waters

" Waters, upon the Defcent of an An-
" gel, who gave a Sanative Virtue to them,
" to the curing of any one, be his Diftem-
" per of what kind foever, who firft
" ftept down into them.

This whole Story is what our Saviour
calls a *Camel* of a monftrous Size for
Abfurdities, Improbabilities and Incredibilities, which our *Divines*, and their implicit Followers of thefe laft Ages, have
fwallowed without chewing; whilft they
have been ftraining at *Knats* in Theology,
and hefitating at frivolous and indifferent
Things of the Church, of no Confequence.

As to *Jefus*'s Miracle in this Story,
which confifted in his healing a Man, of
no body knows what *Infirmity*, there neither is nor can be proved any Thing fupernatural in it, or there had been an
exprefs Defcription of the Difeafe, without which it is impoffible to fay, there
was a miraculous Cure wrought. As far as
one may reafonably guefs, this Man's *Infirmity* was more *Lazynefs* than *Lamenefs*,
and *Jefus* only fhamed him out of his
pretended Illnefs, by bidden him to take
up his Stool and walk off, and not lie a-
ny longer, like a lazy Lubbard and Diffembler, among the Difeafed, who were
real Objects of Pity and Compaffion: Or,

if

if he was no Deſſembler, he was only fancyfully ſick, and *Jeſus* by ſome proper and ſeaſonable Talk touch'd his Heart, to his Relief; and ſo, by the Help of his own Imagination, he was cured, and went his Way. This is the *worſt* that can be made of this *infirm* Man's Caſe; and the *beſt* that can be ſaid of *Jeſus's* Power in the Cure of him, as will appear, by and by, upon Examination into it. But the other Parts of the Story of the healing Virtue of the Waters, upon the Deſcent of an Angel into them, is not only void of all good Foundation in Hiſtory, but is a Contradiction to common Senſe and Reaſon, as will be manifeſt after an In-quiry into the Particulars of it.

St. *John* was the beloved Diſciple of our Lord, and I hope he lov'd his Maſter : or he was worſe than an Heathen, who loves thoſe who love him : But this Story, and ſome others, that are peculiar to his Goſpel, ſuch as, of *Jeſus's telling the Sama-ritan Woman her Fortune*; of *his healing the blind Man with Eye-Salve made of Clay and Spittle*; Of *his turning Water into Wine for the Uſe of Men, who had before well drank*; and of *his raiſing La-zarus from the Dead*, are enough to tempt us to think, that he wilfully deſign'd, ei-ther to blaſt the Reputation of his Maſter,

or

or to try how far the Credulity of Men who through blind Love were running apace into Christianity, might be imposed on; or he had never related such idle Tales, which, if the *Priesthood*, who should be the philosophical Part of Mankind, had not been amply hired into the Belief of them, would certainly have been rejected with Indignation and Scorn before now.

St. *John* wrote his Gospel many Years after the other *Evangelists*: What then should have been his peculiar Business? Certainly nothing more, than to add some remarkable Passages of Life, to *Jesus's* Honour, which they had omitted; and to confirm the Truths which they had before reported of him. But St. *John* is so far from doing this, that the Stories, he has particularly added, are not only derogatory to the Honour of *Jesus*, but spoil his Fame for a Worker of Miracles, which the other *Evangelists* would raise him to. By reading the other *Evangelists*, one would think, that *Jesus* was a Healer of all manner of Diseases, however incurable by Art and Nature, and that where-ever he came, all the sick and the maim'd (excepting a few Infidels) were perfectly cured by him. But this Story before us will be like a Demonstration, that *Jesus* was no such Worker of Miracles and

Healer

Healer of Difeafes, as he is commonly believed to have been; and that he wrought not near the Number of Cures, he is fuppofed to have done, much lefs any great ones. The beft Conception that an impartial Reader of the Gofpel can form of *Jefus*, is, that he was a tolerable good natural *Orator*, and could handfomely harangue the People off hand, and was according to the Philofophy of the Times, a good *Cabalift*; and his Admirers finding him endewed with the Gift of Utterance, which was thought by them more than human, they fancy'd he muft have the Gift of healing too. and would have him to exercife it; which he did with Succefs, upon the Fancies and Imaginations of many, who magnified his divine Power for it. And the Apoftles afterwards, to help forward the Credulity and Delufion of the People, amplified his Fame with extravagant Affertions and ftrange Stories of Miracles, paffing the Belief of confiderate and wife Men. Whether this Reprefentation of the Cafe, according to the *Letter* of the Gofpels, be falfe and improbable, let my *Readers* judge by the Story before us, which I come now to diffect, and make a particular Examination into the feveral Parts of it. Accordingly it is to be obferv'd

Firft,

First, that this Story of the *Pool* of *Bethesda*, abstractedly considered from *Jesus*'s Cure of an infirm Man at it, has no good Foundation in History : It merits no man's Credit, nor will any reasonable Person give any heed to it. St. *John* is the only Author that has made any mention of this Story ; and tho' his Authority may be good, and better than another Man's in Relation to the Words and Actions of *Jesus*, in as much as he was most familiar and conversant with him ; yet, for foreign Matters, that have no immediate Respect to *Jesus*'s Life, he's no more to be regarded than another *Historian*, who, if he palm upon his *Readers* an improbable Tale of senseless and absurd Circumstances, will have his Authority questioned, and his Story pry'd into by the Rules of *Criticism*, and rejected or received as it is found worthy of Belief and Credit. If there had been any Truth in this Story before us, I cannot think but *Josephus* or some other *Jewish* Writers, it is so remarkable, peculiar and astonishing an Instance of the Angelical Care and Love to the distressed of *Jerusalem*, would have spoken of it : But I don't find they have ; or our modern *Commentators* would have refer'd to them, as to a Testimony of the Credibility of the Gospel-

Gospel-History. *Josephus* has professed-
ly written the History of the *Jewish*
Nation, in which he seems to omit nothing that makes for the Honour of his
Country, or for the Manifestation of the
Providence of God over it. He tells us
of the Conversation of Angels with the
Patriarchs and Prophets, and intermixes
Extra-Scriptural Traditions, as he thought
them fit to be transmitted to Posterity.
How came he then and all other *Jewish*
Writers to forget this Story of the Pool
of *Bethesda* ? I think, we may as well
suppose that a Writer of the natural History of *Somersetshire* would neglect to
speak of the medicinal Waters of *Bath,*
as *Josephus* should omit that Story, which,
if true, was a singular Proof of God's distinguishing Care of his peculiar People,
or an Angel had never been frequently,
as we suppose, sent to this Relief of the
Diseased amongst them. Is then St. *John's*
single Authority enough to convey this
Story down to us ? Some may say, that
there are several Prodigies, as well as political Events of antient Times, that, tho
they are reported but by one Historian,
meet with Credit ; and why may not St.
John's Testimony be equal to another
Writer's ? I grant it ; and tho it is hardly
probable but that this Story, if true, before
us,

us, muſt have had the Fortune to be told
by others; yet St. *John*'s ſingle Authority ſhall paſs ſooner than another Man's,
if the Matter be in itſelf credible and well
circumſtanc'd. But where it is blindly imperfectly and with monſtrouſly incredible
Circumſtances related, like this before us,
it ought to be rejected. Which brings me,

Secondly, To ask, what was the true
Occaſion of the Angel's Deſcent into this
Pool? Was it to waſh and bath himſelf?
Or, was it to impart an healing Quality
to the Waters for ſome one diſeaſed Perſon? The Reaſon, that I ask the firſt of
theſe two Queſtions, is, becauſe ſome
antient Readings of v. 4. ſay (39) the
Angel ἐλούετο *was waſhed*, which ſuppoſes
ſome bodily Defilement or Heat contract-
ed in the Cæleſtial Regions, that wanted Refrigeration or Purgaton in theſe
Waters : But how abſurd ſuch a Thought
is, needs no Proof. To impart then com-
paſſionately an healing Power to the Waters for the Benefit of the Diſeaſed was
the ſole Deſign of the Angel's Deſcent into them. And God forbid, that any ſhould
philoſophically debate the Matter, and
enquire how naturally the Waters deriv'd
that Virtue from the Angel's corporal

(39) Vid. Milli. Nov. Teſt. *In Loc.*

Preſence

Prefence. The Thing was providential
and miraculous, our *Divines* will fay, and
fo let it pafs. But I may fairly ask, why
one difeafed Perfon only at a Time reap'd
the Benefit? Or why the whole Number
of impotent Folks were not at once healed?
I have a notable Anfwer prefently to be given to thefe Queftions; but I am afraid beforehand, our *Divines* will not approve of
it. Therefore they are to give one of their
own, and make the Matter confiftent with
the Goodnefs and Wifdom of God; or the
faid Queftions fpoil the Credit of the Story,
and make an idle and ridiculous Romance of
it. And when their Hands are in, to make,
what is impoffible, a fatisfactory Anfwer
to the faid Queftions; I wifh, that, for the
fake of *Orthodoxy*, they would determine,
whether the Angel defcended with his
Head or his Heels foremoft, or whether he
might not come, fwauping upon his Breaft
into the Waters, like a Goofe into a Horfe-
pond. But,

Thirdly, How often in the Week, the
Month or the Year did the Angel
vouchfafe his Defcent into the Pool?
And for how many Ages before *Chrift's*
Advent, and why not fince and even (40)

(40) Quare modo non movetur Aqua? *St. Ambr:s de
Sacrament. Lib. C.* 2.

now

now, was this Gracious and Angelical Favour granted ? St. *John* should have been particular as to these Points, which he could not but know Philosophers would be curious to enquire about. If it was but once in the Year, as St. *Chrysostom* (41) hints, little Thanks are due to him for his Courtesy. One would think sometimes, that his Descent was frequent; or such a Multitude of impotent Folk, variously disorder'd had never attended on it. And again at other Times, one would think that his Descent was seldom, or the Diseased as fast as they came, which could not be faster than the Angel could dabble himself in the Waters, had been charitably dismissed with restor'd Health. Here then is a Defect in St. *John*'s Story, and a *Block*, at which wise and considerate Freethinkers will stumble. But,

Fourthly, How came it to pass, that there was not better Care taken, either by the Providence of God, or of the Civil Magistrates of *Jerusalem* about the Disposal of the Angelical Favour to this or that poor Man, according to his Necessities or Deserts : But that he, who

(41) Εις μονος του ενιαυτου εθεραπευτο *In Serm. contra Ebrietatem.*

coul

could fortunately catch the Favour, was to have it. Just as he who runs fastest obtains the Prize: So here the Diseased, who was most nimble and watchful of the Angel's Descent, and could first plunge himself into the Pool, carried off the Gift of Sanation. An odd and a merry Way of conferring a divine Mercy. And one would think that the Angels of God did this for their own Diversion, more than to do good to Mankind. Just as some throw a Bone among a Kennel of Hounds, for the Pleasure of seeing them quarrel for it; or as others cast a Piece of Money among a Company of Boys for the Sport of seeing them scramble for it: So was the Pastime of the Angels here. It was the Opinion of some Heathens, that *Homines sunt Lusus Deorum*, the Gods sport themselves with the Miseries of Mankind; but I never thought, before I considered this Story, that the Angels of the God of the *Jews* did so too. But if they delighted in it, rare sport it was to them, as could be to a *Town-Mobb*. For as the poor and distressed Wretches were not to be supposed to be of such a polite Conversation, as in Complaisance to give place to their betters, or in Compassion to make way for the most miserable; but upon the Sight or Sound of the Angel's Fall into the Pool, would without Respect of Persons strive who should be first: So those who were behind and unlikely to be cured, would like an unciviliz'd *Rabble*, push and press all before them into it. What a Number then, of some hundreds perhaps, of poor Creatures were at once tumbled into the Waters to the Diversion of the City Mob, as well as of God's Angels? And if one arose out of it, with the Cure of his Disease, the rest came forth like drown'd *Rats*, to the Laughter of the foresaid Spectators; and it was well if there was not sometimes more Mischief done, than the healing of *one* could be of Advantage, to those People. Believe then this Part of the Story, let him that can. If any Angel was concern'd in this Work, it was an Angel of *Satan* who delights in Mischief; and if he healed *one* upon such an Occasion, he did it by way of Bait, to draw others into Danger of Life and Limb. But as our *Divines* will not, I suppose, bear the Thoughts of its being a bad Angel; so I leave them to consider upon our Reasonings, whether it was credible that either a good or a bad Angel was concerned, and desire them to remember to give me a better Reason, why but *one* at a Time was healed.

If

If any Pool or Ciftern of Water about this City of *London* was fo bleffed with the Defcent of an Angel to fuch an End, the Magiftrates, fuch is their Wifdom, would, if God did not direct, take care of the prudent Difpofal of the Mercy to the beft Advantage of the Difeafed. And if they fold it to an infirm *Lord* or *Merchant*, who could give for it moft Money, to be diftributed among other Poor and diftrefs'd People, would it not be wifely done of them ? To fuppofe they would leave the Angelick Favour to the Struggle of a Multitude, is abfurd and incredible. And why then fhould we think otherwife of the Magiftrates of *Jerufalem ?* Away then with the Letter of this Story ! And if this be not enough to confute it. Then,

Fifthly, Let us confider, to its farther Confutation, who and what were the impotent Folk, that lay in the Porches of *Bethefda*, waiting the Troubling of the Waters. St. *John* fays they were *Blind*, *Halt*, *Withered*, and as fome Manufcripts (42) have it, *Paraliticks*. And what did any of thefe there ? How could any of them be fuppofed to be nimble enough of Foot to ftep down firft into the Waters, and carry off the Prize of Sanation, be-

(43) Vid. Milli. Nov. Teft. *In Loc.*

fore

fore many others of various Diftempers?
Tho' the troubled Waters might be of
fuch medicinal Force as to heal a Man of
whatfoever Difeafe he had; yet none of
the forefaid Perfons for want of good Feet
and Eyes could expect the Benefit of it.
Tho' the Ears of the Blind might ferve
him to hear, when the Angel plump't
like a Stone into the Waters, yet through
want of Sight for the guidance of his
Steps, he would by others be joftled out
of the right Way down into them. And
if the Lame had good Eyes to difcern
the Defcent of the Angel, yet Feet were
all in all to this Purpofe : Confequently
thefe impotent Folk, fpecified by St. *John*,
might as well have ftay'd at Home, as re-
forted to *Bethefda* for Cure. I know not
what Fools the Difeafed of *Jerufalem* of
old might be, but if there was fuch a Prize
of Health to be ftrove for, by the Diftem-
pered of this City, I appeal to all Men
of common Senfe, whether the *Blind*, the
Lame, the *withered* and *Paralyticks* would
offer to put in for it. St. *John* then forgot himfelf, or elfe blundered egregioufly,
or put the Banter upon us, to try how
far an abfurd Tale would pafs upon the
World with Credit. There might be, if
there was any litteral Senfe in the Story,
many of other Diftempers, but there could
be

be neither *blind*, *halt* nor *withered*, without *such an Absurdity*, as absolutely dis-
parages the Story, blasts the Credit of
the *Relator*, or rather brings to mind the
Assertion of St. *Ambrose*, that the Letter
of the *New* as well as of the *Old Testament*
lies abominably. If what I have here
said does not overthrow the Letter of this
Story; Then what I have,

Sixthly, To add, will do it more effectually, and that is, of the *certain Man*, *that
had an Infirmity thirty and eight Years*, and
lay at this Pool for an Opportunity to be
cured of it. Tho these *thirty* and *eight*
Years are, in our *English* Translation præ-
dicated of this Man's Infirmity, yet more
truly, according to the Original, are they
spoken of the Time he lay there? and the
Fathers so understood St. *John*'s Words.
What this Man's Infirmity was, we are
uncertain: For αϑενεια *Weakness* or *Infirmity*
is a general Name of all Distempers, and
may be equally apply'd to one as well as to
another: Whereupon, tho we can't certainly say from this Man's Infirmity, that he
was a Fool to lay there so long, expecting
that Cure, which it was impossible for
him to obtain; yet what he says to our
Saviour, *I have no Man, when the Waters
are troubled to put me into the Pool, but
while I am coming another steppeth down*
before

before me, does imply his Folly sufficiently, or rather the Incredibility of the whole Story. What then did this *infirm* Man at this Pool, if he had neither Legs of his own good enough, nor a Friend to aſſiſt him, in the Attainment of Sanation? Was he not a Fool, if it was poſſible for any to be ſo great a one, for his Patience? Would it not have been as wiſely done of him to wait, in the Fields ſo long; the Falling of the Sky; that he might catch Larks? The Fathers ſay, this Man's *Infirmity* was the *Palſy*; but whether they ſaid ſo for the Sake of the Myſtery, or to expoſe the Letter, I know not. But that Diſtemper, after *thirty* and *eight* Years Duration, and Increaſe; if it was more curable than another at firſt, had in that time undoubtedly ſo weakened and render'd him uncapable to ſtruggle with others for this Relief, that it is without Senſe and Reaſon to think he ſhould wait ſo long for it. Our *Divines*, if they ſo pleaſe, may commend this Man for his Patience, but after a few Years, or rather a few Days Experience, another Man would have been convinc'd of the Folly and Vanity of his Hopes, and returned Home. If he could not put in for this Benefit, with Proſpect of Succeſs in his more youthful Days, when the Diſtemper was young too,
much

much lefs Reafon had he to hope for it
in his old Age, after *thirty* and *eight Years*
Affliction, unlefs he dream'd of, what was
not to be imagin'd, an Opportunity, without Moleftation and Competition, to go
off with it. Whatever then our *Divines*
may think of this Man and his Patience,
I will not believe there ever was fuch a
Fool ; and for this Reafon will not fuppofe St. *John* could literally fo romance, unlefs he meant to bambouzle
Mankind into the Belief of the greateft
Abfurdity. A Man that Lies with a Grace
to deceive others, makes his Story fo
hang together, as to carry the Face and
Appearance of Truth along with it ;
which this of St. *John*, that for many
Ages has been fwallowed, for the Reafon
before us, has not. But what is the worft
of all againft this Story is,

Seventhly, That which follows, and
abfolutely deftroys the Fame and Credit
of *Jefus* for a Worker of Miracles. *And*
V. 1, 2, 3. *Jefus went up to Jerufalem,*
where there was by the Sheep-Market, a
Pool, called Bethefda, having five Porches,
in which lay a great Multitude of impo-
tent Folk, blind, halt, withered. Why
then did not *Jefus* heal them ? Here was
a rare Opportunity for the Difplay of his
Healing and Almighty Power ; and why

H   did

did he not exercife it, to the Relief of that Multitude of impotent Folk ? If he could not cure them, there's an End of his Power of Miracles? and if he would not, it was want of Mercy and Compaffion in him. Which way foever we take this Cafe, it turns to the Difho-nour of the Holy *Jefus*. What then was the Reafon, that of fo great a Multitude of difeafed People, *Jefus* exerted his Power, and extended his Mercy, on only *one* poor Paralytick? St. *Auguftin* (44) puts this Queftion and Objection into my Mouth ; and tho' neither He nor I ftart it for the Service of Infidelity, but to make Way for the Myftery , yet I know not why *Infidels* may not make Ufe of it, till Minifters of the Letter can give a fatisfactory Anfwer and Solution to it.

The Evangelifts, *Matthew, Mark,* and *Luke*, tell fuch Stories of *Jefus*'s healing Power, as would incline us to think he cured all where-ever he came. He *heal'd,* they fay, *all Manner* of Difeafes among the People, and they make mention of particular Times and Places, where all the Difeafed were healed by him, which

(44) Tot jacebant & unus curatus, cum poffet uno Verbo omnes erigere. Quid ergo intelligendum eft, nifi quia Poteftas & Bonitas illa magis agebat, &c. *In Loc. Joban.*

Affertions imply, that *Jefus*'s healing Power was moft extenfive and (excepting to an hard-hearted and unbelieving *Pharifee* now and then) univerfal; fo far that it might be queftion'd, whether any died, during the Time of his Miniftry, in the Places where he came: And our *Divines* have fo harangued on *Jefus*'s Miracles, as would confirm us in fuch an Opinion: But this Story in St. *John* confutes and confounds all. St. *John* in no Place of his Gofpel talks of *Jefus*'s healing of many, nor of all manner of Difeafes, much lefs of all that were Difeafed; which, if it be not like a Contradiction to the other *Evangelifts*, is fome Diminution of their Authority, and enough to make us fufpect, that they ftretch'd much in praife of their Mafter, and faid more to his Honour than was ftrictly true. But this Place before us is a flat Contradiction to them, and *Jefus* is not to be fuppofed to heal many in any Place, much lefs all manner of Difeafes, or he had never let fuch a Multitude of poor Wretches pafs without the Exercife of his Power and Pity on them. Some good Reafon then muft be given for *Jefus*'s Conduct here, and fuch a one as will adjuft it to the Reports of the other Evangelifts; or *Infidels* will think, that either

they

they romanc'd for the Honour of their Master, or that St. *John* in Spite told this Story to the Degradation of him. I can conceive no better of this Matter according to the Letter.

The *Bishop* of *Litchfield* very remarkably says, (45) *that Jesus where-ever he went, healed all that came to him without Distinction, the impotent, halt, withered.* He certainly had this Text of St. *John* in his Eye, when he said so, because *Impotent, Halt, Withered,* are only mention'd here, where *Jesus* cured *none* of them : Whereupon if his *Lordship* had made but a marginal Reference to this Text, it would have been the best Jest and Banter, with a Sneer, that ever was put upon *Jesus* and his Power of Miracles : As it is, it's a very good one, and I desire my Readers to take Notice of it, that his Lordship may not lose the Credit and Praise of it. It's for such Circumspection of Thought, Exactness of Expression, and Acuteness of Wit, that I admire that *Prelate*, and must needs say of him, whether he ever be translated to *Canterbury* or *York*, or not, that he's an *arch* Bishop.

(45) **Defence of Christianity,** P. 415.

But

But to return and go on. The Conduct of *Jesus*, to all Appearance, is not only blameable, his Power of healing disputable, and his Mercy indefensible, for that he cured but *one* infirm Man out of a Multitude, at *Bethesda*, but,

Eightly, and lastly, it may reasonably be questioned, whether he wrought any Miracle in the healing of this *one* Man. Miracles (to say nothing of the ridiculous Distinction between divine and diabolical ones) are Works done out of the Course of Nature, and beyond the Imitation of human Art or Power. Now whether the Cure of this infirm Man can be brought under this Definition of a Miracle, may be doubted. What this Man's *Infirmity*, which is a general Name for all Distempers, was, we know not. How then can we say he was miraculously cured, unless we knew his Disease to be incurable by Art, which none can affirm? The worst that we know of this Man's Case, is, that it was of a long Continuance, no less than of *eight* and *thirty* Years: And the *Bishop* of *Litchfield* and others in their florid Harangues of *Jesus's* Works, make the Cure of such Chronical Diseases to be miraculous: But why so? Many Instances may be given of Infirmities of human Nature, of a long Duration,

ration, which in Time, and especially in old Age, wear off. If such Infirmities don't occur to the Memory of our *Divines*, I could put them in Mind of them. And who knows but this was the Case of this impotent Man, whose Infirmity *Jesus* observing to be wearing off, bid him to be gone, and take up his Couch, for he would soon be made whole.

The Fathers indeed call this Man's Infirmity the *Palsy*, which in truth is generally worse than better by Time, and after *thirty* and *eight* Years, must needs be very deplorable, and incurable without a Miracle. But why do they call it the Palsy? They have no Authority for it from the Text, without which, as our litteral *Doctors* will not subscribe to their Opinions in other Cases; so why should I here? In short, the Fathers had never call'd it the *Palsy*, but for the sake of the Mystery; and I am not bound to own *that* to have been the Distemper, any more than it was want of Legs; for that would be making of Miracles for *Jesus*, without Reason and Authority.

If *Jesus* here had healed the whole *Multitude of impotent Folk*; without Enquiry what Numbers there might be of them, I should have believed that he wrought there many great Miracles, in as much

much as in such a great Multitude, there must needs, in all Probability, be some incurable by Art or Nature: But since he cured only this *one* Man, it affords Matter of Speculation, whether he was the *most* or the *least* diseased amongst them. Our *Divines*, for the sake of the Miracle, may possibly suppose him to be the most grievously afflicted of any; but *Infidels*, on the other hand, will say, not so: but with their Cavils will urge that this infirm Man was either a Dissembler, whom *Jesus* shamed out of his pretended Disease, or that he was only hippish, and fancyfully more than really distemper'd of a long Time, whom *Jesus* by suitable Exhortations and Admonitions, working upon his Imagination, perfuaded into a Belief of his Cure, and bid him to walk off. Certain it is, that *Infidels* will say, it was not a Power of Miracles in *Jesus* which heal'd him, or he had used it then and there for the Sanation of others also.

And thus have I finish'd my Invective against the Letter of this Story; which, if any are offended at, they enjoy, what is the most reasonable Thing in the World, the same Liberty to write for the Letter, which I have used against it: And so I pass to the Consideration of the Opini-

ons

ons and Expofitions of the Fathers on this
ftrange Story.

The Fathers, upon whofe Authority
I form'd my preceding Invective againft
the Letter, fo univerfally betake themfelves to the myftical Interpretation of this
Story; that it may be queftion'd, whether
any of them, more than myfelf, believ'd
any Thing at all of the Letter of it. St.
Chryfoftom, who is as much a litteral Interpreter of the Scriptures as any of
them, here intirely difcards the Letter,
faying admirably thus, (46) *what a*
ftrange Way and Story of healing the
Difeafed is here ? but what is the Myftery
of it ? that we are to look to. The Mat-
ter could not be fo fimply and unadvifedly
tranfacted litterally, as it is related. There
muft be fomewhat future here, as by a Type
and Figure, fignify'd ; or the Story, it is
fo incredible in itfelf, will give Offence to
many. St. *Chryfoftom* was certainly in
the right on't ; and I wonder, for which
no Reafon but want of Liberty can be

---

(46) Quis hic **Curationis modus ?** quid hoc nobis my-
fterium fignificatur ? non απλως nec εικη hæc, fed futura
nobis, tanquam imagine et figura quadam defcribuntur,
ne res nimium incredibilis et inexpectata, accedente
fidei Virtute, Multitudinis Animos offenderet. *In Loc.*
Johan.

given, that *Infidels* have not before now, with their Jests and Cavils, ridiculed this Story. St. *Augustin*, to the same Purpose, says, (47) *Can any one believe, that these Waters of Bethesda were wont to be troubled in this Fashion, and that there was not Mystery, and a spiritual Significa- tion in it?* Yes, I could tell St. *Augustin*, that our modern *Divines* seem to believe it, tho' he, if he was now alive, would laugh at them for it. But to come to the profound Mystery signified by this Story, which to use the Words of (48) St. *Augustin*, as God shall enable me, I will now speak to.

Our *English* Version says, *There is at Jerusalem by the Sheep-Market, a Pool.* How our *Translators* came by the Notion of a *Market* here, I can't imagine, since there is nothing to favour it in the Ori- ginal, which stands thus, επι τη προϐατικη κολυμϐηθρα : By κολυμϐηθρα, the Fathers un- derstand (49) Baptism, or the spiritual *La-*

(47) Aqua turbata —— credas hoc Angelica Virtute fieri solere, non tamen sine significante aliquo Sacramen- to ? *In Loc. Johan.*

(48) Cujus Rei & cujus signi profundum mysterium, quantum Dominus donare dignatur, loquar ut potero. *Ibid.*

(49) Piscina illa Baptismum designat. *Theophyl. In Loc.* Quænam igitur hæc descriptio ? Futurum erat Baptisma plenum maximæ Potestatis & Gratiæ purga- turum peccata. *Chrysost. In Loc.*

I

ver of Regeneration ; and who is that for, but the Flock of Chrift, fignified by πρό-Cαλιxη ? So we have another and clearer Interpretation of thefe two Words. And as to *Bethefda*, that is a myftical Name of the Church, which according to the Signification of *Bethefda*, is the Houfe of Grace. And if it is faid to be at *Je-rufalem*, it is not to be underftood of the Old *Jerufalem*, but of the *New* and Apocalyptical *Jerufalem*, at the Entrance into which the Flock of Chrift will be baptiz'd by the Waters of the Spirit, as in a myfti-cal Laver.

Bethefda is faid to have five *Porches*, that is, as the Fathers (50) agree, the five Books of *Mofes*, which are as fo many Doors of Entrance into the Houfe of Wif-dom, or of the Grace of *Chrift*.

At thefe *five Porches* of the five Books of Mofes lay *a great Multitude of impo-tent Folk, blind, halt, withered*. And who are thefe myftically ? The ignorant, er-roneous, and unftable in Faith and Princi-ple, as the Fathers often underftand them fpiritually. And what is the Reafon of thefe their myftical Difeafes ? Becaufe, as

(50) Per quinque Porticus, quinque Libros Mofis in-telligo, St. *Theophil. Antioch. in Loc*. Quinque Porticus funt quinque Libri Mofis. St. *Auguft. in Loc*.

St.

t. *Augustin* (51) and other Fathers say, they rest on the Letter of the Law, which throws them into various Errors, like Diseases, of different Kinds, of which they can't be cured without the Descent of the Spirit, like an Angel, to instruct them mystically to interpret.

With these impotent Folk lay *a certain Man who had an Infirmity.* And who is this infirm Man? Mankind in general, say St. *Cyril* (52) and (53) St. *Augustin,* And what is his Infirmity? The Fathers call it the (54) *Palsy,* because of his Instability, and Unsteadiness in Faith and Principles, which is now the Case of of Mankind. St. *John* calls it ασθενιαν *a Weakness,* which being a general Name

(51) Mosis quinque Libros scripsit, sed in quinque Porticibus Piscinam cingentibus languidi jacebant, et curari non poterant. Vide quomodo manet littera, convincens sum non salvans iniquum. Illis enim quinque Porticibus, in figura quinque Librorum prodebantur potius quam sanabantur ægroti. Ergo quicunque amatis litteram sine gratia, in Porticibus remanebitis, ægri eritis, jacentes non convalescentes, de littera enim præsumitis. *In Psal.* lxx.

(52) Est Figura Populi in ultimis temporibus sanandi. *In Loc. Johan.*

(53) Languidus ille, de puo in Evangelio legimns, quia jacebat, Typum Generis humani habere videbatur. *In Serm.* cclxxiv. *Append.*

(54) Paralyticum qui juxta Natatoriam jacebat. *Irenæi.* *Lib.* ii. Chap. 22.

of all Diftempers, we can't guefs what might be here the fpecifical one. But reafonably fpeaking, according to the Rule of Interpretation, this Man's *Infirmity* is the fame with the Woman's *Spirit of Infirmity*, and that is a Weaknefs at the Spirit of Prophecy, which Mankind, as well as the Woman of the Church, is to be cured of in the Perfection of Time.

And how long did this Man with his Infirmity lay in thefe Porches of *Bethefda ?* *Thirty eight Years :* So has Mankind with his Weaknefs at the Spirit of Prophecy lay eight and thirty (hundred) (55) Years, reckoning two thoufand under the Law, and eighteen hundred fince under the Gofpel. St. *Auguflin* (56) has an ingenious and more myftical way of Computation of thefe *thirty and eight Years,* which pleafes me too, but poffibly fome Readers may not fo eafily apprehend it, unlefs they are well acquainted with the Myftery of Prophetical Numbers.

(55) Tempus et Annus funt centum Anni, *Ticbonii in Reg.* 5a.

(56) Quod autem triginta et octo Annos iu Languoribus pofitut erat, do illo Quadraginta numero, quem fuprà diximus duo minus habens; et quæ funt ifta duo, nifi duo præcepta, dilectio Dei et Proximi. Ifta duo, in quibus tota Lex pendet et Prophetæ, fi non habuerit, languidus et Paralyticus jacet. *In Pf.* lxxxiii.

And

And how is Mankind to be cured of his Infirmity at the Spirit of Prophecy? By being inſtructed, by the Spirit of Truth, who is to come at the Concluſion of the ſaid thirty and eight myſtical Years, *to ariſe and take up his bed and walk*, that is, to raiſe his Thoughts to the Contemplation of the divine Myſteries of the Law, and to lift up his Bed of the Letter, on which he has hitherto *reſted*, into a ſublime Senſe, and then he will walk uprightly and ſteadily in the Faith, without wavering like a Paralytick.

And at what Seaſon did *Jeſus* come to this infirm Man? It was at a Feaſt of the *Jews. Irenæus, Chryſoſtom, Theophylact*, and *Cyril* call it the Feaſt of Penticoſt. And the grand Feaſt of Penticoſt is, as St. *Cyril* (57) ſays upon the Place at the Perfection of Time, the Time of the Evangelical Sabbath, and of *Jeſus*'s ſpiritual Advent, which will be a Time of feaſting on intellectual and divine Myſteries, of ſeeing Viſions and of dreaming Dreams; conſequently at that Time, as the ancient *Jews* and Fathers aſſert, Mankind will be cured of this Infirmity at the Spirit of Prophecy.

---

(57) Quod autem ſub finem Hebdomadum Sanctæ Pentecoſtes ipſe revertitur Hieroſolymam, figuraté et ænigmatice ſignificat futurum noſtri Salvatoris Reverſionem ultimis præſentis ævi temporibus. *In Loc. Johan.*

And this too is the *certain Seaſon, that the Angel will deſcend and trouble the Waters.* By Angel is here meant (58) the Spirit of Chriſt. And by Waters the Fathers uuderſtand, (59) the People of all Nations. But how will the Deſcent of the Spirit of Truth, like an Angel, trouble theſe Waters, that is, give any Moleſtations and Diſturbance to the People ? Is there not a Miſtake in the Oracle ? If the *Clergy* will be but greater Lovers of Truth than of their Intereſts ; if they, who ſhould be Teachers of Forbearance of one another in Love, will but keep their Temper, there would be found a miſtake in it. But alas!

Laſtly, The *Jews,* as is intimated, ſeem to have been mov'd with Indignation at the Cure of the infirm Man, ſaying to him, ver. 10. *it is the Sabbath, it is not lawful for thee to carry thy Bed* ; which litterally could not be true. The *Jews* were not ſuch preciſe Obſervers of the Sabbath ; nor *ſo ſtupid and fooliſh,* as St. *Cyril,* (60) ſays, as to

---

(58) Turbabat Angelus, ——dictus eſt Dominus magni conſilii Angelus. *Auguſtin in Serm.* cxxv. *Sect.* 3.

(59) Turbavit Aquam, id eſt, turbavit Populum. *Ejuſdem in Pſ.* cii.

(60) Sabbatum eſt et Grabatum non licet tollere. Quid ſtupidius aut inertius eſſe poteſt ? *In Loc. Johan.*

think

think the taking up and carrying a Stool to be a Breach of it. But myftically, it is to be fear'd, this will be moft true, and that the *Clergy*, who would be *Jews* inwardly, and the Circumcifion in Spirit, will be bitter Enemies to Man's Exaltation of his Couch of the Letter of the Scriptures on or againft the Evangelical Sabbath, and will make it, if poffible, an *unlawful* Work; becaufe it will bring to them Shame, Difhonour and Lofs of Interefts along with it.

After this Manner is every other Circumftance of this Story to be allegorically apply'd out of the Fathers. The Moral or Myftery of the whole, in fhort, is this, that at the Perfection of Time, fignified by the *Sabbath*, the *Pentecoft*, the End of *thirty eight Years*, the Spirit of Truth will defcend on Mankind, to their Illumination in Prophechy, and to the healing of their *Errors*, call'd *Difeafes*; which is admirably reprefented by the Parable before us, that according to the Letter, has neither Reafon nor common Senfe in it.

And thus have I fpoken to *eight* of the Miracles of *Jefus*; and whether I have not fhew'd them, in whole or Part, according to the Propofition before us, to
consist

consist of Absurdities, Improbabilities, and
Incredibilities; and whether they are not
prophetical and parabolical Narratives of
what will be mysteriously, and more wonderfully done by *Jesus*, I appeal to my
Readers.

After another Discourse of some other
Miracles, I intend to take into Examination the several Stories of *Jesus*'s raising of
the Dead as of *Lazarus*, *Jairus*'s Daughter,
and the Widow's Son of *Naim*; which
reputedly are *Jesus*'s grand Miracles;
but, for all the seeming Greatness and Excellency of them, I don't doubt but to give
the Letter of these Stories a Toss out of
the Creed of a considerate and wise Man ;
at least show their Insufficiency for the Purpose for which they have been hitherto
apply'd. And if I should afterwards, by
the Leave and Patience of the *Bishop* of
London, give my Objection against *Christ*'s
Resurrection a Review, and some more
Force, then what will become of the Argument of *Christ*'s Power, Authority, and
Messiahship from his Miracles?

But, besides *Jesus*'s Miracles, I am, as
Opportunity serves, to take into Confideration some of the Historical Parts of
his Life ; and shew them to be no less sens-
less, absurd and ridiculous than his Miracles.

And

And why may I not fometimes treat on the Parables of *Jefus*, and fhow what nonfenfical and abfurd Things they are, according to the Expofitions of our moft famous Commentators of thefe laft Ages. *Jefus* was certainly the abfolute, and moft confummate Perfection of a *Cabalift*, *Myftift*, *Parabolift* and *Enigmatift* ; but according to modern Commentaries and Paraphrafes, he was the mereft Ideot and Blockhead that ever open'd his Mouth, in that fort of Learning, to the Inftruction of Mankind. And I am oblig'd a little to fpeak to the Abfurdities of *Chrift*'s Doctrine and Parables, becaufe one Article of the Profecution againft me was for faying, *that any of the Philofophers of the Gentiles*, or *any rational Man* (meaning according to modern Expofitions) *would make a better Teacher, than Jefus was.*

What a great deal of Work have I upon my Hands, which, if God fpare my Life and Health, I intend to go on with : If what I have already done in it be not acceptable to the *Clergy*, their Way to prevent the Profecution of this great Undertaking, is to battle me upon what's paft. Who knows but they may write, if they would try their Strength, fo acutely in Defence of the Letter of *Jefus*'s Miracles already difcufs'd, as may effectu-

ally

ally ſtop my Mouth, and prevent my giving them any more Trouble of this Kind? And I ſuppoſe I have now gotten an Adverſary in the *Biſhop* of St. *David's*, who has already diſcharg'd one Fool's Bolt at me.

There has nothing been a more common Subject of Declamation among the *Clergy* than the *Reaſonableneſs* of Chriſtianity, which muſt be underſtood of the Hiſtory of *Chriſt's* Life and Doctrine, or the Application of the Word *Reaſonableneſs* to the Chriſtian Religion is impertinent. But if I proceed, as I have begun in this Work, I ſhall ſhew Chriſtianity, as it is underſtood, to be the moſt unreaſonable and abſurd Story, that ever was told; and our modern Syſtems of Theology groundleſs and ſenſleſs in almoſt every Part of them. *Mahometaniſm*, without Offence be it ſpoken, is a more *reaſonable* Religion than the Chriſtian, upon modern *Schemes* and *Syſtems*.

If what I here ſay is offenſive to our *Divines*, the *Preſs* is open for them as well as for myſelf, and they may, if they can, ſhew their Reſentment of it. Thanks unto God and our moſt excellent Civil Government for ſuch a Liberty of the *Preſs*: A Liberty that will lead and conduct us to the Fountain of Wiſdom and Philoſophy

phy, which Reftraint is a down-right E-
nemy to. And that this Bleffing of Liberty may be continued, for all *Bifhop Smal-
brook* and Dr. *Roger's Hobbifm*, is, I dare
fay, the Defire of the curious, inquifitive,
and philofophical Part of Mankind. If
this Liberty fhould be taken away, what
a notable Figure will our *Divines* make
from the *Prefs* and *Pulpit*, declaiming
on the Reafonablenefs, Excellency and Perfection of the Chriftian Religion, without
an Adverfary; and telling their Congre-
gations, that all, their bitteref and acutef
Enemies can object, is clearly anfwered!

The *Prefs*, of late Years, has been pro-
ductive of fo many cogent and perfuafive
Arguments for Liberty of debate, and the
Advocates for this Liberty, in the Judgment of the impartial and confiderate, have
fo far gotten the better of their Adverfaries,
that I wonder any one can appear in behalf of Perfecution. If I was a *Bifhop* or
Doctor in *Divinity*, I fhou'd think it a
Difgrace to my Station and Education to
ask the Affiftance of the Civil Authority to
protect my Religion: I fhould judge my
felf unworthy of the Wages and Emoluments I enjoy'd, for the Preaching and
Propagation of the Gofpel, if I was unable to give an Anfwer to any one, that
ask'd a Reafon of my Faith; Or if I was

ſo Shallow-pated, as to think Hereſy and Infidelity puniſhable by the Civil Magiſtrate, I ſhould think myſelf as much oblig'd to confute by *Reaſon*, as he is to puniſh by the *Sword*. If the *Biſhop* of *London* had taken this Courſe with me; if he had publiſh'd a Refutation of my ſuppoſed Errors, as well as endeavour'd at a Proſecution of me for them, I had forgiven him the Wrongs and Injuries done me, and made no repeated Demands of Satisfaction for them.

Chriſtianity is, as I believe, founded on a Rock of Wiſdom; and what's more, has an omnipotent and omniſcient God on its Side, who can incline the Hearts of Men to believe, and open the Eyes of their Underſtanding to diſcern the Truth of it; conſequently there can be no Danger in the Attempts of our Adverſaries, whether, *Jews*, *Turks* or Domeſtick *Infidels*, againſt it. But Perſecution implys Weakneſs and Impotency in God to defend his own Cauſe; or his Prieſts would not move for the Help of the Arm of Fleſh in Vindication of it. And if, at this Time of Day, after ſo many Treatiſes of *Infidels*, and ſome of them as yet unanſwered, againſt our Religion, this good Cauſe ſhould be taken out of the Hands of God, and committed to the Care of the Civil

Civil Magistrate; if instead of Reason the Clergy should have Recourse to Force, what will By-standers, and even Well-wishers to Christianity say? Nothing less than that *Infidels* had gotten the better of *Christ*'s Ministers, and beaten them at their own Weapons of Reason and Argument.

The two great Pleaders for Persecution, to the Disgrace of themselves and Dishonour of our Religion, that have lately arose are Dr. *Rogers* and the *Bishop* of St. *David*'s. Dr. *Rogers*'s chief Reason against Liberty of Debate, is because, as he says, it is pernicious to the Peace and Welfare of the Community, by unsettling the Minds of the People about the Religion established : But here's no consequence, unless it could be proved, that such as the great Mr. *Grounds* and Mr. *Scheme*, have it in their Hearts to raise Mobbs upon the Government, and to beat out the Brains of the *Clergy*. All the Harm, or rather Good, they aim at, is to exercise the Wits of the *Clergy* with their Doubts and Objections; and if the Passions of our *Ecclesiasticks* are not raised upon it, to the doing of Violence to these *Gentlemen*, the Peace of the Publick will never be disturb'd. As to myself, tho' I have a vast and numerous Party on my my Side, no lefs than all the Fathers and primitive Chriftians for fome Ages; yet as we were peaceable and quiet Subjects of old and paffively obedient to the *Emperors* of *Rome*; fo we will continue to the Civil Authority of this Nation. We only take the Liberty to awaken the Clergy out of a Lethargy of Dulnefs and Ignorance; and hope the Civil Magiftrate will confider the Goodnefs and Charity of our Intentions, and guard us againft their Infults for it.

The *Bifhop* of St. *David's* (61) fays, " It is abfurd to affert, that the Liberties " of any Nation will allow, with Impu- " nity, a Set of diftinguifh'd Infidels to " infult and treat with the greateft Con- " tempt and Scorn the moft facred and " important Truths, that are openly pro- " feffed, by the whole Body of the Peo- " ple, of whatever Denomination." By a Set of Infidels, I fuppofe, he means me and the Fathers: And by *treating with Contempt and Scorn the moft facred and important Truths*, he means, our burlefquing, bantering and ridiculing the *Clergy* for their Miniftry of the Letter: And for *this* he would, I conceive, have incenfed the *Societies* for Reformation of Manners to a Profecution of me. And if they had not

(51) Sermon before the Society for Reformation, &c. p. 12.

been wiser, and more merciful than their
Preacher, I must have gone to Pot. But
why should the *Bishop* dislike this way of
Writing? Don't he know, that the Fathers
of the Church used to jest and scoff at the
Gentiles and their Priests for their foolish
Superstitions? Don't he know, that our
Reformers banter'd and ridicul'd Popery out of Doors, and almost within the
Memory of Man, it was reckon'd but
a dull Sermon, that was not well
humm'd for its Puns and Jests on the
Papists? why then should the *Bishop* be a-
gainst that way of writing, which was of
good Use to the *Reformers*, and first *Christians?* The grand Subject for *Burlesque*
and *Banter*, in my Opinion, is *Infidelity*;
and that *Bishop*, who can't break two Jests
upon *Infidels* for their one upon Christianity, has but a small Share of Wit. The
Christian Religion according to the *Bishop*,
will abide the Test of calm and sedate Reasoning against it, but can't bear a Jest; O
strange!

But to leave these two Contenders for
Persecution to the Chastisement of acuter
Pens. What I have here pleaded for Liberty is not thro' any Fears of Danger
to myself; but for the Love of Truth and
Advancement of Christianity, which, without it, can't be defended, propagated and
sincerely

fincerely embraced. And therefore hope, that the Controverfy before us, between *Infidels* and *Apoftates* will be continued by the Indulgence of the Government, till Truth arifes and fhines bright to the Diffi-pation of the Mifts of Error and Ignorance; like the Light of the Sun to the Difperfion of the Darknefs of the Night. I will by God's Leave, go on to bear my part in the Controverfy ; And, if it was not more a-gainft the Interefts than Reafon of the *Clergy* to believe me, would again folemn-ly declare that what I do in it is with a View to the Honour of *Jefus*, our fpiritual *Meffiah*, to whom be Glory for ever. *Amen.*

F I N I S.

A FOURTH
DISCOURSE
ON THE
MIRACLES
OF OUR
SAVIOUR,

In VIEW of the Present
Controversy between INFIDELS
and APOSTATES.

---

*Canes qui oblatrant contra Inquisitionem
Veritatis.*　　　　　Clem. Alex.

The Third Edition.

By THO. WOOLSTON, B. D. sometime
Fellow of *Sidney-College* in *Cambridge.*

LONDON:
Printed for the Author, and Sold by him
next door to the *Star,* in *Aldermanbury,*
and by the Booksellers of *London,* and
Westminster, 1728.
[Price One Shilling.]

TO THE

Right Reverand Father in GOD

FRANCIS,

Lord Bifhop of St. ASAPH.

MY LORD,

F *the* Convocation *had been fitting, I would have made this* Dedication *to them, and humbly implored of them, what, for their* Love *to the* Fathers, *they would readily have granted, a* Recommendation *of thefe my* Difcourfes *on* Miracles *to the* Clergy: *But being unhappily difappointed of a* Seffion *of that* Reverend *and*

A 2   Learned

Learned *Body*, for *whofe wife Debates*
and orthodox *Votes I have fuch a Vene-*
ration, as is not to be expreſs'd in a few
Words, *I prefently turn'd my Thoughts on*
your Lordſhip, *to whom* a Dedication
is due, becauſe of your Reſpect, often declared, for the Authority of the Fathers,
which induces me to think, you now approve of the Uſe I have made of them.

But what I am here to applaud your
Lordſhip for, is, your Diſcourſe call'd
Difficulties and Diſcouragements, &c.
That admirable Satire againſt modern
Orthodoxy and Perſecution! How was
I tickled in the Peruſal of it! It is
plainly the Senſe of your Soul, or you
had ſet your Name to it : And if the
Temptation of Praiſe for it, had not
been too great to be reſiſted, I could
have wiſh'd you had always conceal'd
your ſelf ; and then you had not written
againſt the Grain, an aukward Piece on
Church Power, like a Retractation,
to reingratiate your ſelf with ſome Eccleſiaſtical Noodles, whom you no more,
than, I need to care for.

I

I have sometimes wondered, My Lord, *where and when the Great* Mr. Grounds *imbibed his notable Notions about Religion and Liberty ; for he suck'd them not in with his Mothers Milk, who, I suppose, train'd him up in the Belief of Christianity : But when I consider'd, that he was once the* Pupil *of* Mr. Hare *at* Cambridge, *my wonder ceas'd. Under your* Lordship's *Tuition, it seems he laid the Foundation of his distinguish'd Learning and Opinions! His Pupillage will be your immortal Honour! I wonder, none of the Writers against him have as yet celebrated your* Praise *for it ! How does he imitate and resemble his* Tutor *in Principles! I can't say, he surpasses you, since there is such a Freedom of Thought and Expression in your* Difficulties, &c. *so strongly favouring of Infid--ty, that he has not as yet equall'd.*

Upon your Lordship's *Advancement to a* Bishoprick, Difficultys *and Discouragements* not withstanding, I. *wish'd, without prescribing to the* Wisdom

dom of the Government in the choice of a learned Prelate, that the great Mr. Grounds, *for the good of the Church too, might be soon consecrated: And I should not have despair'd of it, but that he is a* Gentleman *of real Probity and Conscience, and might possibly boggle at Subscriptions, unless you and Bishop* Hoadly *could help him to some of your Reserves and Distinctions, wherewith you must be both well Stock'd, to overcome that* Difficulty. *And why should not* Dean Swift *for his Writings, as well as some others, be made a Bishop? I should like to see him one; if the then Right Reverend Bishop* Grounds *would not think him, for his Tale of a* Tub, *too loose in the Faith, for his Company.*

Don't, imagine, My Lord, *that I am forming of Schemes for my self to be a Bishop. Tho these my Discourses on* Miracles *are of very great Merit, as well as your Lordship,s Difficulties, &c. yet you may be assured, I have no such View, when I tell you, that the*
Honour,

Honour, the Fathers have exalted me to, of a Moderator *in this Controversy, sets me above all Ecclesiastical Prefer-ment, excepting the* Arch-Bishoprick *of* Canterbury, *which I'm afraid will be void, before the King is ap-prised of my singular Worth and Qua-lifications for it.*

But however, if such excellent Pre-lates, *as* Grounds, Hoadly, Swift, Hare *and my self were at the Head of Ecclesiastical Affairs, what would we do? What should we not do? What would not this free-thinking Age expect from us? Nothing less, than that, ac-cording to our Principles, we should en-deavour to set Mankind at perfect Li-berty, and to lay open the dirty Fences of the Church, call'd Subscriptions, which are not only the Stain of a good Con-science, but the* Discouragements, *your* Lordship *hints at, in the Study of the Scriptures: And if we made a Push for an Act of* P——t *to turn the* Clergy *to Grass, after King* Henry VIIIth's *Monks and Fryars; where*
would

would be the Harm of it? Nay, the Advantage to the Publick, as well as to Religion, would be great, if their Revenues were apply'd to the Payment of National Debts ; with a Reserve to our selves (remember, My Lord) of large Emoluments out of them, according to our great Merits ; otherwise worldly-wise Men will repute us impolitick Fools, which you and Bishop Hoadly, *I humbly presume, will never endure the Reproach of.*

So, hoping your Lordship will accept of this Dedication to your Praise, in as much Sincerity as it is written, I subscribe myself,

My LORD,

London *May,* 14. 1728.

The Admirer of your

Difficultys and

Discouragements,

Thomas Woolston.

A FOURTH

DISCOURSE

ON THE

MIRACLES

OF OUR

SAVIOUR, &c.

N O W for a *fourth* Discourse on *Jesus*'s Miracles, which, as before, I begin with a Repetition of the three general Heads, at first proposed to be treated on; and they are,

I. To show, that the Miracles of healing all manner of bodily Diseases, which

B   *Jesus*

Jesus was famed for, are none of the proper Miracles of the *Messiah*; neither are they so much as a good Proof of his divine Authority to found a Religion.

II. To prove that the literal History of many of the Miracles of *Jesus*, as recorded by the *Evangelists*, does imply Absurdities, Improbabilities and Incredibilities; consequently they, either in the whole or in part, were never wrought, as it is commonly believed now-a-days, but are only related as prophetical and parabolical Narratives, of what would be mysteriously, and more wonderfully done by him.

III. To consider what *Jesus* means, when he appeals to his Miracles, as to a Testimony and Witness of his divine Power; and to show that he could not properly and ultimately refer to those he then wrought in the *Flesh*, but to the mystical ones, he would do in the Spirit; of which those wrought in the Flesh are but mere Types and Shadows.

I am upon the second of these Heads, and according to it, have, in my *former Discourses*, taken into examination *eight* of the Miracles of *Jesus*, *viz.* those:

1. Of

1. Of his driving the Buyers and Sellers out of the Temple.

2. Of his exorcifing the *Devils* out of the Mad-men, and fending them into the Herd of Swine.

3. Of his Transfiguration on the Mount.

4. Of his Healing a Woman, that had an Iffue of Blood, twelve Years.

5. Of his curing a Woman, that had a Spirit of Infirmity, eighteen Years.

6. Of his telling the *Samaritan* Woman, her fortune of having had five Husbands, and being than an Adulterefs with another Man.

7. Of his curfing the Fig-tree for not bearing Fruit out of feafon.   And,

8. Of his healing a Man of an Infirmity at the Pool of *Bethefda.*

Whether it be not manifeft, that the Literal and Evangelical Story of thefe Miracles, from what I have argu'd and reafon'd upon them, does not confift of Abfurdities, Improbabilities, and Incredibilities, according to the Propofition before us, let my Readers judge; and fo I come to the Confideration of

9. A ninth Miracle of *Jefus, viz.* that (1) of his giving fight to a Man who was

(1) John. ix.

born blind, by the means of Eve-falve, made of Dirt and Spittle.

Blindnefs, as far as one may guefs by the Evangelical Hiftory, was the Diftemper that *Jefus* frequently exercis'd his Power on: And there is no doubt to be made, but he heal'd many of one Weaknefs, Defect and Imperfection, or other in their Eyes, but whether he wrought any Miracle upon any, he is fupppofed to have cured, is uncertain. There are, as it's notorious, many kinds of Blindnefs, that are incurable by Art or Nature: and there are other kinds of it, that Nature and Art will relieve a Man in. But whether *Jefus* ufed his healing Power againft the former, as well as the latter fort of Blindnefs, is more than can be affirm'd, or at leaft proved by our *Divines*. And unlefs we knew of a certainty, that the fore or blind Eyes, *Jefus* cured, were abfolutely out of the reach of Art and Nature; *Infidels* will imagine, and fuggeft, that he was only Mafter of a good Ointment for fore Eyes, and being fuccefsful in the ufe of it, ignorant People would needs think, he wrought Miracles.

The World is often blefs'd with excellent *Oculifts*, who thro' Study and Practice have attain'd to wonderful Skill in Eye-Maladies, which, tho they are of various

rious

rious forts, yet, by Cuftom of Speech all pafs under the general Name of *Blindnefs*. And fometimes we hear of famous *Chance-Doctors*, like *Jefus*, who by a Gift of God, Nature, or Fortune, without any Skill in the Structure of the Eyes, have been very fuccefsful in the Cure of one Diftemper or other incident to them : Such was Sir *William Read*, who, tho no Scholar, nor of acquir'd Abilities in *Phyfick* and *Surgery*, yet cured his Thoufands of fore or blind Eyes; and many of them too to the furprife and aftonifhment of profefs'd *Surgeons* and *Phyficians*. Whether He, or *Jefus*, cured the greater number of Blindnefs may be queftion'd. To pleafe our *Divines*, it fhall be granted that *Jefus* cured the greater Numbers; but that he cured worfe or more difficult Diftempers in the Eyes, can't be proved. Sir *William* indeed met with many Cafes of blind and fore Eyes, that were out of the reach of his Power; and fo did *Jefus* too, or he had never let great Multitudes of the blind, and otherwife diftemper'd People, go unheal'd by him. Our *Divines* will here fay, that it was never want of Power in *Jefus*, but want of Faith in the difeafed, if he did not heal them; but in other *Surgeons* and *Phyficians*, it is confeffedly their own Infufficiency: To which I have only this Anfwer,

Anſwer, that our *Phyſicians* and *Surgeons* are to be commended for their Ingenuity, to impute it to their own Defect of Power, and not to lay the Blame upon their Patients, when they can't cure them: And it is luckly for us Chriſtians, that we have *this Salvo* for the Credit of *Jeſus*'s miraculouſly healing Power, that it was not fit, he ſhould exert it againſt Unbelief; otherwiſe reaſonably ſpeaking, He with Sir *William Read*, *Greatrex*, *Veſpaſian*, our former *Kings* of *England*, and *Seventh-Sons*, muſt have paſs'd but for a *Chance-Doctor*.

But to come to the particular Conſideration of the Miracle before us. *Jeſus* reſtored, it ſeems, a blind Man to his Eyeſight, by the uſe of a peculiar Ointment, and waſhing of his Eyes, as directed, in the Pool of *Siloam*. Where lies the Miracle? I can't ſee it; but hope our *Divines* will take their opportunity to point it out to me. Our *Surgeons*, with their Ointments and Waſhings can cure ſore and blind Eyes of one ſort or other; and *Jeſus* did no more here; and yet he muſt be reckon'd a Worker of Miracles; and they but artificial Operators: where's the Senſe and Reaſon of this difference between them? If Mr. *Moor*, the *Apothecary*, for the notable Cures he performs, by the

means

means of his Medicines, fhould write himfelf, and be accounted by his Admirers, a
Miracle-worker; he and they would be
but laugh'd at for it: And yet *Jefus* for
his curing the fore Eyes of a poor Man
with an Ointment, muft be had in veneration for a divine and miraculous Operator, as much as if by the breath of his
Mouth he had removed an huge Mountain!

A Miracle, if I miftake not the Notion
of our *Divines* about it, is a fupernatural
Event, or a Work out of the Power of Nature or Art to effect. And when it is fpoken of the Cure of a Difeafe, as of Blindnefs or Lamenefs, it ought to be fo reprefented, as that skilful and experienced *Surgeons* and *Phyficians*, who can do ftrange
and furprizing Cures by Art, may give it
upon their Judgment, that no Skill of
Man could reach that Operation; but that
it ought to pafs for the Work of a divine
and almighty Hand and Power. But
there is no fuch care taken in the Defcription of any of the Difeafes, which
Jefus cured; much lefs of this before us;
againft the miraculoufnefs of which, confequently, there are thefe two Exceptions
to be made:

Firft, that we know nothing of the
Nature of this poor Man's Blindnefs; nor
what

what was the defect of his Eyes; nor whether it was curable by Art or not: Without which Knowledge, it is impossible and unreasonable to assert, that there was a Miracle wrought in the Cure of him. If his blindness or weakness of Eye-sight was curable by human means, and Jesus did use those means, there's an end of the Miracle. If the *Evangelist* had given us an accurate Description of the Condition of this Man's Eyes before Cure, we could have judg'd better: But this is their constant neglect in all the Distempers *Jesus* heal'd, and is enough to induce us to doubt of his miraculous Power. There are, as I have said, some sorts of sore or blind Eyes curable by Art, as Experience does testify; and there are others incurable, as *Physicians* and *Patients* do lament. Of which sort this Man's was, we know not. The worst that we know of his Case, is, that he was blind from his Birth, or Infancy, which might be: and yet Time, Nature and Art, may give relief to him. As a Man advances in Years, the diseases of Childhood and Youth wear off. What we call the *King's-Evil*, or an Inflammation in the Eyes, in time will abate of its Malignity. Nature will not only by degrees work the Cure it-self, but the seasonable help of a good *Oculist* will soon expedite

it,

It, tho in time of Infancy he could be of no uſe. And who knows but this might be the Caſe of this blind Man, whoſe Cure *Jeſus* by his Art did only haſten and help forward. However, there are Grounds enough to ſuſpect, that it was not divine Power which heal'd this Man, or *Jeſus* had never prepared and and order'd an *Ointment* and *Waſh* for him.

Should our *Divines* ſuppoſe or deſcribe, for the *Evangeliſt*, a ſtate of Blindneſs in this Man, incurable by Art; that would be begging the Queſtion, which no Unbeliever will grant. But to pleaſe them, I will yield, without Enquiry into the Nature of this Man's Blindneſs, that, if *Jeſus* had uſed no Medicines; if with only a word of his Mouth he had cured the Man, and he had inſtantaneouſly recover'd, as the Word was ſpoken; here would have been a real and great Miracle, let the Blindneſs or Imperfection of the Man's Sight before, be of what kind or degree ſoever. But *Jeſus*'s uſe of Waſhings and Ointments abſolutely ſpoils and deſtroys the Credit of the Miracle, and we ought by no means to aſcribe *that* to the immediate Hand and Power of God, which *Medicines* and *Balſams* are apply'd to the Effect of. And this brings me to the

Second Exception againſt the miracu-
louſneſs of the Cure of this blind **Man**,
which is, that *Jeſus* uſed human means
for the Cure of him ; which means,
whether they were at all proper and effectual in themſelves, do affect the Credit
of the Miracle, and give occaſion of ſuſpicion, that it was Art and not divine
Power that heal'd him, or *Jeſus*, for
his Honour, had never had recourſe to
the uſe of them. And what were thoſe
Means, or that Medicine, which *Jeſus*
made uſe of? Why, " He ſpit upon the
" Ground, and made a Balſam of Dirt
" and Spittle, and anointed the poor
" Man's Eyes with it, and he recover'd."
A ſtrange and odd ſort of an Ointment,
that I believe was never uſed before, nor
ſince, for ſore and blind Eyes ! I am
not Student enough in *Phyſick* and *Surgery* to account for the natural and rational uſe of this Balſam ; but wiſh that
ſkilful Profeſſors of thoſe Sciences would
help me out at this difficulty. If they
could rationally account for the uſe of
this Eye-ſalve, tho it was by ſuppoſing,
that Jeſus imperceptibly had in his Mouth
a proper unctuous and balſamick Subſtance, which he diſſolv'd into Spittle,
they would do great ſervice to a certain
Cauſe ; and I wonder none of them,
whe-

whether well or ill affected to Religion, have as yet bent their Thoughts to it.

In the Practice of *Physick* and *Surgery*, there are sometimes very odd and unaccountable Medicaments made use of; and now-and-then very whimsical and seemingly ridiculous ones, by old Women, to good Purpose: But none of them are to be compared to *Jesus*'s Balsam for sore Eyes. I have heard of a merry *Mountebank* of Distinction, whose catholick Medicine was *Hasty-Pudding*, which indeed is a notable Remedy against the *Esuriency* of the Stomach, that the Poor often labour under. But *Jesus*'s Eye-Salve, for absurdity, whim, and incongruity, was never equall'd, either in jest or in earnest, by any *Quack-Doctor*. Whether *Infidels* think of this Ointment of the Holy *Jesus* with a smile; or reflect on it with disdain, I can't guess. As to myself, I should think with St. *Chrysostom* (2), that this Eye-Salve of *Jesus* would sooner put a Man's Eyes out, than restore a blind one to his Sight. And I believe that our *Divines*, for the Credit of the Miracle, and our *Surgeons*, for the Honour of their Science, will

---

(2) Quid Lutum i linere opporet ? hoc potius excum reddere, quis unquam hoc pacto curatus est ? *In Loc. Johan.*

agree,

agree, that it could not be naturally operative and effective of the Cure of the blind Man.

What then was the Reason of *Jesus*'s using this strange Eye-Salve; when, for the fake of the Miracle, and for the honour of his own Power, he should have cured the Man with a word speaking? This is a Question and Objection in St. *Cyril* (3) against Ministers of the Letter, who are obliged to give an Answer to it, that will confist with the Wisdom and Power of *Jesus*, otherwise they must give up the Miracle or make him a vain, insignificant and trifling Agent. St. *Cyril*, of whose mind I am, says (4) that the Reason of the use of this Balsam made of Dirt and Spittle is to be fetch'd from the Mystery. But, in as much as our *Divines* will never agree to that, which would be of ill Consequence to their Ministry, they must give a good Reason of their own, which I despair of seeing, that will comport with the Letter.

(3) Quam ob causam dicet aliquis, cum omnia solo Verbo præstare possit, nulloque negotio, Lutum quidem sputo macerat? *In Loc. Johan.*

(4) Sed Rationem quandam mysticam habet Vis Rei istius de sputo. *Ibid.*

St.

St. *Irenæus* too, fays (5), that the *Clay and Spittle* was of no fervice to the Cure of the blind Man; and yet *Jefus* did not ufe it *in vain*. Is not this an Inconfiftency? How will our *Divines* adjuft it? With *Irenæus*, I am fure they'll not myftically folve the Difficulty; therefore if they don't provide another Solution of it to fatisfaction; either their Miniftry of the Letter, or the Reputation of *Jefus*, and this Miracle muft fuffer for it.

I am puzzled to think, how our *Divines* will extricate themfelves out of this Strait, and account for the ufe of this Eye-Salve, without any Diminution of the Miracle. Surely, they will not fay that *Jefus* ufed this fenflefs and infignificant Ointment to put a *Slur* upon the Practice of *Phyfick* and *Surgery*, as if other Medicines were of no more avail than his *Dirt* and *Spittle*. They have more wit than to fay fo; leaft it incenfe a noble and moft ufeful Profeffion, not fo much againft themfelves, as againft *Jefus*, and provoke them to a

(5) Ei autem qui cæcus fuerat a Nativitate, jam non per fermonem fed per operationem præftitit vifum; non vanè, neque prout evenit, hoc faciens, fed ut oftenderet manum Dei, eam quæ ab initio plafmavit Hominem, &c. Contra Hæref. L. v. c. 15.

nicer

nicer and stricter Enquiry, than I can make into his Miracles, the Diseases he cured, and his manner of Operation; and to infer from thence, that he could be no miraculous Healer of Diseases who used Medicines; nor his *Evangelists* orthodox at Theology, who were so inexpert at Anatomy and the Description of bodily Distempers. This might be of bad Consequence to Religion: And yet I wonder that none of them, who may be supposed a little disaffected to Christianity, have taken the Hint from this pretended Miracle before us, and some others, to endeavour at a Proof of *Jesus*'s being little better than a *Quack-Doctor*.

If I was, what I am not, an *Infidel*, I should think, from the Letter of this Story, that *Jesus* was a *juggling Impostor*, who would pass for a miraculous Healer of Diseases, tho he used underhand, proper Medicines. The *Clay and the Spittle* he made an open shew of, as what, to Admiration, he would cure the blind Man with; but in reserve he had a more sanative Balsam, that he subtilly slip't in the room of the Clay, and repeatedly to good purpose anointed the Man's Eyes with it. But as the Authority of the Fathers, and their mystical Interpretation of this Story is alone my

safe-

safe-guard againſt ſuch an ill opinion of *Jeſus* ; ſo I would now gladly know upon what Bottom the Faith of our *Divines* can ſtand, as to this Miracle, and *Jeſus*'s divine Power in it.

I have peruſed ſome of our *Commem-tators* on the Place, and don't perceive that they heſitate at this ſtrange Eye-Salve; nor make any Queſtions about the pertinent or impertinent Uſe of it. Whether it is, that they ſleep over the Story, or are aware of greater Difficultys in it, than can be eaſily ſurmounted, and therefore dare not touch on't, I know not. But now that we enjoy Liberty of debate, which will make us Philo-ſophers, and I have taken the Freedom to make a ſtricter Scrutiny than ordinary into *Jeſus*'s Miracles, and to conſider what Abſurditys, their Srories, and *this* in par-ticular, are clog'd with; it is incumbent on our *Divines* to anſwer ſolidly theſe Queſtions, *viz.* What was the Reaſon of *Jeſus*'s Uſe of this Eye-Salve made of Clay and Spittle? Whether, if it was of ſervice to the Cure of the blind Man, it does not deſtroy the Miracle? And if it had no effect in the Cure of him, whether *Jeſus* was not a *vain* and *trifling* Operator, making uſe of inſignificant and impertinent Medicines to the Diminution

of

of his divine Power? Thefe Queſtions are not ludicrous, but *calm and fedate Reafoning*, which *Bifhop Smalbroke* (6) does not difapprove of. Therefore a grave, rational, and fubſtantial Anſwer is expected to them, ſuch as will be a Vindication of the Wiſdom and Power of *Jefus*, without any Diminution of the Miracle.

Should our *Divines* ſay, that this Matter was an Act of unſearchable Wiſdom and muſt be left to the Will of our Saviour, and not curiouſly pry'd into, any more than ſome other Diſpenſations of Providence, that are paſt finding out: This Anſwer, which I believe to be the beſt, that can be given, will not do here. The Miracles of *Jefus* are, as our *Divines* own, Appeals to our Reaſon and Senſes for his Authority; and by our Reaſon and Senſes they are to be try'd, condemn'd or approved of. If they will not abide the teſt of Reaſon and Senſe, they are to be rejected, and *Jefus*'s Authority along with them, Therefore a more cloſe, pertinent and ſerious Anſwer is to be given to the ſaid Queſtions; which as I believe to

(6) *See his Sermon before the Societys for Reformation.* p. 32.

be impoffible, confiftently with the Letter ; fo our *Divines* muft of neceffity go
along with me to the Fathers for a myftical and allegorical Interpretation of the
Story of this Eye-Salve ; or the Miracle
will fall to the Ground, and *Jefus's*
divine Power be in great danger with
it.

St. *Cyril*, (who is one of *Bifhop Smalbroke's* Greek Commentators, that fhould
ftrictly adhere to the Letter) fignifies, as
I before obferv'd, that *Jefus's* Ufe of this
Clay and Spittle would be an Abfurdity,
if it was not to be accounted for, from the
Myftery.

Eufebius Gallicanus, treating on this
Miracle, fays (7) ; " that our Saviour
" apparently manifefts that his Miracles
" are of a fpiritual and myftical Signifi-
" cation, becaufe in the Work of them,
" he does fomewhat, or other, that lite-
" rally has no Senfe nor Reafon in it.
" As for Inftance, in the Cure of this
" blind Man, what occaffion was there

(7) Ipfe Salvator nofter apertiffime oftendit, quod
ejus Miracula aliquid fignificent, dum ea faciendo, aliquid agit, quod Ratione carere videatur. Nifi enim
aliquid fignificaret, quid neceffarium fuit, in hujus cæci
Illuminatione, ut Lutum faceret, quo oculos ejus lini-
ret, cui folum dicere fufficiens erat. Quæramus igitur
fignificationem, & videamus quid cæcus ifte fignificet.
In Homil. quartâ poft quartam Dominicam.

" for

" for *Clay and Spittle* to anoint his Eyes,
" if it was not of a mystical meaning,
" when with a Word of his Mouth,
" *Jesus* could have cured him? Let us
" then set aside the Letter of the Story,
" and Search for the Mystery, and con-
" sider who is meant by this Blind
" Man, *&c.*"

Origen too, upon occasion of this
Miracle, and its Absurdity according to
the Letter, says (8); " that whatever
" *Jesus* did in the Flesh was but a Type
" and Figure of what he would do in
" Spirit, as is apparent from the Miracle
" of his curing a blind Man, which no-
" body knows why it was so done, if
" it be not to be understood of a mys-
" tical Ointment to open the Eyes of the
" blind in Understanding."

And who then is this blind Man mystically? St. *Augustin* (9), St. *Jerome* (10,

---

(8) Similitudo erat & Typus futurorum unumquodque
quod fiebat in Corpore. Veluti nescio quis à Nativitate
cæcus Visum recuperavit. Vere autem cæcus iste erat à
Nativitate Gentilium Populus, cui Salvator reddidit
Visum, Saliva sua ungens oculos ejus & mittens ad *Siloam*,
quod interpretatur missus, mittebat quippe illos quos
spiritu unxit ad Apostolos. *In Isai. c. vi.*

(9) Genus humanum est iste cæcus, *In Loc. Johan.*

(10) Cæcus humanum Genus significatar. *In Com.
Johan.*

Eusebius Gallicanus (11), St. *Theophilus*
of *Antioch* (12), *Origen* (13), St. *Cyril* of
Alexandria (14), and St. *Theophylact* (15),
(Four of them, *Bishop Smalbroke*'s Greek
and literal Commentators!) say, this *blind
Man* is a Type of Mankind of all Nations,
who in the Perfection of Time signified
by the Sabbath (16) in the Story, is to
be cured of this Blindness in Understanding.

And what is Mankind's Blindness here
signified? St. *Augustin* (17), St. *Cyril* (18)
and St. *Thyophylact* (19), say, it is Ignorance, Error and Infidelity, or the want
of the intellectual Sight and Knowledge of

(11) Cæcus iste a Nativitate, Genus humanum esse
videtur à primo homine.——Hæc enim cæcitas non Corporis sed Animæ est. *In Loc. supra laudat.*

(12) Per cæcum naturaliter non videntem & illumina-
tum significat Genus humanum. *In Loc. Johan.*

(13) Vere autem cæcus iste erat à Nativitate Gentilium
Populus. *In Isai. c. vi.*

(14) Cæci hujus Curationem in figuram & typus voca-
tionis Gentium accepimus. *In Loc. Johan.*

(15) Intellige hoc Miraculum spiritualiter. Nam cæcus quidem erat omnis homo à Nativitate, id est, ab
Initio Mundi. *In Loc. Johan.*

(16) Im Sabbato est figura ultimi Temporis. *St. Cyril
in Loc. Johan.*

(17) Cæcitas est Infidelitas. *In Loc.*

(18) Cæcus qui destituitur divino Lumine. *De Adorat.*
p. 414.

(19) Cæcus qui sedet in tenebris omnis Ignorantiæ,
& non potuit videre Conditorem Mundi. *In Loc. Johan.*

God

God and his Providence. *Origen* (20), St. *John* of *Jerusalem* (21), and St. *Theophylact* (22), (Still *Bishop Smalbroke's* literal and Greek Commentators!) tell us the Reason of this spiritual Blindness of Mankind, that is, because they adhere to the Letter of the Scriptures.

And how will *Jesus*, or right *Reason* and *Truth*, which are his mystical Names, cure Mankind of this his spiritual Blindness? By his mystical *Spittle* temper'd with mystical *Dirt*. And how shall we do to understand this mystical Ointment, so as to make it a proper Medicine for Mankind's spiritual Blindness? St. *Theophilus* of *Antioch* (23), has an allegorical Interpretation of this *Clay* and *Spittle* of our Lord; but as it is hard to apprehend his meaning, I shall not here insist on it. *Origen* says (24), that the anointing of the blind Man's Eyes with

(20) Literam Legis sequentes, in Errores, Superstitiones & Infidelitatem incurrunt. *In Matt. Tract.* xxvi.

(21) Cæcus ille est cæcus in Litera, & hoc statu Sanari non potest. *In Marc.* c viii.

(22) Cæci qui imperiti Scripturarum. *In Loc. Johan.*

(23) Lutum vero factum de Saliva oris Domini, ac positum super oculos cæci, significat hic, quod naturæ deerat, opere suo implere Figulum. *In Loc. Johan.*

(24) Saliva sua ungens Oculos caci & mittens ad *Siloam* quod interpretatur *Missus*, mittebat quippe illos, quos spiritu unxit. &c. *In Isa. c.* vi.

Spittle,

Spittle, is to be underſtood of the Unc-
tion of the *Spirit* of Chriſt. But this
does not give us rightly to underſtand
the Metaphor and Figure. St. *John* of
Jeruſalem ſays, that by the *Clay* and *Spittle* is meant (25) *perfeçt Doçtrine*, which
in Truth may open the Eyes of Mens
Underſtanding : But what is *perfeçt Doctrine ?* Why, to help the Fathers out here,
without departing from their Opinions,
by the *Spittle* of Jeſus muſt be underſtood the *Water* of the Spirit inſtill'd into
the *Earth* of the Letter of the Scriptures,
which temper'd together, does, in the
Judgment of them all, make *perfeçt Doctrine* to the opening of the Eyes of our
Underſtanding in the Knowledge of the
Providence of God of all Ages; which
Knowledge, Light, Sight, or Illumination,
Mankind has hitherto wanted.

St. *Irenæus* (26), gives an excellent and
myſtical Reaſon, by himſelf, for the uſe

(25) Saliva eſt perfeçta Doçtrina. *In Marc.* c. viii.

(26) Ei autem qui cæcus fuerat à Nativitate, jam non
per ſermonem ſed per operationem præſtitit Viſum ;
non vane neque prout evenit hoc faciens, ſed ut oſtenderet manum Dei, eam quæ ab Initio plaſmavit hominem.
Quapropter expuit in Terram, & fecit Lutum, & ſuper-
linivit illud Oculis, oſtendens antiquam Plaſmationem,
quemadmodum façta eſt, & manum Dei manifeſtans his
qui intelligere poſſunt, per quam è Limo plaſmatus eſt
homo. *Cont. Hæreſes. L.* v. *c.* 15.

of

of this Ointment of *Clay* and *Spittle*, to the Cure of this blind Man, which I shall not stay to illustrate, but only have cited it for the Meditation of the Learned and Curious.

The Story of the blind Man, as St. *John* has related it, is long, and would take up more time, than I have to spare at present, to go thro' all the Parts of it. What I have done at present is enough to awaken others to the Consideration, not only of the Absurdities of the Letter, but of the mystical Interpretation of the rest.

The Miracle, which consisted literally in the Cure of a blind Man by the use of an Ointment made of *Dirt* and *Spittle*, is absurd, senseless and unaccountable; but in the Mystery, there is Wisdom and Reason. And the Cure of Mankind of the Blindness of his Understanding, by the *Spirit*'s being temper'd with the *Letter* of the Scriptures, which is the mystical *Eye-Salve*, will not only be a most stupendous Miracle, but a Proof of *Jesus*'s *Messiahship* beyond all contradiction, in as much as by such an opening of the Eyes of our Understandings, which have been hitherto dark, we shall see, how he is the Accomplishment of the Law and the Prophets. And so I pass to a

10. Tenth

10. **Tenth Miracle of Jesus,** *viz.* (27) *That of his turning Water into Wine, at a Marriage in* Cana *of* Galilee. This is call'd the beginning of *Jesus*'s Miracles; but whether it is to be understood of the *First* of his whole Life, or of the *First* that he wrought in *Cana* of *Galilee,* is not agreed amongst *Divines.* I shall not enter into the Dispute, which as it is of no Consequence to my Cause in hand; so I shall pass it by, and not urge any Arguments for or against either side of it.

Tho I would not for the World be so impious and profane as to believe, what is contain'd and imply'd in the Letter of this Story; yet I am still too grave to handle it as ludicrously as I ought; and it is now against the grain, that I write so freely, as I shall against it, being unwilling, not only to put the *Clergy* out of all Temper, but, to give *Scoffers* and *Infidels* so great an Advantage against their Ministry of the Letter. Some may wonder that I, who have gone so far in the ludicrous display of the gross Absurdities of some other Miracles, should boggle at this. But to be ingenuous, and speak the Truth sincerely,

(27) John ii.

I am

I am still a Christian (for all what
the *Bishop* of St. *David's*, (28) *Arch-
deacon Stubbs*, and others would make of
me) upon the Principles of the Fathers,
and have a greater Veneration for the
Person of the Holy *Jesus*, than to be forward to make such sport with him, his Mother, and his Disciples, as this Story affords
Scope for. And if it was not for the necessity of turning the *Clergy*'s Heads to the Consideration of Mysteries, this Miracle should
have been pass'd by in silence.

There were some antiently, whom St.
Chrysostom (29) writes of, whether *Jews*,
Gentiles, or *Hereticks*, I know not, who
took great offence at the Story of this
Wedding, accounting it, from what is related in St. *John*, as a riotous Feast,
and that *Jesus* and his Mother, and his
Disciples, not only bore a part in the
Revellings, but were most to blame for
them; or he should not have countenanced
them with his Presence, much less pro-
moted them, by the Change of a large
quantity of Water into Wine for the use
of a Company, who were already *drunk*

(28) *See his Speech in Convocation, printed in the* Post-
Boy *of March the 30th.*

(29) Rursus hoc in loco calumniantur nonnulli hunc
ebriosorum fuisse Conventum, &c. *In Loc. Johan.*

with

with it. But I, with St. *Chryſoſtom,* am inclined to believe, that, if *Jeſus* did grace this Wedding with his Preſence, there was no Exceſs encouraged, or ſo much as ſuffer'd at it. If he did accept of the Invitation of the Bridegroom, it was for an Opportunity, not ſo much to turn *Water* into *Wine,* as to make a proper Diſcourſe to the People of conjugal Duties.; and, as he was a Searcher of the Hearts, ſecretly to admoniſh the Married of the Sin and Miſchief of Adultery; tho we read not of a ſeaſonable and good Word ſpoken at it.

And the Empreſs *Eudocia,* a nurſing Mother of the Church, has given us a Poetical, and I hope a fictitious Deſcription of this Wedding. She makes a ſumptuous and voluptuous Feaſt of it; and writes (30) of *Muſick* and *Dancing* in abundance, enough to make us think of ſuch Mirth and Paſtime here, as was unbecoming of a Company of Saints to be preſent at. Whether it was, that this

---

(30) Pueri aut Saltatores volutabantur, in his autem Tibiæ, Lyræque Vocem habebant. Mulieres autem Cantum accipientes, volvebantur per medias Quæcunque optimatum erant uxores atque filiæ. Illi vero ad Saltationem & deſiderabilem Cantum Converſi delectabantur, &c.

In *Homero-Centon.*

E

Empreſs,

Emprefs, being only accuftom'd to the Exceffes of a Court, could form no meaner Conceptions of a Country Wedding; or whether fhe had any extra-fcriptural Authority for what fhe writ, I know not : But I believe, that, if *Jefus* was at all at a Marriage-Feaft, the whole was conducted with Decency, Order, and Sobriety; and if he there wrought any Miracle, it was to manifeft his Glory, to the Converfion of fome, and Confirmation of the Faith of others.

And our *Tranflators* of the *Bible* too have given occafion to fufpect fomewhat of Excefs at this Wedding; or they need not have made the Waterpots to hold two or three Firkins apiece. If I had been the Tranflator, they fhould not have held above two or three *Pints* apiece, which Meafure is as agreeable to the Original as *Firkin*; neither can I imagine, that *Jefus*, if he did convert Water into Wine, would do it in fo large a Meafure, for fear of an intemperate abufe of it, but only gave the Company a caft of his miraculous Power, and a little Tafte of his Love and Goodwill to them.

Such are the Conceptions, that, to the Honour of *Jefus*, I am willing to form of this *Wedding*; and wifh that the

Letter

Letter of the Story did fuggeft no worfe Thoughts of it to us. I fhould be pleas'd, if no *Infidel* really could, what I, but for the fake of the Myftery moft unwillingly fhould, write any ludicrous Defcants on it. But if this Story had been related of *Apollonius Tyranæus*, as it is of our *Jefus*, I would have ridicul'd and fatiriz'd it to the utmoft of my Power, and have render'd him and his Difciples of all Nations, as contemptible as I could, for the Belief of it; and I don't doubt, but our Chriftian *Priefts* would have given me ample Praifes and Commendations for fo doing. It is faid of *Apollonius*, that for the Entertainment of his Friends, he commanded variety of nice Difhes of Meat, together with Bowls of choiceft Wines, all on a fudden to defcend upon his Table and range themfelves in good Order. Whether there was any Truth in this Miracle of *Apollonius*, is not the Queftion; but Mr. *Chandler* (31) could fee a Fault in it, (tho none in *Jefus*'s Wine at this Wedding) as if it was done for the Pleafure of luxurious Appetites, tho we read of no Intemperance at it, which can't be faid of the *Wedding-Feaft* before us. Our

(31) *Vindication of the Chriftian Religion.* p. 82.

Divines

Divines I suppose, no more than myself,
believe any thing of the said Miracle in
Apollonius ; but, if it was really wrought,
I fancy, I could have lampoon'd him for
it, and would have made it a diabolical
Work, like that, as Fables go, of the
Feastings of *Wizards* and *Witches* ; and
our *Divines* (passing by *Jesus's Wine*
here) would readily, as they are Believers of the Storys of Witchcraft, have
struck in with me.

But setting aside that miraculous Story
of *Apollonius*, which has but *one* Voucher ;
the Case before us is *Jesus's turning Wa-*
ter into Wine for the use of Men, who
had before *well drank*. How shall I
force Nature and Faith to ridicule this
Story ? How shall I lay aside that profound Veneration for the Holy *Jesus*,
which Conversation with the Fathers,
more than the Prejudice of Education
has begotten in me, and ludicrously here
treat him and his Miracle too, as is incumbent upon me, to make way for the
Mystery ? In short, I can't do it, in my
own Name ; but having met with a satirical Invective of a supposed Jewish *Rabbi*
to this purpose, I here publish it, that
our *Clergy*, as well as myself, may
think of an Answer to it, and so prevent that Mischief it may do by being
handed

handed about among *Jews* and *Infidels*, in Manuscript. It is as follows;

" You Christians pay Adoration to
" *Jesus*, whom you believe to be a di-
" vine Author of Religion, sent of God
" for the Instruction, Reformation and
" Salvation of Mankind, and what in-
" duces you to this Belief of him, is,
" (besides some obscure Prophecies, which
" you can't agree upon, and which nei-
" ther your selves, nor any body else
" understands the Application of) the
" History of his Miracles: But I won-
" der, you should have a good opinion
" of him for his Miracles, which, if he
" wrought no better than what are re-
" corded of him, by your *Evangelists*,
" are, if duly consider'd, enough to a-
" lienate your Hearts from him. I can't
" spare time now to examine into all of
" them, but according to the cursory
" Observation I have made on them, there
" is not one so well circumstanced, as to
" merit a considerate Man's belief, that
" it was the Work of an omnipotent,
" all-wise, just and good Agent. Some
" of them are absurd Tales, others foo-
" lish Facts, others unjust Actions, others
" ludicrous Pranks, others jugling Tricks,
" others magical Enchantments ; and if
" many

" many of them had been better and
" greater Operations than they are, and
" of a more useful and stupendous Na-
" ture than they seem to be ; yet the
" first Miracle that he wrought, *viz.*
" that of his *turning Water into Wine*
" at an extravagant and voluptuous Wed-
" ding at *Cana* of *Galilee*, is enough to
" turn our Stomachs against all the rest.
" It is in itself enough to beget in us
" an ill opinion of *Jesus*, and to prepof-
" fefs us with an averfion to his Religion,
" without farther Examination into it,
" It is enough to make us fufpect his o-
" ther Miracles, of what Name foever,
" to be of a bafe, magical, and diaboli-
" cal Extraction ; or he had never fet
" up for a divine worker of Miracles
" with fo ill a grace. Would any fo-
" ber, grave, ferious and divine Perfon,
" as you Chriftians fuppofe *Jefus* to have
" been, have vouchfafed his Prefence at
" a Wedding ; where fuch Levities, Di-
" verfions and Exceffes (in our Nation of
" the *Jews*, as well as in all others)
" were indulg'd on fuch Occafions, as
" were not fit to be feen, much lefs
" countenanc'd by the *Saint*, you would
" make of him. If your *Jefus*, his Mo-
" ther, and his Difciples had not been
" merry Folks in themfelves, they would
" have

" have declined the Invitation of the
" *Bridegroom*; nay, if they had been at
" all graver and more ferious People
" than ordinary, no Invitation had been
" given to fuch *Spoil-Sports :* But boon
" Companions they were, and of comi-
" cal Converfation, or there had been
" at a Wedding no Room for them. You
" Chriftians may fancy, what you pleafe,
" of *Jefus* and his Mother's Saintfhip ;
" but the very Text of the Story im-
" plies, they were Lovers of good Fel-
" lowfhip and Excefs too, upon occa-
" fion ; or he had never, upon her Inti-
" mation, turn'd fo large a quantity of
" Water into Wine, after all or moft of
" the Company were far gone with it.
" You may fuppofe, if you pleafe, that
" all were fober, and none intoxicated,
" and that the Want of Wine pro-
" ceeded from the abundance of Com-
" pany, rather than excefs in drinking ;
" but why then did *John* the *Evange-*
" *lift* ufe the word μεθυσθωσι, which im-
" plies, they were more than half Seas
" over ? And if *Jefus* and his Mother
" had not both a mind to *top* them up ;
" the one would not have requefted, nor
" the other have granted a Miracle to
" that purpofe. Whether *Jefus* and his
" Mother themfelves were at all *cut*, as
" were

" were others of the Company, is not
" so certain. She might be an abstemi-
" ous Dame for ought we know; tho if
" old Stories are true of her familiarity
" with a *Soldier*, of whom came her
" *chara Deûm Soboles*, in all probabi-
" lity she would take a *Dram* and a *Bot-*
" *tle* too. But it looks as if *Jesus* him-
" self was a little *in* for't, or he had
" never spoke so waspishly and snap-
" pishly to his Mother, saying, *Woman,*
" *what have I to do with thee? mine*
" *Hour is not yet come:* which was ve-
" ry unbecoming of a dutiful Son, who,
" excepting when he ran away from
" his Parents, and put them to (32)
" *Sorrow* and *Trouble* to look him up,
" was, and is still in Heaven, say the
" *Roman Catholicks* a most obedient Child.
" You modern Christians may put what
" Construction you can upon the words
" above of *Jesus* to his Mother, to salve
" his Credit; but the Fathers of your
" Church (33) confess them to be a sharp
" and surly Reply to her, which, if it
" did not proceed from the natural bad-

(32) Luke ii. 48.

(33) Christus asperius respondit, quid tibi & mihi,
Mulier? *St. Chrysost. in Loc. Johan.* Vide & *Theophy-*
lact. in Loc.

" nefs

" ness of his Temper, derived, *ex traduce,*
" from his supposed Father yet, was cer-
" tainly the effect of Drinking, and
" that's the more likely, because it is
" a *broken* and *witless* Sentence, such as
" *Fuddlecaps* utter by halves, when the
" *Wine's in,* and the *Wit's out.* Your
" modern *Commentators* are sadly puz-
" zled to make good Sense of this bro-
" ken and abrupt Sentence of *Jesus,* and
" a pertinent Reply of it, to what his
" Mother said to him, *they have no*
" *Wine:* If you will bear with me, I'll
" help you out at this dead lift, and
" give you the true meaning of it *thus.*
" *Jesus's* Mother being apprised of a
" deficiency of Wine, and willing, as well
" as the *Bridegroom,* that the Company
" should be thorowly merry before they
" parted, intimates to her Son, (whom
" she hnew to be initiated in the My-
" sterys of *Bacchus*) *that they had no*
" *Wine:* But before she could finish her
" Request to him, He, mistaking her
" meaning, imagines, she was caution-
" ing against drinking more Wine, and
" exhorting him to go home; where-
" upon he takes her up short and quick,
" saying, *Woman, what have you to do*
" *with me?* (for that too is the *English*
" of the *Greek*) I'll not be interrupted

F   " in

" in my Cups, nor break Company;
" *for mine Hour is not yet come* to de-
" part : But after he rightly apprehend-
" ed her, he goes to work, and rather
" than the Company fhould want their
" fill, by trick of Art, like a *Punch-*
" *maker*, meliorates Water into what they
" call'd Wine. That this is the obvious
" Interpretation, and natural Paraphrafe
" of the Words before us, fhall be try'd
" by the Abfurd Comments now-a-days
" put upon them, that are enough to
" make a confiderate Man laugh, if not
" hifs at them.

" Some antient Hereticks (34), very
" gravely inferr'd from this Expreffion,
" *Woman, what have I to do with thee,*
" that *Mary* was neither a Virgin, nor
" *Jefus* her Son; or he had never ac-
" cofted her with fuch blunt Language,
" that implys, they could not be fo a-
" kin to each other. This was a per-
" plexity to St. *Auguftin*, and gave him
" fome trouble to explain the Expref-
" fion, confiftently with her Virginity
" (for all fhe cohabited with the old Car-
" penter) and his Filiation. But this
" being a quibble, that has been long
" fince dropt, I fhall not revive, nor in-

(34) Vide Sanctum Auguftinum. *In Loc. Johan*

" fift

" fift on it. But that the Expreffion
" above do's fuppofe a little Inebriation,
" in *Jefus*, I may avert, neither is
" there a better Solution to be made of
" it.

" The Fathers of your Church, be-
" ing fenfible of the abfurdity, abrupt-
" nefs, impertinence, pertnefs, and fenflef-
" nefs of the Paffage before us accord-
" ing to the Letter, had recourfe to
" a myftical and allegorical Interpreta-
" tion, as the only way to make it con-
" fiftent with the Wifdom, Sobriety and
" Duty of the Holy *Jefus*. But you
" *Moderns*, abandoning Allegories and
" Myfteries on Miracles, have endea-
" vour'd, I fay, to put other Conftruc-
" tions upon it, as may comport with
" the Letter and Credit of Jefus : But
" how infipid and fenflefs they are,
" I appeal to a reafonable Man, who
" will give himfelf the trouble to con-
" fult them, upon the Place, and fave
" me the Pains of a tedious and nau-
" feous Work to recount them for him.

" But to Humour the Chriftian Prieft-
" hood at this Day, I will fuppofe that
" *Jefus*, and his Mother, and Difciples,
" tho Fifhermen, to have been all fober,
" grave and ferious at this Wedding,
" fuitably to the Opinion that their Fol-

" lowers

" lowers now would have us to enter-
" tain of them. But then it is hard
" to conceive them, lefs than Spectators
" and even Encouragers of Excefs and
" Intemperance in others; or *Jefus*, af-
" ter their more than fufficient drink-
" ing for the fatisfaction of Nature,
" had never turn'd Water into Wine,
" nor would his Mother have requefted
" him to do it, if, I fay, they had not
" a mind, and took Pleafure in it too, to
" fee the Company quite *flitch'd up*.

" A fober, prudent and wife Philofo-
" pher or *Magician*, in the place of
" *Jefus*, if he had an Art or Power to
" turn Water into Wine, would never
" have exercifed it upon fuch an occa-
" fion; no, not to pleafe his beft Friends,
" nor in obedience to the moft indul-
" gent Parent. What would he have
" faid in fuch a Cafe? That the Com-
" pany had drank fufficiently already,
" and there was no need of more Wine:
" The Bridegroom had kindly and plen-
" tifully entertain'd his Guefts, and he
" would not for the Honour of God,
" who had endow'd him with a divine
" Power, be at the Expence of a Mi-
" racle to promote the leaft Intemperance.
" Whether fuch a Speech and Refolu-
" tion in *Jefus*, upon this occafion,
" would

" would not have been more commen-
" dable, than what he did, let any one
" judge.

" If I was a Christian, I would, for
" the Honour of *Jesus*, renounce this
" Miracle, and not magnify and extol
" it as a divine and good Act, as many
" now-a-days do. I would give into,
" and contend for the Truth of *that*
" *Gloss*, which the *Gentiles* of old (35)
" by way of Objection put upon it,
" *viz. That the Company having ex-*
" *hausted the Bridegroom's Stock of Wine,*
" *and being in Expectation of more;*
" *Jesus, rather than the Bridegroom should*
" *be put to the Blush for deficiency,*
" *palm'd a false Miracle, by the help*
" *of the Governour of the Feast, upon*
" *a drunken Crew; that is, having some*
" *spirituous Liquors at hand, mingled*
" *them with a quantity of Water, which*
" *the Governour of the Feast vouch'd*
" *to be incomparable good Wine, mira-*
" *culously made by* Jesus: *and the Com-*
" *pany being, thro' a vitiated Palate,*
" *uncapable of distinguishing better from*
" *worse, and of discovering the Fraud,*
" *admired the Wine and the Miracle;*
" *and applauded* Jesus *for it, and per-*

(35) Apud St. Chrysostomum *In Loc. Johan.*

" haps

" haps became his Disciples upon it. If
" I, I say, was a Disciple of *Jesus*, I
" would give this Story such an old
" turn for his Credit. And I appeal
" to indifferent Judges, whether such a
" daubing of the Miracle, to remove the
" Offence of *Infidels* at this Day, would
" not be politically and wisely done of
" me. Whether modern Christians may
" be brought into such a Notion of
" this supposed Miracle, I know not;
" but really there is room enough to
" suspect such a Fraud in it.

" But supposing *Jesus's* Change of
" Water into Wine to have been a real
" Miracle; none commission'd of God
" for the Reformation and Instruction
" of Mankind would ever have done it
" here. Miracles (as Mr. *Chandler* (36)
" says excellently well) *must be such*
" *things, as that it is consistent with*
" *the Perfections of God, to interest*
" *himself in*; and again, *they must ar-*
" *gue not only the Power of God, but*
" *his Love to Mankind, and his Inclina-*
" *tion to do them good*; which this of
" *Jesus* is so far from, that it has an
" an evil Aspect and Tendency, as is
" above represented; consequently it is

(36) *Vindication of the Christian Religion*, p. 82.

" to

" to be rejected, and no longer esteem'd
" a divine Miracle; neither is *Jesus* to
" be received as a Revealer of God's
" Will for it, as Mr. *Chandler* will
" bear me witness.

" No doubt on't, but you Christian
" Priests would have us *Jews* and *In-
" fidels*, to believe the whole Com-
" pany at this Wedding, for all what
" is intimated by St. *John* to the con-
" trary, to consist of sober and demure
" Saints. I will suppose so; but then,
" what occasion had they at all for
" Wine? What reason could there be
" for God's Power to interpose and make
" it, especially in so large a quantity,
" for them? I can conceive none. If
" any of the Company had been taken
" with fainting Fits; and *Jesus* for
" want of a Cordial Bottle, had created
" a chearing Dram or two, I could not
" have found fault with it; tho even
" here, if he had restored the *Patient*
" with a word of his Mouth, it had
" been a better Miracle, than making
" of Wine for him: But that he should
" make for a Company of Sots, a large
" quantity of Wine, of no less than
" twelve or eighteen Firkins of *English*
" Measure, enough to intoxicate the
" whole Town of *Cana* of *Galilee*, is
" what

" what can never be accounted for by
" a Chriſtian, who ſhould, one would
" think, wiſh this Story, for the Repu-
" tation of *Jeſus* expunged out of the
" New Teſtament.

" Beſides, if *Jeſus* had really and mi-
" raculouſly made Wine, which no Power
" or Art of Man could do, he ſhould,
" to prevent all ſuſpicion of deceit in
" the Miracle, have done it without
" the uſe of Water. You Chriſtians ſay,
" he is the original Cauſe of all Things
" out of nothing; why then did he
" not (37) create this Wine out of no-
" thing? why did he not order the
" Pots to be emptied of their Water,
" if there was any in them, and then
" with a word of his Mouth command
" the filling them with Wine inſtead of
" it? Here had been an unexceptiona-
" ble Miracle, which no *Infidels* could
" have cavil'd at, for any thing, but the
" *needleſsneſs* of it. But this ſubject
" Matter of Water ſpoils the Credit of
" the Miracle. The Water-Pots, it ſeems,
" are to be fill'd, before *Jeſus* could do

(37) Sed quanam gratia, antequam implerentur, non
fecit Miraculum, quod longe fuiſſet admirabilius? Siquidem aliud eſt ſubjectæ Materiæ qualitatem mutare, aliud ipſam ſubſtantiam ex nihilo facere. *Chryſoſ. in Loc.*

" the

" the notable Feat ; is not this enough
" to make us think, that Jefus was but
" an artificial *Punch-maker?* Could not
" he create Wine without Water for a
" Tranfmutation? Yes, you'll fay he
" could : what was the Reafon then, that
" he did not? This is a reafonable Quef-
" tion to a learned Priefthood : and a ra-
" tional Anfwer fhould be given to
" it. And a Queftion too it is that
" heretofore has been under debate.
" Some faid that the Water might be
" ufed to abate of the (38) immenfity
" of the Miracle, which otherwife for
" its greatnefs might have furpafs'd all
" Belief. But this Reafon will not do.
" A Miracle can't be too great in itfelf,
" if well attefted, to tranfcend Credit :
" but it may eafily be too little to con-
" ciliate the Faith of a Free-Thinker.
" The Fathers of your Church fetch'd a
" Reafon, for the ufe of Water here,
" from the Myftery ; but fince Myfterys
" on Miracles are fet afide by the Prieft-
" hood of this Age, they are to affign
" another and good Reafon of their own ;
" or this Miracle is to be rejected, as a
" Piece of Art and Craft in the Ope-

(38) Sæpe obeft Magnitudo, ne Miracula creditu fint
facilia. *Theophylact. in Loc.*

" rator, if for no other Reaſon than this,
" that *Jeſus* uſed Water to make Wine.

" All that I have to ſay more to this
" Miracle, is, that it is to be wiſh'd, if
" Jeſus could turn Water into Wine, that
" he had imparted the Secret and Power
" to his Diſciples of the *Prieſthood* of
" all Ages ſince, which would have been
" of greateſt Advantage to them in this
" World. He has empower'd them, they
" ſay, to remit Sins, which few old
" Sinners think themſelves the leſs in
" danger for : And he has enabled them,
" ſome ſay, to tranſubſtantiate Bread in-
" to Fleſh, and Wine into Blood,
" which none but fooliſh and ſuperſti-
" tious Folks believe they ever did :
" And he promiſed to inveſt them with
" a Power to do greater Miracles than
" himſelf, even to remove Mountains,
" and to curſe Trees ; but I thank God,
" they never were of ſo ſtrong a Faith,
" as to put it in Practice, or we might
" have heard of the *natural* ſtate, as well
" as we do now of the *civil* ſtate of ſome
" Countrys, ruin'd and overturn'd by
" them. But this Power to tranſmute
" *Water into Wine*, without Labour and
" Expence, would have been of better
" worth to them, than all their other
" Prieſtly Offices. Not, that our Con-
" duits

" duits would thereupon run with Wine,
" inftead of Water ; or that Wine would
" be cheaper and more plentiful than it
" is now, excepting among themfelves, if
" they could withal curfe Vineyards.
" They would make the beft Penny they
" could of their divine Power. And as
" furely as they can now fell the Water-
" drops of their Fingers at a Chriftening,
" at a good Rate, they would fet a better
" Price on their miraculoufly made Wine,
" and give a notable Reafon for its dear-
" nefs, *viz.* that Miracles fhould not be
" *cheap*, which would bring them into
" Contempt, and leffen the Wonder and
" Admiration of them."

So ends the Invective of a fuppos'd
Jewifh *Rabbi* againft this Miracle ; which
our *Divines*, as well as myfelf, are to
confider of an Anfwer to. Whether they
fhall think themfelves able to anfwer the
rational Parts of it, confiftently with the
Letter, I know not ; but I own myfelf
unable, and believe it impoffible for them,
to do it : And therefore they muft of neceffity go along with me to the myftical
Interpretation of the Fathers ; or this Miracle will turn to the difhonour of *Jefus*,
and difadvantage of his Religion.

Juftin

Juſtin Martyr (39) ſays, it is abſurd to take the Stories of the Marriages and Concubinages of the *Patriarchs* of the Old Teſtament in a literal Senſe. And indeed, literally conſider'd, they are ſome of them too luſcious Tales to be related by divine and inſpired Penmen: whereupon he, as well as St. *Paul* and *Philo-Judæus* (40), turn theſe Stories for the Honour of God and Edification of his Church, into an Allegory. Conſequently, if *Juſtin* had had an occaſion to ſpeak of this Marriage before us, there's no doubt on't, but he would have made Myſtery of all and every Part of it.

To the ſame purpoſe *Origen* (41) ſays, " That ſince the Law is a ſhadow of " good Things to come, and writes ſome- " times of Marriages and of Husbands " and Wives ; we are not to underſtand " it of Marriages according to the Fleſh, " but of the ſpiritual Marriage between " Chriſt and his Church. As for Inſtance, " *Abraham* had two Sons, *&c.* here we " ought not to confine our Thoughts to " carnal Marriages, and their Offsprings ; " but to extend them to the Myſteries

(39) In Dialog. cum Tryphone, *p.* 364.
(40) In Lib. de Abrahamo.
(41) *In Matt. Tract.* xxii.

" here

" here fignified. And there are almoft a
" thoufand other places in Scripture a-
" about Marriages; but in every place
" (*unufquifque Locus caftum & divinum*
" *de Nuptiis continet Intellectum fecun-*
" *dum Expofitionem moralem*) is to have
" a divine, moral, and myftical Con-
" ftruction put on't. Whoever therefore
" reads the Scriptures about Marriages,
" and underftands no more by them, than
" carnal Marriages; he errs, not knowing
" the Scriptures, nor the Power of God."
From hence may be eafily concluded,
what was *Origen*'s opinion about this Marriage in *Cana* of *Galilee*, if there were
no other Paffages in him for a Confirmation of it. But to come clofer to the Purpofe.

St. *Auguftin* (42) fays, there is Myftery fignified in the Story of this Marriage,
as in all *Jefus*'s Miracles, which it becomes us to open and fearch for; till, if
poffible, we are *inebriated* with the fpiritual and invifible Wine, that *Jefus* made

(42) Aliquid enim & in ipfis factis innuit nobis, puto,
quia non fine caufa venit ad Nuptias. Excepto Miraculo, aliquid in ipfo facto Myfterii & Sacramenti latet.
Pulfemus ut aperiet & de Vino invifibili inebriet nos.
In Loc. Johan.

at

at this Feaft. And again (43) fays, Let us then confider the feveral Particulars of the Story, and what is meant by the fix Waterpots; and the Water that is turn'd into Wine ; and the Governor of the Feaft ; and who are the Bridegroom and the Bride; and who is the Mother of *Jefus* in a Myftery ; and what is to be underftood by the Marriage.

And again, fays St. *Auguftin* (44), there is Myftery in this Marriage, or *Jefus* upon no invitation had gone to it. The Bridegroom is our Lord himfelf, to whom it is faid thou haft referv'd the good Wine of the Gofpel *until now*, that is, until the typified Time of the Celebration of this myftical Marriage, which according to St. *Auguftin* (45) is to be on the fixth Age of the World, fignified by the fix Water-Pots, holding two or three Firkins apiece,

(43) Nihil dicemus, quid fibi velint Hydriæ, quid Aqua in Vinum converfa, quid Architriclinius, quid Sponfus, quid' Mater Jefu in Myfterio, quid ipfæ Nuptiæ? *Ibid.*

(44) Per hoc invitatus Dominus venit ad Nuptias, ut oftenderetur Sacramentam Nuptiarum, ——Illarum Nuptiarum Sponfus Perfonam Domini figurabat, cui dictum eft, fervafti bonum Vinum ufque adhuc, Bonum Vinum id eft Evangelium fervafti ufque adhuc. *Ibid.*

(45) Sex Hydriæ fûnt fex Ætates Temporum capientes Prophetiam pertinentem ad omnes gentes five in duobus generibus hominum, id eft, Judæis & Græcis, five in tribus propter Noe tres Filios. *Ibid.*

that

that is, all Mankind, as they are divided into the *two* forts of *Jews* and *Gentiles;* or into *three*, as they are defcended of the *three* Sons of *Noah*.

And in another Place, the fame St. *Auguftin* interpreting this Story, fays (46) thus; " Our Saviour is invited to a Mar-
" riage ; what can that mean but that the
" Holy Spirit is courted and invocated by
" the Church, wifhing to be efpoufed to
" him ? *Jefus* comes with his Difciples,
" that is, into a holy Place of a Company
" of Saints. *Mary* the Mother of our Lord
" fignifies to him, *that they have no Wine* ;
" fo the Church makes known to him,
" the Deficiency of the Spirit, which fhe
" waits for the Power of. And if *Jefus*
" calls *Mary*, a Woman ; he means the
" Church, who by Transfiguration may
" be a Virgin, the Mother, the Spoufe of
" Chrift, and a Whore too."

(46) Vocatur Salvator ad Nuptias, hoc eft, Ecclefiæ voto fpiritus fanctus invocatur ——Venit cum Difcipulis fuis, id eft, in Loco fancto, Turba fanctorum. Mirabi-lia Dei Maria Mater expectat, hoc eft, Virtutem Chrifti expectat Ecclefia. —— Maria ait, ecce Vina deficiant, hoc eft, Vinum Spiritus Ecclefia optat excipere.—— Numquid Mulierem dicit Jefu Mariam, quæ Virgo poft Pactum inventa eft? Sed Ecclefiam alloquitur, quæ non folum Mulier, fed meretrix nuncupatur. *In Sermon* xcii. *Append.*

And

And again St. *Auguſtin* explaining (47)
what is meant by the Water, and the
Wine that it wou'd be turn'd into, at
the Time of the ſpiritual Celebration of
this Marriage of Chriſt with his Spouſe of
the Church, ſays plainly enough; that by
Water is meant the Letter of the Scriptures ; and by the beſt *Wine* is to be underſtood ſpiritual Interpretations, which
would tranſport the underſtandings of Men
with divine knowledge ; and warm their
Hearts and Affections into a ſpiritual *Inebriation*; after the ſimilitude of Wine
natural.

St. *Theophilus* of *Antioch*, a moſt antient
Greek Commentator (who according to
Biſhop Smalbroke ſhould ſtrictly adhere to
the Letter) ſays (48), that by this Mar-

(47) Vinum multis Locis accipimus Scripturas Sanctas
meraciſſimum Vigorem cœleſtis ſapientiæ continentes;
quibus incaleſcant ſenſus & inebrientur Affectus. Ope-
rante Chriſto in Cana Galileæ Vinum defecit & Vinum fit, id eſt, Umbra removetur & Veritas præſenta-
tur. Recedit Lex, Gratia ſuccedit. Carnalia ſpiritua-
libus commutantur. Bonum quidem Vinum eſt vetus
Teſtamentum, ſed ſine ſpirituali Intellectu vaneſcit in
Litera. *In Sermon* xc. *Append.* Sed illud quod in Litera Legis aquam ſapiebat, dum ſpiritualiter intelligi fecit, aquam in Vinum convertit. *In Sermon* xci. *Append.*

(48) Per Nuptias, Conjunctionem Chriſti Eccleſiæ,
hoc eſt Veteris & Novi Teſtamenti Traditionem debemus accipere. Sponſus eſt Chriſtus. Architriclinius eſt
Moſes. *In Loc. Johan.*

riage,

riage is meant the Conjunction of Christ and his Church, as it is the Tradition of the Old and New Testament. And that *Jesus* himself is the Bridegroom; and *Moses* the Governor of the Feast.

Other Fathers, such as St. *Cyril*, St. *Theophylact* and St. *Jerome* are of the same mind about the mystical Interpretation of this Marriage, as might be prov'd by Passages out of them, if I had room here to cite them. But I must observe here, that according to the Fathers, the Story of this Marriage is but another Emblem of the Marriage of the Lamb with the Bride of the *New Jerusalem*, spoken of in the *Revelations*, to which all the Fowls of the Air will be invited, that is, spiritual and heavenly minded Christians, who (49) soar and fly aloft in their divine and sublime Contemplations on the anagogical Sense of the Scriptures, which will exhibit those intellectual Dainties, they are there to be entertain'd with.

What I have here said out of the Fathers to the Story of this Marriage, is enough to quicken our *Divines* to search for the like mystical Interpretation of the whole. The Part of it that's most

(49) Voluores Cœli funt verè puri & ad cælestis sapientiæ Cognitionem evolare parati. *Clem. Alex. Strom L. iv.*

difficult

difficult to be fpiritually expounded, is that faying of *Jefus* to his Mother, *Woman, what have I to do with thee? mine Hour is not yet come.* For the clear interpretation of which, I own, I meet with little in the Fathers. But St *Auguftin* (50) affures us, there's latent Myftery in the words. How then fhall we come at it? Why, if we caft away the *Interrogation,* and look upon the Sentence, as ellyptical, like an infinite number of prophetical ones, the Senfe paraphraftically, and agreeably to the reft of the Myftery, arifes thus: In anfwer to the Woman of the Church's Expectation of the Wine of the Spirit; *Jefus* will tell her or make her to underftand of what importance it is to her (and himfelf) to be fupply'd with that myftical Wine to her Edification, which it was not his time to pour forth upon the Church, till the Celebration of his Nuptials with her.

And thus have I done with the Miracle of *Jefus*'s turning Water into Wine at a Marriage of *Cana* of *Galilee.* Whether it be not an abfurd and offenfive Story acording to the Letter, let any

(50) Quid mihi & tibi eft, Mulier? Procul dubio, Fratres, latet ibi aliquid Myfterii. *In Loc. Jehan.*

one judge. If the fuppofed Jewifh *Rabbi* has forced a worfe Senfe upon it, than it will naturally bear, our *Clergy* may expoftulate with him for it, which they hardly will any otherwife than by Exclamations againft him, without Reafon and Authority. But in the myftical Operation of this Miracle at the Marriage of Chrift with his Church, there will be the Wifdom and Power and Goodnefs of God vifible. And it will be a demonftration of *Jefus*'s *Meffiahfhip*, in as much as the Water of the Letter of the Law and the Prophets can't be turn'd into the Wine of fpiritual Interpretations, but we muft difcern how he is the Accomplifher and Fulfiller of them. And fo I pafs to an

11. *Eleventh* Miracle of Jefus, *viz.* (51) That of his healing a Paralytick, for whom the Roof of the Houfe was broken up to let him down into the Room where *Jefus* was.

And this Story (without excepting that of the Pool of *Bethefda*) is the moft monftroufly abfurd, improbable and incredible of any according to the Letter. There is not one Miracle of *Jefus* fpecifically related, that does not labour un-

der

der more or lefs Abfurdities, either in
Subftance or Circumftance : But this, for
number and greatnefs of Abfurdities, I
think furpaffes them all : And the Abfurdities of it too are fo obvious and ftare
a Man in the Face, that I wonder they
are hitherto overlook'd; and that confiderate and intelligent Perfons have not
before now hefitated and boggled at them.
If Intereft had not blinded the Eyes of
our learned *Clergy*, they would eafily
have defcry'd the Incredibilities and Abfurdities of this Story ; and in another
Impoftor's Cafe prefently have pointed
them out to the ridicule of his Admirers
and Adorers.

If a Man was to torture his Brains for
the Invention of a romantick Tale of improbable and furprizing Circumftances,
that he might, withal, hope to palm for
a Truth, if it was but for a Week or a
Day, upon the Faith and Underftanding
of the Credulous; he could never have
prefumed, I think, fo far upon the weaknefs of their Intellects, as to imagine any
thing fo grofly and notoriously contradic-
tory to Senfe and Reafon, would have
gone down with them, as is *this* before
us, which has pafs'd currently thro' many Ages of the Church, has been read
with attention by the Learned, and re-
vered

vered by the reſt of Chriſtians, without any exception, heſitation, or doubt of the Truth of it. In ſhort, ſo palpable is the falſity of the Story of this Miracle, that it requires no Sagacity to detect it; and was it not for the ſake of the Myſtery more than to expoſe the Folly of the *Clergy* in believing of it, I had never beſtow'd the following Pains on it.

The People, it ſeems, ſo preſs'd and throng'd about the Door of the Houſe, where *Jeſus* was, that the Paralytick and his Bearers could not get near it. What did they ſo throng and preſs for? Was it to ſee *Jeſus*, who was *without Form and Comelineſs*, according to the Prophet *Iſaiah*; or, who was one of the moſt graceful of the Sons of Men, as *Painters* and *Publius Lentulus* do deſcribe him? This could not be the Reaſon of the Croud. Tho a Perſon extraordinary, either for Beauty or Deformity may attract the Eyes of the People, and occaſion too a Throng about him; yet this could be no Reaſon for a *Preſs* about *Jeſus*, at *Capernaum*, where he dwelt, and was commonly ſeen and well known.

Was it then to hear him preach? Nor this neither. Tho an excellent Preacher does ſometimes, and a very indifferent one does oftener draw multitudes

tudes after him; yet *Jesus*, as a Prophet, was without Honour at *Capernaum*, his own Country; consequently, it is not to be supposed that, for his Doctrine, he was so much follow'd here, tho we read, that he *preach'd the Word unto them.*

Was it then to behold him working of Miracles and curing of the diseased? This is the likeliest Reason of the Crouds and Throng about him. And perhaps it was a Day appointed beforehand for his healing of the diseased, which might occasion a more than ordinary Concourse of the People. But then this Reason would have induced the People to make way for the *Lame, Blind,* and *Paralyticks* to come to *Jesus*; or they frustrated their own Hopes and Expectations of seeing Miracles wrought; and acted more unreasonably than ever Mob did, or can be supposed to do.

But whatever was the Reason of this tumultuous Crouding, which is hard to be accounted for; it's said, the poor *Paralytick* with his Bearers could not get to the Door of the House for the *Press,* and therefore in all haste is he haul'd to the Top of the House, and let down, thro' a breach of the Roof, into the Room where *Jesus* was. What need

was

was there of such Haste and Pains to get to *Jesus* for a Cure? It was but waiting a while, not many Hours, and in all probability the Tumult would be appeas'd, and accefs easily had to him. But that the Bearers of the poor Man should enterprise a trouble and difficulty, that could not require lefs Time, than the Tumult could be supposed to last, is a little strange and somewhat incredible.

St. *Chrysostom* says (52), that the *Paralytick* saw that the Market-place or Street was throng'd with People, who had obstructed all Passage to the House, where *Jesus* was; and yet he did not so much as say to his Friends and Bearers, " What's the Reason of this Tu-
" mult? Let's stay till it is appeas'd,
" and the House clear'd of the People,
" who ere long will depart; and then
" we shall privately and quietly get ad-
" mittance to Jesus," But why did he not say so? Any one beside himself and his Bearers, if they had any Reason and

---

(52) **Paralyticus reppletum videret Theatrum, Aditus Interclufos, Portum obfeptum, ——Non tamen dixit Propinquis fuis, quid hoc Rei eft? Expectemus quoufque Domus evacuetur, Theatrum dimittatur, recedent, qui congregati funt, poterimus privatim ad illum accedere.** *In Homil. de hoc Paralyt.*

Senfes about them, would have fo argued. St. *Chryfoftom* fays, it was their *Faith* that made them in fuch hafte to get to *Jefus*: But I fhould have thought their *Faith* might have work'd *Patience*, and difpofed them to ftay till Jefus could come out to them, or they get in to him: And it is an Addition to the ftrangenefs and incredibility of this Story, that it did not.

But fuppofing this *Paralytick* in fuch hafte and danger of Life, that he could not wait the difperfion of the Tumult, but, for want of a free entrance at the Door, is, coft what it will, to be rais'd to the top of the Houfe, and a breach muft be there made for him. The Queftion is, whether fuch an Enterprize was or could be feifable and practicable? I have no Conception of the poffibility of it. If they could not get to the Door of the Houfe for the Prefs; of confequence they could not come at the Sides of it. How fhould they? over the Heads of the People? That's not to be imagined; confequently here's another difficulty in the Story, that renders it yet more ftrange and incredible.

But, without queftioning the poffibility and eafinefs of getting the *Paralytick* and his Couch over the Heads of

the

the Mob, to the sides of the House; thi-
ther he is brought, where we now behold
him and his Bearers with their Pullies,
Ropes, and Ladders (that were not at
hand, nor could suddenly be procured)
hauling and heaving him to the top of
the House. Of what height the House
was, is not of much Consequence. Some
for the Credit of the Story may say
(53), it was a *very low one*; tho antient
and modern *Commentators* are pretty well
agreed, that it was an *upper-Room*, where
Jesus was; consequently the House was
at least two Stories high: But if it was
much higher, I'll allow that Art and
Pullies (which they wanted for the present) would raise the Man and his Bed
to the top of it: So we will not dispute nor differ upon that matter. On
the top of the House then, we are now
to behold the *Paralytick* and his Bearers
with their Hatchets and Hammers, *&c.*
(which they forgot to bring with them,
for they could not think of any use
they should have of them) uncovering
the Roof of the House; breaking up
Tiles, Spars, and *Rafters*, and making a
Hole, capacious enough for the Man and

(53) Dicet aliquis valde dimissum fuisse Locum, à quo
per Tegulas deposuerunt Paralytici Lectum. *Johan. Nepot. Hierof. in Loc. Luc.*

his

his Bed to be let thro'. An odd, ftrange, and unaccountable Work *this*, which, if they had not been cunning Fellows, would hardly have enter'd into their Heads to project. But at work they are, when it was well, if Jefus and his Difciples e-fcaped with only a broken Pate, by the fal-ling of Tiles, &c, and if the reft were not almoft fmother'd with the Duft ; for it was over their Heads that the breach was made. Where was the good Man of the Houfe all this while ? Would he fuffer his Houfe to be thus broken up, and not command them to defift from their foolifh and needlefs Attempt, till the Mob was quell'd, and there was a free entrance at the Door of his Houfe, which could not be long firft ? Is there nothing in all this, of difficulty and obftruction in the way of the belief of this Story ?

Some modern *Commentators*, being a-ware of thefe difficulties in this Story, and willing to reconcile Men to the ea-fier belief of it, fay, as *Drufius* (54) did, that the Houfes of *Judæa* were *flat-roof'd, and not ridg'd :* And Doctors, *Lightfoot* and *Whitby* (55) fay, there was

(54) Judæorum Tecta plana erant, & non in Coni-formam faftigiata. *In Loc. Luc.*

(55) *In Loc. March.*

a

a Door on their flat Roofs, by which the
Jews ufed to afcend to the top of their
Houfes, where they difcours'd on the
Law and religious Matters ; and that it
was thro' fuch a Door, by a little wide-
ning of the fides of it, that the *Paralytick* was let down in the prefence of
Jefus. To which Opinion I would yield,
if it was not liable to thefe Objections,
viz. that it is not reconcilable to what
St. *Luke* fays, of *their letting the Paralytick down thro' the Tiling with his
Couch, in the midft, where Jefus was;*
nor hardly confiftent with what St. *Mark*
fays of their *uncovering* and *breaking
up the Roof of the Houfe :* which Expreffions the *Evangelifts* had never ufed,
if there had been a Door for him to defcend by. But to indulge *Lightfoot* and
Whitby in their Notion ; I may ask them,
what occafion was there then of wide-
ning the door-way, and breaking down
the fides of it ? They'll fay, becaufe the
Paffage otherwife was too narrow, for the
Man's Couch to get thro'. Why then
did not they take him out of his Couch,
and let him down in a Blanket, a Chair,
or a Basket ? Or rather, why did not
Jefus, to prevent this Trouble and Damage
to the Houfe, afcend thro' this Door, to
the Top of it, and their fpeak the healing

I 2   Word

Word to this poor Man? To fay, that *Jefus* could not or would not go up to the Paralytick, I would not, for Fear of an Imputation of Blafphemy againft me. Our *Divines* therefore are to look for, what they'll hardly find, an Anfwer to the faid Queftion, which will confift with the Wifdom, the Goodnefs and Honour of *Jefus*; or here will be another and infuperable Bar to the Credibility of this Story.

In fhort, there are more and greater Difficultys affecting the Credit of this Miracle, on the fide of *Jefus*, than any before urg'd. Could not he, as it was antiently (56) objected, have made the Accefs to himfelf more eafy? Could not he, to prevent all this Trouble and Pains of getting to the Top of the Houfe, and of breaking up the Roof of it, have defired or even forc'd the People to make way for this poor Man and his Bearers? This was not impoffible for him to do. If it was hard for another; it was not for him, who was omnipotent. He that could drive his Thoufands before him out of the Temple; and draw as many after him into the wildernefs, might furely, by Force or Per-

(56) Numquid enim facilem illi potuit Acceffum red_ere ? *Apud Chryfoftom. de hoc Paralyt.*

suasion have made the People, how unreasonably mobbish soever, to retreat. And why did he not? Without a good and satisfactory Answer, which I can't conceive, to this Question, here is the most unaccountable and incredible part of the whole Story, that reflects on the Wisdom, the Power and Goodness of *Jesus*. If there had been no other absurd Circumstances of it, this is enough to spoil its Credit, so far as that I believe it impossible for *Ministers* of the *Letter*, with all their Wit, Penetration and Sagacity to get over it.

Believe then the Story of this Miracle, thus taken to Pieces, who can? It is such an Accumulation of Absurdities, Improbabilities, and Incredibilities, that a Man of the most easy Faith, if he at all think, can't digest. It's not credible, I said, to suppose, the People of *Capernaum*, where *Jesus* dwelt, and was well known and little admired, would at all *press* to see or hear him: And if the occasion of their Concourse was to behold his Miracles; it is less reasonable to think they would tumultuate to their own disappointment; but rather make way for the diseased, for the satisfaction of their own Curiosity, to come to him: And if they did mob it to their own disappointment, about the

Door

Door of the House; it was next to impossible for the poor Man and his Couch to be heav'd over their Heads, and rais'd to the top of it : More unreasonable yet to think, the master of the House would suffer the Roof of it to be so broken up: But most of all against Reason to suppose, *Jesus* would not give forth the healing word, and prevent all this Labour, or by his divine Power disperse the People, that the *Paralytick* might have present and easy access to him.

Whether all this be not absolutely shocking of the Credit of this Story, let my Readers judge. In my Opinion, no Tale more monstrously romantick can be told. I don't here question *Jesus*'s Power to heal this Paralytick, nor the miraculousness of the Cure of him : The trouble of that Question is saved me, by the many other incredible Circumstances of the Story, which are such a Contradiction to Sense and Reason, as is not to be equall'd, in any thing, that's commonly receiv'd and believ'd by Mankind. *Cicero* says, that there is nothing so absurd, which some of the Philosophers have not held. And they might and did, some of them, hold gross Absurdities. But the Letter of the Story of this Miracle before us, which is the Object of the Faith

of

of our learned Priesthood at this Day is a Match for the worst of them.

But as absurd, as this Story is, I expect that our *Clergy* will be disgusted at my ludicrous display of it; and that Arch Deacon *Stubbs* in particular will again be ready to exclaim against me, and say, that this is turning a *miraculous Fact* and a *divine Testimony* of our Religion into Ridicule. Whereupon it is to be wish'd, *that Arch-Deacon* would write, what would be a Pleasure to see, a Vindication of this Story. If he can account for the possibility and credibility of the Letter of it, he shall have my leave to make another dull Speech in *Convocation* against me. And it is not unlikely, but he may say as much for it, as another Man : For as the Story is senseless, so it is the better suited to his Head and Brains. But if he don't, I much question, whether any other Clergyman of more Wit will, appear in Defence of it.

So absurd is the Letter of this Story, that for the Honour of *Jesus*, and Credibility of his Gospel, it is absolutely necessary to turn it into Allegory. To the Fathers then, let us go for their help in this Case. If they did not read me a better Lecture upon this Miracle, than do our

modern

modern *Commentators*, I fhould be almoft tempted to renounce my Religion upon it : But as they have rationally and rightly inftructed me in its true meaning, fo I retain my Chriftian Faith, and admire the Sublimity of the Myftery, which I am now to give an account of.

By this *Paralitick*, St. *Hilary* (57) fays, is to be underftood *Mankind* of all Nations, which opinion too the Fathers held of the *Paralitick*, who was heal'd at the Pool of *Bethefda*. And by his Palfy is not meant any bodily Diftemper, but the fpiritual Palfy of the Soul, that is, as St. *Auguftin* (58) and St. *Jerome* (69) interpret, a diffolutenefs of Morals, and an unfteadinefs of Faith and Principles, which is the Condition of Mankind at prefent, who want *Jefus*'s help for the Cure of it. *Eufebius Gallicanus* (60) fays, our Saviour's words fignify,

(57) In Paralytico Gentium univerfitas offertur me denda. *In Loc. Matt.*

(58) Paralyticus poteft intelligi Anima diffoluta Membris, id eft, bonis operibus. *Inter. Quæft. Evang.*

(59) Paralyfis Typus eft Torporis, quo piger jacet in Malitia Carnis, habens defiderium Salutis, & Torporis Ignavia & duplis Cogitationibus, ac fi enervatus Membris oftendit. *In Loc. Marci.*

(60) In hoc enim quod ait, remittuntur tibi Peccata, interiorem hominem, id eft, fpiritum paryliticum effe demonftrat. Hoc enim non dixiffet, fi ad Corporis Infirmitatem refpexiffet. Non ideo Corpus fanatur, quia Anima à peccatis liberatur. *In Homil. in Dominic. xix. poft Pentecoft.*

that

that it is not a bodily but a spiritual Disease here meant; or he had never said to the Paralytick, *Son, thy Sins are forgiven thee,* which words respect the inward Man, and demonstrate the Palsy here to be a disease of the Soul.

The Man sick of the Palsy had *four Bearers.* And who are they mystically in this Case? Why, the Fathers (61) understand by them the *four Evangelists,* on whose Faith and Doctrine Mankind is to be carry'd unto Christ; for no Soul can be brought unto him, for the Sanation of his Sins and Errors, but by these *four.*

But to the top of the House is Mankind, thus paralytically diseased, to be carry'd by the four Evangelists, his Bearers. And what then is this House and its Top? The House of *Jesus* is the intellectual Edifice of the World, otherwise call'd Wisdom's House; of the beautiful Buildings of which the Scriptures prophetically

(61) Sed qui sunt isti quatuor, qui hunc Paralyticum portant & Domino offerunt. Per hos enim nescio, qui melius quam quatuor Evangelistæ intelligi possunt. Nulla enim Anima nisi per istos Domino offertur, nulla Anima nisi per istorum fidem sanatur. *Euseb. Gallican. ibid.* Sum Paraliticus, quia non operantur & immobiles sunt Vires Animæ meæ ad bonum, sed si a quatuor Evangelistis gestatus & adductus fuero ad Dominum, tunc audiam, remittuntur Peccata. *Theophylact. in Loc. Marci.*

treat:

treat : therefore to the *fublime Senfe* of
the Scriptures, call'd the Top (62) of the
Houfe, is Man to be taken : He is not
to abide in the *low and literal Senfe*
(63) of them, where People *prefs* and
ftrive in vain to come to *Jefus :* But if
he is taken to the Sublimity of the Scriptures and there *open* (64) *the Houfe* of
Wifdom, he will prefently be admitted to
the Prefence and Knowledge of *Jefus.*

Venerable *Bede*, who is altogether a
Tranfcriber of the Fathers, for which
Reafon I cite him among the Fathers,
fays (65), that by the *Tiles* of the Houfe

(62) Tectum Domus qua Chriftus docet, afcendendum,
id eft, Sacræ Scripturæ Sublimitas eft appetenda. *Bedæ
in Loc. Lucæ.*

(63) Non utique in Infimis exterius, qua turbæ tumul-
tuantur remanendum, fed Tectum Domus, &c. *Ibid.*

(64) Patefacto Tecto ægerad Jefum fummittitur, quia
referatis Scripturarum Myfteriis, ad Notitiam Chrifti
pervenitur. *Bedæ in Loc. Marci.* Eft Paralyfis interior,
ut pervenias ad Chriftum (forte enim latet Medicus &
intus eft, hoc eft, ifte verus Iutellectus in Scripturis occul-
tus eft) exponendo quod occultum eft aperi Tectum, &
depone Paraliticum. *Auguftin. In Serm.* XLVI. *Sect.*
13. Impediri turbis nifi Tecta id eft operta Scripturarum
aperiat, ut per hæc ad Notitiam Chrifti perveniat.
Ejufdam in Quæft. 4ta *in Evangel. Lucæ.*

(65) Et bene Domus Jefu juxta alterius Evangeliftæ
Narrationem tegulis effe contecta reperitur, quia fub con-
temptibili Literarum Velamine, fi adfit, qui referet, divina fpiritualis Gratiæ Virtus invenietur. Denudatio
etenim Tegularum in Domo Jefu, Apertio eft, in utili-
tate Literæ, fenfus fpiritualis & arcanorum cœleftium.
In Loc. Marci.

spoken of in St. *Luke*, is meant the *Letter* of the Scriptures, which is to be laid open for the manifestation of Christ and of divine Mysteries to the healing of Man's spiritual Palsy, the unsteadiness and dissoluteness of his Morals and Principles.

So much, in short, then to the mystical Interpretation of the Story of this Miracle. The literal Sense of it is so encumber'd with romantick Circumstances, as are enough to turn a Man's Heart against Christianity it self: But in the Mystery there will be a most stupendous Miracle, which will be not only an Argument of *Jesus*'s divine Power, but of his *Messiahship*, as certainly as his House of Wisdom, of which the Scriptures write, is open'd to the Manifestation of his Presence, and to the Cure of Mankind of his paralytical Disease, call'd an instability of Faith and Principles.

And thus have I, in this *Discourse*, taken into Examination three more of *Jesus*'s Miracles; which I submit to the Judgment of my Readers, whether the literal Story of them does not consist of Absurdities, Improbabilities and Incredibilities according to the Proposition before us; and whether there is not a necessity, for the Honour of *Jesus*, to

turn

turn them into prophetical and parabolical Narratives of what will be myfterioufly and more wonderfully done by
him.

My next *Difcourfe*, if my mind hold,
fhall treat on the three Stories of *Jefus's*
raifing of the dead, *viz.* of the Widow
of *Naim*'s Son, of *Jairus*'s Daughter, and
of *Lazarus*; after which I will give the
literal Hiftory of Chrift's Refurrection,
that fandy Foundation of the Church, a
Review; and fo conclude my Difcourfes
on the Miracles of our Saviour.

To run thro' all the Miracles of *Jefus*,
and handle them in the manner I have
done the foregoing, would be a long and
tedious Work. But if our *Divines* fhall
think, I have felected only thofe Miracles, which are obnoxious to Cavil and
Ridicule ; and have omitted others, that
literally are a more unexceptionable
Teftimony of *Jefus*'s divine Power, and
Authority ; I will, for their Satisfaction
take more of them to Task, and give
the Letter of their Stories, the like ludicrous treatment. If I miftake not, the
Miracles already fpoken to, together with
thofe of *Jefus*'s raifing of the dead, and
of his own Refurrection, are the moft
famous and remarkable of any others :
And according to the Obfervation I have
made

made on the reft, they are no lefs but rather more liable to Ridicule and Exception. But if any are of a contrary Opinion, and will let me know, which in
their Judgment are more unexceptionable Miracles, I will vouchfafe them
an Examination. I am fure there is not
one Miracle, which the Fathers of the
Church did not turn into Allegory; and
if we don't at this Day make myftical
Operations of them, they will none of
them according to the Letter, ftand their
Ground, nor abide the Teft of a critical
Inquiry into them.

I don't expect, that this *Difcourfe* will
be any more pleafing and acceptable to
the *Clergy*, who are *Minifters* of the *Let-*
ter of *Jefus*'s Miracles, as well as of the
Prophecies of him, than any of my former : But their Difpleafure in the Cafe
will give me no Difturbance, nor am I
concern'd about any Refentment, they
can make of it. If they are offended at
thefe *Difcourfes*, they fhould as they came
forth, have written folid Confutations
of them, and fo have prevented my Publication of any more of this kind : But
inftead of ferious and potent Reafonings
againft me, I have met with little elfe
but oral Railings, Exclamations, Defamations, and attempts for Profecution ;
which

which have been fo far from terrifying
me, that they give me a fecret Pleafure, and animate me to proceed in the
Undertaking in hand.

I did not much queftion but the *Bifhop* of St. *Davids,* whom I look'd upon as a Perfon of Ingenuity and Learning,
would, before this Time, have publifh'd
fomewhat in Confutation of one or other
of my former *Difcourfes.* Whether he
was not obliged to it, or to make me
fome publick Reparation of the Injury
done to my Reputation, by his flande-
rous Sermon, I appeal now to the wor-
fhipful *Societys* for Reformation of Manners ; to whom, and to other Civil Magiftrates, I hope his Sermon, without
Reafon, will be a Caution, that no Pulpit-
Invective move them to profecute or
think the worfe of any Author.

Liberty of thinking, writing aud judging for our felves in Religion is a natural,
a Chriftian, and a proteftant *Right :* It is
a *Right* that the Magiftrates as well as the
Subjects are interefted in, and are to fee
to the Confervation of, or their Underftandings as well as their Purfes will be
ridden and opprefs'd by an ignorant and
tyrannical Priefthood. I urge not this
for my own fecurity againft Profecution
for Infidelity and Blafphemy, declaring
that

that if the *Bishops* of *London,* St. *Davids,* or *Arch-Deacon Stubbs,* who are zealous for Persecution, will but engage me on the Stage of Controversy, and make good their Accusations against me, I will submit to the worst Punishment, that can be inflicted on the worst Offender.

In the mean time I will go on with my Undertaking, to the advancement of Truth, and demonstration of the *Messiahship* of the Holy *Jesus,* to whom be Glory for ever, *Amen.*

F I N I S.

BOOKS written by Mr. WOOLSTON *and Sold by him next Door below the,* Star *in* Aldermanbury, *and by the Book-sellers of* London *and* Weſtminſter.

I. THE old Apology reviv'd, &c.

II. Diſſertatio de Pontii Pilati Epiſtola ad Tiberium circa Res Jeſu Chriſti geſtas.

III. Origenis Adamantii Epiſtolæ duæ circa Fidem vere orthodoxam & ſcripturarum Interpretationem.

IV. The exact Fitneſs of the Time of Chriſt's Advent. demonſtrated by Reaſon, againſt the Objections of the old Gentiles, and modern Unbelievers.

V. Four Free-Gifts to the Clergy, or Challenges to a Diſputation on this Queſtion, Whether the Hireling Prieſts of this Age, who are all Miniſter of the Letter, be not Worſhippers of the Apolalyptical Beaſt, and Miniſters of Anti-Chriſt.

VI. An Anſwer to the ſaid four Free-Gifts.

VII. Two Letters to Dr. *Bennet*, on this queſtion, Whether the People call'd *Quakers*, do not the neareſt of any other Sect in Religion, reſemble the Primitive Chriſtians in Principle and Practice.

VIII. An Anſwer to the ſaid two Letters.

IX. The Moderator between an Infidel and an Apoſtate : or the Controverſy between the *Grounds* and his eccleſiaſtical Opponents, ſet in a clear Light, &c.

X. Two Supplements to the Moderator, &c.

XI. A Defence of the Miracle of the *Thundering Legion*, againſt a Diſſertation of *Walter Moyle* Eſq;

XII. Five Diſcourſes on the Miracles of our Saviour.

A FIFTH
DISCOURSE
ON THE
MIRACLES
OF OUR
SAVIOUR,

In Vɪᴇᴡ of the Preſent
Controverſy between Iɴғɪᴅᴇʟs
and Aᴘᴏsᴛᴀᴛᴇs.

——— ——— *Ridiculum acri*
Fortius & melius magnas plerumq; ſecat Res.

The Second Edition.

By Tʜᴏ. Wᴏᴏʟsᴛᴏɴ, B. D. ſometime
Fellow of *Sidney-College* in *Cambridge.*

LONDON:
Printed for the Author, and Sold by him
next door to the *Star*, in *Aldermanbury*,
and by the Bookſellers of *London*, and
Weſtminſter, 1728.
[Price One Shilling.]

TO THE

Right Reverend Father in God

THOMAS,

Lord Bishop of *Bangor.*

My Lord,

Hatever we poor *Authors* may sometimes pretend to, by the Dedication of our Works to *Great* Men ; it's certain we aim at nothing less than Rewards and Preferments, whether we deserve them or not : That this is my Design in *Dedications,* is so apparent, that it's to no Purpose to deny or dissemble it.

Wherefore else have I made Choice of some of our Learned and Wealthy *Bishops* for the Patrons of

A 2   these

these *Discourses*, which I foresaw would be grateful to their nice and critical Palates ? Wherefore else have I been so profuse of such Compliments on their *Lordships*, as I was sure, they would take great Pleasure in ? Wherefore else, *My Lord*, do I inscribe *this* to your *Right Reverend* Name, but that I expect your Approbation of it, and hope for a Recompence, equal to the Honour, that is here done you.

Some, who are envious, *My Lord*, of my good Fortune in *Episcopal* Patrons, will not believe that I have receiv'd so much as one *Purse* of *Gold* for any of my *Dedications* ; but I would have such Malignants to know, that the less I have receiv'd, the more there is behind : And I can moreover assure them, that their *Lordships* have it in their Heads and their Hearts too, highly to advance me in the World ; and if their Endeavours for my Promotion fail not, I shall be a very *Great* Man.

Such

Such primitive Doctrine, *My Lord*, as I have reviv'd, must, in the Judgment of our *Bishops*, be deserving of their distinguish'd Favours : And if they should Design for me such a *mystical* Crown of Glory, as the *Gentile Priests* help'd some of the Fathers of the Church to ; I profess without Dissimulation, that, for all my Love to *Mysteries*, it will be more than I am ambitious of : But if the Honour is forc'd on me, it will be my Duty to their *Lordships*, to found an *allegorical* Trumpet of their Fame, that their Names, which might otherwise be soon forgotten, may be everlastingly remember'd for their Love and Good-will towards me.

But the chief Foundation, *My Lord*, of my Merits lies, they say, in my Treatment of the Miracles of our Saviour, after the Manner you handled a Scripture-Prophecy, of a *Man's kicking a Serpent on the Pate, for biting him by the Heels :*

And

And if your *Lordſhip* got a *Welſh-Biſhoprick* upon it, what may not I expect for my more meritorious Works of the ſame kind? The Great *Mr. Scheme* has celebrated your Praiſe for that Effort of your Wit: And I muſt needs ſay, to your *Lordſhip*'s Applauſe, that were not your Thoughts unhappily ſhackled with Intereſt and Subſcriptions, (an Unhappineſs you ſadly lament!) you would endeavour to make as pleaſant Work with the *Letter* of the *Old*, as I can do with that of the *New* Teſtament.

I have not here Room, *My Lord,* for a ſufficient and deſerv'd *Encomium* on your *Uſe and Intent of Prophecy*; therefore muſt be content to ſay of it, in ſhort, that it is a moſt curious Piece of, what the Fathers call, *Engaſtromuthiſm*; or ſuch a ſingular Specimen of a Webb, ſpun out of a Man's own Bowels, as one of fewer Brains in his Head can hardly equal.

It

It was wisely done of your *Lord-ship* to caution your Readers against taking your *Book* for an Answer to Mr. *Grounds* ; otherwise it had not been impossible, but some others as well as the *Worshipful Benchers* of the *Temple* might have mistaken the *Use* and *Intent* of it.

After I had gone thro' your *beautifully-printed* Work, I wish d, *My Lord*, for another *Decoration* of it, that some Annotations out of the Fathers had been subjoin'd to it. How would your Notions then and Theirs about Prophecy have stood as a *Foil* to each other ! How should I then have admired the Difference between a *Rich* Bishop and a *Poor* Father as to Wit and Sense *!* How should I then have contemplated the Usefulness of Ecclesiastical Wealth in our *Clergy* for the Understanding of the Inspirations of the poor old Prophets!

When your *Lordship* is call'd upon for another Edition of your *Book*, vouch-

vouchſafe me the Favour of making ſome marginal Remarks on it, which ſhall not be without their good Uſe. As you know, ſavoury Sawce makes ſome ſort of Food go down the better ; ſo a little more of that Salt, which Mr. *Scheme* has too ſparingly ſprinkled on your *Work*, will give your *Readers*, a right Reliſh of it : But whether I am indulg'd this Favour or not ; I ſhall take another opportunity, according to Promiſe elſewhere made, of teſtifying to the World, how much I am,

My LORD,

The Admirer of

October 25.
1728.

Your Uſe *and*

Intent *of Prophecy,*

Thomas Woolſton.

A FIFTH

DISCOURSE

ON THE

MIRACLES

OF OUR

SAVIOUR, &c.

Ccording to Promiſe in my laſt *Diſcourſe*, I am in *this* to take into Examination the three Miracles of *Jeſus*'s raiſing the dead, *viz.* Of *Iairus*'s Daughter (1); of the Widow of *Naim*'s Son (2) ; and of *Lazarus* (3): The literal Stories of which

(1) Mat. ix. Mark v. Luke viii.
(2) Luke vii.
(3) John xi.

B

I shall show to consist of Absurdities, Improbabilities and Incredibilities, in Order to the mystical Interpretation of them : And because some of our *Bishops* and *Clergy* were a little disgusted at the ludicrous Treatment of the *Letter* of some foregoing Miracles, I will handle these with the more Caution ; being as unwilling, as any Man of my primitive Faith can be, to offend weak Brethren.

Whether *Jesus* rais'd any more from the dead, besides the foresaid three Persons is uncertain from the Evangelical History. St. *Augustin* (4) thinks, he rais'd many others ; and he founds his Opinion on the modest *Hyperbole* of St. *John*, who supposes (5) *the World it self could not contain the Books that might be Written of Jesus.* And *Eusebius Gallicanus*, of whose Mind entirely I am, says (6) the Reason lies in the Mystery, why these *three*, and no more than these *three* Miracles of this

(4) Quot autem mortuos visibiliter suscitaverat quis novit ? non enim omnia quæ fecit scripta sunt. *Johannes* hoc dicit, multa alia fecit Jesus, quæ si scripta essent, arbitror totum Mundum non posse Libros capere. Multi ergo sunt alii sino dubio suscitati, sed non frustra tres commemorati. *In Serm.* xcviii.

(5) John xxi. 25.

(6) Non autem vacat a Mysterio, quod, cum plures Dominus suscitaverat, tres tantum Evangelistæ eum suscitasse scripserunt, *In Homil. Feria quinta post Dominic. 4tam.*

Kind

Kind are recorded by the *Evangelists*. But since our *Divines* are averse to Mysteries on Miracles, I would gladly know their Opinion, whether *Jesus* rais'd any others from the dead, or not: I have made some search into modern Writers for their Opinion in this Case, but can't find it: And unless I knew their Opinion, it would be lost Labour to argue against either Side of the Question, and much more against both Sides of it: But I can assure our *Divines*, that, which Side of the Question soever they should hold, the Consequence upon the Argument would be neither better nor worse, than that they must of necessity espouse the mystical and allegorical Interpretation of these Miracles, or grant that *Jesus* literally rais'd none from the dead at all.

But waving that sort of Argument for the present against the *Letter*; these three Miracles are reputed the greatest that *Jesus* wrought: And I believe, it will be granted on all hands, that the restoring a Person, indisputably dead, to Life again, is a stupendous Miracle; and that two or three such Miracles well circumstanced, and credibly reported, are enough to conciliate the Belief of Mankind, that the Author of them was a divine Agent, and invested with the Power of God, or he

could

could not do them. But God knows, (and for the fake of the Myftery, I am not forry to fay it) this is far from being the Cafe of thefe three Miracles before us, or of any one them.

That thefe three Miracles are not equally great, but differ in Degree, is vifible enough to any one, that but curforily reads, and compares theirs Stories one with another. The Fathers of the Church (7) have taken Notice of fuch a Difference amongft them. The greateft of the three, and indeed, the (8) greateft Miracle, that *Jefus* is fuppos'd to have wrought, is that of *Lazarus*'s Refurrection; which, in Truth, was a moft prodigious Miracle, if his Corps was putrified and ftank; or if there were no juft Exceptions to be made to the Credibility of the Story. Next to that, in magnitude, is *Jefus*'s raifing of

(7) Sufcitaverat Dominus filiam Jairi Principis Synagogæ, fed adhuc mediante morte, adhuc viante Spiritu, adhuc Anima Clauftra Tartari nefciente. Sufcitavit & unicum Matris filium, fed fic ut retineret Pheretrum, ut anticiparet Sepulchrum, ut Corruptionem fufpenderet, & præveniret fætorem ; ut ante mortuo Vitam redderet, quam tota mortuus jura Mortis intraret. Circa Lazarum vero quod geritur totum fingulare eft, quem circa Vis tota Mortis impleta eft. *In Pet. Chryfol. Serm.* lxiii.

(8) Inter omnia Miracula quæ fecit Dominus nofter Jefu Chriftus, Lazari Refurrectio præcipue prædicatur. *St. Auguft. in Loc. Johan.*

the

the Widow's Son, as they were carrying him to his Burial : And a great Miracle it was to bring him to Life again; if none before or since had been miftaken for dead, and carried to their Graves alive ; or if no Impoftor and his Confederates could frame fuch a feemingly miraculous Scene, as is that whole Story, to his own Glory. The leaft of the three is that of his raifing *Jairus*'s Daughter, which in Appearance is fo far from a Miracle, that according to the Story itfelf, fhe was but afleep, or by the Shrieks of By-ftanders frighted out of her Senfes for the prefent.

But however it really might be with thefe three fuppofed dead and revived Perfons ; the Cafe of none of them was well enough circumftanced to ferve the Purpofe of our D*ivines.* I am apt to believe with the Fathers, that *Jefus* actually did raife the dead ; but then, as thefe Miracles are only recorded for the fake of the *Myftery*, I affirm that none of them, as to the *Letter*, will abide the Teft of a critcal Examination, nor ftand its Ground againft fuch Exceptions as may be made to them. If *Jefus* was to raife any dead Bodies to Life, for a Teftimony of his divine Power and Authority, he would and fhould have made Choice of other dead Perfons, under other Circumftances of Death ; and
the

the History of their Refurrection fhould have been more credibly and carefully tranfmitted to Pofterity, fo as there fhould have been no Room left to make a reafonable Doubt of the Truth of it. But this, I fay, is not the Cafe in the Refufcitation of any of thefe Perfons, as will appear from the following Remarks and Obfervations upon them. And

1. Obferve, that the unnatural and prepofterous Order of Time, in which thefe Miracles are related, juftly brings them all under fufpicion of Fable and Forgery. The greateft of the three is indifputably that of *Lazarus*'s Refurrection; but fince this is only mention'd by St. *John*, who wrote his Gofpel after the other *Evangelifts*, and above fixty Years, according to the beft Computation, after our Lord's Afcenfion; here is too much Room for Cavil and Queftion, whether this Story be not entirely his Invention. What could be the Reafon that *Matthew*, *Mark*, and *Luke*, who all wrote their Gofpels before *John*, and many Years nearer to the Death of our Saviour, fhould omit to record this remarkable and moft illuftrious Miracle of *Lazarus?* They could not forget it, nor be ignorant of it, if the Story had been really true; and to affign any
other

other Reason than Ignorance or Forgetfulness, is hard and impossible. To aggrandize the Fame of their Master, for a Worker
of Miracles, was the Design of all the *Evangelists*, especially of the three first, who
may be presumed to make a Report of
the greatest, if not of all, that *Jesus*
wrought : But that there should come
after them an *Evangelist* with an huge and
superlatively great Miracle, and meet with
Credit for it, is against all Sense and Reason ; neither is there any Story, so disor-
derly told, in all History, that *Critics* will
admit of the Belief of. The first Writer
of the Life of an *Hero*, to be sure makes
mention of all the grand Occurrences of
it, and leaves no Room for *Biographers* afterwards, but to enlarge and paraphrase
upon what he has written, with some
other Circumstances and Additions of less
Moment. If a third or a fourth *Biogra-
pher* after him shall presume to add a more
illustrious Transaction of the *Hero*'s Life,
it will be rejected as Fable and Romance,
tho' for no other Reason than this, that the
first Writer must have been appris'd of it,
and would have inserted its Story, if there
had been any Truth in it. And whether
St. *John*'s Story of *Lazarus*'s Resurrection,
that Miracle of Miracles, ought not to be
subjected to the like Criticism upon it,

Christians

Chriſtians may conſider, and *Infidels* will judge.

What then was the Reaſon, I ask again, that the three firſt *Evangeliſts* neglected to record this renown'd Miracle of *Lazarus?* And why too (may I enquire here) did not *Matthew* and *Mark* mention the Story of the Widow of *Naim*'s Son, as they could not but know of it, if true, more certainly than *Luke*, the Companion of *Paul*, who alone has made a Report of it ? *Grotius* ſays, (9) *it may ſeem ſtrange that this illuſtrious Miracle of the Widow's Son* was omitted by *Matthew* and *Mark :* And what is the Reaſon that *Grotius* gives for this ſtrange Omiſſion ? Why, he tells us (10) *that theſe two Evangeliſts were content with one miraculous Inſtance of this Kind, by which Chriſtians might judge of* Jeſus's *Power in others alſo.* And is this Reaſon ſufficient ? True it is, they were content with one Inſtance ; but if they had made a Report of two or three more of the ſame ſort, no body would have thought their Hiſtory of *Chriſt* overcharg'd with impertinent and tautological Repeti-

---

(9) Mirum videri poteſt Hiſtoriam hanc tam illuſtrem a Matthæo & Marco omiſſam. *In Loc. Luc.*

(10) Sed videtur mihi horum uterq; contentus fuiſſe uno Exemplo redditæ Vitæ in Jairi filia ex quo ſimilia alia poſſunt intelligi. *In Loc. Luc.*

tions.

tions. But one Inftance of a Pérfon rais'd from the dead, they were, fays *Grotius*, content with : And I'll grant one to be fufficient : But which then fhould they, as wife and confiderate *Hiftorians* have made Choice of, the greateft or the leaft Miracle? The greateft, to be fure, and that was of *Lazarus*, or of the Widow's Son, if they knew of either. But inftead of either of thefe, they tell us the Story of *Jairus*'s Daughter, that is (11) an imperfect and difputable Miracle, in Comparifon of the other two, which confequently they knew nothing at all of, or they would have preferr'd the Report of them.

If *Matthew*, the firft Writer, had recorded only the Story of *Lazarus*, whofe Refurrection was the greateft Miracle ; and if *Luke* had added *that* of the Widow of *Naim*'s Son ; and *John* laftly had remember'd us of *Jairus*'s Daughter, which the other *Evangelifts*, not through Ignorance or Forgetfulnefs, but ftudying Brevity, had omitted, then all had been well ; and no Objection had hence lain againft the Credit of any of thefe Miracles, or againft the Authority of the *Evangelifts* : But this unnatural and pre-

(11) Nondum perfecta Mors eft in Puella. *St. Auguft.* in Serm. xcviii.

pofterous

pofterous Order of Time, in which thefe
Miracles are recorded (the greateft being
poftponed to the leaft) adminifters juft
Occafion of fufpicion of the Truth and
Credibility of all their Stories. And it is
lucky for Chriftianity, that *Jews* and *Infidels* have not hitherto hit upon the *Abfurdity* of this prepofterous Narration, or
they might have form'd a cogent Objection againft thefe Miracles thus, faying ;

" *Jefus*, it is manifeft, rais'd not the
" dead at all. The only Perfon, that
" Chriftians can reafonably pretend, he
" did raife, was *Jairus*'s Daughter, whom
" *Matthew* writes of ; and fhe, according
" to the Story was only in a Sleep, or an
" Extacy, when *Jefus* revived her. But
" the *Galileans*, who were after a Time
" call'd *Chriftians*, finding their Account
" in a Refurrection-Miracle ; *Luke*, for
" the former Advantage of the Caufe, de-
" vifed another Story of better Circum-
" ftances, in the Widow of *Naim*'s Son :
" But this not being fo great a Miracle, as
" the Church ftill wanted ; *John*, when
" no body was alive to contradict and ex-
" poftulate with him for it, trumps up a
" long Story of a thumping Miracle, in
" *Jefus*'s raifing of *Lazarus*, who had
" been not only dead, but buried fo long
" that

" that he ftank again. But to prove the
" Story of this Miracle to be falfe and fa-
" bulous, we need fay no more than that
" it was laft recorded. If there had been
" any Truth in it, the firft *Evangelift*
" would have remember'd us of it.

" We don't fuppofe, that you Chriftians,
" becaufe of your Prejudices, will fub-
" fcribe to this Account, that we thus
" give of the Rife of thefe Miracles : But
" this is certain, that if thefe three Mira-
" cles had not been reported of *Jefus*,
" but of *Mahomet*, in the fame diforder of
" Time, by three different Hiftorians,
" you would prefently have fcented the
" Forgery and Impofture : You would
" juftly have affirm'd that the three Stories
" were apparently three Fables and Falf-
" hoods ; and that the three Hiftorians
" vifibly ftrove to outftretch each other :
" That the *firft* was fparing and modeft in
" his Romance ; and the *fecond*, being fen-
" fible of the Infufficiency of the former's
" Tale, devifes a Miracle of a bigger
" Size ; which ftill not proving fufficient to
" the End propofed ; the *third* Writer,
" rather than his Prophet's Honour fhould
" fink for want of a Refurrection-Miracle,
" forges a Story of a monftroufly huge
" one ; againft which it is, and always will
" be Objection enough, that it was not

　　　" related

" related by the first Historian. So would
" you Christians argue against these three
" Miracles in another Impostor's Case;
" and there is not a judicious *Critic* in the
" Universe, that would not approve of
" the Argument, and applaud the Force
" of it, tho' you will not endure the
" Thoughts of it in the Case of your
" *Jesus.*

" But to come nearer home to you;
" supposing *John* (who was then above a
" Hundred, and in his Dotage) had not
" reported this Miracle of *Lazarus*; but
" that *Clement* (joining it with his (12) in-
" credible Story of the Refurrection of a
" *Phænix*) or *Ignatius*, or *Polycarp*, or the
" Author of the *Apostolical Constitutions*
" had related it; would not your Chrif-
" tian *Critics* have been at work to ex-
" plode it? There is not an antient extra-
" evangelical Tradition of any Note about
" *Jesus*, that some or other of your *Cri-*
" *tics* have not boggled at; but such a
" Story as this of *Lazarus* would have
" been received by none. I question,
" whether Mr. *Whiston* would not have
" rejected the *Constitutions* upon such a
" Story in them; or if his Fancy for some
" other Things in them had overcome his

(12) In Epist. prima ad Corinth. Cap. xxv.

" Reafon

" Reason against this ; yet *Bishop Small-*
" *broke*, who has written against the Ca-
" nonicalness of the *Constitutions*, with
" his judicious Animadversions upon this
" Story, would absolutely have over-
" thrown their Authority. And what
" would he have said here ? Not only
" that the Miracle smells rankly of Forge-
" ry and Fraud, or the *Evangelists*, especi-
" cially *Matthew*, had never forgotten to
" record it ; but he would have reminded
" us of intrinsic Notes (*hereafter to be men-*
" *tion'd*) of Absurdity, and Incredibility,
" that would for ever have cashier'd the
" Belief of it. And whether we *Infidels*
" ought not to take the same Liberty to
" criticize on *John's* Gospel, which you
" do on your Apostolical Fathers, who
" wrote before him, let the impartial and
" unprejudiced judge : If in justice we
" ought to take it ; we are sure we could
" give two or three notable Reasons (but
" that We will not now put Christians
" out of Temper with them) why *John*
" may be suspected of a Mistake or Fraud
" in this Miracle, rather than any other
" *Christian* Writer of the *first* or *second*
" Century.".

To such an unhappy Objection, arising
from the unnatural and preposterous Order
of Time, in which they are recorded,

are these three Miracles before us obnoxious. And I am thinking how Ministers of
the Letter will be able to get over it. As
for my self, who am for the mystical Interpretation of these Miracles, I have a solid
and substantial Answer at hand to the foresaid Objection, an Answer that curiously
accounts for the Order of Time in which
these Miracles are related; but my Answer
will not please our *Divines*, nor stand them
in any stead; therefore they must look up
another good one of their own, that will
comport with the *Letter*; or the said Objection, improved with another presently
against *Lazarus*'s Resurrection, will be too
hard, not for Christianity it self, but for
their Ministry.

Grotius, being aware of the foresaid
Objection, has given us such a (13) Solu-
tion of it as then occurr'd to his Thoughts.
Dr. *Whitby*, not being satisfied with *Gro-*

___

(13) Quæri folet, cur hanc tam nobilem Hiſtoriam
priores Evangelii ſcriptores non attigerint. Mihi hoc
ſuccurrit, cum illi ſcriberent, vixiſſe reſuſcitatum Lazarum, & periculum ei fuiſſe a judæis, ſi quod illi acciderat,
palam vulgaretur. Nam etiam mox narratur C. xii. 10,
ob hoc ipſum ſtructas ei inſidias. Quare viſum illis hoc
ad tempus ſubticeri poſſe, cum alia Exempla reſuſcitato-
rum ſuppeterent. At mortuo Lazaro, cum jam nemini
Periculum ex rei Narratione fieri poſſet, additum hoc a
Johanne in hac quaſi prætermiſſorum Collectione. *In Loc.*
Johan.

tius's Solution, has given us (14) another: But how weak and insufficient both their Solutions are, I will not spare Time to confider, till some *Writer* shall appear in Defence of the Sufficiency and Strength of one or other of them. And so I pass to a

2. Second Obfervation, by Way of Objection to the *Letter* of these Miracles, and that is, by enquiring, what became of these three Perfons after their Refurrection? How long did they live afterwards? And of what Ufe and Advantage were their reftored Lives to the Church or to Mankind? The Evangelical and Ecclefiaftical Hiftory is entirely filent as to these Queftions, which is enough to make us fufpect their Stories to be merely romantick or parabolical; and that there were no fuch Perfons rais'd from the dead; or we muft have heard fomewhat of their Station and

(14) The laft of the three *Euangelifts* writing but fifteen Years after our Lord's Afcenfion, might think it needlefs to mention a Miracle concerning a Perfon, living fo near *Jerufalem*, where there was fo great a Fame thereof, and fo many living Witneffes. St. *John*, writing his Gofpel, fay the Ancients, above fixty Years after our Lord's Afcenfion, when by the Deaths of the Perfon, and moft of the Witneffes that were prefent at his Refurrection, the Memory and Fame of it might be much impair'd, had great Reafon to perpetuate the Memory of it, by this large Rehearfal of it. *In Loc. Johan.*

Con-

Conversation in the World afterwards:
It's true, that *Ephiphanius* (15) says, what
he found among Traditions, that *Lazarus*
lived thirty Years after his Resurrection:
But how did he spend his Time all that
while? Was it to the Honour of *Jesus*,
to the Service of the Church, and Propagation of the Gospel? Of that we know
nothing; tho in Reason and Gratitude to
Jesus, his Benefactor, it ought to have
been so spent; and if it had been so employ'd, History surely would have inform'd
us of it. According to the Opinion of
Grotius, in a Citation above, *Lazarus* for
the rest of his restored Life abconded, and
skull'd about the Country for Fear of the
Jews, who lay in Wait for him ; which is
a Suggestion, not only dishonourable to
Jesus, as if the same Power, that rais'd
him from the dead, could not protect him
against his Enemies ; but reproachful to
Lazarus himself, who should have chosen
to suffer Death again, rather than not bear
an open Testimony to *Jesus*, the Author
of his Resurrection. However it was, we
hear no more of *Lazarus*, than that he
lived thirty Years afterwards, which Tra-

(15) Quin & illud inter traditiones reperimus triginta
tum Annos natum fuisse Lazarum, cum a mortuis excitatus
est; atq; idem ille postea triginta aliis annis vixit. *In
Haref.* lxvi. *Sect.* 34.

dition, without other Memorials of his Life, brings the Miracle more under fufpicion of Fable, than if he had dy'd foon after it. And of *Jairus*'s Daughter, and of the Widow of *Naim*'s Son, which is aſtoniſhing, we read nothing at all. Does not this Silence in Hiſtory about them, make their Miracles queſtionable, and but like *Gulliverian* Tales of Perſons and Things, that out of the Romance, never had any Being.

Jeſus did but (16) *call a little Child, and ſet him in the midſt* of his Diſciples; and that Act was remember'd in the Piety and Zeal (17) of *Ignatius*, who made a renown'd Biſhop. But the Favour and Bleſſing conferr'd on theſe three rais'd Perſons was exceedingly greater; and one might have expected, that *Lazarus* and the Widow's Son would have been eminent Miniſters of the Goſpel. But inſtead of that, their Lives afterwards were paſs'd in Obſcurity, or, what's as bad, Eccleſiaſtical Hiſtory has neglected a Report of them. What can any one hereupon think leſs, than that the Favour of the Miracles was loſt on undeſerving Perſons, which I abhor the Thoughts of; or that their Stories

(16) Matt. xviii. 2.
(17) In Nicephor. Calliſt. Eccl. Hiſt. L. ii. c. 35.

are but Parables, which I rather incline to.

Minifters of the *Letter* may here fay, " That the Ecclefiaftical Hiftory of the A- " poftolical Age is very fcanty ; and that " many Memorials of other Perfons and " Tranfactions are loft and buried in Ob- " livion : Which unhappy Fate has at- " tended the after-Lives and Actions of " thefe rais'd Perfons, or undoubtedly we " fhould have had a famous Record of " them." This is not impoffible ; tho' in the Wifdom of Providence it is hardly probable, but that fome more Remem- brance muft have been left of one or o- ther, if not of all the three Perfons ; in as much as fuch a Remembrance of them would now-a-days have no lefs gain'd a Belief of the Miracles, than this Hiftorical Silence tends to the Difcredit of them.

It's fomewhat ftrange, that we hear no more of the after-Fame and Life of any of the difeafed Perfons, whom *Jefus* mi- raculoufly cured ; excepting of the Wo- man, heal'd of an Iffue of Blood ; who, tho' fhe *fpent* A L L *fhe had, even* A L L *her Living* upon *Phyficians* ; yet out of the Remains of it erected, fays (18) *Eu- febius*, at *Cæfarea Philippi*, two moft coft- ly Statues of Brafs, to the Memory of

(18) In Eccl. Hift. L. vii. c. 18.

Jefus

Jesus and of herself, and of the Miracle wrought by him ; which Dr. *Whitby* (19) as if he was tainted with Infidelity, endeavours to make an idle Tale of. But excepting, I say this Story of this Woman, we hear nothing of any other heal'd Person ; which is Matter of some Speculation : But that the Persons rais'd from the dead should not at all be mention'd in History for their Labours and Lives afterwards to the Honour of *Jesus*, is absolutely unaccountable. Whether such a profound Silence in History about them be not shocking of the Credit of the Miracles, let our *Divines* consider. I am of Opinion that if *Jesus* really rais'd these Persons from the dead ; this and no other Reason, in the Providence of God, can be given for the Silence of Ecclesiastical History about them afterwards, than to make *dead-letter'd* Stories of their Miracles, in order to turn our Heads entirely to the Consideration of their mystical Signification, without which the *Letter*, for the Argument before us, is deserving of no Regard nor Credit. But

3. By way of Objection to the *Letter* of these three Miracles, let us consider the

(19) In Loc. Matthæi.

Con-

Condition of the Perfons rais'd from the dead ; and whether they were at all proper Perfons for *Jefus* to work fuch a Miracle upon, in Teftimony of his divine Power. If they were improper Perfons according to the *Letter*, it's not credible that He, who was the Wifdom of God, would raife them ; or if he did, it was becaufe they were the propereft to make myftical Emblems of their Stories.

That *Jefus* ought to have rais'd all that dy'd, where-ever he came, during the Time of his Miniftry, none, I prefume, can hold. Two or three Inftances of his almighty and miraculous Power of this Kind will be allow'd to be fufficient : But then they muft be wifely and judicioufly made Choice of, out of a vaft Number of Perfons, that muft needs die in that Time. Where then was his Wifdom and Prudence to chufe thefe three Perfons above others to that Honour ? Why were all of them, or indeed any one of them preferr'd to other Perfons of a different Age and Condition in the World ? Nay, if the *Letter* of their Stories is only to be regarded, were not all thefe three Perfons almoft the impropereft and moft unfit of any for *Jefus* to exercife that Power on ?

Jairus's

Jairus's Daughter was an infignificant
Girl of twelve Years old: And there
could be no Reafon for raifing her, but to
wipe Sorrow from the Hearts, and Tears
from the Eyes of her Parents, who ought
to have been better Philofophers, than im-
moderately to grieve for her. And was
here a good Reafon for *Jefus* to interpofe
with his Almighty Powe ? No certainly ;
a Lecture of Patience and Refignation in
this Cafe had been enough. And tho
Jefus could raife her from the dead ; yet
for as much as that Favour was to be conferr'd but on a few ; and his Miracles
ought to be ufeful as well as confpicuous,
fhe fhould have been pafs'd by, as an improper Object of his Power, in Comparifon of many others, prefently to be na-
med. If therefore a better Reafon, than
what's difcernible in the *Letter*, is not to
be fetch'd from the Myftery ; I can't fuppofe that *Jefus*, the Wifdom of God would
raife this *Girl*; but that the modern Be-
leif of her Refufcitation, exclufive of the
myftical Signification, is, as fhall be by and
by argued, altogether groundlefs.

The Widow of *Naim*'s Son too was
but a νεανισκος *Youth*, and whether any
thing older than the *Girl* above is doubt-
ful; but his Life certainly was of no
more Importance to the World after, than
be-

before his Refurrection. And why was he then one of the *three* to be rais'd from the dead? Why had he this Honour done him, before others of greater Age, Worth, and Ufe to Mankind? Some will fay, for the Comfort of his forrowful Mother. And is this Reafon fufficient? A Difcourfe on the Pleafures of *Abraham's* Bofom, where fhe would e'er long meet her Son, had been enough to chear her Heart. If therefore the Fathers don't help me to a folid myftical Reafon, why the Son and *only Son* of a Widow was to be rais'd by *Jefus*, as they were carrying him to his Burial, I'll not believe, He would raife this dead *Boy* rather than many others, for the Manifeftation of his Power; but that the Story of his Refurrection, as fhall foon be reafonably proved, was all Sham and Cheat.

Lazarus indeed was *Jefus's* Friend, whom he Loved; and as I will not queftion but *Jefus's* Affection was wifely and defervedly placed on him; fo here, to Appearance, was a better Reafon for the raifing of him, than of either of the other Two. But even this Reafon, fuppofing *Jefus* was to raife but three Perfons, is not fufficient againft the Cafes of many others, that may be put for the Manifeftation of his Power, for the Illuftration of his Wifdom and Goodnefs, and for the

Con-

Converſion of Unbelievers : Conſequently, if this Story of *Lazarus* be not parabolical, the litteral Fact is diſputable, and obnoxious to ſuch Exceptions preſently to be obſerved againſt it, as will not be eaſily got over.

Jeſus rais'd the dead, and wrought other Miracles, ſay our *Divines* often, not only to manifeſt his own Power and Glory, but his Love to Mankind, and his Inclination to do them good: For which Reaſon his Miracles are uſeful and beneficial as well as ſtupendous and ſupernatural Acts, on purpoſe to conciliate Men's Affections as well as their Faith to him. On this Topick our *Divines* are copious and rhetorical, when they write on *Jeſus's* Miracles, as if no more uſeful and wonderful Works could be done, than what he did. And I do agree with them, that (what Reaſon beſpeaks) the Miracles of a pretended Author of Religion ought to be both as uſeful and great as well as could be. But ſuch were not *Jeſus's* Miracles according to *Letter*, and leaſt of all his Acts of raiſing the dead. For if we conſider the Perſons rais'd by him, we ſhall find, he could hardly have exerted his Power on any of leſs Importance to the World, both before and after their Reſurrection. A young *Girl* indeed is fitter to be rais'd

than

than a decripid old Woman, who by the
Courfe of Nature was to return to Corruption again, as foon as reftored to Life :
And a *Boy* rather than an infirm old Man
for the fame Reafon : And *Lazarus* the
Friend of *Jefus*, perhaps, and but perhaps,
rather than his profefs'd Enemy. But
what are thefe three Perfons in Comparifon of many others of other Circumftances ? Inftead of a *Boy*, and a *Girl* and
even of *Lazarus*, who were all of no
Confequence to the Publick, either before
or fince; I fhould think, *Jefus* ought to
have rais'd an ufeful Magiftrate, whofe
Life had beed a common Bleffing; an in-
duftrious Merchant, whofe Death was a
publick Lofs; a Father of a numerous
Family, which for a comfortable Subfift-
ance depended on him. Such dead Objects of *Jefus*'s Power and Compaffion
could not but offer themfelves, during the
Time of his Miniftry, and if he meant to
be as ufeful as he could, in his Miracles,
he would have laid hold on them. If a
few Perfons only were to be rais'd from
the dead, the forefaid were the propereft,
whofe Refurrection and Return to Life
would have begotten the Applaufe as well
as the Wonder of the World; would
moft extenfively have fpread *Jefus*'s Fame;
and would have gain'd him the Love and
Dif-

Difciplefhip of all that heard of his being fo great a Benefactor to Mankind. Such Inftances of his Power would have demonftrated him to be a moft benign as well as a mighty Agent; and none in Intereft or Prejudice could have open'd their Mouths againft him, efpecially if the Perfons rais'd from the dead were felected upon the Recommendation of the People of this or that City. But that an infignificant *Boy* and a *Girl*, (forfooth!) and the obfcure *Lazarus*, are preferr'd by *Jefus*, to fuch publick and more deferving Perfons is unaccountable. Their Story therefore, upon this Argument, favours of Romance and Fraud; and unlefs the *Myftery* help us to, what the *Letter* can't, a good Reafon for *Jefus*'s Conduct here, the Miracles may be hence juftly queftion'd, and the Credibility of their Report difputed.

But now I am fpeaking of the Fitnefs and Unfitnefs of deceafed Perfons to have this grand Miracle wrought on them; it comes into my Head to ask, why *Jefus* rais'd not *John* the Baptift to Life again? A Perfon of greater Merits, and more worthy of the Favour of *Jefus* and of this Miracle, could not be. If *Jefus* could raife any from the dead he would furely have raifed him; and why did he not? This is a reafonable Queftion, and an

E   An-

Anfwer fhould be thought on for it. Was it a Thing out of *Jefus*'s Power? Not fo; He was Omnipotent, and could by Force or Perfuafion have refcued *John*'s Head out of the Hands of his Enemies; and the tacking it again to his Body, and the infufing new Life into him was no more difficult to *Jefus*, than the Refufcitation of a ftinking Carcafs. If *Jefus* had here exerted his Power, and rais'd his deareft Friend and choiceft Minifter for the Preparation, if not Propagation of the Gofpel, none could queftion his Ability to raife any others, tho he had rais'd no more. But in as much as *John* the *Baptift*, one of his fingular Merits and Services to *Chrift*, was overlook'd and neglected by him; and three ufelefs and infignificant Perfons had this Honour done them, the Facts may reafonably be called into queftion, and, if the Myfteries don't folve the Difficulty, their litteral Stories may hence be accounted foolifh, fictitious and fabulous; efpecially if we confider,

4. That none of thefe three rais'd Perfons had been long enough dead to amputate all Doubt of *Jefus*'s miraculous Power in their Refurrection. As to *Jairus*'s Daughter, fhe was but newly expired, if at all dead, when *Jefus* brought her to

Life

Life again. *Jesus* himself says, she was but asleep. And according to *Theophanes Cerameus* (20), and *Theophilact* (21) there is Room to suspect that this *Girl* was only καλοχ& *beside herself*. And it is not impossible, but the passionate Skreams of the Feminine By-standers might fright her into Fits, that bore the Appearance of Death ; otherwise why did *Jesus* turn these inordinate Weepers out of the House, before he could bring her to her Senses again ? And why did he tell her Parents, that she was only in asleep, but to Comfort them with the Possibility of his awakening her out of it ? Is not this destructive of the Miracle, and making no more of it, than what another Man might do ? And is there not some Probability, that here's all of this Story ? But supposing she was really dead, yet for the sake of an indisputable Miracle in her Resurrection, it must be granted, that she ought to have been much longer, some Days if not Weeks, dead and buried.

As to the Widow of *Naim*'s Son, there was somewhat more of the Appearance of Death in him, than in *Jairus*'s Daughter. He was carried forth to his Burial, and so may be presumed to be really a dead

(20) Puellam ex illo Tumultu plangentium stupore correptam esse, non vero defunctam. *In Homil. de Juri filia.*
(21) In Loc. Matthæ.

Corpse.

Corpfe. But might not here be Fraud or
Miftake in the Cafe? Hiftory and common Fame affords Inftances of the miftaken Deaths of Perfons, who fometimes
have been unfortunately buried alive, and
at other Times happily, by one Means or
other, reftored to Life: And who knows
but *Jefus*, upon fome Information or
other, might fufpect this Youth to be
in a lethargick State, and had a Mind to
try, if by chafeing, *&c.* he could not do,
what fuccefsfully he did, bring him to his
Senfes again: Or might not a Piece of
Fraud be here concerted between *Jefus*,
a fubtil Youth, and his Mother and others;
and all the Formalities of a Death and Burial contrived, that *Jefus*, whofe Fame for
a Worker of Miracles was to be rais'd,
might here have an Opportunity to make a
fhew of a grand one. The Mourning of
the Widow, who had her Tears at Command and *Jefus*'s cafual meeting of the
Corpfe upon the Road, looks like Contrivance to put the better Face upon the
Matter. God forbid, that I fhould fufpect, there was any Fraud of this Kind
here; but of the Poffibility of it, none
can doubt. And where there is a Poffibility of Fraud, it is Nonfenfe, and
mere Credulity to talk of a real, certain
and ftupendous Miracle, efpecially where
the

the Juggler and pretended Worker of Miracles has been detected in some of his other Tricks. All that I have to say here to this Matter, is, that if *Jesus* had a Mind to raise the Son of this Widow, in Testimony of his divine Power, he should have suffer'd him to have been buried two or three Weeks first ; otherwise, if the Mystery don't account for *Jesus*'s stopping the Bearers of the Corpse upon the Road, here is too much Room for suspicion of Cheat in the Letter of the Story,

Lazarus's Case seems to be the less exceptionable of the three. He had been buried *four Days*, and supposed to be putrified in the Opinion of his Sister *Mary*, and of modern Christians : And if so, his Resuscitation was a most grand and indisputable Miracle. And I could have wish'd, if I had not loved the *Mystery* rather than the *Letter*, that no Cavil and Exception could have been made to it. Whether *Lazarus*, who was *Jesus*'s Friend and beloved Disciple, would not come into Measures with his Lord, for the Defence of his Honour, and Propagation of his Fame, *Infidels*, who take Christianity for an Imposture, will not question : And whether he would not consent to be interr'd alive, in a hollow Cave, where there was only a Stone laid at the Mouth of it, as long as

a

a Man could faſt, none of them will doubt.
Four Days was almoſt too long for a Man
to faſt without danger of Health ; but if
thoſe *four Days* are number'd according to
the Arithmetick of Jeſus's *three Days* in his
Grave, they are reducible to two Days and
three Nights, which Time, if no Victuals
were ſecretly convey'd with him, a Man
might faſt in *Lazarus's* Cave. As to the
ſtinking of *Lazarus's* Carcaſs : that, *Infidels*
will ſay, was but the Aſſertion of his Siſter
beforehand, like a Prologue to a Farce.
None of the Spectators at his Reſurrection
ſay one Word of his ſtinking. And as to
the Weepings and Lamentations of *Jeſus*
and of *Lazarus's* Siſters, they will ſay
that was all Sham and Counterfeit, the
better to carry on the Juggle of a feign'd
Reſurrection. And what's worſt of all,
they will ſay, that tho *Jeſus* did call *Lazarus*
forth with a *loud Voice*, as if he had
been as deaf as a dead Man ; yet his *Face
was bound about with a Napkin*, ſo that
the Spectators could not diſcern what was
of the Eſſence of the Miracle, the Change
of his Countenance from a dead to a live
one, which is a plain Sign, that it was all
Fraud and Impoſture.

God forbid, that I ſhonld have the ſame
ſenſe with *Infidels*, of this Matter ; but to
be juſt to their Suggeſtions and Imaginations

tions here, I muſt needs ſay, there are ſome other unhappy Circumſtances, preſently to be conſider'd, in this Story, which, if they are not emblematical, make it the moſt notorious Cheat and Impoſture that ever was put upon Mankind. In the mean Time, from what is here argued, it is plain, that *Lazarus* was not ſo long dead and buried, as that there is no Room to doubt of the Miracle of his Reſurrection.

Now whether theſe Arguments againſt theſe three Miracles, drawn from the Shortneſs of the Time, in which theſe Perſons lay for dead, have any Force in them, let our *Divines* conſider. If nothing of all this is in their Opinion affecting of the Credit of the Miracles; yet they muſt allow, that *Jeſus*, if he could raiſe the dead, might have made Choice of other Inſtances of Perſons, more unqueſtionably dead, who had lain longer in their Graves, and were in a viſible State of Putrefaction. And if this grand Miracle of raiſing the dead was to be wrought by *Jeſus* for the Manifeſtation of his Glory, and in Teſtimony of his Authority; he ſhould have exerciſed his Power on ſome ſuch Perſons, nominated by the Magiſtrates of this or that City, who with the People ſhould be preſent at the miraculous Operation, beholding the putrified Bodies,

(with-

(without a Napkin before their Faces) and how they were suddenly enliven'd and invigorated with new Flesh, after the Similitude of their pristine Form, when in Health and full Strength. Because that *Jesus* rais'd not some such Persons to Life, I must take the Stories of the three Miracles before us to be but typical of more mysterious Works; or believe them for the Arguments above to be downright Cheats and Fables. And what is enough to induce a modern *Divine* to this Opinion. ᵀs

5. The Consideration, that none of these rais'd Persons did or could, after the Return of their Souls to their Bodies, tell any Tales of their separate Existence otherwise the Evangelists had not been silent in this main Point, which is of the Essence of Christianity. Are not our *Divines* here reduced to an unhappy *Dilemma*, either to deny the separate Existence of the Soul, or the precedent Deaths of these rais'd Persons? As Christians, we profess to believe both, which seemingly are incompatiable; or the Evangelists had made such a Relation, as their return'd Souls had given of the other World. Was any Person, in this Age, to be rais'd to Life, that had been any time dead; the first Thing that

that his Friends and Acquaintance would enquire of him, would be to know, where his Soul had been ; in what Company ; and how it had fared with him ; and Hiftorians would certainly record his Narrative. The fame Curiofity could not but poffefs People of old, when thefe Miracles were wrought ; and if the rais'd Perfons had told any Stories of their feparate Exiftance, the Evangelifts no lefs unqueftionally would have reported them, in as much as fuch a Report would have been, not only a Confirmation of that Doctrine, which is of the Effence of our Religion ; but an abfolute Confutation of the *Sadducees* and *Sceptifts* of that Age, and of the *Materialifts* of this. But this their Silence in this Cafe is of bad Confequence, either to the Doctrine of the Soul's Exiftence in Separation from the Body, or to thefe Miracles themfelves, fince we muft hereupon almoft neceffarily hold, that thefe rais'd Perfons were not at all dead, or that their Souls dy'd with them.

The Author of a Sermon, afcrib'd to St. *Auguftin* tells us (22) that *Lazarus* after

F

---

(22) Atque ut miraculum divinæ Virtutis accrefceret, dum Convivis interrogantibus triftia Loca pænarum, fedefq; alta nocte femper obfcuras, Lazarus indicat diligenti narratione per ordinem. Diu quæfiti longifq; tempo-

ter his Resurrection made a large Report of *Hell*, where he had been : But as this is a mere Fiction of that Author, without the least Authority from Scripture ; so I presume it will be accounted a *Blunder* in him, to suppose the Soul of *Lazarus*, the Friend and beloved of *Jesus*, was in Hell. The Soul of *Jesus* indeed, for Reasons best known to himself, upon his Death, descended into Hell, when some think he should rather have gone, with the penitent Thief, into Paradise. But the Thoughts, that any of *Jesus*'s Friends should go to Hell, I suppose will not be born with ; or what will become of the Preachers of this Age, who would be accounted Men of that Denomination. And if *Lazarus*'s Soul had been in Paradise, it was hardly a good Work in *Jesus* to recall it, for thirty Years afterwards, to the Miseries and Troubles of this wicked World. I wish therefore our *Divines* could determine, where *Lazarus*'s Soul was for the four Days of his Burial ; because I can't possibly conceive any thing else, than that he was not really dead, or that his Soul dy'd with him, or went to a bad place, otherwise after his Resurrection he had never

temporibus ignorati invenerunt tandem Inferi Proditorem. *In Serm.* cxvi. *Append. St. August.*

ab-

abſconded for fear of the *Jews*, as if he was unwilling to die agaîn, and return to the Place from whence he came.

But however it was with the Souls of theſe rais'd Perſons before their Re-union to their Bodies, here is another Difficulty and Objection againſt theſe Miracles ; and how will our *Divines* get over it ? Perhaps they may ſay, that tho' theſe rais'd Perſons were before really dead ; yet their Souls were not as yet gone to their Places prepared of God for them, but continued hovering about their Bodies, like the Flame about the Snuff of a Candle, with deſires

> ── *iterumq; reverti*
> *Corpora* ──

to be again rejoin'd to them. And withall my Heart let this Anſwer paſs, if our *Divines* and *Infidels* can ſo agree upon it. As for my own Opinion, it is this, that theſe Miracles of *Jeſus* are Parables, and that it was beſide the Purpoſe of the Parable, and of the *Evangeliſts* to ſay any thing of the Place and State of the Soul upon its Separation from the Body ; otherwiſe the Letter of their Stories is manifeſtly obnoxious to the Objection above, or the Deaths of theſe pretended rais'd Perſons, upon Chriſtian Principles, are queſtionable. But

6. And

6. And laftly, Let us confider the in-trinfick Abfurdities and Incredibilities of the feveral Stories of thefe three Miracles. And fuch Abfurdities fhall we find in them, that, if they had been intended as Tefti-monies of *Jefus*'s divine Power, had never been inferted in their Narratives,

As to *Jairus*'s Daughter, and her Refur-rection from the dead, St. *Hilary* (23) hints that there was no fuch Perfon as *Jairus* whofe Name was fictitious, and coin'd with a fpiritual Signification for the Ufe of the Parable ; and he gives this Reafon, and a good Reafon it is, why he thought fo, becaufe it is elfewhere (24) intimated in the Gofpel, that none of the Rulers of the Synagogues confeffedly be-lieved on *Jefus*. Is not here then a ftum-bling-Block at the Threfhold of the Let-ter of this Story? But why did *Jefus* fay, this Girl was but in a Sleep? If he was going to work a Miracle in her Refufcita-tion, he fhould not have call'd Death,

(23) Princeps hîc, Lex effe intelligitur, quæ Domi-num orat pro Plebe, quam ipfa Chrifto prædicata ejus Adventûs Expectatione nutriverat, ut Vitam mortuæ reddat. Nam nullum Principem credidiffe legimus, ex quo Perfona hujus principis orantis merito in Typum ap-tabitur. *In Loc. Math*.

(24) John vii. 48. and xii. 42.

Sleep ;

Sleep; but if others had been of a contra-ry Opinion, he fhould firft have convinced them of the Certainty of her Death, be-fore he did the great Work on her. And why did he charge the Parents of the Girl not to fpeak of the Miracle? If he meant it as a Teftimony of his divine Power, he fhould rather have exhorted them, in juftice to himfelf to publifh it, and make it well known. And why, as St. *Ambrofe* (25) puts the Queftion, did he turn the People out of the Houfe, before he would raife her? The more Witneffes are pre-fent at a Miracle, the better it is attefted, and the more readily believed by others; and who fhould be prefent at the Miracle rather than thofe who were incredulous of *Jefus's* divine Power? Are not all thefe Circumftances, fo many *Abfurdities*, which, if they are not to be accounted for in the *Myftery*, are fo far deftructive of the *Let-ter*, as that it is Nonfenfe and Folly in our *Divines* to talk of a Miracle here, againft *Jefus's* exprefs Word and Prohibition to the contrary.

As to the Story of the Widow of *Naim's* Son, excepting what is before obferved of

(25) Quæ tamen tantæ diverfitatis Caufa? Supra pub-lice Viduæ filius fufcitatur, hic removentur plures arbitri. *In Loc. Luc.*

the

the ſhortneſs of the Time, in which he lay dead, and of the Unfitneſs of his Perſon to be rais'd before an Husband and Father of a Family, to the Comfort of his Wife and Children, (which are enough to overthrow the Credility of the Miracle) I have here no more Fault to find in the Letter of it.

But the long Story of *Lazarus* is ſo brimful of Abſurdities, that, if the Letter alone is to be regarded; St. *John*, who was then above a hundred, when he wrote it, had lived beyond his Reaſon and Senſes, or he could not have committed them.

I have not Room here to make Remarks on all theſe Abſurdities, which would be the Work of a Volume ; but ſhall ſingle out three or four of them at preſent, reſerving the reſt for another Opportunity, when the whole Story of this Miracle will appear to be ſuch a Contexture of Folly and Fraud in its Contrivance, Execution, and Relation, as is not to be equall'd in all Romantick Hiſtory; and our *Divines* will find themſelves ſo diſtreſs'd upon the Diſſection and Diſplay of it, as that they muſt of Neceſſity allow this Story to be but a Parable; or, what's moſt grievous to think on, give up their Religion upon it.

First then, obferve that *Jefus* is faid to have *wept* and *groan'd* for the Death of *Lazarus*: But why fo, fays (26) St. *Bafil*? Was not this an *Abfurdity* to weep at all for the Death of him, whom he could, and was about to recover to Life again? Another Man may as reafonably grieve for the Abfence of his Friend, whofe Company and Prefence he can retrieve in an Inftant, as that *Jefus* fhould fhed Tears for *Lazarus* in this Cafe. If *Jefus* could not or would not raife him from the dead, he ought not, as a Philofopher, who knows Man is born to die, to betray fo much Weaknefs as to weep for him. Patience and Refignation unto God upon the Death of our deareft Friends and Relations is what all Philofophers have rightly taught; and *Jefus*, one would think, fhould have been the moft Heroical Example of thefe Graces; and how came he to fail of it here? A Stoical Apathy had better became him than fuch childifh and effeminate Grief, which not only makes him a mean and poor-fpirited Mortal; but is a grofs *Abfurdity* and *Incredibility* upon Confideration of his Will and Power to fetch

(26) Qua igitur Ratione, qui tanta hæc erat facturus, id quod evenit, judicaffet merito Lacrymis effe profequendum? *In Homil. de Gratiarum Actione.*

Lazarus to Life again. If there be not, according to the Fathers, Myſtery in theſe Tears of *Jeſus*, they are a fooliſh and unnatural Prelude to a Farce, he was acting in the pretended Reſuſcitation of *Lazarus*.

Some antient Catholicks, not being appriſed of the Myſtery, were ſo offended at theſe Words, *Jeſus wept*, that, as *Epiphanius* (27) ſays, they expung'd them out of their Bibles ; and I wonder, they have not, before now, diſturb'd the Faith of Miniſters of the Letter, to the utter Rejection of the Miracle.

Secondly, Obſerve that *John* ſays, it was with *a loud Voice*, that *Jeſus* call'd *Lazarus* forth out of his Cave. And why, I pray, a louder Voice than ordinary ? Was dead *Lazarus* deafer than *Jairus*'s Daughter, or the Widow's Son ? Or was his Soul at ſo great a Diſtance from his Body, as he could not hear a ſtill and low Voice ? Some ſuch ſilly Reaſon as *this* muſt be given for this *loud Voice* here ; but how abſurd it is according to the Letter, Infidels will judge, till Chriſtians can aſſign a better. The dead can hear the Whiſper of the Almighty, if Power go along with it,

---

(27) *Lacrymatus eſt Jeſus,* quod aliquando eraſum fuiſſe a Catholicis quibuſdam ſcribit Epiphanius. Vid. *Druſium in Loc. Johan.*

as foon as the Sound of a Trumpet. St.
John then fhould not have written of a
loud Voice, unlefs he meant to adapt his
Story to the Capacities and Conceptions of
the Vulgar, who have no Apprehenfions
of God's Power, out of fenfible and human Reprefentations of it.

Thirdly, Becaufe that a Miracle fhould
be well guarded againft all Sufpicion of
Fraud, I was thinking to make it an *Ab-*
furdity, that the Napkin, before *Jefus* rais'd
Lazarus, was not taken from his Face, that
the Spectators might behold his mortified
Looks, and the miraculous Change of his
Countenance from Death unto Life. What
Infidels think of this Circumftance I know
not: I hope it is not with them a Token
of Fraud and Impofture; tho I muft needs
fay, that if the Fathers did not let me into the Myftery of the Napkin about *Laza-*
rus's Face when *Jefus* call'd him forth, I
fhould not my felf like it.

Fourthly, and laftly, Obferve, St. *John*
fays, v. 45. that *many of the Jews, who*
had feen the Things that Jefus did here;
believed on him; and *fome of them*, v. 46.
who did not believe, *went their Ways to*
the Pharifees and told them what Things
Jefus had done in this pretended Miracle,
G   and

and how the Bufinefs was tranfacted : Whereupon the Chief Priefts and Phari-fees were fo far incens'd as v. 53. *from that Day forth they took Council together to put him to Death* ; and Ch. xii. 10. *confulted, that they might put* Lazarus *alfo to Death.* Jefus *therefore* (and his Difciples and *La-zarus* fled for it, for they) v. 54. *walk'd no more openly among the Jews*, but *went thence into a Country near to the Wildernefs* (a convenient hiding Place) *and there con-tinued with his Difciples* ; otherwife in all Probability they had been all facrificed.

I dare not argue upon thefe Circum-ftances, neither would I, for the Honour of *Jefus* have mention'd them ; but that my old Friend, the Jewifh *Rabbi*, who help'd me to the Satirical Invective againft *Jefus's* Miracle of *turning Water into Wine*, has hence form'd an Objection againft *La-zarus's* Refurrection, and fent me a *Letter* upon it, defiring me to publifh it, and ex-hort the *Clergy* to anfwer it ; otherwife he would clandeftinely hand it about to the Prejudice of our Religion : Whereupon I, rather than Chriftianity fhould fo fuffer, do here publifh it, and it is as follows.

" *Sr.* When we laft difcours'd on *Jefus's* " Miracles, I promifed to fend you my " Thoughts on *Lazarus's* Refurrection, " which I look upon as a notorious Im-
" pofture,

" posture, and for the Proof of it, need go no
" farther, than to the Circumstances of its
" Story, which your *Evangelist* has related.

" If there had been an indisputable Mi-
" racle wrought in *Lazarus*'s Resurrecti-
" on ; why were the *Chief-Priests* and *Pha-*
" *risees* so incens'd upon it, as *to take*
" *Council to put both Jesus* and *Lazarus* to
" *Death for it?* Where was the Provoca-
" tion? I can conceive none. Tho' the
" *Jews* were ever so canker'd with Ma-
" lice and Hatred to *Jesus* before ; yet
" such a most stupendous Miracle was e-
" nough to stop their Mouths, and turn
" their Hearts: Or if their Prejudices a-
" gainst *Jesus* were insuperable, and they
" hated him but the more for the Num-
" ber and Greatness of his Miracles ; yet
" why is poor *Lazarus*, inoffensive *Laza-*
" *rus*, upon whom this good and great
" Work was wrought, an Object of their
" Hatred too? Your *Divines* are to give a
" credible and probable Account of this
" Matter, such a one as will comport with
" Reason and Sense; or we shall conclude,
" that it was *Fraud*, detected in this pre-
" tended Miracle, which justly provok'd
" the Indignation of our Ancestors.

" To say, what is all you can say, that
" it was downright Inhumanity, Barbarity
" and Brutality in the *Jews* to hate *La-*

G 2
" *zarus*

" zarus as well as *Jesus*, will not do here.
" Tho' this may pass with many Christians,
" who are ready to swallow, without
" chewing, any evil Reports of our Na-
" tion ; yet it can't go down with rea-
" sonable and unprejudic'd Men, who
" must have other Conceptions of human
" Nature in all Ages and Nations, than
" to think it possible, that a Man, in *La-*
" *zarus*'s Case, can be hated and persecu-
" ted for having had such a good and won-
" derful Work done on him. And why
" then was he hated and persecuted ? I
" say, for this, and no other Reason, than
" because he was a Confederate with *Jesus*
" in the wicked Imposture, he was putting
" upon Mankind.

" But supposing, what is never to be
" granted, that the *Jews* of old were so
" inhuman, brutish, and barbarous as to
" hate and persecute *Lazarus* as well as
" *Jesus* for this Miracle ; yet why did
" *Jesus* and his Disciples, with *Lazarus*,
" run away and abscond upon it ? for they
" v. 54. *walk'd no more openly among the*
" Jews, *but went thence into a Country near*
" *to the Wilderness, and there* Jesus *continued*
" *with his Disciples.* Is not here a plain
" Sign of Guilt and of Fraud ? Men, that
" have God's Cause, Truth and Power on
" their Side, never want Courage and Re-
" solution

" folution to ftand to it. And however
" your Chriftian *Priefts* may palliate the
" cowardly and timerous Conduct of *Je-*
" *fus* and his Confederates in this Cafe ;
" yet with me, it's like Demonftration,
" that there was a difcover'd Cheat in the
" Miracle, or they would undauntedly
" have faced their Enemies, without Fears
" And Apprehenfions of Danger from them.

" Our Anceftors then, who unquef-
" tionably detected the Fraud, were in the
" right on't to profecute with Severity,
" the whole Party concern'd in it : And if
" they had aveng'd the Wickednefs of it
" upon *Lazarus* as well as they did upon
" *Jefus*, I fhould have commended them
" for it. Whether fuch a monftrous Im-
" pofture, as was this pretended Miracle,
" happily difcover'd does not call aloud for
" Vengeance and moft exemplary Punifh-
" ment ; and whether any Nation of the
" World would fuffer the like with Im-
" punity, let any Man judge.

" For all the Reports of your Gofpels,
" it is unnatural to hate a miraculous
" Healer of Difeafes ; and there muft be
" fomewhat fuppreft about the Inveteracy
" of the *Jews* to *Jefus*, or his healing
" Power, if it was fo great as is imagined,
" muft have reconciled them to him : But
" that they fhould hate not only *Jefus* for
                                    " raifing

" raifing the dead, but the Perfon rais'd
" by him, is improbable, incredible, and
" impoffible.

" If Hiftorians can parrallel this Story of
" the Malignity of the *Jews* towards
" *Jefus* and *Lazarus* upon fuch a real Mi-
" racle, with any Thing equally barbarous
" and inhuman, in any other Sect or Na-
" tion; we will acknowledge the Truth
" of it againft our ancient Nation : Or if
" fuch Inhumanity, abftractedly confider'd,
" be at all agreeable to the Conceptions any
" one can form of Human Nature in the
" moft uncivilis'd and brutifh People, we
" will allow our Anceftors, in this Cafe,
" to have been that People.

" Was fuch a real and indifputable Mi-
" racle, as this of *Lazarus* is fuppofed, to be
" wrought at this day in Confirmation of
" Chriftianity, I dare fay, it would bring
" all us *Jews*, to a Man, into the Belief
" of it : And I don't think it poffible, for
" any People to be fo begotten, byafs'd,
" and prejudiced, as not to be wrought
" on by it. Or if they would not part
" with their Interefts and Prejudices upon
" it, they would have more Wit and
" Temper, than to break forth into a
" Rage againft all or any of the Perfons
" concern'd in it. And, for my Life, I
" can entertain no worfe Thoughts of our
" old Nation.   " Sup-

" Suppofing God fhould fend an Am-
" baffador at this day, who, to convince
" Chriftians of the Mifchiefs and Incon-
" venience of an *Hireling Priefthood,*
" fhould work fuch a Miracle as was this
" of *Lazarus's* Refurrection, in the Pre-
" fence of a multitude of Spectators ; how
" would your *Bifhops* and *Clergy* behave
" themfelves upon it ? Why, they would
" be as mute as Fifhes ; or if they did
" fret and grieve inwardly for the Lofs
" of their Interefts ; yet they would have
" more Prudence (ask them elfe,) than to
" fhow their Anger openly, and perfecute
" both *Agent* and *Patient* for it. Where-
" fore then are they fo cenforious and un-
" charitable as to preach and believe ano-
" ther Notion and Doctrine of our An-
" ceftors ?

" But if a falfe Prophet, for the fubver-
" fion of an *Hireling Priefthood,* fhould,
" in fpite to the *Clergy,* counterfeit fuch a
" Miracle, and be detected in the Opera-
" tion ; how then would Priefts and Peo-
" ple, Magiftrates and Subjects behave up-
" on it ? Why, they would be full of In-
" dignation, and *from that day forth would
" take Council to put* the Impoftor and his
" Confederate to Death, of which they
" would be moft deferving ; and if they
" did not abfcond and fly for it, like *Jefu*
" and

" and his Difciples *to a Wildernefs in the* " *Country* to hide themfelves, the Rage of " the Populace would hardly wait the " Leifure of Juftice to difpatch and make " terrible Examples of them. Was not " this exactly the Cafe of *Jefus*'s Impo- " fture in the Refurrection of *Lazarus;* " and of the Punifhment he was threaten'd " with, and afterwards moft juftly under- " went for it ?

" Mankind may be in fome Cafes very " obdurate, and fo hard of Belief, as to ftand " it out againft Senfe, Reafon and De- " monftration : But I will not think worfe " of our Anceftors than of the reft of " Mankind ; or that they any more than " others would have withftood a clear and " indifputable Miracle in *Lazarus*'s Refu- " fcitation. Such a manifeft Miracle, let " it be wrought for what End and Pur- " pofe, we can poffibly imagine, would " ftrike Men with Awe and Reverence ; " and none could hate and perfecute the " Author of the Miracle ; leaft He who " could raife the dead, fhould exert his " Power againft themfelves, and either " wound or fmite them dead with it. " For which Reafon, the Refurrection of " *Lazarus*, on the certain Knowledge of " our Anceftors, was all Fraud, or they " would have reverenc'd and adored the " Power of him, that did it. " It

" It may be true, what *John* fays, that
" *many of the Jews, who had feen the*
" *Things that Jefus did, believed on him,*
" that is, believed that he had wrought
" here a great Miracle : But who were
" thefe ? the ignorant and credulous, whom
" a much lefs *juggler* than Mr. *Fawkes*
" could eafily impos'd on. But on the o-
" ther hand, it is certain, according to *Chrif-*
" *tian Commentators,* that *fome of them* did
" not believe the Miracle, but *went their*
" *ways to the Pharifees and told them what*
" *Things Jefus had done,* that is, told
" them, after what manner the Intrigue
" was managed ; and complain'd of the
" Fraud in it. How they came to fufpect
" and difcover the Fraud, was not *John's*
" Bufinefs to relate ; and for want of
" other ancient Memorials, we can only
" guefs at it. Perhaps they difcern'd fome
" motion in *Lazarus*'s Body, before the
" Word of Command, to *come forth,* was
" given ; perhaps they difcover'd fome
" Fragments of the Food, that for *four*
" *days* in the Cave, he had fubfifted on :
" But however this was, they could not
" but take Notice of the *Napkin about his*
" *Face* all the while ; which *Jefus,* to pre-
" vent all fufpicion of Cheat, fhould have
" firft order'd to be taken off, that his
" mortify'd Countenance might be view'd,

" be-

" before the miraculous Change of it to
" Life was wrought. This neglect in
" *Jesus* (which I wonder *John* had no
" more Wit than to hint at) will be a laft-
" ing Objection to the Miracle. *Jesus*
" was wifer, than not to be aware of the
" Objection, which he would have obvi-
" ated, if he durft, by a Removal of the
" Napkin, to the fatisfaction of all Spec-
" tators there prefent. Becaufe this was
" not done, we *Jews* now deny, there
" was any Miracle wrought; and, whe-
" ther our Unbelief upon this Circum-
" ftance be not well grounded, we appeal
" to Chriftian Priefts themfelves, who
" muft own, that if there was a Miracle
" here, the Matter was ill conducted by
" *Jesus*, or foolifhly related by his *Evan-*
" *gelift.*

" It is a fad Misfortune, that attends our
" modern enquiry after Truth, that there
" are no other Memorials extant of the
" Life and Miracles of *Jesus*, than what
" are written by his own Difciples. Not
" only old Time has devour'd, but Chri-
" ftians themfelves, (which in the Opini-
" on of the impartial makes for us) when
" they got Power into their Hands, wil-
" fully deftroy'd many Writings of our An-
" ceftors, as well as of *Celfus* and *Porphi-*
" *ry* and others, which they could not an-
" fwer ;

" fwer ; otherwife I doubt not but they
" would have given us clear Light into
" the Impofture of *Lazarus*'s Refurrecti-
" on : But if *Jefus*, according to his own
" *Evangelifts*, was arraign'd for a *Decei-*
" *ver* and *Blafphemer*, in pretending to the
" Sonfhip and Power of God by his Mi-
" racles ; in all Probability this Piece of
" Fraud in *Lazarus* was one Article of the
" Indictment againft him ; and what makes
" it very likely, is that the *Chief Priefts*
" and *Pharifees*, from the Date of this pre-
" tended Miracle, *took Council together to*
" *put him to Death*, not clandeftinely or
" tumultuoufly to murder him, but judici-
" ally to punifh him with Death, which,
" if they proved their Indictment by cre-
" dible and fufficient Witneffes, he was
" moft worthy of.

" As it is plain from the Story in *John*,
" that there was a Difpute among the By-
" ftanders at *Lazarus*'s Refurrection, whe-
" ther it was a real Miracle or not ; fo it
" is the Opinion of us *Jews*, which is of
" the Nature of a Tradition, that the
" *Chief-Priefts* and civil Magiftrates of *Be-*
" *thany*, for the better Determination of
" the Difpute and quieting of the Minds of
" the People, requir'd that *Jefus* fhould
" re-act the Miracle upon another Perfon,
" there lately dead and buried. But *Je-*

" *sus* declining this Test of his Power, the
" whole Multitude of Believers as well as
" of Unbelievers before, question'd the
" Resurrection of *Lazarus*; and were high-
" ly incens'd against both him and *Je-*
" *sus* for the Deceit in it. And this was
" *one* Reason among others of that vehe-
" ment and universal Outcry and Demand,
" at *Jesus*'s Tryal, for his Crucifixion. I'll
" not answer for the Certainty of this
" Tradition or Opinion, but as the Expe-
" dient was obvious, so it has the Face of
" Truth and Credibility ; and for the
" Proof of it, I need only appeal to Chris-
" tain *Priests* and *Magistrates* ; whether,
" under a Dispute of a Miracle of that
" Consequence, they would not require,
" for full Satisfaction, it should be acted
" over again ; and, if the *Juggler* refused,
" whether there would not be a general
" Clamour of People of all Ranks for his
" *Execution.*

" *Matthev, Mark* and *Luke,* who knew
" as much of this Sham-Miracle as *John,*
" had not the Confidence to report it ;
" because, when they wrote, many Eye-
" Witnesses of the Fraud were alive to
" disprove and contradict them; therefore
" they confined their Narratives to *Jesus*'s
" less juggling Tricks, that had pass'd more
' current : But after the *Jewish* State
" was

" was diſſolved, their judicial Records were
" deſtroy'd, and every Body dead that
" could confute him, *John* ventures a-
" broad the Story of this Miracle ; and if
" the good Providence of God had not
" infatuated him, in the Inſertion of the
" Circumſtances here obſerved, it might
" have paſs'd through all Generations to
" come, as well as it has done for many
" paſt, for a grand Miracle.

" Thus, *Sir*, have you a few of my
" Thoughts on the pretended Miracle of
" *Lazarus*'s Reſurrection. I have more to
" beſtow on it, but that I would not be
" tedious. There's no need to argue a-
" gainſt the other two Reſurrection-Stories.
" You know *omne majus includit minus*,
" and if the greateſt of the three Miracles
" be an Impoſture, the two leſs ones of
" Conſequence are Artifice and Fraud.
" And rather than the Miracle of *Lazarus*
" ſhall ſtand its Ground, I'll have t'other
" Bout at it from ſome other Circum-
" ſtances ; the Conſideration of which will
" make it as fooliſh and wicked an Impo-
" ſture, as ever was contrived and tran-
" ſacted in the World ; ſuch a *wicked Im-*
" *poſture* of moſt pernicious Conſequence to
" the Welfare of the Publick, that it is
" no Wonder, the People, by an unani-
" mous Voice, call'd for the Releaſement
" of

" of *Barabbas*, a Robber and Murderer,
" before *Jesus*. I don't suppose these Ar-
" guments against this Miracle will be con-
" vincing of your Christian *Clergy*, who are
" hired to the Belief of it. But howe-
" ver, a *Bishop* of many *thousands* a Year
" to believe, can't in Conscience deny,
" that the Arguments above are a sufficient
" Justification of our *Jewish* Disbelief of
" it.

" If you, Sir, should write a Discourse
" gainst the Letter of the Story of *Je-*
" *sus*'s Resurrection, I beg of you to ac-
" cept of a few of my Conceptions on that
" Head, which, I promise you, shall be
" out of the common Road of thinking.
" Your *Divines* think they have exhausted
" that Subject, and absolutely confuted
" all Objections that can be made against
" it, but are much mistaken. Sometimes
" we *Jews* dip into their Writings on this
" Head, and always smile with Indigna-
" tion at their foolish Invectives against the
" Blindness of the Eyes, and Hardness of
" the Hearts of our Ancestors. If they
" would but favour us with a Liberty to
" write for our selves, a reasonable Liber-
" ty, which in this Philosophical Age we
" don't despair of, especially under so wise
" just and good a Civil Administration, as
" this Nation is happily bless'd with, we
                                   " would

" would cut them out some more Work,
" which they are not aware of. In the
" mean Time I am your assured Friend,

N. N.

So ends the Letter of my Friend, the *Jewish Rabbi*, which consists of *calm* and *sedate* Reasoning, or I would not have publish'd it ; for I am resolv'd he shall no more impose upon me with his ludicrous and bantering Stuff, like his Satirical Invective against *Jesus*'s Miracle of *turning Water into Wine*, so offensive to our Godly *Bishops*. And because it consists of *calm* and *sedate* Reasoning, which *Bishop Smalbroke* allows of, I hope his *Lordship* will take it into Consideration, and write an Answer to it, which I, without the Help of the Mystery, can't do.

If the foresaid *Letter* be offensive to our *Clergy*, who don't judge it meet that the *Jews* should take this Liberty to write against the Miracles of our Saviour, and in Vindication of their own disbelief of Christianity, I beg of them, for the Love of *Jesus*, not to let their Displeasure be visibly seen ; because the *Jews* will then laugh in their Sleeves, and perhaps openly insult and triumph upon it : But if they will privately acquaint me with their Displeasure

at

at it, I'll promise them to hold no more Correspondence with such *Jewish Rabbies*; neither will I ever hereafter publish any other Objections against *Christ*'s Religion and Miracles, than what come from the *Hotentots* and *Pawawers :* and then it will be strange, if our dignified *Clergy*, of most grave and demure Looks, can't solidly confute the worst, that such ignorant and illiterate People can urge against them.

And thus have I done with my Objections against the Letter of these three Miracles. If our *Divines* shall think there is little or nothing of Force in them; then an Answer, which I should be glad to see, may the more easily be made to them. As for my part, without being conceited of the Acuteness and Strength of any of the Objections, I think it impossible satisfactorily to reply to them, without having Recourse to the Opinions of the Fathers, that these three Miracles, whether they were ever litterally transacted or not, are now but emblematical Representations of mysterious and more wonderful Operations to be perform'd by *Jesus*.

To the Fathers then let us go for their mystical Interpretation of these Miracles. St. *Augustin*, in his Introduction to a Sermon on the Widow of *Naim*'s Son, says

(29) thus, " There are some so silly as *to*
" stand amazed at the corporal Miracles
" of *Jesus*, and have no Consideration of
" his greater and spiritual Miracles, signi-
" fied by them : but others who are wiser
" can hear of the Things that *Jesus* did
" on Men's Bodys, without being astonish'd
" at them, chusing rather to contemplate
" with Admiration his more wonderful
" Works on Men's Souls; after the simili-
" tude of bodily Miracles. And these are
" the Christians that conform their Studies
" to the Will of our Lord ; who would
" have his corporal Miracles, spiritually
" interpreted : For He wrought not Mi-
" cles in the Flesh, for the sake of such
" Miracles abstractedly consider'd ; but

---

(29) Quidam corporalia ejus Miracula stupentes, majora intueri non norunt. Quidam vero ea, quæ gesta
audiunt in Corporibus nunc amplius in Animis admirantur.——Dominus enim noster Jesus Christus ea quæ faciebat corporaliter, etiam spiritaliter volebat intelligi ;. neque enim Miracula propter Miracula faciebat, sed ut illa
quæ faciebat, mira essent Videntibus, vera essent Intelligentibus.—— Alii & facta mirati & intellecta assecuti.
Tales nos esse debemus in Schola Christi.—— Hoc dixi
(de ficu arefacta) ut persuaderem Dominum Jesum Christum ideo Miracula fecisse, ut aliquid illis Miraculis sig-
nificaret ; ut excepto eo, quod mira & magna & divina
erant, aliquid inde etiam disceremus. Videamus ergo
quid nos discere voluit in tribus mortuis, quos suscitavit.
In Serm. xcviii.

I

" that

" that, if they were surprifing to fome
" Mens Senfes, they fhould be more afto-
" nifhing to the Underftanding of others,
" who apprehend the fpiritual Meaning of
" them. And they who by Contempla-
" tion can attain to the myftical Signifi-
" cation of *Jefus*'s Miracles, are the beft
" Scholars and moft learn'd Difciples in
" his Church and School. And, (*fpeaking
" of the Abfurdity of Jefus's curfing the
" Figtree according to the Letter*) prefent-
" ly after fays, that this he obferv'd, that
" he might perfuade his Hearers to think,
" that our Lord *Jefus* therefore wrought
" Miracles, that he might fignify fomewhat
" by them, which he would have his Dif-
" ciples to learn and confider of. Come
" now, *fays he*, and let us fee what we are
" miftically and fpiritually to underftand
" by the Stories of the three Perfons rais'd
" from the dead."

There are two Ways, that the Fathers
took in the moral and myftical Interpretation of thefe Miracles : One was from the
Number *three*, and their Difference in Magnitude. According to which they faid
with St. *Auguftin* (30) that thefe three
forts

(30) Ifta tria Genera Mortuorum, funt tria Genera
eecato rum, quos hodie fufcitat Chriftus. —— Sunt
o rgo

fort*s* of dead Perfons, fo rais'd to Life,
are Figures of three forts of Sinners,
whom *Jefus* raifeth from the death of Sin
to the Life of Righteoufnefs. They who
have conceiv'd Sin in their Hearts, and
have not brought it forth into Act; are
figured by *Jaïrus*'s Daughter, who lay
dead in the Houfe of her Father, and was
not taken forth to her Burial. Others,
who after Cogitation and Confent, pafs into
actual Sin are figured by the Young Man,
carried towards his Grave. But thofe
Sinners, who are habituated and long accuftom'd to Sin, are like *Lazarus* bury'd,
and in a ftinking Condition under the Cor-

---

ergo inftar filiæ Synagogæ Principis, qui peccatum
intus in Corde babent, in facto nondum habent. Con-
demnatur Confenfus ad Iniquitatem; refpiratur ad Sa-
lutem atq; Juftitiam. Surgit mortuus in Domo, revivif-
cit Cor in Cogitationis Secreto. Facta elt ifta Refurrectio
Animæ mortuæ intus intra Latebras Confcientiæ, tanquam intra Domefticos Parietes.—— Alii poft Confen-
fum eunt in factum, tanquam efferentes mortuum, ut quod
latebat in Secreto, appareat in publico. Nonne illi juve-
ni dictam elt. *Tibi dico, furge* & redditus elt Matri; fic
qui jam fecerit, fi forte admonitus & commotus Verbo
Veritatis ad Chrifti Vocem refurgit, vivus redditur Ecclefiæ. —— Qui autem faciendo quod malum eft, etiam
mala Confuetudine fe implicant, tales Confuetudine ma-
ligna preffi, tanquam fepulti, ita fepulti ut de Lazaro
dictum eft, jam *putet.* In Serm. xcviii.

ruption

ruption of it; whom *Jesus*, for all that, with the *loud Voice* of the Prædication of his Gospel, will call forth out of the Death and Grave of their Sins to a new Life. So does St. *Augustin* make these three dead Persons and their Resurrections, Emblems of the said three Sorts of Sinners, who are dead in Trespasses and Sins, and by the Power of *Jesus* quicken'd to a Life of Righteousness. And to this Opinion of St. *Augustin*, do St. *Ambrose*, *Eusebius Gallicanus*, and Venerable *Bede* agree. And according to this Notion of these Miracles they descend to a particular Explication of the several Parts of their Stories. As to give you two or three Instances.

The People who were turn'd out of the House, upon the raising of *Jarius*'s Daughter, which is an *Absurdity* according to the *Letter* are, says (31) *Bede*, a Multitude of wordly and wicked Thoughts, which, except they are excluded from the Secrets of the Heart, are a Hindrance of the Resurrection of a Sinner to a new Life.

(31) *Cum ejecta esset Turba, intravit*. Moraliter non resurgit Anima, quæ intrinsecus jacet mortua, nisi prius a secretioribus Cordis excludatur inopportuna sæcularium Cogitationum Multitudo. *In Loc. Matt.*

The

The Bearers of the Young Man (32) to his Burial are Vices, evil Spirits, Hæreticks, and Seducers ; and the *Widow*, his Mother, to whom he was reftored, is the *Church*, who mourns for the Death of fuch Sinners, as are typified by that Young Man.

Jefus's weeping for dead *Lazarus*, which is an *Abfurdity* according to the *Letter*, is a Sign (33) of the deplorable State, that habitual Sinners are in, enough to excite the Sorrows and Mournings of good Chriftians, who have the Spirit of *Chrift*, for them. And the Stone that lay at the Grave of *Lazarus*, is (34) a figure of the Hardnefs of the Heart of fuch a Sinner

---

(32) Mali ifti Portit**o**res, qui ad fepeliendum hominem ferunt, funt Vitia & maligni fpiritas, Hæretici & feductores. Hos enim nifi Dominus fifteret, quofcunq; femel acciperent, fepulturæ & æternæ Damnationi traderent. Sufcitatus igitur Adolefcens fedet, loquitur & Matri redditur, quia ad Penitentiam **co**nverfus in Ecclefiæ pace quiefcit, Dei Magnalia loquitur, fua peccata confitetur ; & Ecclefiæ reconciliatur. *Eufeb. Gallic. in Homil. Feria quinta poft Domin.* 4tam.

(33) Et *lacrymatus eft Jefus.* Lacrymemur igitur & nos pro omnibus illis, quos in Fætore Vitiorum jacere fentimus. *Eufeb. Gallic. in Homil. Feriæ* 5tæ *poft Domin.* 4tam.

(34) Lapis autem revolutus a Monumento fignificat Infidelitatis Duritiam ab Hominum Corde fubmotam. *Theop. Antioch- in Loc. Johan.*

which

which muſt be taken away before *Jeſus*
will call him to a new Life. So do the
Fathers moraliſe and allegoriſe every Minute Circumſtance of theſe three Miracles,
as any one, who will conſult them, may
find, and ſave me the Trouble of a tedious
Recital of their Authorities.

But the other myſtical Way of interpreting theſe three Miracles is by making
them Types of three great Events at the
Time of *Chriſt's* ſpiritual Advent. Accordingly the raiſing of *Jairus's* Daughter is
a Type of the Converſion of the *Jews* at
that Day, as *Euſebius Gallicanus* (35) and
venerable *Bede* (36) and others expound
it. By *Jairus*, the Ruler of a *Synagogue*,
is meant *Moſes* (37); and by his Daughter is to be underſtood the *Jewiſh Church*,
which, being at preſent in a State of Spiritual Death, will be revived and converted in the Perfection of Time. And to
the myſtical Reſurrection or Reſtitution of
the *Jewiſh Synagogue*, call'd *Jairus's*

(35) Quod enim tunc temporis factum eſt in una
Puella, hoc in fine Temporum futurum eſt, ut fiat in
tota Sonagoga. *In Homil. Feriæ 5ta poſt Domin. 4tam.*

(36) Synagoga circa finem ſæculi erit reſtituta ſaluti.
In Loc. Matt.

(37) Jairus illuminatus vel illuminans, Moſes intelligitur. *Bed. in Loc. Mat.*

Daughter

Daughter, will *Jesus* come (38) at the same Time he heals the Woman of the Church of her Issue of Blood. And this is the Reason that the Stories of these two Miracles are blended together by the *Evangelists*, with their synchronical Numbers of the Age of the *Girl* and of the Disease of the Woman; because they are Types of that blessed Scene of Affairs at the Conversion of the *Jews*, when the Fulness of the *Gentiles* is come in. Concerning which blessed state of the Church, *Origen* (39) says, *Jesus* wrought many Miracles, by Way of Type and Figure.

Among all the Miracles that *Jesus* wrought, and are recorded by the *Evangelists*, I think, as far as I have had Occasion to observe, the Fathers are most scanty in their Interpretations of that of the

---

(38) Ad hanc ergo Principis filiam dum properat Dei Verbum, ut salvos faceret filios Israel, sancta Ecclesia de Gentibus congregata, quæ inferiorum Lapsu Criminum deperibat, paratam aliis fide præripuit Sanitatem. *St. Ambros. in Loc. Luc.* Quod vero post restitutam immundæ Mulieri Valetudinem, defuncta Puella a mortuis restituitur ; ne hoc quidem ab exquisita Allegoria alienum. Nam Reliquiæ salvæ fiant, juxta Apostolum, cum ingressa fuerit Gentium Plenitudo. *Theop. Ceram. in Homil. de Jairi filia.*

(39) Quarum Rerum Causa multa fuere Jesu Miracula. *In Johan. Cap. XI.*

Widow of *Naim*'s Son: Excepting what
is before noted of his being a figure of a
Sinner dead in actual, tho not habitual
Sin, I find very little. But if *Origen*'s
Comments on this Miracle had been extant, I dare say he would have given us
this following Interpretation of it. This
Widow, he would have call'd the Church;
and her *only Son* or masculine Offspring, he
would have call'd the *Spiritual Sense* of
the Scriptures, which is now dead, and
that the *Ministers* of the *Letter*, who are
his Bearers, are for interring him within
the *Earth* of the *Letter* : But *Jesus*, upon
his Spiritual Advent will put a stop to the
Intention of such Bearers, by reviving the
Spiritual Sense of the Scriptures; and by
restoring it, like a *quicken'd Son*, to the
Comfort of his Mother, the Church; who
has been in a sorrowful and lamentable
Condition upon the Death and Want of
it. This, I am sure, would be *Origen*'s
Interpretation of this Miracle, which, if I
had Room here, by a little Circumlocution, I could prove.

As to *Lazarus*'s Resurrection, it is in the
Opinion of the Fathers (40) a Type of the
general

---

(40) Per Lazarum Genus humanum ostenditur.
Theop. Antioch. in Loc. Johan. Nostra Resurrectio
figuratur per Lazari Resurrectionem. ———— Spelunca
sive

general and myſtical Reſurrection of Mankind in the Perfection of Time. But this
is a moſt copious Subject ; and unleſs I
could here throughly handle it, I had much
better ſay nothing.

And thus have I done with the three
Reſurrection Stories. If the *Convocation,*
next Seſſion, would determine by an Orthodox Vote, whether *Jeſus* rais'd any
more, than the ſaid three Perſons, from
the dead or not ; I would preſent them
with a new and more entertaining Chain
of Thoughts againſt theſe Miracles ; ſuch
a Chain of Thoughts, as, upon the Concluſion, let them hold which Side of the
Queſtion they pleaſe, will neceſſarily induce us to hold the myſtical Meaning of
theſe Miracles, or to grant that *Jeſus*
rais'd none from the dead at all.

My next and laſt *Diſcourſe* on *Jeſus*'s
Miracles ſhall be againſt the Letter of the
Story of his own Reſurrection, in which,
if our *Biſhops* will keep their Temper
and Patience, till I publiſh it, I'll cut
out ſuch a Piece of Work for our *Boy-*

ſive Sepulchrum Lazari Litteram Legis umbratilem de-
ſignat. ——*Magna Voce clamavit Jeſus,* id eſt, Præ-
dicatio Evangelii per quam humana Natura Peccatorum
Vinculis & in Sepulchro Infidelitatis jacens vocatur ad
Vitam. *Theop. Ceram. in Homil. de Lazaro.*

lean

lean Lectures, as shall hold them tug, so long as the *Ministry* of the *Letter* and an *Hireling Priesthood* shall last. If *Christ be not risen*, then, according to the Inference of St. *Paul*, *is their Preaching vain* ; and why should the People be any longer charg'd with the Maintenance of an ignorant and idle Order of Men, to no Use and Purpose ?

If I had not had Experience of it, I could never have believed that, for all the ludicrous Nature of these *Discourses*, our *dignified Clergy* could have been so foolish or malicious as to prosecute me for an *Infidel* and *Blasphemer* upon them. How a Man may be mistaken in himself! I took my self for a real Advocate for the Truth of Christianity ; and was so vain as to imagine these Discourses tended to a Demonstration of *Jesus's* Messiahship: And tho the *Bishop* of *London* may be of a contrary Opinion, yet I am still so conceited of my Ability to defend our Religion, that I'll stake my Life against his *Bishoprick*, which I'll not be troubled with, if I win it, that he can't form an Objection against Christianity, which I can't solidly confute, and make our Readers merry too, with his Weakness and Impertinence in it. But perhaps it may be unbecoming of his Lordship's Character, and against the

Grain,

Grain, to make an Objection to that Religion, which he finds much *temporal*, as well as some *spiritual* Comfort in the Profession of; I will therefore descend to another Proposal, *viz.* If he'll but |publish an Answer to the *Jewish Rabbi*'s Letter in this Discourse, and vouchsafe me the pleasure of a Reply to him; then (to save the Civil Magistrate's Trouble) I will suffer any Punishment that in his Clemency he shall think fit to inflict on me, for what's past. Oh, what a Hazard do I here run of Life or Liberty!

Some Christians, in my Case, would think it a sad Misfortune to be odiously represented as an *Infidel* and *Blasphemer*; but I, in Temper and Principle, despise such Obloquies, Slanders and Defamations; and would not give a Rush to remove them, so long as I had the Answer of a good Conscience that I was undeserving of them: But considering, that it is the Duty of a Christian to seek the Peace and Friendship of all about him, and especially of our good *Bishops*, who, in Compassion to the Danger they think my Soul is in, have taken zealous and laudable Pains with the *Civil Magistrate* for my Conviction and Conversion; I do here, for the sake of a Reconciliation with their *Lordships* and other good People, make a for-

mal

mal and solemn Confession of my Christian Faith, which tho' I don't express in the Words of the *Apostical*, *Nicene* or *Athanasian* Creeds; yet will do it in such Terms as will be a Demonstration that at the Bottom I am found as a *Rock*. Be it known then to all Christian People, that

Imprimis, I believe upon the Authority of the Fathers, that the Ministry of the Letter of the *Old* and *New* Testament is downright *Antichristianism.*

Item, I believe upon the Authority of the Fathers, that the Miracles of *Jesus*, as they are recorded by the Evangelists, *litterally* understood, are the *lying Wonders* of Antichrist.

Item, I believe upon the Authority of the Fathers, that all opposition and Contradiction to spiritual and allegorical Interpretations of the Scripture, is the Sin of *Blasphemy* against the Holy Ghost.

Item, I believe upon the Authority of the Fathers, that the *Ministry* of the *Spirits* or allegorical Interpretations of the Law and the Prophets will be the Conversion of *Jews* and *Gentiles.*

Item,

Item, I believe upon the Authority of the Fathers, that the *Ministry* of the *Letter,* and an Hireling-Priesthood have been the Cause of the Infidelity and Apostacy of these latter Times.

Item, I believe upon the Authority of the Fathers, that the Spirit and Power of *Jesus* will soon enter the Church and expel Hireling-Priests, who make Merchandise of the Gospel, out of her, after the manner he is suppos'd to have driven the *Buyers* and *Sellers* out of the Temple.

These are a few Articles of that Faith, once deliver'd to the *Saints* of the primitive Church, which I firmly believe, and will earnestly contend for. Now I appeal to the Christian World, whether a Man of such a Faith, like Heart of Oak, can be an Infidel or Blasphemer. Upon this ingenuous Confession of my Faith, which I make by way of Atonement for my past supposed Errors and Offences, I hope the *Bishops* and all good Christian People will be reconciled to me.

St. *Jame's* says, that *Faith without Works is dead,* and how a Man ought to show his Faith by his Works, without

which

which Faith is an empty and airy Nothing.
Accordingly I am making what hafte I can
to fhow the Sincerity of my Faith by
thefe my *Works* and *Difcourfes* of this Kind.
And by the Grace of God, I hope our
Bifhops will find me as unmoveable as a
Rock in the faid Faith.

According to the forefaid Articles of
this my Faith, I am fo fully convinced, not
only of the Error of the *Miniftry* of the
Letter, but of the Mifchiefs and Inconveniences of an *Hireling-Priefthood*, that,
having fet my Shoulders to the Work, I
am refolv'd, by the Help of God, to endeavour to give *both* a Lift out of this
World. This is fair and generous Warn-
ing to our *Clergy* to fit faft, and look to
their own Safety, or they may find me a
ftronger Man than they may be aware of.
And tho I don't expect long to furvive
the Accomplifhment of fo great and
glorious a Work; yet I am delightfully
ravifh'd and tranfported with the Fore-
thought and Contemplation of the Happinefs of Mankind, upon the Extinction of
Ecclefiaftical *Vermin*, out of God's Houfe;
when the World will return to its *Primo-
genial* and *Paradifaical* State of Nature,
Religion and Liberty; in which we fhall be
all taught of God, and *have no need* of a
foolifh and contentious Prieft, hired to harangue

rangue us with his Noife and Nonfenfe.
Which bleffed State of the World God of
his infinite Mercy haften, for the fake of
our Spiritual Meffiah, Mediator and Re-
deemer *Jefus Chrift*. To whom be Glory
for ever, *Amen.*

F I N I S.

BOOKS written by Mr. WOOLSTON,
and Sold by him next Door below the,
Star *in* Aldermanbury, *and by the Book-*
sellers of London *and* Westminster.

A SIXTH

DISCOURSE

ON THE

MIRACLES

OF OUR

SAVIOUR,

In View of the Prefent Controverfy between INFIDELS and APOSTATES.

Jamque Opus exegi,———

The SECOND EDITION.

By THO. WOOLSTON, B. D. fometime
Fellow of *Sidney-College* in *Cambridge*.

LONDON:
Printed for the AUTHOR, and Sold by him
next Door to the *Star*, in *Aldermanbury*, and
by the Bookfellers of *London* and *Weftminfter*.
MDCCXXIX.

[*Price One Shilling.*]

TO THE

Right Reverend Father in GOD,

J O H N,

Lord Bishop of *Oxford*.

MY LORD,

 HEN *the following Dis-course was finish'd and ready for the* Press, *I con-sider'd to what* Bishop *the* Dedication *of it would be most acceptable (for I am resolv'd that none but* Bishops *as yet shall have the Honour of my* Dedications*) and*

A 2 *I had*

I had not long ponder'd upon the Matter, before I hit upon your Lordſhip, *who muſt needs be pleas'd with this* Diſcourſe, *becauſe of the Advantage, that you, as well as my ſelf, in the End, will reap by it.*

BY *Virtue of your* Profeſſorſhip *at* Oxford, *you,* my Lord, *are a* Moderator *at theological* Diſputations, *as I am here: And whether the Execution of your Office be as troubleſome as mine is, I know not: But if the Deſign of this* Diſcourſe *takes Place, we ſhall find that modern Controverſies about Religion are all vain; and thereupon be* both *of us ſoon eas'd of the Trouble of our* Moderations *at them.*

IT *may be,* my Lord, *you are not ſo weary of your* Moderatorſhip, *as I am: Beſides, that you are better paid for your Pains, your* Diſputants *are more amicable, and, in the midſt of their* Diſputes, *more tractable: Tho' they may warmly contend, at the preſent, for and againſt the* Point

in

in Debate; yet like Lawyers *who are no less zealous for their* Clients *in the Day, they commonly agree to drink a Bottle together at Night, and go to Bed, good* Friends. *And this is very well done of them.*

BUT *my Difputants,* my Lord, *call'd* Infidels *and* Apoftates, *at whofe Controverfy I have the Trouble, by the Appointment of the* Fathers, *to prefide, are more ftubborn, turbulent and refractory. What ill Treatment they would give each other, if it was in their Power, I know not : But my* Apoftates, *fince they can't be aveng'd on their Adverfaries, are full of Refentment againft their* Moderator, *becaufe I am not altogether partial to their Side; and how I fhall efcape their Indignation,* God *alone knows.*

WHATEVER *the* Clergy, my Lord, *whom I dignify with the Title of* Apoftates, *may think, I look upon my felf as a notable* Modera-

Moderator *of the Controversy* ; *I have shewn them all the Favour I can in it, and would have brought them off with Honour, but for a* little **Flaw**, *here discover'd, in the Foundation of their Church, which, for the Determination of our Disputes, must be confess'd and granted.*

IF *your* Lordship, *upon reading this* Discourse, *should be of the same Mind with me, I beg of you to stroak the* Clergy *into Temper, Patience and Compliance : Tell them, they have been long orthodox and glorious Victors over* Infidels, *and that it would be now an Act of Generosity to yield to them in a* small Point ; *upon which such a Pacification would ensue, as nothing hereafter would be able to dissolve.*

BUT *I have another Favour,* my Lord, *here to crave of you,* viz. *that you would be pleas'd to persuade my old* Friend, *the* Bishop *of* London, *to stay*
at

at Home this Lent, *and keep to his* Prayers *and* Fasting, *for the casting out a certain* Kind *of——, that by Fits he's unhapily troubled with ; or upon the* Publication *of this* Discourse, *I shall be in Danger of being soon knapp'd for it.*

IF *your* Lordship *will do me that Favour, then I will do you as good a Turn; and praise you for your* Doctrine *of* Passive Obedience, *preach'd at the* Coronation : *Tho' many may laugh at your Revival of that* Doctrine, *saying the* Clergy *upon an Occasion, which our most excellent* Sovereign *will never give them, would again have Recourse to their* Reserves *and* Distinctions; *yet I say it was well done of your* Lordship *to preach it, that the* Tongues *and the* Hands *(to say nothing of the* Hearts*) of the* Clergy *might go together in Subscriptions to* Articles *and* Homilies; *and so avoid that* Prevarication *and Inconsistency, which some now have no more Wit than to charge them with.*

So

So *not questioning your* Lordship's *Approbation of this* Discourse *and the* Dedication ; *nor doubting but you'll make me as bountiful a Recompence for it, as any of my other Episcopal Patrons have done; I subscribe my self,*

My Lord,

The Admirer of your

Feb. 15th
1728-9
Paſſive Obedience Sermon,

Thomas Woolſton.

A SIXTH
DISCOURSE
ON THE
MIRACLES
OF OUR
SAVIOUR, &c.

HERE goes my fixth and laft *Difcourfe* on *Jefus*'s *Miracles*; the Subject whereof is the literal Story of his own Refurrection; which, according to the Propofition in Hand, I am to fhew to confift of Abfurdities, Improbabilities and Incredibilities. And I hope our *Bifhops* will quietly permit the Publication of this *Difcourfe*, efpecially

B

if

if I affure them that I mean nothing worfe by it, than to make way for the underftanding what the Fathers write of the myftical Refurrection of *Jefus* out of the Grave of the Letter of the Law and the Prophets; of which myftical Refurrection of our *fpiritual Jefus*, the Evangelical Story of the Refurrection of a *carnal Chrift* is but mere Type and Shadow.

I am fo far from defigning any Service to Infidelity by this *Difcourfe*, that I aim at the Accomplifhment of fome of St. *John*'s Apocalyptical Vifions. The Fathers fay that a *Church*, built on the Letter of the Scriptures, particularly on the Letter of *Jefus*'s Miracles, is *Babylon*; and that antiliteral Arguments and myftical Interpretations will be the Downfal of her. Whether there is any Truth in this Opinion of the Fathers, I am minded to make the Experiment; and tho' I fhould bring the old Houfe of the Church over my Head, and be crufh'd to Pieces in its Ruins, I can't forbear it : But however, I would advife the *Clergy* to make Hafte and *come out of Babylon*, for Fear of the worft; or they, who upon the Authority of the Fathers are *the Merchants of Babylon*, will *weep* (1) *and mourn* upon her

(1) Revelations, Chap. xviii. 11.

Fall,

Fall, becaufe *none will buy their Merchandize* of the Letter *any more.* Dear *Jefu,* that fuch a *Student* as I am in the *Revelations* of St. *John,* and an Interpreter of them too, upon the Authority of the Fathers, fhould be charg'd with Blafphemy and Infidelity!

So to Work I went ; and I had not been long mufing by myfelf, how to fap this Foundation of the Church, before I was fenfible of my own Infufficiency for it. Whereupon I fent to my old Friend, the *Jewish Rabbi,* for his Thoughts on this grand Miracle of *Jefus's* Refurrection, which he gave me fome Promife of. But I defired him to forbear all Ludicroufnefs, Satire and Banter, for fear of Offence : For tho' our *Clergy* liked Volumes of Jefts and Facetioufnefs, if they were difcharg'd againft *Jews, Turks,* and *Infidels ;* yet when they were levell'd at *Minifters* of the *Letter,* the *Cafe was alter'd,* as quoth *Plowden,* and they were not to be borne with. Therefore he was to remember that Decency, Serioufnefs and Calmnefs of Argument, required by the *Bifhop* of *London* (2) or I durft not print it.

In Compliance with my Defires he fent me the following *Letter,* which, having

(2) *In his Paftoral Letter,* P. 35.

purg'd

purg'd it of a few *Puns* and *Cunundrums*, becaufe all Appearance of *Wit*, as of *Evil*, was to be abſtain'd from, I here publiſh, and it runs thus.

S I R,

ACcording to your Requeſt, I here ſend you my Thoughts on *Jeſus*'s Reſurrection, in which I ſhall be ſhorter than I would be, becauſe of the cuſtomary Bounds of your *Diſcourſes*.

The Controverſy between us *Jews* and you *Chriſtians* about the *Meſſiah* has hitherto been of a diffuſive Nature : But as the Subject of *this* is the Reſurrection of your *Jeſus* ; ſo, by my Conſent, we'll now reduce the Controverſy to a narrow Compaſs, and let it turn intirely on this grand Miracle and Article of your Faith. If your *Divines* can prove *Jeſus*'s Reſurrection againſt the following Objections, then I will acknowledge him to be the *Meſſiah*, and will turn Chriſtian, otherwiſe he muſt ſtill paſs with us for an Impoſtor and falſe Prophet.

I have often lamented the Loſs of ſuch Writings, which our *Anceſtors* unqueſtionably diſpers'd againſt *Jeſus*, becauſe of the clear Sight they would give us, into the Cheat and Impoſture of his Religion.
But

But I rejoice and thank God, there is little or no Want of them, to the Point in Hand. For I had not long meditated on the Story of *Jesus*'s Refurrection, as your *Evangelists* have related it, but I plainly difcern'd it to be the moft notorious and monftrous Impofture, that ever was put upon Mankind. And if you pleafe to attend to my following Arguments, which require no Depth of Judgment and Capacity to apprehend, I am perfuaded that you and every one difinterefted, will be of the fame Mind too.

To overthrow and confute the Story of this monftrous and incredible Miracle, I was thinking once to premife an Argument of the Juftice of the Sentence denounc'd againft and executed upon *Jesus*, who was fo far from being the innocent Perfon, you Chriftians would make of him, that, as may eafily be proved, he was fo grand a *Deceiver*, *Impoftor* and *Malefactor*, as no Punifhment could be too great for him. But this Argument (which I referve againft a Day of perfect Liberty, to publifh by it felf in Defence of the Honour and Juftice of our *Anceftors*) would be too long for the Compafs of this Letter; and therefore I pafs it by, tho' it would give Force to my following Objections; it being hard and even impoffible to imagine,
that

that God would vouchfafe the Favour of a miraculous Refurrection to one, who for his Crimes defervedly fuffer'd and underwent Death.

But waving, I fay, that Argument for the prefent, which of itfelf would be enough to prejudice a reafonable Man againft the Belief of *Jefus*'s Refurrection; I will allow *Jefus* to have been a much better Man, than I believe him to have been; or as good a one in Morals as your *Divines* do fuppofe him; and will only confider the Circumftances of the Evangelical Story of his Refurrection; from which, if I don't prove it to have been the moft bare-fac'd Impofture that ever was put upon the World, I deferve for the Vanity of this Attempt, a much worfe Punifhment, than he for his Frauds endured.

I have fometimes wonder'd, confidering the Nature and Heinoufnefs of *Jefus*'s Faults, for which he dy'd, that our *Chief Priefts* and *Pharifees* had any Regard to his Prediction (which was fo like a Bambouzlement of the Populace) that he was to rife again the *third Day* after his Crucifixion. There's no other Nation in the World, which would not have flighted fuch a vain Prognoftication of a known Impoftor. Let him foretel with ever fo much Confidence

fidence his fpedy Return to Life, I dare fay, any other Magiftrates of ordinary Prudence would have defpifed him for a prefumptuous *Enthufiaft*: But, when I reflected on the Impofture of *Lazarus*'s Refurrection, and of what pernicious Confequence it had like to have proved to the Peace and Welfare of our Nation, if it had not been happily difcover'd, my Wonder here ceas'd; and I as much admire now the Wifdom, Caution and Circumfpection of our *Chief Priefts* againft all poffible Fraud and Deceit in the foretold Refurrection of *Jefus*. Tho' *Jefus* himfelf, the Head of the Confederacy, and prime Projector of the defign'd Cheat in the Cafe of *Lazarus* was cut off, yet his Affociates were ftill numerous; and it was not impoffible, but they might concert a Project of a counterfeited Refurrection of him, in Accomplifhment of his Prophecy, that might be of more fatal Confequence, and tend to fuch Confufions and Diftractions among the People, as would not be foon quell'd and quieted. Whereupon our *Chief Priefts* very prudently confider of Precautions againft Cheat here, and wifely make Application to *Pilate* the *Governour*, that proper and effectual Meafures may be taken againft a falfe and feign'd Refurrection, for Fear of the ill Effects of it.
And

And one of them, as the *Spokesman* of their Company, seems, according to *Matthew*, Ch. xxviii. to have made the Speech following.

  S I R, " We remember that this De-
" ceiver and Impostor *Jesus*, who was
" yesterday crucified, and justly suffer'd
" Death for his Blasphemy and many De-
" lusions of the People (that were of bad
" Consequence, and might have been of
" much worse, if he had not been timely
" brought to condign Punishment) said
" repeatedly before, that notwithstanding
" the Death he was to undergo, he should
" rise again to Life the *third Day* after.
" It is not that we are at all apprehensive
" of such a wonderful and miraculous
" Event, which knowing him to have
" been a false Prophet as well as a de-
" ceitful Juggler, we have no Fears nor
" Belief of. But as it is not long since,
" that the Inhabitants in and about *Be-*
" *thany* had like to have been fatally de-
" luded and imposed on by him, in the
" pretended Resuscitation of *Lazarus*, one
" of his Disciples and Confederates in Ini-
" quity ; so it is not altogether impossible
" nor improbable but his Disciples and
" Accomplices, who are many, may pro-
" ject a feign'd Resurrection of *Jesus* (in
                                   " Accom-

" Accomplifhment of his Prediction) by
" ftealing his Body away, and pretend-
" ing he is rifen from the dead. Should
" fuch a Sham-Miracle be contrived
" amongft them, and cunningly executed,
" it would be πλανη (*not an Error but*) an
" Impofture of worfe Confequence to our
" Nation and Religion, than the former
" in *Lazarus* could have been, if it had
" never been detected: We crave there-
" fore the Favour of your *Excellency*, to
" give Command for the making his Se-
" pulchre fure, till the *third* Day is paft,
" that neither his *dead* Body may be ta-
" ken away, and a Refurrection pretend-
" ed ; nor a *living* one flipt into its Place,
" and a Miracle counterfeited on that Day,
" when we will be prefent at the opening
" of the Sepulchre, and give Satisfaction
" to the People of his being a falfe
" Prophet.

Whether *Pilate* was at all intent on the
Prevention of Fraud in this Cafe, or would
not willingly have connived at it, to increafe the Divifions and Diftractions of our
then unhappy Nation, may be queftion'd :
But the Requeft of our *Chief Priefts* was
fo reafonable, and their Importunities fo
urgent, that he could not refift them; and
therefore order'd them a *Watch* for the

Sepul-

Sepulchre, which they might make as sure, as they could, againſt Fraud and Impoſture, till the *third Day*.

Whereupon our *Chief Prieſts* deliberate, what Meaſures were fitteſt to be taken to this Purpoſe. And as I can't, and don't believe any Man elſe can, deviſe any better for the Security of the Sepulchre againſt Fraud, than what they took; ſo I admire and applaud their Prudence, Circumſpection, and Precaution in the Caſe. They *ſeal'd the Stone* at the Mouth of the Sepulchre, and placed a Guard of Soldiers about it; which were *Two* ſuch certain Means for the Prevention or Detection of Cheat in a Reſurrection, as are not to be equall'd by any other.

They *ſeal'd the Stone* of the Sepulchre, which, tho' it was no Security at all againſt Violence, yet was an abſolute one againſt Fraud. How the *Stone* which fitted the Mouth of the Sepulchre, as a Door does the Entrance into a Room, was ſeal'd, I need not deſcribe. The Uſe and Manner of ſealing the Doors of Cloſets, of Cheſts, and of Papers is common; and as it is an obvious Expedient, for the Satisfaction of the Signators, againſt Deceit; ſo it has been an antient as well as a modern Practice. *Darius*, King of *Babylon*, (3) ſeal'd the

(3) Daniel, Chap. vi. 17.

Door

Door of the Den of Lions, wherein
Daniel was caſt, with his own Signet:
And wherefore did he ſo? For the Satisfaction of himſelf and of his Courtiers,
when he came again to open and compare the Signature with his Signet, that
no Art nor Artifice had been uſed for the
Preſervation of *Daniel*. So our *Chief
Prieſts* ſeal'd the Stone of *Jeſus*'s Sepulchre, which they deſign'd to be preſent at
the opening of, on the *third Day*, the
Time appointed by *Jeſus* for his Reſurrection, and then give ample Satisfaction
to the People, that there was a real, or
could be no Reſurrection of his Body.
Wherefore elſe did they *ſeal* the Stone of
his Sepulchre?

Your *Grotius* (4) thinks, that *Pilate*'s
Seal was affix'd to the Stone of the Sepulchre; but, as I believe, *Pilate* little concern'd himſelf about the Prevention of
Deceit here; ſo I much queſtion it. It is
more reaſonable to think that the *Chief
Prieſts* and other Civil Magiſtrates of
Jeruſalem with their ſeveral Seals, which
could not be open'd, but by themſelves,
without Suſpicion of Fraud, ſign'd the

(4) Adducor ut credam Pilati Annulo & hunc Lapidem
ſignatum. *In Loc. Matt.*

Stone,

Stone, and intended to be prefent, on the
Day appointed, at the opening of the
Sepulchre; not doubting, what no body
could queftion, but *Jefus* would wait their
coming, and arife to Life, if he could, in
the Sight of themfelves, and of a vaft Con-
courfe of People, that were fure to attend
on them to behold the Miracle. Such a
Refurrection would have been of Satif-
faction to the whole Nation; and fuch a
Refurrection, reafonably fpeaking, *Jefus*
would, if he could, have vouchfafed in
Accommodation to the *fealing* of the
Stone.

But, notwithftanding this Precaution,
in fealing of the Stone, the beft that could
be taken againft Fraud, *Jefus*'s Body
was privately flipt off, early in the Morning of the Day before, and a Refurrection
pretended by his Difciples; and you
would have us and our Anceftors to believe, there was no Deceit in the Cafe;
tho' confeffedly none of the *Sealers* of the
Sepulchre were prefent: Who can believe
it? Was, or can there be, any Impofture
more againft Senfe and Reafon palm'd
upon the Underftandings of Mankind?
If there had been a real Refurrection, the *Sealers* of the *Stone* would have
been

been the *Openers* of the Sepulchre; wherefore elſe was the *Stone ſeal'd?*

A Queſtion, that here ariſes, is, On
what Day, and what Time of the Day,
did our *Chief Prieſts,* the Sealers of the
Stone, expeƈt, what they could not think
would ever come to paſs, *Jeſus's* Reſurreƈtion? Or what was the Extent of the
Time meant by *Jeſus,* when he ſaid that
after *three Days,* or on the *third Day* after
his Paſſion, he ſhould riſe again? If any
Impoſtor or Prophet like *Jeſus* ſhould in
this Age ſo prediƈt his Reſurreƈtion, and
be executed on *Friday,* the Day for his
Reſurreƈtion would be preſumed to be
Monday, and not *Sunday* Morning before
Day. And I humbly conceive former
Ages and Nations, and our Nation in
particular did compute after this Faſhion.
Accordingly on *Monday* our *Chief Prieſts*
I don't doubt, intended to be preſent at
the opening of the Seals of the Sepulchre,
and to behold the Miracle: But *Jeſus's*
Body was clandeſtinely moved off early
on *Sunday* (the Day before *that* ſignified
and prediƈted for his Reſurreƈtion) to the
Laughter more than the Surprize of our
Anceſtors, at the Notoriety of the Fraud
committed, and at the Vanity of a Reſurreƈtion pretended upon it. And I may
appeal

appeal even to your *Chief Priests* of the
Church, whether here's not another Note
of Cheat and Imposture; and whether
the Disciples were not afraid to trust *Je-sus*'s Body, its full time, in the Grave;
because of the greater Difficulty to carry
it off afterwards, and pretend a Resur-rection upon it.

But because your *Divines* (who have
singular Knacks at making two Nights and
a full Day, that *Jesus* was buried, to be
three Days and *three Nights*; and whose
various Ways of Computation I always
smile at) do assert that *Sunday* was the
third Day, on which, in Accomplishment
of *Jonah*'s Prophecy, and of his own Pre-diction, he was to rise again; I will sup-pose so with them, and will, if they please,
grant that our *Chief Priests*, and the *Sea-lers* of the Sepulchre, expected his Resur-rection on that Day, and intended, for the
opening of the Seals, to be present at it

But at what Time of the Day were they
to come or could be expected at the Se-pulchre? Not long before Noon. But
Jesus's Body was gone betimes in the
Morning, before our *Chief Priests* could
be out of their Beds; and a barefac'd In-fringment of the Seals of the Sepulchre was
made against the Laws of Honour and
Honesty,

Honesty, and a Resurrection confidently talk'd of by the Disciples; and yet your Christian Priesthood at this Day would have us to believe, there was no Fraud and Deceit in all this! O most monstrous!

If our *Chief Priests* had trespass'd upon *Jesus*'s Patience, and would not attend at the Sepulchre for the opening of the Seals, on the Day and Time appointed; if they had been for confining him longer in the Grave than was meet, according to Prophecy, then his Resurrection, without their Presence, had been excusable and justifiable. But this his pretended Rising to Life, not only a Day before the *Chief Priests* could imagine he would, or earlier in the Morning than he should, for the Sake of their requisite Presence, is, together with the Fracture of the Seals against the Law of Security, such a manifest and indisputable Mark and Indication of Fraud, as is not to be equall'd in all or any of the Impostures, that ever were attempted to be put upon the World.

In short, by the sealing of the Stone of the Sepulchre, we are to understand nothing less than a Covenant enter'd into between our *Chief Priests* and the *Apostles*, by which *Jesus*'s Veracity, Power and

Messiahship

Meſſiahſhip was to be try'd. Tho' we read not of the Apoſtles giving their Conſent to the Covenant, yet it was reaſonably preſum'd and could not have been refus'd, if ask'd. The Condition of the ſeal'd Covenant was, that if *Jeſus* aroſe from the dead in the Preſence of our *Chief Prieſts*, upon their opening the Seals of the Sepulchre, at the Time appointed; then was he to be acknowledg'd to be the *Meſſiah:* But if he continued in a corrupt and putrified State of Mortality, then was he to be granted to be an *Impoſtor:* Very wiſely and rightly agreed! And if the Apoſtles had ſtood to this Covenant, Chriſtianity had been nipt in its Bud, and ſuppreſs'd in its Birth. But they had other Views, and another Game to play at all Adventures. The Body was to be removed and a Reſurrection pretended, to the Deluſion, if poſſible, of all Mankind, in which they have been more ſucceſsful than could be imagin'd upon a Project that had ſo little Senſe or Reaſon, ſo little Colour of Truth or Artifice in the Contrivance and Execution of it. Our *Chief Prieſts* were apprehenſive at firſt of their ſtealing the Body away, and pretending a Reſurrection: But after the *ſealing* of the *Stone*, thoſe Fears vaniſh'd; becauſe upon the ſtealing the
Body,

Body, away against such Security and Precaution, the Fraud would be self-evident, and want no Demonstration and Proof of it. But, for all this Precaution, I say, the Body was in a barefaced Manner taken away, a Resurrection talk'd of, and to the Amazement of every one, who can think freely, has been believed thro' all Ages of the Church since. Upon the whole then, I think, you may as well say, when a seal'd Closet is broken open, and the Treasure gone without the Privity of the Signators, that there's no Wrong done; as that in the Resurrection of *Jesus*, there was no Fraud. The Cases are equal and parallel. What then can your Christian *Priests* say to this demonstrative Argument of a manifest and bare-faced Cheat in *Jesus*'s Resurrection? I have been thinking, what they will or can say; and upon the maturest Consideration I don't find they can make any other than one or more of these shuffling Answers to it, *viz.*

1. That it was impossible for the Disciples to steal the Body of *Jesus* away, because of the Watchfulness of the Guards, and therefore there was a real Resurrection, tho' the *Chief Priests* and *Sealers* of the Sepulchre were not present at it.

D   2. That

2. That, tho' the *Chief Priests* and *Sealers* of the Stone of the Sepulchre were not present, as I say they ought to have been, to behold the Miracle; yet his Resurrection was afterwards made as manifest to them, as if they had been there present.

3. That if *Jesus* did not really arise from the dead, the Belief of his Resurrection could never have been so propagated at first, nor would have been retain'd in the World for so many Ages since.

I can think of no other Answers, and believe it impossible for your Christian *Priests* to form any other, to the foresaid Argument of Fraud in *Jesus's* Resurrection: But how weak, frivolous and insufficient they all and every one are, will appear upon a little Examination into them.

1. Then, against the aforesaid demonstrative Argument of Fraud, it may be pretended, *That it was impossible for the Disciples to steal the Body of* Jesus *away, because of the Watchfulness of the Guards; and therefore there was a real Resurrection, tho'* the Chief Priests, *the* Sealers *of the Sepulchre were not present at it.*

To

To which I reply, and confeſs, that if it was impoſſible to evade the Guards of the Sepulchre, then there was a real Reſurrection; but if there was but a bare Poſſibility of evading them, then this Anſwer is of no Force. And I am of Opinion, that the Thing was not only poſſible, but eaſy, feaſible, and practicable. Tho' the *Roman* Soldiers were of as much Fidelity and Integrity as any of their Profeſſion; yet it is well known, that ſuch Creatures are ſubject to Bribery and Corruption, if the Diſciples had any Money to tempt them with: Or if their Faithfulneſs to their Truſt was untainted; yet it is not improbable, but their Officers, at the Direction of *Pilate*, who found his Account in the Diſtractions of our Nation, might give them the Hint to wink hard at the Commiſſion of ſuch a Fraud. But not to inſiſt on either of theſe Ways to evade the *Watch*; our Anceſtors ſaid, what your *Evangeliſt* has recorded, that the Diſciples taking the Opportunity of the Sleep of the Guards, carry'd the Body of *Jeſus* off; which was a thing both poſſible and probable.

Of what Number the *Watch* did conſiſt is uncertain. Your *Whitby* (ſ) ſays they

(ſ) *Upon the Place in* Matthew.

were

were *sixty* ; but he has no Reason nor Authority to think, they were so many. If they had been to be a Guard against Violence, I could easily have believed they were more ; but in as much as they were only a *Watch* against Fraud, and against any casual defacing of the *Seals* on the Stone, before the *Chief Priests* came to open the Sepulchre, *three* or *four* Soldiers were sufficient, and I don't think, there were any more set to this Purpose.

It is not then at all improbable, that so few Soldiers should be fast asleep at that time of Night, or so early in the Morning, when the clandestine Work was done ; especially after keeping such a *Gaudy-day* as was the Feast of the Passover, which, like the Festivals of other Nations, was celebrated with Excess. Foot Soldiers then, you may be sure, upon the Bounty of one or other, did no more want, than they would scruple to take their *Fill*, which like an Opiat, lock'd up their Senses for that Night, when the Disciples, being aware of the lucky Opportunity, carry'd the Body of *Jesus* off safely.

And where's the Absurdity to suppose, that the Disciples themselves might contrive the Intoxication of the Guards ? *Herodotus* tells us a Story of a Dead-
body's

body's being stolen away by such an Artifice. And I don't think the Disciples of *Jesus* either so foolish or conscientious, as not to take the Hint, and enterprize the like Fraud. *Peter*, who, upon Occasion, could *swear* and *curse* like a *Trooper*, would hardly scruple to fuddle a few *Foot-Soldiers*. But which way soever it came to pass, the Watch were asleep, which is neither hard to conceive nor believe; and then the Disciples executed *that* Fraud, which has been the Delusion of Nations and Ages since.

Your *Evangelists* would hint that the *Chief Priests* gave Money to the Soldiers to say, they were asleep, when the Disciples stole the Body of *Jesus* away, as if they were brib'd to a false Testimony; but there neither was nor could be any such thing. If there had been a real Resurrection to their Astonishment and Amazement, as it is represented in your Gospels, no Money could so soon have corrupted them to a false Witness, being under such Fears of God and of *Jesus*. I don't doubt but our *Chief Priests* might reward the Soldiers for speaking the Truth, and exhort them to persist in it, with a Promise to *secure* them

against

against the Anger of *Pilate* for their sleeping and Neglect of their Duty.

Here then is no *Answer* to the foresaid Argument or Objection against *Jesus's* Resurrection. It was not at all impossible for the Disciples, who stole the Body away, to avoid the Guards, who were and may reasonably be supposed to be lull'd asleep, when the Disciples did it. Neither is there any more Force in the

2. Second Answer to it, *viz. That tho' the Chief Priests, the Sealers of the Stone of the Sepulchre, were not present, opening the Seals and beholding the Miracle ; yet his Resurrection was afterwards made as manifest to them, as if they had been there present.*

Ay, this is somewhat like an Answer, if there be any Truth in it. A Manifestation of *Christ* risen afterwards to our *Chief Priests* would have been equivalent to their Presence at and Sight of the Miracle. But how was his Resurrection manifested to them ? did *Jesus* ever afterwards appear personally to them, to their Satisfaction, that he was the same Person, whom they crucified and put to Death for a Deceiver and false Prophet ? No; this is not once asserted by your *Evangelists* or ever insinuated by any antient or modern Writer. How then was *Jesus's* Resurrection made mani-

manifeft to our Chief Priefts? Why; your *Divines* fay, what is all that can be faid here, that the Words of the Difciples, who, being Men of Honefty, Simplicity and Integrity, would not lye, are to be taken for it. Very fine, indeed! our Chief Priefts are to take the Words of the Difciples for *Jefus*'s Refurrection, and look upon them as Men of Veracity, when they knew and experienc'd them to be grand Cheats, not only in ftealing the Body of *Jefus* away, but in the *known Impofture* of *Lazarus*'s Refurrecton, or your *Evangelift* had never implicitly called it fo. When therefore Deceivers will not be *Lyars ;* nor Thieves *Diffemblers* of the Fact they are accufed of, I will own *Jefus*'s Refurrection to have been manifeft enough to our *Chief Priefts.* There's no need of more Argument here: He that beftows more Words on it, lofes Time.

It has been a conftant Objection of us *Jews*, againft the Refurrection of *Jefus*, that he appear'd not perfonally afterwards to our *Chief Priefts*, to *Pilate* and to others his Crucifiers and Infultors, to upbraid them with their Infidelity and ill Treatment of him. Whether *Jefus* would not have done fo, if he really arofe from the dead ; and whether he ought not in Reafon, for the Conviction and Converfion of Unbe-

Unbelievers, to have done fo, with me is no Queftion. *Celfus* of old (6) in the Name of the *Jews* made the Objection; and *Olibio*, a late *Rabbi* (7) has repeated it. But in all my Reading and Converfation with Men or Books, I never met with a tolerable Anfwer to it. *Origen* and *Limborch*, the Writers againft *Celfus* and *Olibio*, gently flide over the Objection, as if it was too hot or weighty to be touch'd and handled by them. To recite the poor, fhort and infufficient Anfwers of thofe two Great Authors, to the Objection, would be the Expofing of them, and giving fuch Strength to the Objection, which it don't want. Therefore I will leave the Objection, which *Origen* (8) owns to be a confiderable one, to the Meditation of your modern Advocates for Chriftianity; and when they can prove, that *Jefus*, after his Refurrection did perfonally appear to his Crucifiers, the *Chief*

---

(6) Si Jefus volebat re vera declarare fuam divinam Potentiam, debuerat fuis Infultatoribus, ipfique Præfidi qui capitalem fententiam contra fe tulerat, denique cæteris omnibus fe oftendere. *In Orig. Lib.* ii. *contra Celfum.*

(7) In *Limborchii* Amica Collatione cum Judæo.

(8) Magna fane Res & miranda occurrit hoc loco, quæ non folum aliquem ex vulgo Credentium exercere poffet, fed perfectiores etiam; cur non Dominus poft Refurrectionem æque ac fuperioribus temporibus confpiciendum fe præbuerit. *In Lib.* ii. *cont.* Celfum.

Priests and *Sealers* of the Sepulchre, to their Confutation; or that, according to the Law of Reason, he ought not to have appear'd to them, then I will turn *Christian*, and grant, that in the Argument above, which proves plain Fraud in the Resurrection, there's no Force nor Truth. In the mean time *Jesus*'s Non-Appearance to the *Chief Priests* is a Confirmation, that he did not arise from the Dead, but that his Body was stolen away, or he would have waited in the Grave, the coming of the Sealers of the Stone, and their regular opening of the Sepulchre, to the Conviction and Conversion of all there present, and Confirmation of the Faith of all Ages and Nations since. But,

3. A third Answer to the foresaid Argument of Fraud in the Resurrection of *Jesus*, drawn from the Nature, Use and Design of sealing the Stone of the Sepulchre, is, *that tho' the* Sealers *of the Sepulchre were not present, opening the Seals and beholding the Miracle*; yet Jesus *did certainly arise from the Dead, or the Belief of his Resurrection could never have been at first propagated by the Apostles, nor would for so many Ages of the Church since have stood its Ground.*

E   Here's

Here's as little Reafon in this Anfwer as in either of the two former. Who knows not, that many Errors in Philofophy, and as many Frauds in Religion have been fometimes accidentally, fometimes defignedly efpoufed and palm'd upon Mankind, who in Procefs of Time become fo wedded to them thro' Prejudice and Intereft, that they will not give themfelves Leave to enquire into the Rife and Foundation of them. Falfe Miracles have been common Things among Chriftians; and as the Refurrection of *Jefus* is their grand and fundamental one, fo it is not at all difficult to account for the Rife, Propagation and Continuance of the Belief of it.

Why it has been believed thro' thefe latter Ages of the Church, is no Wonder at all. The Priefts had their Intereft in it; the ignorant and fuperftitious had their Comfort in it; and the wife and confiderate, for fear of Perfecution, durft not enquire into the Grounds of it.

The only Difficulty here is to know, upon what Principle, the Project and Story of *Jefus*'s Refurrection was at firft devifed. And whether it was Ambition or Revenge upon our ancient and Pharifaical Priefthood, that prompted the Apoftles to it, is all one to me. Such bad

Prin-

Principles too often put Men upon defperate Attempts. But however, an Impofture it was, for the Argument above. To fay the Apoftles and Confederates in the Fraud, would not have ftood to it, and have dy'd for it, if the Refurrection had not been real Fact, fignifies nothing. Many Cheats and Criminals, befides them, have afferted their Innocencey, and deny'd their Guilt in the utmoft Extremity of Death, without the like Views of Honour and Fame. The only Thing that's furprizing and aftonifhing in this Sham-Miracle, is, that tho' it was the moft manifeft, the moft bare-faced, and the moft felf-evident Impofture that ever was put upon the World; yet it has been the moft fortunate and fuccefsful, having paft thro' many Ages and Nations with Reputation and Renown; and might have continued for as many Generations to come, but for the Argument above, that perfectly and clearly overthrows its Credit.

But fome may fay here, where was the Wifdom and Providence of God, all this while, to fuffer fo many Ages and Nations to labour under fuch a Delufion? Why, I'll tell you; The Providence of God in it was, " To humble Mankind, in the End, for their vain

E 2   Often-

Oftentation of Wifdom, Learning and *Science falfly fo call'd*; " To fhame them for their Madnefs and Wickednefs to perfecute one another for different Opinions in that Religion, whofe very Foundation is falfe and groundlefs; " To caution them againft a blind and implicit Faith for the future ; againft believing any thing out of the Sight and Reach of their Underftandings; " To admonifh them of the Neceffity of Liberty to think, fpeak and write freely about Religion, for the Correction of Errors and Difcovery of Truth; and, laftly, " To reduce the World, when it fhould be ripe for it, to the golden Religion of Nature, which upon the Teftimony of our old *Cabaliftical* Doctors, and of your *Jefus* himfelf, is the *End of the Law and the Prophets.*

And thus have I fpoken to the *Anfwers*, which your *Chriftian Priefthood* may be prefumed to make, to the forefaid Argument of Fraud in *Jefus's* Refurrection, drawn from the Defign of our *Chief Priefts* in fealing of the Stone of his Sepulchre. I fhould not have conconcern'd my felf to fpeak to thefe their fuppofed *Anfwers*, but to fave them the Trouble of making them, and the Imagination of there being fome Force in them.

As

As to the Stories in your *Evangelifts* of *Jefus*'s feveral Appearances after his pretended Refurrection, fometimes to the Women, and at other Times to his Difciples, I am not at all obliged to refute them. If thefe Appearances had been more frequent, better circumftanced, and more folemnly averr'd, they would have wanted no Confutation. There's no Doubt on't, but the Difciples, who, for the Argument above, unqueftionably ftole *Jefus*'s Body away, in order to pretend a Refurrection, would talk much of his appearing to them, and of the Converfation afterwards, they had with him. And if they had told better and more plaufible Tales of their Sight of and Converfation with him, it would be nothing to the Purpofe; *better*, I fay, *and more plaufible Tales* than thofe upon Record, which for Abfurdity, Nonfenfe and Incoherence carry their own Confutation along with them.

Whoever blends together the various Hiftory of the four *Evangelifts*, as to *Jefus*'s Appearances after his Refurrection, will find himfelf, not only perplex'd how to make an intelligible, confiftent, and fenfible Story of it; but muft, with *Celfus* (9)

(9) Quamvis Celfus has Jefu poft Refurrectionem Apparitiones conferre conetur cum vulgaribus Spectris & Vifionibus. *In Origen. Lib.* ii. *contra Celfum.*

needs

needs think it, if he clofely think on't, like fome of the confufed and incredible womanifh Fables of the Apparitions of the Ghofts of deceafed Perfons, which the Chriftian World in particular has in former Ages abounded with. The Ghofts of the Dead in this prefent Age, and efpecially in this Proteftant Country, have ceas'd to appear; and we now-a-days hardly ever hear of fuch an Apparition: And what is the Reafon of it? Why, the Belief of thefe Stories being banifh'd out of Mens Minds, the crafty and vaporous forbear to trump them upon us. There has been fo much clear Proof of the Fraud in many of thefe Stories, that the wife and confiderate Part of Mankind has rejected them all, excepting *this* of *Jefus*, which, to Admiration, has ftood its Ground. It's no Wonder indeed, that the *Clergy*, who are more incredulous than other Folks as to Stories of Apparitions, do ftick to *this* of *Jefus*, the only one excepted out of all others. It is a fweet Morfel of Faith, and they readily fwallow and digeft it, becaufe they live by it; otherwife this Story of *Jefus*'s Appearances after Death had hardly efcaped the Fate of other Apparitions; nay, would have been rejected one of the firft of them; there being hardly one, I dare fay it, among all the Stories of

Appa-

Apparitions, were they to be collected together; that's more abfurd and incredible than *this* of *Jefus*.

I have not Room here to make any Remarks on your Evangelical Story of *Jefus's* Apparitions after his Death; and if I had, I durft not do it, for fear of an offenfive Ludicroufnefs, and of tranfgreffing the Rules of *Decency*, *Sobriety* and *Sedatenefs* of Argument, you have confined me to. But however; I can't read the Story without fmiling, and there are two or three Paffages in it, that put me in Mind of *Robinfon Crufo*'s filling his Pockets with Biskets, when he had neither Coat, Waftecoat, nor Breeches on. Sometimes I think your *Evangelifts* wanted Wit to adapt their Tale to Senfe, and to accommodate the Tranfaction to Nature; and fometimes I think them crafty, and were minded, like *Daniel de Foe* in his aforefaid *Romance*, to put the Banter upon the Credulity of Mankind, with fome difguifed and latent Abfurdities, that, in the Conclufion and Difcovery, they might be heartily laugh'd at for the Belief of them. I dare not, I fay, fo much as hint at one of thefe Abfurdities, left I fhould be unwarily tempted to crack a Jeft on it. But the Time, I hope, is coming, when I fhall ufe more Freedom. And fhould your
Prieft-

Priesthood, in Proof of *Jesus*'s Resurrection, urge any of these Stories of his corporal Presence and Appearance after it, then I trust, they'll permit me to make as merry Descants on them, as your *Bishops*, when Academical *Jesters*, used to do on other Men's Bulls and Blunders.

In the mean time I depend on the foregoing single, sober and sedate Argument of Fraud in this grand Miracle, which I found on the Nature and Design of sealing the Sepulchre; and for Confirmation of my Opinion and Proof of Fraud in it, will conclude this Letter with a parallel Case and Story. Not many Years since, one Dr. *Emms*, of the Society of the *French* Prophets, who in their Inspirations were, like *Jesus* and his Disciples of old, Declaimers against the Pharisaical Priesthood of this Age, did by himself, or some of his Fraternity did for him, predict his Resurrection on a certain Day, when there was a Concourse of People about his Grave in vain to behold the Miracle, as there would have been about *Jesus*'s Sepulchre, if he had lain in it, his full Time. But supposing in this Case, that the Magistrates and Priesthood of this City, to prevent a Cheat and Delusion of the People, had interr'd the

Doctor

Doctor in a Church-Vault, and feal'd the
Door of it againft the Day appointed for
his Refurrection, commanding a *Night-
Watch* to look to the Vault, that no Violence or Deceit be ufed: This would
have been a wife Precaution againft Fraud,
as was in the Cafe of *Jefus*. But what
if his Fraternity, having a Mind, like *Jefus's* Difciples, to bambouzle the People
and Priefthood, had, fome of them drawn
the Watch afide to a *Gin-fhop*, whilft
others carry'd the Body off, pretending a
Refurrection? What would all reafonable
Men have faid here? That it was an
impudent and bare-fac'd Impofture. But
to carry on the Farce; fuppofing, the
Doctor's Fraternity had afterwards averr'd
that they had feen and convers'd with him
alive, feveral Times, as before his Death;
and had told particular Stories of their
Converfation with him; as *firft* of all,
how he appear'd to fome of their Women
(who were admonifh'd of the Certainty of
his Refurrection by a Youth or an Angel or two, they could not tell whether,
but they were as like to Angels, which
they never faw before in their Lives, as
Youths could be) who knew him, not by
his Countenance, for *their Eyes were holden,*
but by his Talk on Scripture-Prophecy,
which was his ufual Cant before his
F   Death.

Death. And at another Time he appear'd
to his old Acquaintance, who knew him,
not by the Features of his Face, but by
an habitual Motion and Action of his
Hand in *breaking of Bread*. And at another Time he was corporally present, but
they thought, they saw a Spirit. About
eight Days after that, he appear'd among
more of his old Friends, but for all their
former Intimacy with him, some of them
doubted whether it was the *Doctor* or
not. At another Time he came to them
in *another Form* and Shape, unlike to his
pristine one, but they were sure it was *He*
by his Exposition of the Scripture. At
another Time, when they were assembled
together and the Doors were lock'd, *for
fear of the Clergy*, the *Doctor* slipt unex-
pectedly into their Company, either from
behind a Curtain, or miraculously enter'd at the Key-hole. And the last Time
he appear'd, there was one of his intimate
Friends had not known him, but by a
Sore in his Breast, which the Power of
God, in his Resurrection, did not heal:
After which, they said, he *vanish'd away,
was taken up into Heaven*, and they saw
him no more. Supposing, I say, the
French Prophets had told such like Stories
of *Doctor Emms's* Resurrection and of
his Appearances to them ; what would
your

your Priests and all other wise Men have
said to it ? Why, that it was all idle
Tales, manifest Lyes, Sham, and Imposture; and that if the *Doctor*, in Confutation of the Errors of our Priests, had
risen to Life, God would have kept him
in his Sepulchre, his full time, and have
rais'd him in the Presence of Priests,
Magistrates and People; and that he
would have walk'd afterwards publickly
in the Streets without Danger, to the
Satisfaction of all, who knew him, that
he was the same *Emms* who died and
was bury'd : *Without Danger*, I say, from
the Populace, who would have been so
far from affronting him, that they would
have almost adored him for the miraculous Favour God had done him, in his
Resurrection from the Dead ; and that
he would never have skulk'd about, and
absconded himself for *forty Days* together,
before he was pretendedly translated ;
and therefore there was nothing but notorious Deceit and Imposture in all these
Pretences.

    I need not make the Application of this
Case and Story, which your *Priests* know
how to do for me. To say here, that
there's none would be so desperate to engage in such a Fraud, as is the supposed
Case of Dr. *Emms* above, is a Mistake.

Many

Many Thousands for their Diverfion would enterprife it; and the Stories of the Apparitions of Ghofts, which are almoft all the Frauds of the Crafty to delude the Ignorant, do prove it. I my felf would be forward to concert fuch an Intrigue, if it were but to put the Banter upon the *Clergy*, to ruffle their Tempers, and fecretly to laugh at them. Nothing would deter me from it, but Fears of the Civil Magiftrate, which was not the Danger of the Difciples of *Jefus*, becaufe *Pilate*, for the Sake of Rule over the *Jews*, was a Countenancer of every Faction amongft them; and particularly (10) *Tiberius*, upon *Pilate*'s Reprefentation of the Matter, foon commanded that the Difciples of *Jefus* fhould not be molefted, nor call'd into Queftion: So the Difciples ftood to the Fraud, told the Story of *Jefus rifen* fo often, till they believed it themfelves, and drew Multitudes into the Belief of it: Which Belief muft have continued thro' all Generations to come, but for my Argument of Fraud, before urg'd and argued.

Here, Sir, before I conclude this Letter, I think it my Duty however to give

---

(10) Comminatus eft periculum Accufatoribus Chriftianorum. *Tertul. Apol. Cap.* v.

you my Opinion of the Religion, that
Jesus and his Disciples were for intro-
ducing into the World. Tho' I believe,
what I have proved, his Resurrection, to
be a Piece of Fraud, and his other Miracles to have been all Artifice; and tho'
our *Chief Priests* and ancient Nation are
justifiable in the Sentence, that was pass'd
and executed upon *Jesus*; yet I must
do him and his Disciples the Justice, to
own, that the Doctrine they taught was,
for the most Part of it, good, useful and
popular, being no other than the Law
and Religion of Nature, which, all Nations being wearied with their own Superstitions, and sick of the Burthen of their
Priests, ran apace into. Accordingly one
(11) of your ancient Fathers says, that
they *who lived according to the Law of
Nature, were true Christians.* And I must
needs say, that if Christians, in Process
of Time, had not sophisticated this primitive Religion of *Jesus*; if they had not
built their systematical Divinity upon
him, and brought strange Inventions of
Men into his Worship; if, lastly, they had
not again subjugated and entangled themselves with another and worse Yoke of
Bondage, to an intolerable and tyrannical

(11) Justin Matyr. *In Apol.* ii.

Priest-

Priesthood of the Church, the World might have enjoy'd great Happiness under *Jesus*'s Religion, even *that Happiness* which is now only to be expected upon a Disproof of his miraculous Resurrection, that has been the Foundation of a most confused Superstructure of wild Doctrines and Opinions: Or more truely speaking, *That Happiness* of the State of Nature, Religion and Liberty, which may be look'd for upon the coming of our *Messiah*, the allegorical Accomplisher of the Law and the Prophets; whose Advent, upon the Tradition of our *Cabalists*, will be towards the latter End of the *Sixth* grand Age of the Creation, to remove from our Faces and our Hearts the Veil of the Letter; and in the mean while I adhere to the umbratical Rites, Ceremonies and way of Worship, derived from our Forefathers.

Thus, Sir, have I finish'd my *Letter* on *Jesus*'s Resurrection; and whether I have not said enough to justify our *Jewish* Disbelief of that Miracle, let your *Chief Priests* judge. I don't expect my Argument against it will be convincing of any of your Preachers. They have a potent Reason for their Faith, which we *Jews* can't come at; or I don't know but we might believe with them.

I trust

I truſt you'll meet with no Moleſtation for the Publication of this *Letter*;
neither do I think, it was any thing of
mine, inſerted in your Diſcourſes, that
at any time brought Trouble on you.
It was your own Imprudence to rave,
as you do, againſt *Eccleſiaſticks*. What
need had you to talk of the Miſchiefs
and Inconveniences of an Hireling Prieſthood? What Occaſion had you to call
them Eccleſiaſtical Vermin, and to ſpeak
of the Happineſs of Mankind upon their
Extinction? Theſe things are very pro-
voking. And here's the true Source, in
my Opinion, of all your Troubles!

Tho' I have here ſhewn, that *Chriſt is
not riſen*, yet I have more Wit than to
make the Inference of St. *Paul*, that *their
Preaching is vain*. Their Oratory is
ſtill uſeful, if it be but to tickle the Ears
and amuſe the Underſtandings of the People about Doctrines they underſtand not,
whether true or falſe. And ſuch an
Order of Men, as are your Prieſthood, are,
by their Habit of long Robes, an Orna-
ment to Society; and it is an Honour to
the Country to have them well fed and
clad. Had I Room for it, I could write a
curious *Encomium* in Praiſe of them, and
tell the World of what Uſe and Advantage they have been, in all Ages. O
what

what Wars and Perfecutions might have
been rais'd in the World, but for their
pacifick Tempers! How would Sin and
Immorality have broke in upon Mankind, like a Deluge, but for the Goodnefs
of their Lives, and the Excellency of their
Precepts! How has the Increafe and Multitude of their warm Sermons been the
Ruin of *Satan*'s hot and divided Kingdom
of Darknefs and Error! It's owing to
their Pains and Labours, that every Age,
for many paft, has been improving in Virtue, till the prefent, which for Piety and
good Morals is that perfection of Time,
which is not to be meliorated but by the
Reftitution of the golden Age.

So could I enlarge in Praife of your
Clergy ; and fo fhould you have done ;
and then you might have difputed, as
you do, againft any Doctrines, Miracles
and Articles of Faith, without Moleftation. Try, if you can't correct that fundamental Error, you have commited.
Affert ftill, if you can, with Dr. *Rogers*,
the Neceffity of an eftablifh'd Priefthood,
well paid, for the Service of the *King* and
the Country, under all Changes of Religion ; which may be a Means to retrieve
their Favour, and will beget in me a
better Opinion of your Prudence, than at
present

prefent is entertain'd by your *Affured Friend* N. N.

So ends the Letter of my Friend, the *Jewish Rabbi*, in which, to my Comfort, he has conform'd himfelf to the Rules of *Sedateneſs*, *Decency* and *Sobriety* of Argument, prefcrib'd by the two great *Bifhops* of *London* and St. *David*'s. If the Weight and Solidity of his Argument don't grieve the *Clergy*, I am in no Pain for the Levity and Ludicroufneſs of it. And whether the Weight and Nature of his Argument againſt *Jefus*'s Refurrection will at all ſtartle and ſurprize them, I know not; but I profeſs for my felf, that I might have ſtudy'd long enough for ſuch an Argument againſt it, as this *Rabbi*, with his great grey Beard, has prefently hit of. He told me beforehand, that his Thoughts on *Jefus*'s Refurrection fhould be out of the common Road of thinking; and I muſt needs fay, he has been as good as his Word, or no Man ever kept his Promife.

There are two Things very remarkable in his Argument: The *one* is, the Ufe and Defign of fealing the Stone of *Jefus*'s Sepulchre, which he lays great Streſs on, to the Proof of Fraud in his Refurrection; and the *other* is, his Application of thefe Words, *the laſt Error* (or

G as

as he reads Deceit or Impoſture) *will be worſe than the firſt* or former, in which he makes the *Chief Prieſts* in their Speech to *Pilate*, to refer to *Lazarus*'s Reſurrection as the former known Impoſture. If his Application be juſt and true, the Conſequence is, that the Reſurrections of *Jeſus* and *Lazarus* are both Impoſtures. It grieves me to the Heart to think of this Conſequence, which our *Divines* are to ſee to, and evade, if they can. No ſooner did I read his Application of the foreſaid Words, but I run to our *Commentators* for another and better Expoſition of them: But alas! to my Sorrow, they made nothing of them, but a ſort of a *proverbial Expreſſion*, which the *Chief Prieſts* muſt have ſpoil'd and knock'd out of Joint. Being then under great Trouble for the Truth of Chriſtianity, and the Certainty of theſe two grand Miracles, I refer the Matter to our Learned *Clergy*, deſiring them to be as ſpeedy as they can in another and more proper Interpretation of the foreſaid Words, or *Jews* and *Infidels* will run away with them in the *Rabbi*'s Senſe, to the Confutation of our holy Religion.

I conſider'd lately, that *Eaſter* drew nigh, when it was uſual for our *Divines*

in

in their Pulpits, to infift on the Proof of *Jefus*'s Refurrection ; and therefore I haften'd the Publication of this *Difcourfe*, that they might have thefe two peculiar Texts, *viz.* of *fealing the Stone* of the Sepulchre, and of *the laft Error* or Impofture *will be worfe than the firft*, to treat on. He that produces a Sermon or Sermons, wrefting the forefaid Texts out of the Hands of my *Rabbi*, and puting another Senfe on them, to the Credit of *Jefus*'s and *Lazarus*'s Refurrection,

Erit mihi magnus Apollo,

and by my Confent fhall be the next *Arch-Bifhop* of *Canterbury*.

But my Heart aches a little for our *Divines*, and I almoft defpair of their clean Solutions of the forefaid two Difficulties. What muft they do then ? Why, they muft give up their *Religion* as well as their *Church*, or go along with me to the Fathers for their myftical Interpretation of the whole Story of *Jefus*'s Refurrection.

That the Fathers, without queftioning their Belief of *Jefus*'s corporal Refurrection, univerfally interpreted the Story and every Part of it myftically, is

moft

moſt certain. St. *Hilary* (12) enumerates many Particulars of the Story, and intimates what they are typical and figurative of, as any one may ſee by the Citation referr'd to, which I have not Room to tranſlate and illuſtrate.

St. *Auguſtin* (13) ſays, that *Jeſus*'s Reſurrection from the Dead at that time, was

(12) Quod autem a Joſeph, rogato Pilato ut Corpus redderet, & ſindone involvitur, & in Monumento novo in Petra exciſa reponitur, & Saxum Oſtio Monumenti advolvitur : Quanquam ſit Ordo Geſtorum, & ſepeliri eum erat neceſſe, qui reſurrecturus erat a mortuis, tamen non ſine Rerum aliquarum Momento expreſſa ſunt ſingula. Joſeph Apoſtolorum habet ſpeciem : & idcirco quanquam in duodecem numero Apoſtolorum non fuerit, Diſcipulus Domini nuncupatur. Hic munda ſindone corpus involvit ; & quidem in hoc eodem linteo reperimus de cœlo ad Petrum univerſorum Animantium genera ſummiſſa. Ex quo forte non ſuperflue intelligitur ſub lintei hujus nomine conſepeliri Chriſto Eccleſiam : quia tum in eo, ut in Confuſione Eccleſiæ mundorum atque immundorum Animalium fuerit congeſta diverſitas. Domini igitur Corpus tanquam per Apoſtolorum doctrinam in vacuam & novam requiem Lapidis exciſi, *viz.* in pectus duritiæ Gentilis quodam doctrinæ opere exciſum Chriſtus infertur, rude ſcilicet & novum, & nullo antea ingreſſu timoris Dei pervium. Et quia nihil præter eum oporteat in pectora noſtra penetrare, Lapis Oſtio advolvitur : ut quia nullus antea in nos divinæ Cognitionis Auctor fuerat illatus, nullus abſque eo poſtea inferatur. Metus deinde furandi Corporis, & Sepulchri Cuſtodia atque Obſignatio, Stultitiæ atque Infidelitatis Teſtimonium eſt ; quod ſignare Sepulchrum ejus voluerint, cujus præcepto conſpexiſſent de Sepulchro mortuum ſuſcitatum. *In Loc. Matt.*

(13) Ad hoc enim Dominus hodie reſurrexit, ut Imaginem nobis futuræ Reſurrectionis oſtenderet. *In Serm.* clxviii. *Append.*

to exhibit an Image and Refemblance of his future and myftical Refurrection. And elfewhere fays (14) that it's a holy Pleaſure to confider and fearch for the things fignified by the Story of it.

That *Origen* is of the fame Opinion, no body need queftion. A Multitude of his Teftimonies might be produced to this Purpofe, but I fhall mention only one (15), wherein he afferts, that by the Sepulchre of *Jeſus* is to be underftood the *Letter* of the Scriptures, in which, as in a Rock, he is repofited.

St. *John* of *Jerufalem* (16) by the Crucifiers of *Jeſus* underftands falfe Teachers, meaning *Miniſters* of the *Letter* to be fure, becaufe he himfelf was a great Allegoriſt.

(14) Quid fingula fignificent, quærere fanctæ quidem Deliciæ funt, *In Joban. Evang. C. xx. Tract. 120.*

(15) Monumentum Chrifti eft divina Scriptura, in qua Divinitatis & Humanitatis ejus myfteria denfitate Litteræ veluti quadam muniuntur Petra. *In Diverſos Homil. 2.*

(16) Ne putes, tunc folummodo traditus eft Chriftus Principibus Sacerdotibus & Scribis. ———— Quando enim vides Scripturas Prophetarum & Evangelii & Apoftolorum traditas effe in Manus falforum Sacerdotum & Scribarum; num intelliges quia Verbum Veritatis traditum eft Principibus iniquis & Scribis? *In Mat. C. xx.*

St. *Hi-*

St. *Hilary* ſays that (17) *Barabbas* is a Type of *Antichriſt;* and by *Antichriſt*, as I have elſewhere ſhewn out of the Fathers, is meant the *Letter* of the Scriptures, which modern Commentators and Crucifiers of *Jeſus* would prefer to the Spirit. For theſe are the two, *Letter* and Spirit, the *Chriſt* and *Antichriſt*, that are contrary one to another.

St. *Jerom* (18) ſays, that by the *Vail* of the *Temple* rent at *Jeſus's* Reſurrection, is to be underſtood the opening the *Vail* of the *Letter* of the Law and the Prophets for the Manifeſtation of the divine Myſteries contain'd in them. And by the rending of the Rocks according (19) to him is to be underſtood the Apertion of the Oracles of God, that were before as hard as a Rock, till his ſpiritual Reſurrection for the Illuſtration of them. And by the Earthquake, He ſays is meant the Shaking of the

(17) Interpretatio autem Nominis Barabbæ eſt Patris Filius: Jam itaque Arcanum Infidelitatis futuræ oſtenditur, Chriſto Patris Filium præferendo, Antichriſtum ſcilicet hominem Peccari & Diaboli filium, potiuſque adhortantibus principibus ſuis eligunt, Damnationi reſervatum, quam Salutis Authorem. *In Loc. Matt.*

(18) Velum Templi ſciſſum eſt, & omnia Legis Sacramenta, quæ prius tegebantur, prodita ſunt atque ad Gentium Populum tranſierunt. *In Loc. Matt.*

(19) Petræ ſciſſæ, id eſt, univerſa Vaticinia Prophetarum. *In Epiſt. ad Hedibriam.*

(20) Hearts of Men, and preparing them, by a Dereliction of their old Errors, for the Susception of the true Knowledge of God.

As to the Time that *Jesus* was dead and bury'd, which modern *Divines* call *three Days* and *three Nights*, St. *Augustin* says (21) that according to the Scripture he was not so long dead and buried. Many, says (22) he, have put various Constructions on the Time of *Christ*'s Burial, endeavouring to make three Days of it: But we, without slighting any of their Opinions, are for a mystical Interpretation, and suppose, that by the three Days are to be understood Three Ages of the World.

The Day would fail me to collect all the Passages out of the Fathers, in Interpretation of one or other of the Parts

---

(20) Sed mihi videtur Terræ Motus & reliqua typum ferre credentium, quod pristinis Errorum vitiis derelictis, & Cordis emollita duritia, postea agnoverint Creatorem. *In Loc. Matt.*

(21) Ipsum autem triduum, non totum & plenum fuisse Scriptura Testis est. *In Libro 4to de Trinitate. Sect.* 10.

(22) De tribus diebus, multi sancti multa hinc senserint atque dixerint —— Sed nos neutram eorum vacantes sententiam; melius tamen, si placet in his spiritualem requiramus Intellectum, tres Dies tria Tempora Sæculi ponentes. *In Serm. de Symbolo.*

of

of the Story of *Jesus*'s Refurrection, but what I have here faid in a few Citations, is enough to fhow, that they look'd upon the whole Story, as emblematical of his fpiritual Refurrection out of the *Grave* of the *Letter* of the Scriptures, in which he has been buried about *three Days* and *three Nights*, according to that myftical Interpretation of prophetical Numbers which I have learn'd of them.

And thus have I done with the Miracle of *Jesus*'s Refurrection, which, by the Help of my Friend the Jewifh *Rabbi*, I have fhewn, according to the Letter, to confift of the greateft Incredibilities. And with this I conclude my *Difcourfes* on his Miracles, intending to treat on no more of them, uhlefs I am invited or provoked to it. I had once an Inclination to make another *Difcourfe* on *Jesus*'s miraculous Conception, and on his feeding his Thoufands, in the Wildernefs, with a few Loaves and Fifhes ; but upon a little Confideration on the Letter of thofe two Stories, I found myfelf too grave for the Work ; and my *Rabbi*'s Thoughts are too gay and wanton ; therefore it muft be omitted, till the *Clergy* importune me to it, and fignify their Curiofity to fee it perform'd by me.

My

My Difcourfes hereafter, if God fpare me Life and Liberty, which under his Providence I don't defpair of, to publifh another Volume, fhall treat on fome hiftorical Paffages of the New Teftament, fuch as, " On the Stories of *Jefus*'s Birth; and the Appearances of Angels to the Shepherds keeping Watch over their Flocks by Night: " The Journey and Prefents of the Wife Men to *Jefus:* " The Slaughter of the Innocents at *Bethlehem,* and of *Herod*'s Cruelty: " The Travels of *Jofeph* with the Child *Jefus* and his Mother into *Egypt:* " The Difputation of *Jefus* with the *Doctors* in the Temple, and his Elopement from his Parents: " His riding on an Afs to *Jerufalem*; and on other fuch like Paffages of his Life. For I am refolv'd to give the Letter of the Scripture no Reft, fo long as God gives me Life and Abilities to attack it. *Origen* (23) fays, that *when we difpute againft Minifters of the Letter, we muft felect fome hiftorical Parts of Scripture, which they underftand literally, and fhew that according to the Letter, they can't ftand*

(23) Cum difputamus adverfus eos, & cum conquirimus advicem, tunc quærimus locum Dogmatis illius in litera Legis Hiftoriæ, & oftenditur fecundum Hiftoriam ftare non poffe. *In Pfal.* xxxvi.

H   *their*

their Ground, but imply Abfurdities and Nonfenfe. And how then is fuch a Work to be perform'd to beſt Advantage? Is it to be done in a grave, ſedate, and ſerious Manner? No, I think Ridicule ſhould here take Place of ſober Reaſoning, as the more proper and effectual Means to cure Men of their fooliſh Faith and abſurd Notions. As no wiſe Man hardly ever reprehends a Blunderbuſs for his Bull, any other way, than by laughing at him ; ſo the Aſſerters of nonſenſical Notions in Theology ſhould, if poſſible, be ſatirized and jeſted upon, or they'll never be put out of Countenance for, nor deſert their abſurd Doctrines. And there never was a polemical Divine, that, if he had an Opportunity and Advantage over the Weakneſs of his Adverſary, did not take ſuch a ludicrous and merry Courſe with him.

But on ſuch hiſtorical Paſſages of the Goſpel as before mention'd, do I truſt to publiſh another Volume of *Diſcourſes*, like to theſe on *Jeſus's* Miracles; and at preſent paſs to my third general Head, at firſt propoſed to be ſpoken to, and that is,

III. To conſider what *Jeſus* means, when he appeals to his Works and Miracles,

as

as to a Testimony and Witness of his Authority; and to show that he did not properly and ultimately refer to these done in the *Flesh*, but to those mystical ones he would do in the *Spirit*, of which those done in the Flesh are but mere Types and Shadows.

And on this Head I shall be short, there being no Occasion of many Words on it. The *Bishop* of *London* (24) has collected many Sayings of *Jesus*, wherein he seems to appeal to the Works he then did and had done in Flesh, as to a Witness of him. But why might not *Jesus* then prophesy, and mean the spiritual Works which *He-in-us* would do? It is the known Way of the Prophets to speak of Things to come, as if they were already past, because such Prophecies are not to be understood, till their Accomplishment: Even so did *Jesus* prophesy, when he appeal'd to his Works, as I could prove from the Nature and Manner of his Expressions, but that the Argument would be dry and tedious: And therefore I refer the Matter entirely to the Fathers, who asserted that *Jesus* prophesied in his *Miracles* as well as in his *Parables*, and that the Works he then did in the Flesh were but Types of his mysterious Operati-

(24) *Pastoral Letter*, P. 25.

ons,

ons, that would be the Demonſtration of his Authority and Meſſiahſhip. Hence it is that *Origen* (25) ſays that *Jeſus*'s firſt coming was but a Type and Shadow of his ſpiritual Advent ; and that his (26) true Miracles, by which his Authority is to be proved, are ſpiritual : Hence it is that St. *Hilary* repeatedly ſays (27) that *Jeſus*'s Works were ſignificative and predictive of myſterious Operations, which we were eſpecially to look to. And Hence it is that all the other Fathers interpreted the Miracles of *Jeſus* in a myſtical and allegorical Senſe.

The Queſtion then is, to what Miracles did *Jeſus* truly and properly appeal, in the Opinion of the Fathers, for his Authority and Meſſiahſhip ? Was it to the Typical or Antitypal Works ? was it to the *Shadow* or to the *Subſtance* of his Operations ?

(25) Adventus quidem Chriſti unus in Humilitate completus eſt, alius vero ſperatur in Gloria. Et hic primus Adventus in Carne, myſtico quodam Sermone in Scripturis Sanctis Umbra ejus appellatur. *In Jeſu Nave Homil.* viii.

(26) Vera Chriſti Miracula & Sanatio Infirmorum eſt ſpiritualis. *In Matt. C.* xxv.

(27) Hæc licet in præſens geſta ſunt, quid tamen in futurum ſignificent contuendum eſt. *In Matt. C.* x. *S.* 1. Chriſti Geſta aliud portendunt. *C.* xii. *S.* 1. Peragunt formam futuri geſta præſentia. *C.* xxi.

To

To his fubftantial Operations, to be fure,
which are and will be his fpiritual ones
upon the Soul, that are greater than thofe
once done on Mens Bodies, and which
will be a proper Proof of his divine Power.
And to declare my Opinion freely, I am
only for fuch a fpiritual *Meffiah*, who will
cure the *Errors* call'd the Difeafes of Mankind, which *Jefus* of *Nazareth* has not
as yet done.

But not to difpute this Point with *Bifhop Gibfon*, I will leave him in the Enjoyment of his Opinion of his literal *Meffiah*,
and miraculous Operator on Mens Bodies;
if he'll but indulge me in the Belief of my
fpiritual *Meffiah* to come for the healing of
modern Diftempers call'd the Sins and Errors of Mankind. And in the mean time
let us draw the Comparifon between his
literal and my *fpiritual* Jefus; and let the
World judge, to whom the Preference is
to be given for Power and Authority.

Bifhop *Gibfon* is for *Jefus* of *Nazareth's* Meffiahfhip, becaufe he cured the
bodily Blindnefs of many miraculoufly;
And a good Work it was: But I am for
the Meffiahfhip of a fpiritual *Jefus* to
come, who will open the *blind Eyes* of
our Underftandings to difcern Truth from
Error, which will be a moft glorious
Opera-

Operation, that his *Jesus* of *Nazareth* has not as yet done.

Bishop *Gibson* is for *Jesus*'s Messiahship, who once cured *bodily Deafness* in many, which was indeed well done of him : But I am for the Messiahship of a spiritual *Jesus* to come, to heal the *Deafness* of our Souls, or their *Dulness* in Apprehension of sublime Mysteries, which will be a divine Work, that his *Jesus* has not as yet done.

Bishop *Gibson* is for *Jesus*'s Messiahship, because he cured Mens bodily *Lameness*, for which I do praise him : But I am for a spiritual *Jesus*'s Messiahship, who will heal Mankind of their *Halting* between two and more Opinions; a more blessed Work, that *Jesus* of *Nazareth* has not as yet done for us!

And so, comparing all other Diseases of Body and Soul together, I am for the *Jesus*, who will heal the Diseases of the Soul; and have a much less Regard for *Bishop Gibson*'s *Jesus*, who cured the Diseases of a few Mens Bodies; but for all that, am not angry with the *Bishop* for his high Veneration of his *Jesus*, neither would I by any Means have him prosecuted and punish'd for not being of the same Mind with me.

But,

But, because the *Bishop* suspects me of Infidelity, in that I have ludicrously treated some of the Miracles of his *Jesus*, which by the by he has not vindicated from the Absurdities and Incredibilities I charged them with; I will humour the *Bishop*, and supposing *Jesus* wrought literally those Miracles which are allegorically interpreted by me, will in those very Miracles compare his *literal* and my *spiritual* Jesus together; and appeal to all Men of Consideration, which is the most worthy of the Title and Honour of the true *Messiah*.

Bishop *Gibson* is for his *Jesus*'s Messiahship, who miraculously drove the *Buyers* and *Sellers* out of the Temple, just as if a Man, was God to invest him with Power, should furiously drive the *Butchers* and *Grasiers* with their Cattle, to the Confusion of their several Properties, out of *Smithfield*: A notable Miracle That! But I am for the spiritual *Jesus*'s Messiahship, who according to the Form of that typical Story, will at his Coming expel Ecclesiastical Merchants out of his Church, who make Merchandise of the Gospel, selling their *Bulls* and *Beasts*, and *Fatlings* of the Letter: A most glorious and beneficial Work to Mankind will this be!

be! And to prepare Mens Souls for the Susception of such a spiritual *Jesus*, I intend to publish a *Discourse* of the Mischiefs and Inconveniencies of an *Hireling Priesthood*, wherein it shall be proved, that Mankind can't be either good, wise or happy under the Kingdom of this *Messiah* to come, without an Abolition and Extirpation of them.

Bishop *Gibson* is for the Messiahship of his *Jesus*, who *cast the Devils out of the Madmen, and permitted them to enter into the Herd of Swine*, that *ran violently down a Precipice, and were choak'd in the Sea*: How great a Miracle it was thus to cure the Madmen, the *Bishop* may know best, being perhaps better acquainted with the Devil than I am; but was it not for Pity to the *Swineherds*, for their Losses, I could even now laugh at the Thoughts of the Hoggs running and tumbling down-hill, as if the *Devil* drove them: But leaving the Bishop *calmly, decently*, and *seriously* to admire the Wisdom and Justice of his *Jesus* in that Act, I am for the spiritual *Jesus*, who, according to the typical Form of that Story, exorcis'd the furious and diabolical Tempers out of the *Jews* and *Gentiles* of old, whom no Chains of Reason could hold from doing Violence to the Christians,

till

till they were converted; and tho' He permitted the like perfecuting and diabolical
Spirits to enter into Ecclefiaftical Swine;
yet will they be precipitated into the *Sea*
of the Knowledge of God, wherein they
will be abforpt with divine Vifions and
Contemplations. O moft glorious Work!
that befpeaks the Wifdom, Power and
Goodnefs of our fpiritual *Jefus*, from the
Beginning to the End of it.

Bifhop *Gibfon* admires his *Jefus*, for
his Transfiguration on Mount *Tabor*, tho'
neither He nor any Body elfe can tell,
wherein lay the Miracle, nor into what
various Figures and Shapes *Jefus* was
transform'd: But I am for the fpiritual
Jefus, whofe glorious Transfiguration, after *fix* grand Days of the Creation, will
be confpicuous, when with the Eyes of
our Underftanding we fhall behold him
metamorphofed into the Forms of all the
Types of him under the Law. I am now
ravifh'd with the intellectual View of
this Transfiguration; and believe, was I
to fet about it, I could give others (except
the Bifhop) an Idea and Conception of
it to their Aftonifhment at the Glory of
Jefus in it.

Bifhop *Gibfon* is for the Mefliahfhip of
Jefus of *Nazareth*, becaufe he cured a
Woman of an Iffue of Blood, after fhe had
I   fpent

spent all she had upon Physicians to no purpose, which might be, or might not be a Miracle, for any thing he can argue upon it: But I am for the spiritual *Jesus*'s Messiahship, who, at his Coming, will, acording to that typical Story, cure the *Woman* of the Church of her *Issue of Blood*, that is shed in Persecution and War, which her Ecclesiastical Physicians of the *Clergy* have not been able to stop, tho' they have receiv'd large Fees and Stipends of the Church to that Purpose. Will not this be a desirable and beneficial Work to all Nations? And who knows not, (excepting the *Bishop*) that it is of the Office of the true Messiah, to give *abundance of Peace* to Mankind, to *make the Lion to lye down with the Lamb*; and to induce Men to *break their Swords into Plough-shares*, and *their Spears into Pruning-hooks*; and to *make Wars to cease* in all the World. Which Prophecies are so far from being fulfill'd by *Jesus* of *Nazareth*, that there has been nothing but Wrangling and Jangling, and Scolding and Fighting about him ever since. I wonder the Want of the Accomplishment of the foresaid Prophecies has not long before now occasion'd the Rejection of *Jesus*'s Messiahship, or of the Authority of the Prophets.

Bishop

Bishop *Gibson* is for his *Jesus*'s being the Messiah, because he cured an old *Woman* of a *Spirit* of, no body knows what, *Infirmity*; consequently little or nothing is to be said for the Greatness of that Miracle. But I am for the spiritual *Jesus*'s Messiahship, who, according to the Figure of that literal Story, is to heal the *Woman* of the Church of her *Infirmity of the Spirit* of Prophecy, which *Jesus* of *Nazareth* has not done for her, or there would not be so many Disputes about Prophecies and their Interpretations, so far, as there is hardly one Prophecy that Christians are agreed about the Sense of. It is the grand Characteristick of the true *Messiah*, that he's to restore Prophecy and the Way of Interpretation of the Prophets, upon the allegorical Scheme too. I speak this, not only upon the Authority of the Prophets themselves, but upon an almost infinite Number of Testimonies of ancient *Jews* and *Fathers*; accordingly I expect the Advent of a spiritual Messiah, who alone can do it, to heal the Church of her present *Infirmity*, and to restore the Art and Gift of Prophecy.

Bishop *Gibson* is an Admirer of *Jesus* of *Nazareth*, because he told a poor Whore of *Samaria*, her Fortune of *having had five Husbands*, and being then an

I 2   Adul-

Adulteress with another Man; which, according to the Letter, is such a poor sort of a Miracle, that I can hardly think of it without blushing: But I am an Adorer beforehand of the spiritual *Jesus* who, according to that Type, will out of the Law and the Prophets, allegorically interpreted, tell the present heretical and adulterous Woman of the Church *all that she has done*, and how she has been wedded to the sensible Things of the *five* Books of *Moses*, and is now an Adulteress with the *Anti-Christ* of the Letter. Such an Information of the Church will be a most stupendous and miraculous Work, and a Demonstration of our *Jesus's* Messiahship beyond Contradiction, in as much as it will be agreeable to the Opinion, that all Antiquity entertain'd of the true *Messiah*, *viz* that he was to let us into the Sight, Knowledge and Understanding of the Wisdom and Beauty of Providence thro' all Ages of the World.

Bishop *Gibson* admires *Jesus* of *Nazareth* for *his cursing the Figtree*; *for not bearing Fruit out of Season*: Shame on that Miracle, according to the Letter, and on all Admirers of it! But I am for the spiritual *Jesus*, who, at his coming to the Figtree of his Church, will make its present unfruitful State to *wither away*, and

cause

cause it to produce the Fruits of the Spirit, and allegorical Interpretations of the Scriptures, that are compared to sweet and ripe Figs. For such his Advent to this miraculous and beneficial Purpose I daily pray and say too, Blessed are all those who love his Appearance!

After this Fashion could I go thro' the other Miracles, I have treated on in these *Discourses*; and upon the Comparison set plainly before the Eyes of my *Readers* the Difference between the *literal* Miracles of Bishop *Gibson*'s *carnal* Jesus and the *allegorical* ones of my *spiritual* Jesus, as to Stupendousness, Use and Excellency: But what I have here done in the seven Instances above, is enough to induce us to believe, with the Fathers, that *Jesus*'s first Coming in the *Flesh* was but a Type and Shadow of his second Advent in the *Spirit*; and that *Jesus* of old, when he appeal'd to his Works then done, as to a Witness of his Authority, did only prophesy, and refer ultimately to his mystical Operations, that are alone the Proof of his Godlike and divine Power. Bishop *Gibson* says (28) of me, that *pretending to raise the Actions and Miracles of our Saviour to a more exalted and spiritual Meaning, I*

_____

(28) *Pastoral Letter*, P. 3.

have

have labour'd to take away the Reality of them, and by that to destroy one of the principal Evidences of Christianity. But I presume now, he'll be sensible of the Rashness and Incogitancy of that Accusation. If he be not, I shall say of him, in Case he write any more for *Jesus's literal* Miracles in Opposition to his *allegorical* ones, that he's like the Dog in the Fable (the Bishop will excuse the Coarseness of the Comparison) that let go the *Substance* of his Mutton, and catch'd at the Shadow, and so, like a foolish *Cur* as he was, lost both.

And thus have I done with the *Three* general Heads at first proposed to be handled in these *Discourses.* Now whether I am, upon the whole, an *Infidel,* or *Believer* of Christianity, the World is to judge. I'll make no more solemn Declarations of my Belief of it, much less at this Juncture of Time, when I am under Prosecution for Infidelity; because it would be a sneaking, tame, and cowardly Act in me, and such an Argument of that Meanness of Spirit, as I abhor and detest. My *Works* shall speak for me, in which, being conscious of the Innocency of my Intentions, and of the Usefulness of my Design, I mean to proceed; not doubting but some of our *Clergy,* upon

two

two or three more *Discourses* againft the Letter of the *New Teftament*, will find me out, what I am, and whether I am not a true Profeffor of the Religion of the fpiritual and holy *Jefus*.

In the mean Time I'll not compound the Difference depending between Bifhop *Gibfon* and my felf, upon any other Terms, than his making me ample Satisfaction for the Injuries done to my Reputation and low Fortunes. Tho' he may thirft after my Life, or at leaft, my Liberty; yet under the Providence of God I fear not the Lofs of either. God be prais'd, this Kingdom is blefs'd with fuch a Civil Adminiftration for Wifdom, Juftice and Mercy, as no Nation of the World can equal. Our Magiftrates are all Philofophers, Lovers of Truth, and of an Enquiry into it; and fo tender of the religious as well as of the civil Rights of the Subject, that I have nothing to dread from them.

There is fomewhat *popular* indeed, tho' nothing true nor rational, in the Clamour and Accufations of the *Clergy* againft me. Bifhop *Gibfon* would infinuate (29) that my *Difcourfes* on *Miracles* ftrike *at the Foundation of civil Society*; but by an un-

(29) *Paftoral Letter*, P. 35.

natural

natural Confequence of his own making.
I confefs, it is an heinous Crime to write
any Thing that tends to the Subverfion or
Prejudice of the civil Society : But how
will the *Bifhop* make me guilty of it? If
the *Clergy* will not be Difturbers of the
Peace of the Publick upon my *Difcourfes*;
it's certain, that the Quiet of the World,
which I wifh and aim at, will be inviola-
bly kept and preferv'd for all me. My Followers indeed, when I walk the Streets of
this *City*, are *numerous*; and if any of them
fhould break the Peace, what ferves my
Lord Mayor's Power for, but to chaftife
them for it? As for my felf and my Adherents at home, which, as yet, are *without Number*, we are all *Quietifts* and fhould
act againft our Confciences and Religion,
if we fhould injure any Man in his Perfon
and Property. But I fmile to fee a *Clergyman* all on a fudden, like the *Bifhop*, fo
tender of the Welfare of the Publick, when
Ecclefiafticks, in all Ages paft, have been
the *Bane* of Society and the *Peft* of Mankind, as appears from the Wars and Perfecution they have rais'd in the World ; and
from that Strife, Variance and Difcords,
they have occafion'd in Cities and Families.
And with Submiffion to the *Bifhop*, who
I hope will not be angry for my faying
it, I am fure, the *Clergy* at this Juncture,

are

are like an *high-mettal'd blind Horse*, that
were they not ridden by the Civil Authority with a ſtrait Rein, would be oppreſſing
and trampling upon all, that ſtood in the
Way of their Intereſts, to the Diſturbance
of *Civil Society*.

Profaneneſs too does the *Biſhop* charge
me with. But why ſo? Becauſe I ridicule
the Nonſenſe and Abſurdities of *Jeſus's*
Miracles according to the Letter, which
he venerates. Very fine indeed! The
Biſhop would worſhip the *Head* of an *Aſs*,
and a wiſer Man than himſelf, without
the Charge of Prophaneneſs, muſt not
laugh at his fooliſh Superſtition.

And *Blaſphemy* laſtly does the *Biſhop*
accuſe me of: And this is a ſad *Bugbear*
Word, that has frightned Abundance of
People into dreadful Apprehenſions of my
Guilt, even to the Abhorrence of me.
But the *Biſhop* ſhould firſt have defined,
what is meant by *Blaſphemy*, and have prov-
ed me guilty of it, before he had made his
Exclamations: Or the *Turks* may ſay that
a Jeſt upon their *Alcoran*, in which there
are no Contradictions, is as much a *Blaſ-*
phemy, as any Ludicrouſneſs upon the
Goſpels, which are full of Inconſiſtencies.
That there is ſuch a Sin or Error, call'd
Blaſphemy, according to the Scriptures, is
certain: But our *Divines* are undetermined

K   about

about the Nature of it. I intend to take my Opportunity to treat on the Sin of Blasphemy, and to prove, *Ministers* of the *Letter* are the only Persons that can be guilty of it. *Ministers* of the *Letter*, upon the Authority of the Fathers, are the Worshippers of the *Apocalyptical Beast*; and anti-allegorical Expositions are that *Blasphemy*, St. *John* writes of, which the *Beast* and his Worshippers will open their Mouths in, against the most High. This shall be proved as clear as the Light. But when I do it, I would not have any think, it is with an Intention to bring the Bishops of *London*, *Litchfield*, and St. *David's*, or any other *Divines*, under Profecution for that heinous Sin : No, my God is omnipotent, omniscient and omnipresent; and knows how and when to reckon with such Blasphemers, without calling upon the Civil Magistrate to do it for him. Should I importune the Civil Authority to execute Vengeance upon them, I should make a foolish *Calf* or a Senseless *Idol* of my God, that was unable, or knew not how, nor when to vindicate his own Cause. Surely the *Bishop* of *London*, upon his Profecution of me for *Blasphemy*, must think his God now *asleep* or *gone a Journey* from Home; or he would not be for taking God's own
Work

Work out of his Hands, and commiting
it to the Care of the Civil Magiſtrates.

The *Biſhop* moreover ſhould conſider,
that the Words *prophane* and *blaſphemous*
are of no Uſe and Signification among
Philoſophers, who in Diſputation never
caſt them at each other, however they
may differ in Opinion. Philoſophers are
all ſuppoſed to be ſuch profound Vene-
rators of the Deity, as they would not
be guilty of *Prophaneneſs* and *Blaſphemy*
for the whole World. If any of our
School of *Free-Thinkers* ſhould ſay of his
Opponent that he's *prophane* and *blaſphe-*
mous, he would be reprimanded for want
of Wit, Temper and good Manners ; and
be told that he's like a *Billingſgate Scold*,
who has Recourſe to impertinent bad Language, when her Reaſon fails her for better Rhetorick.

But it may be, for ought I know, the
Biſhop has ſome Deſign in his Accuſations againſt me for *Profaneneſs* and *Blaſ-*
phemy; but I hope it is a better than to
prejudice the Civil Magiſtrate, or to incenſe the Populace.

According to the Fathers I am ſo far
from being a Blaſphemer, that they ſay,
Chriſt upon the literal Interpretation of
his Miracles is metamorphoſed into the
Falſe-Chriſt, call'd *Anti-Chriſt*. Whether
K 2   there

there is any Truth in this their Opinion I can't be pofitive, till the Experiment is fully made. But if our *Clergy* will keep their Temper, and grant me a clear Stage of Battle, I'll try it out; and fee whether I can't, by the Club of Reafon and primitive Authority, give their *Anti-Chrift* a fatal Blow: Who knows but I may give Peace to the Church, and reconcile all Parties by it?

However this may be; I am fure, no Man can wifh for a greater Advantage over his Enemy, than I have over the *Bifhop* in this Controverfy: But he fhall find me a generous Adverfary, who will make no worfe Ufe of my Advantage over him than now and then to put him in Mind of his *Paftoral Letter*, and of the Profecution; unlefs I fhould be tempted, ere long, to publifh my *Moderatorial* Letter, like his *Paftoral* one, to the People of *London* and *Weftminfter*, with *Ten* wholefome Rules in it, not only to caution them againft falfe Prophets and falfe Teachers, without forgetting the *Bifhop* of the *Diocefe*, but to direct them to the Ecclefiaftical Fountain of the growing Sins, Errors and Infidelity of the Age, which the *Clergy* know I am of Ability to lay open.

When

When I began the Publication of these *Discourses*, I own, I laid a *Trap* for some considerable *Clergyman*; but little imagined, the great *Bishop* of *London* would be caught in it. But now I have taken hold of him, I'll not release him out of the Controversy, till he has sorely repented of his Ignorance or Malice in calling me a *Writer, in Favour of Infidelity*.

So much at present for the Bishop of *London*. I have been the quicker of late in the printing of *this*, because I am given to understand, the *Bishop* of St. *David*'s stays for it, intending to make but one Work of it, and answer all *six Discourses* together. I hope my *Rabbi*'s Letter here will be thought by him, a good Payment for his Patience. And now I shall be in Expectation of his Mountainous Production, and where I shall hide myself from the terrible Strokes of his Pen, I have not as yet consider'd.

I am not a little pleas'd to see a *Couple* of Dissenting Preachers, *viz.* Dr. *Harris* and Mr. *Atkinson*, lifted into the Controversy against me. If they had kept their Necks out of the Collar, they might have dissembled and pretended, that, upon the Conclusion of the Battle, when it would have appear'd, I am a real Contender for

Primi-

Primitive Chriſtianity, they had a better Underſtanding of the Fathers, and a clearer View of my Deſign, than to ſuſpect me of Blaſphemy and Infidelity : But now they are engag'd with equal Spite, Ignorance and Defamations againſt me, they muſt take their Share of the Fate and Shame, with the *Clergy*, upon the Concluſion of the Controverſy.

There's no Body can think it worth my while to beſtow a Six-penny *Pamphlet* upon either of theſe *Gentlemen*, but for all that, they ſhall not be altogether ſlighted and neglected by me. I have made a Collection of their Rhetorical Flowers, which occaſionally ſhall be preſented the Publick, to the Admiration of their Wit, Reaſon, Learning and Eloquence. And at preſent only take Notice, that they are *both* for the Perſecution of me ; but not ſo much for my Opinions, as the Indecency, Irreverence, and Immorality of my Stile ; forſooth ! which is juſt ſuch a Diſtinction, as may be eaſily ſtretch'd to the Juſtification of the Perſecution of all Authors, whom the Prieſthood in Power ſhall not like. Mr. *Atkinſon's* Argument for the Perſecution of me, is much the ſame with that, which *John Calvin* uſed for the Perſecution of that great Philoſopher *Servetus* ; the Injuſtice and Cruelty of whoſe whofe Death and Sufferings is a greater Reproach to the Name of *Calvin*, than the Martyrdom of any *Proteſtant* can be to the Memory of any Popiſh Prelate.

To conclude, what I have written, in theſe *Six Diſcourſes*, is with a View to the Glory of God, the Advancement of Truth, the Happineſs of Mankind, the Demolition of *Babylon*, the Edification of *Jeruſalem*, and the Demonſtration of the Meſſiahſhip of our Spiritual *Jeſus*, to whom be Glory for ever. *Amen.*

F I N I S.

BOOKS written by Mr. **WOOLSTON**, *and Sold by him next* Door *below the* Star *in* Aldermanbury, *and by the Book-sellers of* London *and* Weftminfter.

I. **THE** Old Apology reviv'd, &c.

II. Differtatio de Pontii Pilati Epiftola ad Tiberium circa Res Jefu Chrifti geftas.

III. Origenis Adamantii Epiftolæ duæ circa Fidem verè orthodoxam & Scripturarum Interpretationem.

IV. The exact Fitnefs of the Time of Chrift's Advent demonftrated by Reafon againft the Objections of the old Gentiles, and modern Unbelievers.

V. Four Free-Gifts to the Clergy, or Challenges to a Difputation on this Queftion, Whether the Hireling Priefts of this Age, who are all Minifters of the Letter, be not Worfhippers of the Apocalyptical Beaft, and Minifters of Antichrift?

VI. An Anfwer to the faid Four Free Gifts.

VII. Two Letters to Dr. *Bennet* on this Queftion, Whether the People call'd *Quakers* do not the neareft of any other Sect in Religion, refemble the Primitive Chriftians, in Principle and Practice?

VIII. An Anfwer to the faid two Letters.

IX. The Moderator between an Infidel and an Apoftate: Or the Controverfy between the *Grounds* and his Ecclefiaftical Opponents, fet in a clear Light, &c.

X. Two Supplements to the Moderator, &c.

XI. A Defence of the Miracle of the *Thundering Legion*, againft a Differtation of *Walter Moyle*, Efq;

XII. Six Difcourfes on the Miracles of our Saviour.

XIII. His Defence of thofe Difcourfes, againft the Bifhops of St. *David's* and *London*.

Mr. *WOOLSTON*'s

DEFENCE

OF HIS

DISCOURSES, &c.

Mr. *Woolston*'s Defence

OF HIS

DISCOURSES

ON THE

MIRACLES

OF OUR

SAVIOUR,

Againſt the *Biſhops* of St. DAVID's and LONDON, and his other *Adverſaries.*

PART I.

Res Religionis non Verberibus ſed Verbis eſt peragenda.
Lactant.

London: Printed for the Author, and Sold by him, next Door to the *Star* in *Aldermanbury,* and by the Bookſellers of *London* and *Weſtminſter,* 1729.

[Price *One Shilling.*]

TO THE

QUEEN.

Madam,

*OT long since the Bishop of St. David's presented to Your Majesty his Vindication; as I would have done this my* Defence, *if I had known how to get Access to Your Royal Presence.*

Your Majesty will perceive, that here's a sad War broke out between

A 2   *tween*

The DEDICATION.

tween the Bifhop *and my felf, about*
Miracles; *which, in all probability,*
will coft a large Effufion of Words;
and, *unlefs Your* Majefty *can accom-*
modate the Difference, will hardly
be terminated without the Slaughter
of many Notions and Arguments.

The Bifhop *is for making Your*
Majefty *the Arbitrefs of our Con-*
troverfy, which I *confent to; and he*
talks of Your fingular Qualifications
to prefide at it, which I *as certainly*
believe, as that a Bifhop *will not lye*
nor flatter.

Had I *known before of Your Ma-*
jefty's *Abilities at this Controverfy,*
I *fhould have gone near to have ap-*
plauded You for them; and the World
would readily have believed my Praifes
of You to be juft, becaufe I *had no*
Bifhoprick nor Tranflation *in View*
for them.

If

The DEDICATION.

If Your Majesty *has no extraordinary Talent at this Controversy,* I *trust, You are wiser than to think the better of Your self for the Bishop's Compliment. You'll not be vain; tho' he is fulsome.*

But the Bishop, Madam, *has done me wrong. He would insinuate, that I am disaffected to the* King's *Title and Government; which is entirely false. I Love and Honour Your whole Royal Family, and often pray for Your* Majesty *too,* without Pay, *which is more than any* Bishop *in* England *has done for You.*

And what are my Prayers for Your Majesty ? *That God may prolong Your Days to the Comfort of Your Royal Progeny, and the Joy of these Nations ; That the Felicity of Your Life may be uninterrupted by Enemies and Misfortunes ; and That*

after

The DEDICATION.

after a good old Age, when Life is no longer defirable to the happyeft Princes, You may be transferr'd to an heavenly and immortal Crown of Glory. This is the hearty and voluntary Prayer of,

Madam,

London,
September
27, 1729.

Your Majefty's

most humble,

most obedient,

and faithful Servant,

Thomas Woolfton.

A

A

DEFENCE

OF THE

DISCOURSES ON *Miracles.*

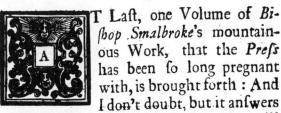 T Laſt, one Volume of *Bi-ſhop Smalbroke*'s mountain-ous Work, that the *Preſs* has been ſo long pregnant with, is brought forth : And I don't doubt, but it anſwers the Expectations of the *Clergy*, who will extol it to the Skies, and applaud it to the Populace, as an abſolute Confutation of my

B *Diſcourſes* ;

Difcourfes ; but I would advife them, if it be not too late, not to be too profufe in their Commendations of it, for fear that an Occafion fhould be given them to blufh for their want of Judgment. We have had Inftances of Books before now (and one very remarkable, in the Cafe of *Boyle* againft *Bently*) that have met with a general Approbation, till they have been fifted into, and upon Examination found empty ; and it is not impoffible, but *this* of the *Bifhop* before us, may meet with the fame Fate.

I had conceived a great Opinion of this *Bifhop*'s Learning and Abilites, and, if he had not fent (*a*) two fimple *Harbingers* before-hand, fhould have been fo apprehenfive of his Acutenefs, that nothing, but a thorough Perfuafion of the Goodnefs of my Caufe, and of my Power to defend it, could have kept me from Flight before him. But I ftand my Ground, and fhall, againft greater Adverfaries than this *Bifhop*, who has more weakly and malicioufly attack'd me, than cou'd have been expected from one of his reputed Candour and Learning ; and given me greater Advan-

---

(*p*) His Sermon before the Societies for Reformation ; and his Charge to the Clergy.

tages to insult and triumph over him, than
I could wish or desire.

Many other little *Whifflers* in Divinity
have before attack'd me with their *Squibs*
and *Squirts* from the *Press*, but I despised
them all, as unworthy of my particular
Regard and Notice, reserving my self for
Defence against this *Bishop*'s grand Assault;
when, by the by, I might have an Opportunity to animadvert on one or other
of them. Some of these *Whifflers*, like
Men of Honour, have set their Names to
their Works; others very prudently have
concealed their Names, which, upon the
best Enquiry I could make, I have not
been able to discover, or I had given them
a Rebuke for their Impudence and Slanders. It may be wonder'd, that any polemical Authors, especially when they
write on the orthodox and establish'd Side
of the Question, should conceal themselves, and that they are not tempted with
the Hopes of Reward and Applause to
make themselves known. I will say what
I think here, that it's never Modesty in
such *anonymous* Authors (for we *Scriblers*
in Divinity, whatever we may pretend,
have always a good Conceit of our selves)
but Apprehensions of a sharp Reply to
their Dishonour. And this is the true Reason, why some of my Adversaries industri-

ously

ously conceal themselves, knowing that they are guilty of wilful and malicious Lies and Calumnies, which I should chastise them for. But, as their Names are suppreft, they know, it's to no Purpose for me to expose their Malice, because no body can be put to shame for it.

The *Bishop* of St. *David's* acts here a more glorious Part : He comes not behind me, like other *Cowards*, to give me a secret Knock on the Pate, but like a couragious Champion, looks me in the Face, and admonishes me to stand upon my Guard. This is bravely done in him ! And I have no Fault to find, but that he is providing himself with *Seconds* in the Controversy, I mean the *Civil Powers*, and calling upon them to destroy me, before the Battle is well begun, and whether he gets the better of me or not. This is not fairly nor honourably done of the *Bishop*, and I have Reason to complain of it. Tho' I think my self equal, if not superior in the Dispute, to any of our *Bishops*, yet I am not a Match for the *King's* Power, neither would I lift up my Hand, or use my Pen against him for all the World. If the *Bishop* will yield to a fair Combat, and desire the Civil Authority to stand by and see fair Play between us, I will engage with him upon any Terms. But to make the

Civil

Civil Powers Parties in our Quarrel, and to befpeak them, right or wrong, to favour his Side, is intolerable, and what we fpiritual Gladiators ought to abhor and deteft.

I liked the *Bifhop*, when he propofed to the *Queen* to be *Arbitrefs* of our Controverfy. As I will not here queftion her Qualifications to judge in it, fo the firft Opportunity I have of waiting on her *Majefty*, I will join my Requefts to her to accept of the Trouble and Office. After fhe has fix'd the Terms of Difputation, and thought of a proper Reward for the *Victor*, or a Punifhment for the *Conquer'd*, then will we proceed, and either difpute the Matter from the Prefs, or fcold it out in the Queen's Prefence, as fhe fhall think it moft conducive to the Edification of herfelf, and of her Court-Ladies.

But the *Bifhop*'s Propofal here, and Compliment on the *Queen*, is but the Copy of his Countenance. He'll fubmit to no Arbitration : No, no, he's for having the Civil Powers to be immediate Executioners (without further hearing what I have to fay for my felf) of his Wrath and Vengeance upon me. He's for having them to take it for granted, that he has proved me an *Infidel* and *Blafphemer*, and would have them to inflict fome exemplary Punifhment

ment upon me, fo as to incapacitate me for ever writing more. Wherefore elfe does he fay thus? (*b*) " Indeed a more proper " Occafion cannot poffibly happen in a " Nation, where Chriftianity is eftablifh'd " by human *Laws*, to invigorate the Zeal " of the Magiftrate, in putting the Laws " in Execution againft fo flagrant a Sort " of Profanenefs, that tramples with fuch " Indignity on the Grounds of the *Chri-* " *ftian* Faith ; and to convince the World " that the *Minifter* of that *God*, who is fo " highly affronted, *bears not the Sword in* " *vain*. And certainly the Higher Pow- " ers have great Reafon to exert their Au- " thority on this and the like Occafions.

I was aftonifh'd at this Paffage, with fome others, in the *Bifhop*'s *Dedication*, and could hardly believe my Eyes when I read it ; that a Scholar, a Chriftian, and a Pro- teftant Bifhop, fhould breath fo much Fury and Fire for the kindling again of *Smithfield* Faggots! That any Thing of human Shape fhould fo thirft after that Deftruction of another, which would turn to the Ruin of his own Reputation and Honour! Does the *Bifhop* believe that he has clearly confuted me, or does he not?

(*b*) In his Dedication.

If

If he believes, and others know that I am absolutely confuted, then there's an End of the Controversy, the Danger of my *blasphemous* Books is over; and why should I undergo any Punishment, which would move the Compassion of many, and give a greater Reputation to my Writings than they do deserve? Does the *Bishop* think he has confuted me? This is Honour and Triumph enough to him; who, of all Men, should not desire me to be otherwise punish'd, for fear of getting the Character of a merciless and implacable Conqueror. Am I in my own Opinion confuted and baffled? This would be Pain and Mortification enough, even worse than Death. For, however we polemical *Writers* may pretend a Readiness to part with our Errors upon Conviction, as if we could easily yield to our Adversaries, yet it goes to the Hearts of us to be out-done in Reason and Argument. As it is said of *Bishop Stillingfleet*, that, being sensible of his Insufficiency to contend with Mr. *Lock*, he grieved and pined away upon it: So I, upon Supposition the Bishop of St. *David's* has confuted me, must not only necessarily afflict my self, but undergo the Shame of the Reproaches of the People, for my wicked and impotent Efforts to subvert their Religion: And what would

the

the *Bishop* have more? He could defire no
more, if he had abfolutely confuted me:
But it's plain he dares not truft to his own
Confutation of me; it's plain he's afraid
of, what he is confcious may be made, a
fmart Reply to him, and therefore he calls
upon the Civil Magiftrate for his Help to
prevent it.

After that the *Bishop* of *London* had
publifh'd his *Pastoral Letter*, and it was
reported that the *Bishop* of St. *David's* was
preparing a ftrenuous Vindication of the
litteral Story of *Jesus's* Miracles, I concluded that the Profecution would immediately be dropp'd, and that the Clergy
were betaking themfelves to that Chriftian,
Rational, and Philofophical Courfe of Confutation, and would no longer make ufe
of Perfecution, which is the Armour of
hot, furious, and ignorant Bigots. And
there is one Paffage in the *Bishop's Pastoral Letter*, which I interpreted as a Grant
of full Liberty; but, whether I am apt
to miftake the Senfe of the Fathers of the
Primitive Church or not, I find I did mif-
conftrue the Words of a Father of our
English Church, and turn'd them to another and better Purpofe than he aim'd at.
His Words are thefe (c) " And as to the

" blaf-

" *blasphemous manner*, in which a late
" Writer has taken the Liberty to treat
" our Saviour's Miracles, and the Author
" of them ; tho' I am far from contend-
" ing, that the Grounds of the Christian
" Religion, and the Doctrines of it, may
" not be discuss'd at all Times in a calm,
" decent, and serious Way (on the con-
" trary, I am sure that the more fully
" they are discuss'd, the more firmly they
" will stand) yet I cannot but think it
" the Duty of the Civil Magistrate, at
" all Times, to take Care that Religion
" be not treated in a *ludicrous* or *reproach-*
" *ful* Manner, and effectually to discou-
" rage such Books and Writings as strike
" equally at the Foundation of all Reli-
" gion, *&c*" What the *Bishop* of *L.*
here says, of his *thinking it the Duty of*
the Civil Magistrate at all Times, to take
Care that Religion be not treated in a lu-
dicrous manner, I understood as an Excuse
for what he had done in stirring up the
Civil Magistrate to a Prosecution of me ;
and that now, like a Philosopher, he was
for letting Truth and Religion to take its
Course, and for leaving it to a free Dis-
cussion, whether in a *ludicrous* or in a
calm, decent or *serious* Way. But I confess, I have mistaken the *Bishop*'s Words,
finding by Experience, that (for all the
C   natural

natural Import of his Expreſſion, that Liberty ſhould be uſed to diſcuſs the Grounds
of Religion in a *ſerious* Manner) he'll no
more ſuffer it, if he can help it, to be con-
teſted in a *ſerious*, than in a *ludicrous*
Way ; wherefore elſe did he move for the
Proſecution of a late *London Journal*,
which was all *calm*, *decent*, and *ſerious*
Argument. And the Biſhop of St. *David's*
his furious *Dedication* now, confirms me
in this Opinion, that our *Clergy* (for all
their preaching up Liberty with as much
Force and Strength of Reaſon as any Men,
and for all their Invitations to *Infidels*, to
ſay and print their worſt againſt Chriſtianity) will by no means, if they can hinder it, ſuffer any Attacks to be made upon
their Religion, nor ceaſe their Importunities and Sollicitations of the Civil Magiſtrate to Perſecution. Bleſſed be God, the
Biſhops are not my *Judges* as well as my
Accuſers, or I know, what would become
of me.

Mr. *Atkinſon*, a little Writer againſt me,
ſays, (*d*) " That I call the pretended Di-
" vines of the Church my Proſecutors,
" when they were not my Proſecutors.
" And *again*, That there was no need of
" my Suppoſition, that the *Clergy* would

(*d*) *Vindication of three Miracles*, p. 76, 77.

" have

" have more Wit than to profecute me
" again for this *Difcourfe* ; for he did not
" know that they had been concern'd in
" any Profecution of me. And again he
fays, " If the Civil Magiftrate thinks it
" his Duty to chaftife me for my Sin and
" Folly, I am to blame my felf, and not
" the *Clergy*, till I can prove the Zeal of
" our Chriftian Government to be exci-
" ted by the malign Influence of the
" *Clergy*." Mr. *Atkinfon* is thus far certainly in the right on't, that, ftrictly fpeaking, the *Clergy* are not my Profecutors,
but the King, who, in all probability,
knows no more of my Books than the
Man in the Moon. But whether Mr. *Atkinfon* could be fo ignorant, as not to
know the *Clergy* were the grand Inftigators
to Profecution, let others judge. If he
really was fuch a poor *Ignoramus*, I have
no more to fay : Otherwife, his Expreffions above, will be look'd upon as the vileft
Piece of Hypocrify and Prevarication that
can be, purpofely utter'd to take off the
Odium of the Profecution from the *Clergy*,
and to caft it upon the Civil Government ;
which, whether Mr. *Atkinfon* believes it
or not, had never, but for the Sollicitations of the *Bifhops*, given me any Trouble. Mr. *Atkinfon* above, acts the Part of
the Popifh Clergy of *France*, upon the Re-

vocation

vocation of the Edict of *Nants*. After that the King, upon the urgent Importunities of the Clergy, had resolv'd to revoke that Edict; the Clergy were for excusing themselves to the Protestants, and laying the Blame only on the King, saying, *The King was bent and resolv'd on't, and they could not help it*; which was such Jesuitical Prevarication in the Popish Clergy, that the Protestants could not forbear *roguing* them for it. Mr. *Atkinson* knows how to apply this Story; which I had not told, but for the Use of the Bishop of *L.* who, upon a certain Occasion could say, that it was not He, but the *Government* that prosecuted Mr. *Woolston*. If Mr. *Atkinson* was really so ignorant as he seems to be, I suppose he is now of another Mind, upon reading the *Bishop* of St. *David's* Dedication; and convinced that the Prosecution against me was began and carried on at the *malign Influence*, as he calls it, of the Clergy.

I will here use no Arguments for Liberty of Debate, which Subject has already been copiously handled, and wants nothing, that I can add unto it. But before I enter into the Body of the *Bishop's* Book, and upon a profess'd Defence of my Discourses against him, let us consider the manifest Lies, Prevarications, and wicked

Insi-

Infinuations in his *Dedication*, whereby he would move the Secular Powers to a fevere Punifhment of me. I will pafs by the *Motto* of his Book, *viz. But Jefus faid unto him, Judas, betrayeft thou the Son of Man with a Kifs*; Whereby he would fignify and intimate, not to *Scholars* (for they have more Wit than to think the worfe of me for his Abufe of Scripture) but to the ignorant Multitude, that I am another *Judas*, a Traitor and Rebel to *Jefus*. Commonly *Mottos* of Books are fuited to their Authors, and the Defign of them; whether the *Bifhop* will be willing to take this *Motto* to himfelf or not, I will upon another Occafion give it a pleafant and pertinent Turn upon him. At prefent I fhall only fay, what the Learned will obferve, that *this* is of a wicked and malicious Ufe and Intention, of no lefs, than to create in the Minds of the People an Hatred and Deteftation of me; of no other, than by dreffing me up, as it were, in a Bear's Skin, to excite the Ecclefiaftical and mercilefs Mob to worry and deftroy me. Such has been the roguifh Artifice of Priefts of all Ages, to reprefent their Adverfaries, whom they would deftroy, under odious and borrow'd Names, that their Perfecutions of them

might

might be thought the less cruel. But paſ-
ſing this by for the preſent, the

I. Firſt wicked and wilful Miſrepreſentation that the *Biſhop*, in his Dedication, has made of me, is that of being an
Infidel, and an *Apoſtate* Clergyman. Wherefore elſe does he ſay thus to the Queen :
" What is now preſented to your Royal
" View, is an Apologetical Defence of our
" holy Religion, againſt one of the moſt
" virulent Libels on it, by an *Apoſtate*
" *Clergyman*, that has appear'd in any
" Chriſtian Country ; and in Compariſon
" of which, other *Infidels* have acted a
" modeſt Part." And again he calls my
Diſcourſes, " A flagrant Sort of Profane-
" neſs, that tramples with Indignity on
" the Grounds of the Chriſtian Faith."
And again he ſignifies, " That I am warm-
" ly engaged in ſubverting the Chriſtian
" Religion, and active in propogating In-
" fidelity." This is all wilful and downright Calumny, to incenſe the Queen and
the Government againſt me. The *Biſhop*
knows in his Heart that I am no *Infidel*,
but a Believer of Chriſtianity, notwithſtanding my *Diſcourſes* on Miracles, that
have occaſion'd ſuch a Clamour againſt
me. In my *Diſcourſes*, I have repeatedly
and moſt ſolemnly declared, that my De-
ſigns

signs are not to do Service to Infidelity, but to advance the Glory of God, the Truth of Christianity, and to demonstrate the *Messiahship* of the holy *Jesus*. If I have sometimes ridiculed the litteral Story of our Saviour's Miracles, I have profess'd as often that it was with Design to turn Men's Hearts to the mystical Interpretation of them, on which alone *Jesus*'s Authority and Messiahship is founded. I could collect a great Number of Passages out of my *Discourses* to this Purpose, if it would not be wasting of Time and Paper. And do all these solemn Declarations of my Faith, and of the Integrity of my Heart, and of the Sincerity of my Intentions, stand for nothing ? Why should not my Word here be taken ? I can think of no other Reason, than because some other Folks are accustom'd to dissemble and prevaricate with God and Man in their Oaths and Subscriptions, therefore I may be suspected here of Hypocrisy, notwithstanding my Professions to the contrary.

Besides, the *Bishop* knows by my other Writings, that I am certainly a Christian, and a true Believer of the Religion of Christ, though I may have some different Conceptions from other Men about it. It has been my good Luck before, not only to publish more Treatises purposely and

pre-

profeffedly in Defence of Chriftianity,
than any *Bishop* in *England*; but fome of
them are of fuch a Nature, as it's impoffible for a Man to write without being a
Chriftian, and impoffible for him to depart
from the Principles of them. This is my
good Fortune and Happinefs at this Juncture. The *Bishop* has perufed, I fee, fome
of my other Writings, and particularly,
my *Old Apology for the Truth of Chriftianity revived*; and to his Praife, as well
as my Comfort be it fpoken, he appre-
hends and rightly relifhes it. And as I
was well pleafed with his Reprefentation
of the Defign of that Book, from the
Principles and allegorical Scheme of which,
he fays (in Twenty-four Years fince) I
am not departed; fo I would appeal to his
Confcience, Whether a Man, who wrote,
as I did then, of the Typical and Antitu-
pal Deliverance of the *Jewish* and *Chriftian* Church, can poffibly be an Infidel,
or ever depart from the Chriftian Faith?
If the *Bishop* has Ingenuity equal to his
Penetration into that Book, he muft own
and confefs to the World, that I was then,
and am ftill a Chriftian, a Man of fix'd
and unalterable Principles from that Day
to this.

The *Bishop* would be thought in his
Preface to enumerate all my Writings;
but

but there are three others, whether wilfully or negligently omitted by him, I know not, that are direct Defences of the Truth of Christianity; and there is not a learned *Clergy-man* in *England* (I humbly presume to say it) who can read them, and not applaud them. If the *Bishop* will be pleas'd to read one of them, *viz. The Defence of the Miracle of the Thundering Legion,* and say it from his Heart, that I might write that Book, and believe the Ecclesiastical Story of that Miracle, and yet be no Christian, then I will yield to his Accusation against me for Infidelity.

But why do I trouble my self thus to assert and vindicate my Belief of Christianity? The *Bishop* would readily come into the Acknowledgment of my being a sincere Christian, but for his Interests and Prejudices, and other political Considerations, which influence him and the *Clergy* so to decry and defame me, that, it possible, I must be destroy'd, or at least have my Mouth stopp'd.

In short then, it is not because I am an *Infidel,* that the *Clergy* so exclaim against me and my *Discourses*; but because, as a Christian, I have particular Designs in view, which, if I can compass, will tend to their Dishonour, and the Ruin of their Interests; and therefore, by Defamations

D   and

and Profecutions, they will, if they can,
in time put a ftop to them. The Defigns
that, for the Truth of Religion, and Good
of Mankind, I have in view, and which,
maugre all Oppofition, Terrors, and Sufferings, I will purfue to the utmoft of my
Power, are thefe three.

1. To reftore the Allegorical Interpretation of the Old and New Teftament,
that is call'd, fay the Fathers, the fublime Mountain of Vifion, on which we
fhall contemplate the Wifdom and Beauty of the Providence of God ; and behold
the glorious Transfiguration of *Jefus* with
Mofes and *Elias*, that is, the Harmony
between the Gofpel and the Law and the
Prophets, agreeably to *Jefus's* typical
Transfiguration. And this is fuch a glorious and beatifick Vifion, that it's enough
to ravifh our Hearts with the Hopes and
Defires of attaining to it. The old *Jews*
fay, that the allegorical Interpretation of
the Scriptures will lead us to the fight of
God, and convert even *Atheifts*. The Fathers fay, that the allegorical Interpretation will be the Converfion of the *Jews* in
the Perfection of Time; and St. *Auguftin*
fpeaks of a great allegorical *Genius*, (*e*)

(*e*) Cum venerit ergo Elias exponendo Legem *Spiritaliter*, convertit Corda Patrum ad filios. *De Civit Dei.*
Lib. XX. c. 29.

that

that will be sent to that Purpose. I believe all this, and being convinced of the Truth of it, I am much addicted to Allegories. And it is plain enough, and wants no Proof, that the Revival of the allegorical Scheme, which I am fond of, portends Ruin to the *Ministry of the Letter*; and will be such an Argument of the Ignorance and Apostacy of our *Clergy*, that it's no wonder they defame, calumniate, and persecute me for my Attempts towards it.

Origen says, (*f*) that *litteral Interpreters will run into Infidelity*, which is a Saying I am well pleased with, and thereupon will try if I can't turn the Tables upon our *Clergy*; I'll try if I can't shift from my self the present Load of Reproaches for Infidelity, and lay it upon them. What would the Wise and the Learned then say? That the great *Bishops* of *London* and St. *David's* had caught a *Tartar*.

I have indeed ludicrously treated the Letter of the Scriptures (in my *Discourses*) which by the said *Bishops* is falsly called *Blasphemy:* But should they either *ludicrously* or *sedately* write against

---

(*f*) Litteram Legis sequentes in Infidelitatem & vanas Superstitiones incurrunt. *In Matt. Tract.* 26.

the

the allegorical Senfe of them, I could prove *that* to be real *Blafphemy.* However, I would not complain to the Civil Powers againft them ; no, it's God's peculiar Prerogative to punifh that Sin, which ought not to be committed to the Care of the Civil Magiftrate.

But what need I *ludicroufly* to handle the Letter of our Saviour's Miracles ? Becaufe fome Sort of Stories are the proper Subjects of *Ridicule* ; and becaufe, *Ridiculum acri fortius & melius,* Ridicule will cut the Pate of an Ecclefiaftical Numbskull, which calm and fedate Reafoning will make no Impreffion on.

To fpeak then the Truth in few Words. As I am refolv'd at any Rate to run down the *Letter,* in order to make way for the *Spirit* of the Scriptures, fo certainly will our Clergy, for their Interefts and Honour, as Minifters of the Letter, vilify and reproach me, and purfue me with an implacable Hatred : But I fhould think it meet for them to ufe a little more Temper in their Revilings, for fear the Torrent of Reproaches fhould fometime or other turn on them. It is afferted and predicted by the Fathers that, after a certain Time of the Church's Apoftacy to the *Letter,* the *Spirit of Life,* or the allegorical Senfe will re-enter the Scriptures, to the Advancement

vancement of divine Knowledge and true
Religon ; in the mean while the *Clergy*
will do well to fee to it. But,

2. The Second Defign which, as a Chriftian, I hawe in View, and which occa-
fionally I write for, is an univerfal and
unbounded Toleration of Religion, without any Reftrictions or Impofitions on
Men's Confciences ; for which Defign, the
Clergy will hate and defame me, and, if
poffible, make an Infidel of me, as well as
for the former. Upon an univerfal Toleration the World would be at quiet : That
Hatred of one another, which is now fo
vifible among different Sects, would then
be terminated by a Unity of their Interefts, when they are all upon the Level
in the Eye of the Civil Magiftrate, who
would choofe Men to Places of Truft, not
for their Faith and Affection to Theological Doctrines, but for their Abilities to
ferve the Publick. In this Cafe, Ten thoufand different *Notions* in Religion would
no more obftruct the Welfare of the Community, than fo many different *Nofes* do
the Happinefs of this City. The Variety
of their Theological Opinions, would be
the Diverfion and Amufement of each
other ; and fo long as it was out of their
Power to opprefs, they could not hate
one another for them. Such a Tolerati-

on,

on, the *Clergy* would perſuade us, tends to Confuſion and Diſtraction, as if Men would go to *Loggerheads* upon it. But this is one of their Miſtakes; there would be a perfect Calm upon it, if ſuch Incendiaries as they are did not diſturb the publick Tranquillity. They'll tell us again, that ſuch a Toleration makes Way for Diſſoluteneſs of Morals, and would let in Sin like a Deluge upon us; but this is another of their Errors. Such a Toleration would promote Virtue, in as much as different Sects of Religion are a Check upon each other againſt Looſeneſs of Morals, becauſe every Sect would endeavour to approve itſelf above others, by the Goodneſs of their Lives, as well as by the Excellency of their Doctrine. But the *Clergy* will never hearken to ſuch a Toleration, becauſe it would be the Downfall of Eccleſiaſtical Power; for which Reaſon, among many others, I am

3. For the Abolition of an hired and eſtabliſh'd Prieſthood. And for this, if for nothing elſe, I am ſure to be proſecuted with Hatred and Violence, and loaded with the Calumnies and Reproaches of Infidelity and Blaſphemy: And the *Clergy*, if poſſible, will have my Mouth ſtopp'd, and my Hands tied, before I proceed too

far

far in my Labours and Endeavours to this End.

And why fhould not the *Clergy* of the Church of *England* be turn'd to Grafs, and be made to feek their Fortune among the People, as well as Preachers of other Denominations? Where's the Senfe and Reafon of impofing Parochial *Priefts* upon the People to take care of their Souls, more than Parochial *Lawyers* to look to their Eftates, or Parochial *Phyficians* to attend their Bodies, or Parochial *Tinkers* to mend their Kettles? In fecular Affairs every Man choofes the Artift and Mechanick that he likes beft; fo much more ought he in Spirituals, in as much as the Welfare of the Soul is of greater Importance than that of the Body or Eftate. The Church-Lands would go a good, if not a full Step, towards the Payment of the Nation's Debts.

I have promifed the World, what, by the Affiftance of God, and the Leave of the Government, fhall be publifh'd, a *Difcourfe* on the Mifchiefs and Inconveniencies of an Hired and Eftablifh'd Priefthood: In which it fhall be fhewn,

I. That the Preachers of Chriftianity in the firft Ages of the Church (when the Gofpel was far and near fpread, and triumph'd

triumph'd over all Oppofition of *Jews*
and *Gentiles*) neither received nor infifted
on any Wages for their Pains, but were
againft preaching for Hire ; and, as if they
had been endew'd with the Spirit of Prophecy, before an Hireling Priefthood was
eftablifh'd, predicted their Abolition and
Ejection out of Chrift's Church.

II. That fince the Eftablifhment of an
Hire for the Priefthood, the Progrefs of
Chriftianity has not only been ftopt, but loft
Ground ; the Avarice, Ambition, and Power of the Clergy having been of fuch un-
fpeakable Mifchief to the World, as is e-
nough to make a Man's Heart ake to think,
read, or write of.

III. That upon an Abolition of our prefent eftablifh'd Priefthood, and on God's
Call of his own Minifters, the Profeffion of
the Gofpel will again fpread ; and Virtue,
Religion, and Learning, will more than
ever flourifh and abound.

The Clergy are forewarn'd of my Defign to publifh fuch a *Difcourfe*; and this
is the fecret Reafon, whatever openly they
may pretend, of their Accufations againft
me for Blafphemy and Infidelity. Their
Zeal and Induftry will be never wanting
to prevent the Publication of this *Dif-*
courfe ; neither need I doubt of Perfecution,

on, if they can excite the Government to it, to that End.

In my firſt Diſcourſe on Miracles, I happen'd to treat on that of Jeſus's driving the Buyers and Sellers out of the Temple; which, upon the Authority of the Fathers, I ſhew'd to be a Figure of his future Ejection of Biſhops, Prieſts, and Deacons out of his Church, for making Merchandiſe of the Goſpel. The *Biſhop* has taken me and that Miracle to task; and if ever any Man ſmiled at another's Impertinence, I then heartily laugh'd when I read him. I begg'd of the *Biſhop* before-hand (g) not to meddle with that Miracle, becauſe it was a hot one, and would burn his Fingers. But for all my Caution, he has been ſo Fool-hardy, as to venture upon it; but has really touch'd and handled it, as if it was a *burning Coal*. He takes it up, and as ſoon drops it again to blow his Fingers; then endeavours to throw a little Water on *this* and *that* Part of it to cool it, but all would not do. The moſt fiery Part of it, *viz.* that of its being a Type of Jeſus's future Ejection of mercenary Preachers out of the Church,

___

(g) In Dedication of Third *Diſcourſe.*

he

he has not, I may fay it, at all touch'd,
except by calling it (*h*) *my allegorical Invective againft the Maintenance of the
Clergy*; which is fuch a Piece of *Corin-
thian* Effrontery in the *Bifhop*, that was he
not refolv'd to lye and defame at all Rates,
for the Support of their Interefts, he could
never have had the Face to have utter'd.
If the *Bifhop* had proved that *that* Miracle (which litterally was fuch a———, as
I dare not now call it) neither was nor
could be a Shadow and Refemblance of Jefus's Ejection of hired Priefts out of the
Church at his fecond Advent, and that the
Fathers were not of this Opinion, he had
knock'd me down at once. As he has done
nothing of this, fo he might have fpared
his Pains in Support of the Letter of this
Story. But I fhall have a great deal of
Diverfion with the *Bifhop*, when I come,
in a proper Place, to defend my Expofition of that Miracle. In the mean Time,
as the Bifhop has publifh'd one of the Articles of my Chriftian Faith, thinking to
render me odious for it; fo here I will
infert another, *viz.* (*i*) " I believe upon
" the Authority of the Fathers, that the

(*h*) Page 177.
(*i*) *Difcourfe* the Fifth, *p.* 69.

" Spirit

" Spirit and Power of Jesus will *soon* en-
" ter the Church, and expel Hireling
" Priests, who make Merchandise of the
" Gospel, out of her, after the manner he
" is supposed to have driven the *Buyers*
" and *Sellers* out of the Temple."

Now upon all this, whether the *Bishop*, modestly speaking, has not been unjust, uncharitable, and insincere, to represent me as an *Infidel*, I appeal to all learned and ingenuous Gentlemen. I am a Christian, though not upon the *litteral* Scheme, which I nauseate, yet upon the *allegorical* one. And by the following easy and short Argument it may be proved that I am most certainly a Christian. I heartily and zealously contend for the allegorical Interpretation of the Scriptures, which the *Bishop* allows to be true of me; consequently I must, and do believe the Scriptures to be of divine Inspiration, or I could not think there were such Mysteries and Prophecy latent under the Letter of them. Whether then a Believer of the divine Inspiration of the Scriptures can be an Infidel (O most monstrous Paradox!) or any other than a Christian, judge Readers. Nay, if *Origen's* and St. *Augustin's* Testimony on my Behalf may be admitted, I am more truly a Christian and Disciple of the Holy Jesus, than any *litteral Schemist*

can

can be. *Origen* fays, (*k*) That the Perfection of Chriſtianity conſiſts in a myſtical Interpretation of the Old and New Teſtament, of the Hiſtorical, as well as other Parts of it. And St. *Auguſtin* fays, (*l*) That they who attain to the Underſtanding of the ſpiritual Signification of Jeſus's Miracles, are the beſt Doctors in his School. The *Biſhop* underſtands this Argument as well as any Man, and therefore I charge it home upon him, as a wilful and malicious Slander, to call and account me an Infidel in his *Dedication*, on purpoſe to incenſe the Government againſt me at this Juncture.

But the *Biſhop* moreover calls me, as above, an *Apoſtate Clergyman* ; And why ſo ? Becauſe I have deſerted the *Miniſtry of the Letter*, and betaken my ſelf to the *Miniſtry of the Spirit* of the Scriptures. That's like the Wit and Reaſoning of his Pate ! The *Biſhop* is old enough, and has read enough to know that *Apoſtacy*, in the Senſe of the Fathers, is a Deſertion of

(*k*) Inveniatur enim in Chriſtianiſmo nón minot (nequid dicam arrogantius) fide Ratio & Enarratió Propheticorum ænigmatum, parabolarumque evangelicarum, aliarumque innumerarum figurarum, quæ vel in *Geſtis* continentur vel Legibus. *Cont. Celſum. Lib.* I.

(*l*) Quidam corporalia ejus Miracula ſtupentes, majora intueri non horunt. Quidam vero ea, quæ geſta audiunt in Corporibus, nunc amplius in animis admirantur,——— Tales nos eſſe debemus in Schola Chriſti. *In Serm.* xcviii.

the

the *Miniſtry of the Spirit*, and a Falling into the *Miniſtry of the Letter* of the Scriptures; whereupon I make bold to retort upon the *Biſhop*, and ſay of him, and his Epiſcopal Brethren, that they are *Apoſtate Biſhops*.

But to humour the *Biſhop* in his fond *Dedication*, I will ſuppoſe my ſelf to be, what I am the fartheſt of any Man living from being, an *Infidel* and *Apoſtate*; yet

II. The *Biſhop* is a wilful Calumniator, or, at beſt, an unhappy Miſrepreſenter of me, and of other Infidels, ſaying in his *Dedication*, that our Deſign is *Tu ſap the Foundation of all Government*, and———*That we were purſuing ſuch Methods, as have a natural Tendency to introduce Confuſion.* If this was true of us Infidels (for now I ſpeak of my ſelf as one of them) it behoves Civil Governors to look about them, and to puniſh and ſuppreſs us with all ſpeed ; and we ſhould be the moſt unreaſonable Men alive, if we complain'd of Perſecution, or call'd it hard Uſage. And the *Biſhop* of *London*, and other *Divines* (like this *Biſhop*) do commonly declaim on the Danger of Infidelity to Civil Society, but this is all Eccleſiaſtical Cant and Jargon. I thought I had given (*m*) the

---

(*m*) In *Diſcourſe* the Sixth.

Bishop of *London* so much on this Head of Complaint against Infidelity, as I could not suppose the *Bishop* of St. *David's* would ever have repeated it. It is true, what the *Bishop* says, that *Religion is the firmest Support of Government*, and *Christianity especially lays the greatest Obligations, on Men's Consciences, of Obedience to the Civil Powers.* I believe all this, and that the better Christians Men are, the more quiet, peaceable, and useful Subjects, and the greater Friends would they be to the Civil Authority. But does it follow from hence, that we *Infidels*, because we have rejected the Belief of some systematical Divinity, as the *Clergy* are fond of, should consequently be Enemies to the Civil Government, and Foes to the Peace, Order, and Welfare of Society ? O fie upon the Drawers of such Consequences! We are, I believe, a numerous and growing Sect in these Nations, though I am acquainted with none, no, not so much as with the Great Mr. *Grounds* : But I could never perceive that any of us, in Principle, were against Civil Government, and the Welfare of the Community ; or were for *Confusion*, for setting the People together by the Ears, to the Disturbance of the publick Peace and Tranquillity. No, no, our Interests in the World, as well as

other

other Men's, oblige us to confult the publick Welfare; and our Confciences, from
the Religion of Nature, bind us to O-
bedience to Government; and, was it not
agreeable to our Inclination, the Neceffity of Affairs would force us to be as quiet
and obedient as are any Chriftians: And
I thank God, we have hitherto behaved
our felves very peaceably, clear of all Sufpicion of Treafon and Rebellion to any
Prince or State. The *Bifhop* hints at Experience to the contrary, but it will puz-
zle him to give an Inftance. One would
think, by this common Harangue, of *Ecclefiafticks* againft us *Infidels*, that Chriftians, efpecially the Priefthood, being, as
the *Bifhop* fays, both *under the Penalties
of human Laws, and the ftronger Impref-
fions of a future State*, were of a Lamb-
like Nature, and never given to difturb
the Civil Authority: And I will own
the Chriftian *Laity* might be acquitted
here, but for the *Clergy*, who have been
repeatedly the *Peft* and *Bane* of human Society, the Trumpeters of Sedition and
Rebellion, and mere Make-bates in Cities
and Families. And I dare fay, that if the
Civil Powers don't curb, and keep our
Priefthood in awe, they will upon this
prefent Occafion be the Difturbers of the
publick Peace. So little Senfe and Truth

is

is there in the *Bishop's* present Invective
against us Infidels! If he had not been infatuated to a Forgetfulness of the *Rogue-*
ries of Priests, in all Ages, against the Civil Powers, he could never have insinuated such a groundless and senseless Charge
against us, to the Provocation of the Civil Magistrate to fall on us. But

III. The *Bishop* calumniates us Infidels
(for against his Conscience, whether I will
or not, he will have me to be one of
them) not only for being Enemies to
Government in general, which he will
have us to advance Principles destructive
of; but insinuates and asserts that we are
disaffected to the particular and present
Government of these Kingdoms, saying,
that as " we are active in propagating In-
" fidelity, we do in the last Resort, not
" only insult the Title of *Defender of the*
" *Faith*, but undermine the undoubted
" Right of his Majesty and his Royal Fa-
" mily to the Crown of these Realms, as
" it is founded on the Profession of *Chri-*
" *stianity*, reform'd, and now legally set-
" tled among us; and therefore Persons
" of that Character may well be consi-
" der'd, as equally false to the Author of
" our Faith, and to the present Govern-
" ment.———Therefore in a just Sense of
" that Allegiance which is due to the
" King,

" King, and for the Security of your Ma-
" jesties, and the Royal Family, and there-
" by of the Publick it self, as well as out
" of a deep Concern for the Honour and
" Preservation of our most holy Faith,
" the ensuing Treatise is now offer'd, un-
" der your Majesty's Protection, to the
" View of the Publick." This is all such
foolish and manifest Slander, that I can't
but think the *Bishop* mad with Rage and
Indignation at me, when he writ it. I
dare say the *Queen*, who is firmly attach'd
to the Interests of the Christian and Protestant Religion, did, when she read all
this, almost grieve for the *Bishop*, and pity him for his Weakness and Ignorance. It
is a *Maxim* among all Parties, that *Infidels* are heartily affected to the present E-
stablishment of the State; yea, so far a
Maxim, that *Jacobites* and *High-Church-
men* are apt to accuse all the well-affected
to the Government, of Infidelity. From
none of the Writings or Practice of Infidels, much less of my self, could the *Bishop* gather any of these his *childish* Sur-
mises. The Government, since the Suc-
cession of the Illustrious House of *Hano-
ver*, has been twice attempted to be disturb'd, and both times by profess'd Christians. The Rebellion at *Preston* consisted
of *Papists* and *High-Church-men*, and tho'
F   there

there were but few *Clergy-men* in Arms, yet they were join'd with the Prayers and Wishes of many Thousands of the *Clergy*, and even, as it was suspected, of some *Oxonian Bishops*. Bishop *Atterbury*'s Plot too consisted of Rebellious Christians, without the least intermixture of us *Infidels*, who are the more zealously affected to the Government, because of the Danger it is sometimes in from the *High-Church Clergy*. Away then with the *Bishop*'s Slander, which, for all we may be Unbelievers of Christianity, our Civil Magistrates will laugh at and deride him for. But,

IV. Another Misrepresentction, more foolish and absurd than the former, that the *Bishop* has made of us *Infidels*, is, that we are making Way for Popery and Slavery: For thus he says of us, " Nothing " is more demonstrable, than that those " Adversaries (meaning us *Infidels*) of the " Christian Religion, who are now so bu- " sily employ'd in infusing Doubts into " some weak Minds, in giving an Indiffe- " rence and Coldness to other well-mean- " ing Persons, and in making others, that " are viciously inclin'd, actual Proselites " to Infidelity, are pursuing such Me- " thods as have a natural Tendency to in- " troduce Confusion, and thereby betray " us into *Popery*." And again he says of
Infidels,

Infidels, " That in Confequence of their
" own Infidelity, and their wicked Dili-
" gence in fpreading that Infection, are
" bringing in upon us the real Perfecuti-
" ons of the Church of *Rome* ; who like-
" wife, whilft they rail fo plentifully at
" the moft rational Religion in the World
" as Superftition, give great Advantages
" towards reftoring the infupportable *Su-*
" *perftitions* of that Communion. Thefe
" are the Perfons indeed that appear in
" favour of an unbounded Liberty, but
" God grant it may not terminate in an
" abfolute *Slavery.*" *Rifum quis teneţat ?*
Who in his Wits could write fuch Stuff?
And who without Impatience can read it?
I was going about a particular Diffection
of thefe two Paragraphs, and to lay open
the Wit, Senfe, and Oratory of the *Bi-*
fhop, to the Contemplation of his Admirers ; but I find it unneceffary, as well as
tedious to do it : The very tranfcribing of
them, and expofing them to View, is e-
nough to render him ridiculous. If there
be no more danger of Popery, Slavery,
Superftition, Tyranny, and real Perfecution from our *Clergy,* than from us *Infi-*
dels, the Nation is fafe. *Infidels* find too
much Inconvenience in the Power, Craft,
and Follies of a Proteftant *Clergy,* to make
Way for *Popery* ; which, as the *Bifhop*

rightly

rightly fays, is a *Complication* of Errors.
There are, what the *Bifhop* fhould have
thought of, many Proteftant Priefts for
an Accommodation with the Church of
Rome; and, if I miftake not, upon fuch
eafy Terms as *this*, *viz.* If fhe'll but part
with fome of her Superftitions that are of
no Ufe to her; our *Clergy* will admit of
others as will be of Advantage to them.
But *Infidels* are irreconcilable Enemies to
the Church of *Rome*, and fo far from Wifhes
and Endeavours to reftore Popery, that it
is mere Nonfenfe to charge them with
either direct or confequential Defigns fo to
enflave Mankind. But

V. The *Bifhop* fays, that we Infidels
(for I am one it feems) *labour induftrioufly to root out all Senfe of Virtue and
Religion among us.* This is fad indeed, if
true; and very bad Men fhould we be,
and deferving of the worft Punifhment.
But this wants Proof. How does he know
that we are for rooting out all Senfe of
Virtue and Religion amongft Men? Does
it appear fo by our Writings or our Practices? Does he find in our Books any Exhortations to Loofenefs and Immorality?
Nothing of this I am fure. Is he then fo
well acquainted with Infidels, as to know
them to be of more depraved and de-
bauch'd Lives than profefs'd Chriftians?
Nor

Nor this neither. I have not as yet heard
that any of my Difciples have been
hang'd, lamenting his Misfortune of reading my *Difcourfes*, as what encouraged
him to Sin, and brought him to the Gal-
lows. No, thofe unhappy People, hitherto, die in the Faith and Communion of
the Church, either of *England* or of *Rome*,
and hope to be faved through the Merits of their Saviour, Neither do I hear
of any Gentleman, old or young, who
has given a greater Loofe to his Lufts and
Paffions, fince he read my Books. Such
News would trouble me.

But becaufe of this Out-cry of the *Bifhop*, and of other Preachers againft us,
that we labour induftrioufly to root out
all Senfe of Virtue and Religion amongft
Men, I wifh (for Proof) that *Infidels*
were diftinguifhable from Chriftians, that
a Comparifon might be made, and the Difference difcern'd between them, as to true
Religion and Virtue. Tho' I am one of
little Acquaintance with Infidels, yet it
is my Opinion that, on this Score, they
may vie with, and, all things confider'd,
do furpafs Chriftians. One would think,
by the *Bifhop*'s Infinuation above, that
none but *good* People were of his Chriftian Faith ; and that all Infidels were
profligate Sinners ; but he knows better,
and

and what's more, he should have been more ingenuous than to charge *Infidels* with *Labours to root out all Senfe of Virtue and Religion amongft Men*, if it was but in Regard to that learned Gentleman who is fuppofed to be at the Head of Infidelity, and who, they fay, is as exemplary for all focial Virtues, as any *Bifhop*; and diflikes Vice and Immorality as much as any Saint can do.

Whatever be the *Virtue* and *Religion* of *Infidels*, it is all genuine, natural, and fincere; and confequently more Praife-worthy than *that* of hired Priefts, who may be fufpected of Hypocrify, becaufe of their Interefts. I heard a wild Spark fay, that he could be as grave as the *Bifhop* of *London*, if he was but as well paid for it. Whether he believ'd the *Bifhop* would have been as loofe as himfelf, but for his *Hire*, I can't tell. But this is certain that, what can't be faid of Infidels, there are Priefts who put on the Face and Form of Godlinefs, and want the Life and Power of it; who lift up their Hands and Eyes unto God, when their Hearts are far from him; and were not their Interefts more than their Faith, a Reftraint to their Lufts, it is commonly believ'd they would be a Company of loofe *Blades*.

What

What a Pother is here of the Danger and Mifchief of Infidelity to Church and State? Do but take away the Caufe of Infidelity, and the Effect ceafes. And what is the Caufe of Infidelity? Why, what *Origen* predicted, I experience to be true, that the *Miniftry of the Letter* is the Caufe of it; and I appeal to Mr. *Grounds*, Whether litteral Expofitions on the Scripture, and the abfurd Doctrines which the *Clergy* have built upon the *Letter*, have not been one Caufe of his calling into Queftion, the Truth of Chriftianity, and the divine Infpiration of the holy Scriptures? But this is not the only Caufe of Infidelity; there are other grand ones, which Dr. *Moore* writes of, faying thus: (*n*) " That Men are exceedingly tempted " to think the whole Bufinefs of Religi- " on is at beft but a Plot to enrich the " Priefts, and keep the People in awe, " from obferving that they, who make " the greateft Noife about Religion, and " are the moft zealous therein, do neglect " the Laws of Honefty and common Hu- " manity; that they eafily invade other " Men's Rights; that they juggle, diffem- " ble, and lye for Advantage; that they

---

(*n*) *Myftery of Godlinefs*, B. x. c. 2.

" are

" are proud, conceited, love the Applause
" of the People, are envious, fierce, and
" implacable, unclean and sensual, merci-
" less and cruel; care not to have King-
" doms flow in Blood, for maintaining
" their Tyranny over the Consciences of
" poor deluded Souls." If then there is
any Danger of any kind in Infidelity, let
the *Clergy* take the Blame and Shame of
it to themselves, and not lay that Fault,
which is their own, upon other Men.

But observing that Dr. *Moore* above
speaks of Priests, their *neglecting the Laws
of Honesty* and *common Humanity*, as a
Cause of Infidelity, I must here do a piece
of Justice to Infidels, who place the very
Essence of all Religion (as I believe the
Essence of Christianity consists) in *common
Honesty*. If they keep to their Principles,
and act agreeably, they will work such a
Reformation in the World for the better,
as the *Priests* of all Ages have not been
able to do. The *Clergy* have made such a
Noise in the World about *Faith* and *Doctrine*, that the People hardly think they
need be *Honest* to be good Christians; and
even many *Clergy-men* are conceited of
their being *orthodox* and *sound Divines*,
though by their Dishonesty, Profuseness,
and Neglect of a Provision for their Families,

milies, they have, in the Judgment of (*o*) St. *Paul*, deny'd the Faith, and are worfe than Infidels.

And thus have I confider'd the Slanders and Mifreprefentations of my felf and Infidels, contain'd in the *Bifhop*'s *Dedication* to the *Queen*, which entirely is fuch a Piece of Fury, Railing, and Impertinence, as a Man fhall hardly meet with. Surely he was not awake when he wrote his *Dedication*, it is fo like the *Dream* of a diforder'd Brain, which confifts of confufed Notions, and fcatter'd Ideas, that are never to be fo compacted together, as to make tolerable Senfe, Reafon, and Truth. If I had not met with much fuch flaming Stuff in the Body of his Book, I fhould have fufpected that fome-body, more a Foe than a Friend to him, had palm'd it upon him, and over-perfuaded him to print it, as what would recommend him to her Majefty's Favour.

Whether he'll merit a *Tranflation* to an *Arch-Bifhoprick*, for this Dedication, with me is no Queftion. For all he may take me for his Enemy, I wifh him *tranflated*, as certainly as the Government has *tranfported* fome other Folks, who are no

(*o*) 1 Tim. v. 8.

more

more the Bane of Society. *Buggs* in a
Houſe, and *Caterpillars* in a Garden, are
not a greater Grievance, than ſome ſort
of Eccleſiaſtical *Vermin* in Chriſt's Church
and Vineyard.

That the *Biſhop* himſelf admires his
Dedication, and is pleas'd with it, I don't
doubt. Like as *Bears* are fond of their
ill-favour'd *Cubbs*, ſo the Brats of ſome
Men's Brains, as well as thoſe of their Bodies, are pleaſing to them ; and however
deform'd and irrational in themſelves, are
hugg'd by them as ſo many Wits and
Beauties. But whether many, beſide the
Biſhop himſelf, will like his *Dedication*, is
a great Queſtion. I don't doubt, but there
may be ſome for Perſecution as well as
the *Biſhop*, and ſo far may approve of the
Dedication : But whether there is any
one that can think, he has not greatly in-
jured *Infidels*, and made a falſe Repreſentation of them, for being Enemies to our
Civil Government, and to our preſent E-
ſtabliſhment, can't ſurely be queſtion'd. If
he be not look'd upon here, by all Mankind, as a wilful and malicious Miſrepreſenter of them, I ſhall much wonder at it.

But what's the *Dedication* to the Book
it ſelf, will ſome here ſay ? Tho' the *Biſhop* may have made ſome Slips in his *Dedication*, which betray Weakneſs and Ignorance ;

norance; yet his following Performance
may be Strenuous and Nervous, and a
compleat Confutation of my *Discourses*.
I answer, that such a Dedication bodes ill
to the Book; and a Man may as well
expect to find the inside of a House beautiful and richly adorn'd, when the Porch
and Entrance into it is mean and nasty;
as that an admirable Treatise for Wit,
Reason, and Learning, should follow upon such a poor, simple, and insipid *Dedication.* Commonly Authors take more
care in their *Dedications*, than in their
following Treatise; that is, they see better to the Accuracy of their Expressions,
the Exactness of their Stile, and Beauty
of their Thoughts; and if they err at all
in them, it is only in Flattery, and excess of Compliments on their Patrons.
Such Care too, after the best manner he
was able, has the *Bishop* taken in his *Dedication* above; and whatever his Readers
and Admirers may think, the *Dedication*
is the best Part of the Book. The Exceptions I have taken at the *Dedication*
are but small, in Comparison of the Faults
I shall find and expose in the *Book* it
self; which is such a Complication of Impertinence and Errors, of Rage and Confidence, and of Calumnies and Reproaches,
as is not to be equall'd; and is so far

from

from deferving the Character of a Confutation of my *Difcourfes*, that it has
done them Service; and will be, after the
Animadverfions I fhall make on it, a Confirmation of the Goodnefs, Ufefulnefs, and
Excellency of my Defign in them.

I have not here room to make a compleat Diffection of the *Bifhop*'s Work, and
to difplay its Infufficiency, in anfwer to
my *Difcourfes*; neither was it my Defign
in this *firft Part* of my *Defence* to do it.
But however, I will fpare a Place here for
a fhort Character and Reprefentation of
his Performance, which take as follows.

" The *Bifhop*'s fole Aim and Defign is
" to vindicate the *litteral Story* of our Sa-
" viour's Miracles, againft my rational
" and authoritative Objections to it. And
" to this Purpofe he wrangles with me,
" where he can, about the Senfe of this
" and that Citation out of the Fathers;
" and after he has forc'd another Senfe on
" it, than the Words do naturally bear,
" then he infults me for a Mifreprefenta-
" tion. And where he meets with a plain
" Teftimony out of the Fathers, which
" he can't mangle nor ftrain to his Pur-
" pofe, he filently paffes by it; tho' he
" would have his *Readers* to believe, he
" has vindicated the litteral Story againft
" my

" my Authorities, and fhewn that the Fa-
" thers were all on his Side.

" He complains of my Mutilations of
" the Fathers, and of making too curt
" Citations out of them ; which is true,
" but more to my own Difadvantage than
" to his. But, what is Matter of grand
" Triumph to the *Bifhop*, is, that I have
" quoted *fpurious* Works of the Fathers
" for *genuine* ones. And here he takes
" great Pains, and waftes Time and Pa-
" per, to prove that *this* and *that* Book
" does not belong to the Author under
" whofe Name I cite it ; and then has a
" Fling at me for want of Skill in *Criti-*
" *cifm.* But can the *Bifhop* be fo weak,
" as to think, I did not know when I quo-
" ted a *fpurious* Work? Suppofing the
" *Book* I quoted do not belong to the re-
" puted Author, but to fome other Wri-
" ter, what's that to the Queftion be-
" tween us? The Citation is no lefs the
" Teftimony of Antiquity, and it's no
" matter whofe Name it bears. If the *Bi-*
" *fhop* had thought a little on this, he
" might have fpared fome Sheets of Pa-
" per, which he has in vain wafted, to
" the Lofs of his Readers Time and Mo-
" ney.

" Again, where my rational Arguments
" againft the *Letter* feem to the *Bifhop* to
" be

" be weak and inconclufive; there, to
" do him Juftice, he handfomly turns
" upon me with his Reafoning, and ad-
" monifhes me of my Spitefulnefs againft
" the *Letter*, or I would never ufe fuch a
" flight Argument. But where I pinch
" and bear hard upon the *Letter*, and the
" Jeft is not to be digefted, there, inftead
" of Reafoning againft me, he makes a
" hideous Out-cry of Buffoonery, Blaf-
" phemy, and Infidelity; and calls upon
" the Civil Magiftrate for his Help, or
" their Religion, and their *All* is in Dan-
" ger, through the impious Writings of
" untoward Infidels.

" The *Bifhop* in fome Cafes gives up
" the Caufe, and feems himfelf to be al-
" moft afhamed of the *Letter*; and for
" the Maintenance of the Honour of *Je-*
" *fus*, and the Dignity of his miraculous
" Operation, flies to Allegory; allowing
" that *this* and *that* Miracle might be
" typical and figurative of fomewhat elfe,
" as his Thoughts did fuggeft to him. But
" here he difcovers his poor Talent at Al-
" legories, making no more Refemblance
" between the *Type* and *Antitype*, than
" between an *Apple* and an *Oyfter*.

" I am repeatedly charg'd by the *Bi-*
" *fhop* with Infidelity, for writing againft
" the *Letter*, tho' I am as grave as a Judge
" at

" at the allegorical Interpretation ; and
" he can't but know that Infidelity and
" Allegorifm are incompatible in the fame
" Perfon. To prove me an Infidel, he
" fhould have fhewn that I meant to pour
" Contempt upon the allegorical, as well
" as litteral Senfe of Jefus's Miracles;
" but he has not once hinted at this. A
" certain great Writer, call'd Mr. *Grounds*,
" plays a double Game upon the *Clergy*,
" he laughs at the *allegorical* as well as
" *litteral* Scheme, and diftreffes the *Clergy*
" with his Objections againft both. But
" I have not done fo ; I really am, or
" feem to be, a fincere Contender for the
" allegorical Senfe. And to make an *In-*
" *fidel* of an *Allegorift*, is more difficult
" and impoffible than to make a *Monkey*
" of a *Bifhop*.

" The *Bifhop*, as a *Minifter of the Let-*
" *ter*, has fpoken too favourably of the
" allegorical Scheme ; he has treated it
" with too much Refpect, both as to the
" Origin and Ufe of it, and done enough
" to fap the Foundation of his Church ;
" for which, I am afraid, he'll meet with a
" Reprimand from his Epifcopal Brethren.
" The *Bifhop* of *Lichfield* is the Man for
" my Money, to write againft the alle-
" gorical Scheme ; he tells us, that
" (*p*) *St.*

" (p) St. Paul *suffer'd in the Esteem of*
" *the Jewish Christians for his Neglect of*
" *Allegories*; *and seems to he brought in-*
" *to the Use of them against his own good*
" *liking.* And again, (q) *It seems to have*
" *been in compliance with Jewish Christi-*
" *ans, who were affected with allegorick*
" *Interpretations, that St. Paul used that*
" *way.* Which is as much as to say, St.
" *Paul* was more a *Minister of the Spi-*
" *rit,* than of Inclination he was disposed
" to be, or, in truth, ought to have been;
" and that, if he took upon him the Mi-
" nistry of the Spirit for the present, it
" was only craftily and politically done
" of him, to catch the *Jews* in their own
" Snare of Allegories. He was consent-
" ing that the Preachers of the Gospel,
" in future Times, should desert the *Mi-*
" *nistry of the Spirit,* and betake them-
" selves to the *Letter* of the Scriptures,
" as what is more agreeable to Truth,
" and conducive to the Defence and Pro-
" pagation of Christianity. Such a *Crafts-*
" *man* was the inspir'd St. *Paul,* in the
" Opinion of the *Bishop* of *Lichfield!*

(p) *Defence of Christianity,* p. 347.
(q) Ibid. p. 353.

" How-

" However, the *Bishop* of St. *David's*
" ought to be of the same Mind ; he should
" assert, that the *Ministry* of the *Spirit*
" was all apostolical Craft and antient Er-
" ror ; and that the present Generation
" of Priests, being wiser, more learned,
" and more sincere than the Primitive
" and Apostolical ones, do adhere to the
" *Ministry of the Letter*. Because the *Bi-*
" *shop* has not gone thus far by much, he
" leaves more room, than he should, for
" the Revival of the *Ministry of the Spi-*
" *rit* ; that is, of the spiritual and alle-
" gorical Interpretation of the Scriptures.

" The *Bishop* often reproves me for my
" primitive Interpretation of *this* and *that*
" Text of Scripture, and then palms his
" own forc'd Sense on us, for natural
" and genuine, contrary to the Judgment
" of all Antiquity.

" He is so *grave*, serious, and sedate at
" some simple Doctrines and Arguments,
" that his *Readers* must of necessity laugh,
" if not scoff at him. Was I *ludicrously*
" to handle the said Doctrines, my *Rea-*
" *ders* would hardly smile. Such a wide
" Difference is there between the *Levity*
" of a Buffoon (as he is pleased to call
" me) and the *Gravity* of an Ass, to the
" exposing of Religion to the Ridicule and
" Contempt of Mankind.

H   " Lastly,

" Laftly, He entirely miftakes the De-
" fign of my *Difcourfes*; he knows not
" what I aim and drive at. There's one
" Paradox runs through his whole Book,
" *viz.* That the litteral Story of our Sa-
" viour's Miracles muft of neceffity be
" true, or I fhould have no Foundation
" to build Allegories upon ; which is a
" grofs Miftake of other Writers againft
" me, as well as of himfelf. Who knows
" not that the profeft Parables of *Jefus*
" have nothing of *Letter* in them, yet are
" a good Foundation for Allegory ? And
" let me tell him here again, that what-
" ever was true, more or lefs, in the lit-
" teral Story of *Jefus*'s Miracles, there
" is abfolute Neceffity, for the Honour
" and Credit of them, to have Recourfe
" to the Myftery ; or litterally they are,
" and fhall be farther proved fuch———
" Stories, as I dare not at prefent call
" them.

Thus have I given a brief Account of
the *Bifhop*'s mighty and pompous Performance ; like to which he has promis'd us
another Volume, that I fhall long for the
publication of, next *Winter.* This my
brief Account is but introductory to future and larger Defences of my *Difcourfes*
on Miracles ; which, by the Help of God,

and

and Permiffion of the Civil Authority, fhall be likewife publifh'd.

I have not, I fay, room here fo much as to defend my felf on any one Miracle; and if I had, I would not do it. For as I can't do it without writing in the fame Stile and Strain for which I am profecuted, fo I will do nothing that may be interpreted as an Act in Defiance and Contempt of the Power of the Civil Magiftrate. I did indeed publifh two *Difcourfes* after the Commencement of the Profecution, becaufe I imagined that our *Bifhops* were more in Jeft than in Earneft; or if their Paffions were raifed for the prefent, I thought, that after a little Confideration of the unreafonablenefs of Perfecution in general, they would cool upon it, and drop the Profecution. But fince they are in Earneft, and I muft anfwer to the Civil Powers for fome fuppofed Crimes in my *Difcourfes*, I'll not repeat here the like Acts, but be quiefcent in refpect to the faid Powers, to whom Reverence and Obedience is juftly due. For, tho' I look upon the Ecclefiaftical Power as an Ufurpation on the Confciences of Mankind, yet the *Civil* is Sacred, is God's Ordinance, and ought to be regarded as fuch. But if I furvive the Profecution, and efcape with my Life and Liberty, which I don't

defpair

despair of, under so wise, just, and good a Magistracy as this Nation is bless'd with, the *Bishop* may expect a strenuous Defence of my self against his weak Assaults on me.

If our *Bishops* were any thing *Heroical*, they would stop the Prosecution, and let the Controversy take its free Course. If they had any Sense of Honour and Reputation, any Regard for their Learning, they would set any Adversary of their Church at Defiance, and disdain the Assistance of the Civil Magistrate to punish him, whom they could not confute. It is the Office of the *Bishops* and *Priests* of the Church, or I know not what is, to convert *Infidels*, to refute *Hereticks*, and by Reason and Argument to put to Silence all *Gain-sayers.* Wherefore have they a liberal and academical Education, but to qualify them for this Work? Wherefore do they receive large Revenues of the Church, but to oblige and encourage them to it? Nothing more unreasonable, than that Men should receive Wages, when they don't their Work. What will the People say hereupon less, than that an Army of at least Twenty thousand Blackguards of the Church are hired to little or no Purpose? The meanest of the People may as well be taken to Church Preferments,

ments, as our reputed learned Divines. They can difcharge other Eccleſiaſtical Offices; and when they are diſtreſs'd with an Objection to their Religion, can do no worſe than call upon the Civil Magiſtrate for his Aid and Aſſiſtance. But after all, I am inclin'd to think our *Biſhops*, in Honour, would forbear Perſecution, but for their Intereſts, call'd their *All*, which depend on the Iſſue of this Controverſy.

However, not to urge the Argument for Liberty of Debate any farther, which has been already by others treated on to Perfection, and will be again refumed, I doubt not, by fome body elſe, on occaſion of this *Biſhop*'s *Dedication*, I can't but take Notice here how unpolitick, as well as unchriſtian, fome Diſſenters are in this Controverſy, being, ſuch as Dr. *Harris*, and Mr. *Atkinſon*, no leſs for Perſecution than the *Clergy*. If they had a Regard to their own Intereſts and Liberties, they would be ſilent. Infidels (of whom I am none) ſhould be conſider'd as Diſſenting Brethren, whom they ſhould not be forward to oppreſs, for fear in time, and by degrees, it ſhould come to their own Turn. Our *Diſſenters* indeed, collectively, are vaſtly numerous, and a potent Party, but may truſt too much to their own Strength and Numbers. Taking
them

them feparately, they may poffibly be Extinguifh'd by Ecclefiaftical Art and Craft. If Blafphemy is a juft Pretence for the Profecution of me, the *Clergy*, upon Occafion, can urge the fame Crime againft them. I'll tell them a Story. The *Calvinifts* and *Socinians* were once equally tolerated in *Poland*, and if they had been faft Friends to each other, the *Papifts* could never have fupprefs'd them : But the *Calvinifts* joining with the *Papifts*, and urging them to complain againft the *Socinians* for Blafphemy, in denying the Divinity of the Son of God, moved the Civil Authority to a Banifhment of them; and the *Socinians* had not been long fupprefs'd, before the *Papifts* accus'd the *Calvinifts* of no lefs Blafphemy, in denying Adoration to the Virgin *Mary*; and fo they were fent packing too; otherwife they might both have enjoy'd their Liberty to this Day. The Application of the Story is eafy. So if all we *Diffenters* from the Church, whether we like one another's Principles or not, don't hold together for the Prefervation of our Liberties, it's eafy for Ecclefiafticks to feign an Accufation of *Blafphemy* againft any of us. We have no Security, but in the Wifdom and Goodnefs of an excellent Government, which, if the *Clergy*
fhould

should ever get on the Back of, its hardly a Question, whether they would not drive, *Jehu* like, most furiously.

But to return to my *Bishop*. I once thought he would never have been drawn into this Controversy. Sometime after the Publication of my Third *Discourse*, which, for a visible Reason, I dedicated to him, and invited him to Battle, I ask'd a dignify'd *Clergy-man*, Whether the *Bishop* would write against me? He answer'd, No: Whereupon I concluded, that he had a Scent of somewhat, not here to be mention'd. But my repeated Provocations of him afterwards, have forc'd him, against Inclination, to engage me. His Passion got the better of his Reason, or he had been certainly quiescent: And the Violence of his Passion is so visible thro' his whole Book, that it's God's great Mercy it did not throw him into a Fever and Convulsions, to the Danger of his Life and Health.

I own here again, what I have done before, that I did lay a Trap for our *Clergy*; but little imagined that two such great *Bishops*, as of *London* and St. *David's*, would, to my Pleasure and Satisfaction, have been caught in it. If I had not baited my Trap well with *Ridicule*, I dare say,

they

they would have kept themſelves clear of it.

But when I experienc'd the hard Uſage the Biſhops had given me upon my *Diſcourſes*, and the Fury with which they attack'd me, it ſurpriſed me, and brought to my Mind *Origen*'s Prediction (r) of this *very* War and Controverſy of the *Spirit* againſt the *Letter* of the *Scriptures*, and of the Violence it would be carried on with. For all my Veneration for the Authority of the Fathers, I did here ſuſpect the Truth of *Origen*'s Prediction, believing him to be miſtaken, and that the Controverſy would be manag'd in a *calm, decent*, and *ſedate* Manner ; and ſo it had been, but for the Intereſts of the *Clergy* that are at Stake in it, which I was not aware of. Finding then the Truth of *Origen*'s Prediction contrary to my Expectations, I had the Curioſity further to conſult the Fathers about the Iſſue of this Controverſy ; and they preſently, with their myſtical Fingers, pointed to a Prophecy of it in the *Revelations* of St. *John* ; but, to ſay no more at preſent, aſſur'd

---

(r) Eſt adhuc alia Pugna his omnibus violentior ; quod ii, quod Legem ſecundum Carnem intelligunt, adverſantur his, qui ſecundum ſpiritum ſentiunt, & perſequuntur eos. *In Geneſin Hom.* vii.

me,

me, that the *Spirit* would get the Better of the *Letter* in the Conclusion of it. Tho' I am accounted an Infidel, I am so easy and credulous a Christian as to believe all this ; and I thank God have so much Courage in me, as to try the Truth of it.

But I must observe here, that besides my two *Bishops*, of *London* and St. *David's*, (and some other inconsiderable *Triflers*) there are two *anonymous* Authors against me, whose Works have acquir'd some Fame. The One is intitled, *The Miracles of Jesus vindicated*, in *Three Parts.* If I could have gotten to the certain Knowledge of the Author, I should have been tempted to have had a Bout with him ; and to have expostulated with him, both with Regard to his Arguments and good Manners. I would have taught him a better Use, and a more proper Application of the Words *Dishonesty, and want of Honesty*, than to reproach me with them. Common Fame says, Dr. *Pearse*, of St. *Martin's*, is the Author ; but I am apt to think, the *King*'s Parish Priest, and other City *Divines*, have more Wit and Craft than to upbraid me as above, for fear a just Charge of *Dishonesty*, for their Extortions and Exactions on the People,

I   should

fhould be retorted on them. Upon the
Publication of the *Firft Part* of the forefaid Treatife, my *Jewifh Rabbi* comes to
me in all hafte, faying to me, " Look
" you here, do you fee how this Author
" has new vampt the old *mumpfimus* Ar-
" gument of *Jefus's* Refurrection ? Do
" you obferve how imperfectly, here and
" there, he anfwers my Objections to it;
" and filently flips by fome knotty Pieces
" of them, that were too hard for him to
" untie?" Yes, *Rabbi*, faid l, I do obferve all this; (and what I have obferv'd
fince, he argues, awkwardly and back-
wardly, for the Certainty of *Jefus's* other
Miracles, from his Refurrection.) My *Rabbi* prefently re-inforc'd his Refurrection-
Objection againft this Author, and would
have had me to print it. No, no, *Rabbi,*
faid I; you may print it your felf, if you
dare. I muft wait to hear how Caufes
will go in *Weftminfter-Hall*, next Term,
before I involve my felf in another Law-
Suit. Befides, *Rabbi*, they fay, I don't really thus correfpond with a *Jew*, but do
only perfonate one; and the *Bifhop* of St.
David's hints, that I am anfwerable to
publick Juftice for fo doing. Here my
my Rabbi ftampt with Indignation; faying, What if you did perfonate a *Jew* ?
Is it not lawful, and in Ufe with your
Divines,

Divines, to write Conferences between a Chriſtian and a *Jew*? And do you any more in this Caſe? Yes, *Rabbi*, ſaid I, it is lawful to write ſuch like Conferences, and to make *Jewiſh* Objections to Chriſtianity, when they are no ſtronger than may be eaſily diſſipated: But when Men write from the Heart, as you do, and raiſe a D - - - l that our *Clergy* can't eaſily lay, it is, they ſay, intolerable, and puniſhable; and either you or I, in the Opinion of the *Biſhop*, ought to ſuffer for it.

The other conſiderable *Treatiſe* againſt me, is that of *The Trial of the Witneſſes of the Reſurrection of Jeſus*; which is an ingenious Piece, and I was well pleaſed with it. Some time after the Publication of this *Treatiſe*, I made my Jewiſh *Rabbi* a Viſit, when, drinking a *Diſh* of *Tea* together, we talk'd it over; and my *Rabbi* was pleas'd to deliver his Sentiments of it in this faſhion: " Whoever was the " Author of this Treatiſe, God knows, " but he's certainly a Friend to my Ob- " jections againſt *Jeſus*'s Reſurrection, " which he has fairly ſtated; but is ſo " far from fully confuting all of them, " that he diſcovers a Conſciouſneſs, here " and there, that they are unanſwerable. " It is commonly reported that Biſhop " *Sherlock* is the Author of this *Treatiſe*,

" but

" but this Report I look upon as an Ar-
" tifice of the Bookfellers, to make it fell
" well; or rather the Author's contrived
" *Banter* upon the *Clergy*, and their weak
" Chriftian Brethren, to try how far they
" may be impofed on, and drawn into
" the Approbation and Admiration of a
" Treatife, that really makes againft them.
" There is but very little in this Trea-
" tife, to make it reputed a fufficient An-
" fwer to my Objections, excepting the
" Verdict of the *Jury*, who brought in
" the Witneffes of the Refurrection, *Not*
" *Guilty*, of either Fraud or Miftake in
" it. *Bifhop Sherlock* can't be the Author
" of this Treatife, if for no other Rea-
" fon than this, that *that* Author is vifi-
" bly againft that Ecclefiaftical Wealth
" and Power, which the *Bifhop* is pof-
" fefs'd of, and does think not difagree-
" able to the Mind of Chrift and his poor
" Apoftles. If any *Bifhop* is the conceal-
" ed Author of this Treatife, he muft fe-
" cretly be of the Opinion of the athe-
" iftical Pope, who faid, *quantum nobis*
" *profuit hæc de Chrifto Fabula*, what vaft
" Advantage has the Story of Chrift been
" to us Popes and Bifhops." I readily gave
into the Opinion of my *Rabbi*, and wonder'd, *Bifhop Sherlock* did not fo much as by
a publick Advertifement clear himfelf of
being

being the Author of this Treatise, and so put a Stop to the Report. It may be the *Bishop* is above the Scandal of it; but I was so concern'd for his Reputation, that I drew up a *Vindication* of him from the Slander of it; which I had publish'd, but for my *Rabbi's* farther Thoughts about the Resurrection of Jesus inserted in it, that our *Bishops* might have possibly taken Offence at. So I dropp'd that Design at present, but hope still for an Opportunity to publish the said Vindication of the *Bishop*, by which, I don't doubt, but to merit his Friendship and Favour.

But whoever was the real Author of the foresaid Treatise, I humbly and heartily beg of him to publish, what in the Conclusion of it, he has given us some Hopes of, *The Trial of the Witnesses of the Resurrection of* LAZARUS, because my *Rabbi's* Objections to it are a Novelty and Curiosity, which, by way of such a Reply to them, I should be glad to see handled.

But having here by Chance mention'd my *Rabbi's* Letter concerning *Lazarus's* Resurrection, it brings to my Mind a Challenge I made to the *Bishop* of *London* upon it, *viz.* (s) " If he would publish an

---

(s) In Fifth *Discourse*, p. 67.

" Answer

" Anſwer to that Letter, and vouchſafe
" me the Pleaſure of a Reply to it; then
" (to ſave the *Civil Magiſtrates* Trouble)
" I would ſuffer ſuch Puniſhment that
" he in his Clemency ſhould think fit to
" inflict on me, for what's paſt." An ingenuous *Clergy-man*, upon reading this,
ſaid, that the *Biſhop* was bound, in Honour, to accept of my Challenge, or, what
was in his Power, in Generoſity, to put a
Stop to the Proſecution. But the *Biſhop*
is not of his Mind. And for what Reaſon he does not accept of my Challenge,
is beſt known to himſelf, and others will
conjecture. If he had not condeſcended
to write againſt me in his *Paſtoral Letter*,
I ſhould have imagined, that he thought
it beneath the Dignity of One of his exalted Station in the Church, to ſet his
Wit (for dignified Prieſts, for the moſt
part, think their Wit and Learning pro-
portion'd to their Wealth and Power) a-
gainſt ſuch a poor Author as I am. But
this is not the Reaſon. It may be, he
thinks his Reputation and Honour ſecure
in the Height of his Grandeur, and that
his Dependents will admire his Learning
nothing the leſs for his Neglect of my
Challenge. However it be, this I will ſay,
that were we upon the Level in the World
as to Fortune, as well as we are to Age
and

and Education, the Learned would despise him for declining the reasonable Challenge of one, whom he has injuriously treated and persecuted. It's to no Purpose to challenge him here afresh; he, being purpos'd to carry the Matter with an high Hand, has taken other Measures, and is resolv'd to make use of his Power and Interest to suppress him, whom with Reason and Argument he can't convince.

However, I will here make another Proposal to the *Bishop* of St. *David's*. Because he thirsts after a very severe Punishment of me, or he would not be so warm in his Exhortations of the Government to that Purpose, I'll tell him how he may glut his Revenge, and inflict a greater Punishment on me, than, in all probability, the Civil Magistrate will humour him in. If he'll but put a Stop to the Prosecution at present (which is not out of the Power of our *Bishops*, whatever they may pretend) and let the Controversy go on, till I have finish'd my Reply to his *two Volumes*, which shall be done with all Expedition; then, if his Passion is not allay'd, I will submit to any Punishment, he in his Wisdom and Justice, without Mercy, shall think fit to have laid on me, whether it be to Death or Imprisonment. And what would he, or any implacable

Priest

Prieſt, deſire more? This Propoſal makes him my Judge as well as my Accuſer, and if he be not the moſt unreaſonable Man alive, he muſt accept of it. All my Hopes here are, that his Reaſon may recover its Dominion over his Paſſion, againſt the Concluſion of my *Defence*, or it will go hard with me. If the *Biſhop* will not comply with this Propoſal, I ſhall conclude, he's poſſeſs'd with the only certain and allegorical *Satan*, mention'd in my *Diſcourſes* ; and I ſhall be confirm'd in the Opinion of St. *Hilary* (whoſe Teſtimonies about Devils, the *Biſhop* has ſilently paſs'd by, without any Charge upon me for Miſrepreſentation) that there are no worſe *Devils* in the World, than the calumniating, furious, and perſecuting Tempers of Mankind. The *Biſhop*, by the by, has taken Pains to prove there are other *Devils*, of an infernal, frightful, and independent Nature, and of a more certain Exiſtence than *Hobgoblins* ; and he gravely aſſerts, that three of thoſe *Devils* enter'd into each *Hog*, that ran violently down-hill ; thereby making the little *Pigs* to carry as great a Burden as the old *Boars* and *Sows*, which ſhould have been better thought of by him. The *Biſhop*, perhaps, for theſe my Deſcants, will ſay I am an Infidel ; but I aſſure him, it is one

of

of the Articles of my Primitive and Christian Faith, that the old *Dragon*, *Satan*, the *Serpent*, or the *Devil*, mention'd in the *Revelations*, is no other than the furious, violent, and persecuting Spirit in Man; which, upon the World's getting Liberty of Religion, will be bound and chain'd. And it is the Opinion of Thousands, as well as of my self, that Mankind will never be Happy, nor at Rest, till this *Devil* is exorcised out of the Priesthood, and so of consequence chain'd up. According to the primitive Way of interpreting the *Revelations* of St. *John*, the Time is near at Hand for the *binding* this Apocalyptical old *Dragon* or *Satan*, that has pester'd the World through all Ages past. All the Honour that I desire, is, by my Studies and Endeavours to be contributing to so great a Work, for the Good and Happiness of Mankind.

To conclude. I have been the more expeditious in printing of this Discourse, not only for fear the *Bishop*'s *Vindication* (as it is call'd) should have a *malign Influence* upon some People, I don't mean our *Civil Magistrates*, who are wiser and more learned than to be guided by such outragious Stuff; but because he should not long triumph in a Conceit of the Po-

K   tency

tency and Excellency of his Performance, as if no Reply could or would be made to it. If I had at this Time enjoy'd free Liberty of Debate, I should not have thought it worth my while to meddle with his *Dedication*, which with a Scorn I should have pass'd by, and left to the Animadversions and Chastisement of other Enemies to Persecution ; but would immediately have enter'd upon a Defence of my *Discourses* against him. If I do retrieve my Liberty, and the free Use of my Pen, and should not publish Defences of my self, I should deserve (what *one* said the *Bishop* of *London*, for his declining my Challenge, deserv'd) to be piss'd upon for a vain Pretender to Argument and Authority.

In the mean time, I have nothing to request of our *Clergy*, but that Liberty of Debate may be indulg'd us ; *that* Liberty of theological Disputation, which would be granted, if they did not industriously labour to obstruct it. When will they cease to disgrace Truth, to dishonour their Religion, and to disparage their own Education and Learning ; and no longer envy Mankind the blessed Enjoyment of such a Liberty !

But

But their Religion, they fay, would be in Danger upon fuch a Liberty. How can that be? How can Chriftianity be in Danger, that has not only the Omnipotence of God on his Side, but a numerous ftanding Army of Priefts, hired for the Defence of it? It is not then their Concern for Religion, that prompts them to fo much Zeal here; but their Fears for their Interefts, that depend on the Iffue of this Controverfy.

Was I to write againft any other honeft *Trade*, that is practifed in this City, the Artificers of it, being fenfible of the Ufefulnefs of their Craft, would let me go on unmolefted; and only pity and defpife me for the Vanity of my Attempt to fubvert them : But the *Clergy*, being prick'd with a Confcioufnefs of the Mifchiefs and Inconveniencies of their Eftablifhment, do therefore thus winch and kick.

And who, befides the *Clergy*, are at this time Enemies to Liberty? None hardly, but their immediate Dependents, whom they can eafily infufe their fiery and furious Notions into. Was it to be voted this Day among the learned *Laity*, I dare fay, the Friends of Perfecution would be found vaftly fhort of the Numbers of their Adverfaries. And I hope to God, the Le-

giflative

giſlative Authority of theſe Nations will ſoon take the Matter into their Conſideration; and either limit or enlarge the Bounds of Liberty, that honeſt and well-meaning Men may be no longer harraſs'd and moleſted, for their ſincere Endeavours to ſerve the Publick.

No Body, I truſt, can complain of any diſreſpectful Uſage, I have here given the *Biſhop* of St. *David's*, that conſiders, how he has treated me in *his Sermon before the Societies for Reformation*; and *in his Charge to the Clergy of his Dioceſe*; as well as *in his Vindication.* It would be ſufficient, if I had no other Excuſe for my ſelf than *this*, That Controverſy is like a *Game* at *Foot ball*, in which, if a *Lord* will engage with a *Plowman*, and ſhould meet with a Kick on the Shins, he ought not to complain of the ill Manners of it: So if a *Biſhop* will diſpute with one of lower Degree, he muſt look for a Rub on his Intellects, a Rap on his Pate, and if his Adverſary cuts him on a ſoft Place, he ſhould know how to bear it with Patience. But the *Biſhop*, contrary to this *Game-Rule* in Controverſy, complains (t) of my *unmannerly* Treat-

---

(t) In his Preface, p. 17, 18.

ment

ment of him, and cries out of the Sufferings and Reproaches he undergoes, as if he was already more than half a Martyr for Religion. I can't pretend to equal him in Reproaches and Sufferings, having not so quick a Senfe of them ; and therefore I am willing, that good Christian People should pity my poor *Bishop*, rather than me, in a persecuted and sorrowful Condition.

How long it will be, before I publish another, and *second* Part of my *Defence*, is uncertain, for a Reason, that I need not again mention. But if it please God, that I enjoy Life, Health, and Liberty, I'll go on with my Designs. I am resolv'd to give the *Letter* of the Scriptures no Rest, so long as I am able by Reason and Authority to disturb it. If our Ministers of the *Letter* will not ascend with me, the sublime and allegorical *Mountain* of divine Contemplation, they shall have no Comfort nor Enjoyment of themselves in the low *Valley* of the *Letter*, if I can disquiet them. Notwithstanding what the *Bishop* has written in *Vindication* of *Jesus*'s Miracles, the litteral Story of them, by the Leave of God, and of the Civil Magistrate, shall be afresh attack'd, and perhaps with more *Ridicule*, than I used before.

fore. What should I flinch for ? The litteral Story of *Jesus*'s Miracles is not, in the Opinion of the Fathers, as well as of my self, agreeable to Sense and Reason; neither can *Jesus*'s Authority and Messiahship be founded on the *Letter* of them. I am not for the *Messiahship* of a carnal *Jesus*, who cured the bodily Diseases of Blindness and Lameness; but for the Messiahship of the spiritual *Jesus*, who will cure the Blindness and Lameness of our Understandings. I am for the Messiahship of the spiritual *Jesus*, who will expel the mercenary Preachers out of his Church, after the manner that *Jesus* in the Flesh is supposed to have driven the Sellers out of the Temple, which litterally is but a sorry Story. I am for the Messiahship of the spiritual *Jesus*, who exorcised the furious and persecuting Devils out of the Mad-men of *Jews* and *Gentiles*; and tho' he permitted them to enter into a Herd of Ecclesiastical Swine, yet will precipitate them into the Sea of Divine Knowledge. I am for the spiritual *Jesus*, who will cure the *Woman* of the Church, of her *Issue of Blood*, that is shed in Persecution and War; which her Ecclesiastical Physicians, and Quack-Doctors of the *Clergy*, have not been able to do, tho' they have

received

received large Fees and Revenues to that End. I am for a spiritual *Messiah*, who will cure the Woman of the Church of her *Infirmity*, at the Spirit of Prophecy, of whose Infirmity this Age is her *eighteenth* Year. So could I write of all *Jesus*'s Miracles; for the whole Evangelical History is Figure and Shadow of the spiritual *Jesus*, whom we should *know to be in us of a Truth, unless we be Reprobates*. The *Clergy*, if they are not wilfully blind, may hence see my Christian Faith and Principles; and be assured, that what I do in this Controversy, is with a View to the Honour of God, the Advancement of Truth, the Edification of the Church, and Demonstration of the Messiahship of the Holy *Jesus*, to whom be Glory for ever. *Amen.*

F I N I S.

Mr. *WOOLSTON's*

DEFENCE

OF HIS

DISCOURSES

ON THE

Miracles of our *Saviour.*

Againſt the Bishops of St. *David's*
and *London*, and his other Adverſaries.

PART II.

---

*Nec Religionis eſt cogere Religionem, quæ ſponte
ſuſcipi debeat, non Vi.* Tertull.

LONDON:

Printed for the Author, and Sold by him
next Door to the *Star*, in *Aldermanbury*, and
by the Bookſellers of *London* and *Weſtminſter.*
MDCCXXX.

[*Price One Shilling.*]

TO THE

RIGHT HONOURABLE

Sir *Robert Raymond*, Kt.

Lord Chief Juſtice of the Court of *King's Bench*.

MY LORD,

T HAT I am no Flatterer of *Patrons*, appears by my other *Dedications* : If therefore I ſhould tell your *Lordſhip*, what I can in Sincerity, that I think you as wiſe and good a Magiſtrate, as any of your *Predeceſſors* in that *High Court* of *Juſtice*, you may be aſſured, I don't diſſemble.

A 2   Tho'

Tho' I was so unfortunate, *My Lord*, as to receive a Sentence in your Court, which I wish'd to avoid; yet I have no worse Opinion of your Wisdom and Justice. Your Conduct towards me, from first to last, has rather heighten'd than lessen'd my Esteem and Veneration for you. I observ'd in you such a Tenderness for our religious Liberties; such an Aversion to Persecution; and such Moderation towards my self, that if I had been absolutely acquitted, it would have been but with somewhat more Satisfaction.

And if I now write to clear my self of all Suspicions of Infidelity, for which I was sentenced; your *Lordship*, I humbly presume, will not think the worse of me. It is not expected that the Innocent should

con-

confeſs Guilt, in a Compliment to any Court of Juſtice : Nor does the Condemnation of the Guiltleſs, at any time almoſt, ſo much affect the Juſtice of the Magiſtrate, as the Honeſty of the Evidence : So I, *My Lord,* know how to lay the Blame entirely on my Eccleſiaſtical Accuſers, and believe your *Lordſhip* will be rather pleas'd than offended at any good Defence I can make for my ſelf.

From the Beginning of the Proſecution againſt me, *my Lord,* I hardly believed, that any Sentence would be paſs'd on me, till the Day I received it : And the Reaſon was, not only becauſe the good Tendency of my *Diſcourſes* was ſo viſible, that I thought it could not be overlook'd by the Wiſe and Learned ; but becauſe I imagin'd our *Biſhops* would have better conſulted their Reputation,

tion, than to let Matters come to this Iſſue.

That it is a Tranſgreſſion of the Law of the Land to write againſt Chriſtianity, eſtabliſh'd in it, I'll not queſtion, ſince I have your *Lordſhip*'s Word for it : But for all that, I could wiſh, for the Sake of Chriſtianity, that ſuch a Liberty was indulg'd to *Infidels*. Whatever our zealous *Clergy* may think, one Perſecution of an *Infidel* does more Harm to Religion, than the Publication of the worſt *Book* againſt it.

Liberty is ſo eſſential, *My Lord*, to the Enquiry after Truth, that where It is wanted, Truth will want that Splendor, which it receives from Diſputation : And Chriſtianity would be the more tryumphant over its Enemies, for that unbounded

ed Liberty, they may enjoy to con-
test it from the *Press*. I say this,
not for the Security of my self,
against future Prosecutions but,
from a Heart, full of Zeal for the
Religion of the Holy *Jesus*.

Ever since the *Reformation*, which
was founded on our Natural and
Christian Rights to Liberty of Conscience, has this great Blessing of
Liberty, at Times, been interrupted
by Persecutions : But whether any
of them hitherto have done any
Service to *Church* or *State*, your
Lordship is a good Judge.

However, tho' the Prosecution
of my self, which was founded on
a grand Mistake, is attended with
no ill Consequence ; yet I hope
our *Ecclesiasticks* will grow cautious
by it, and no more sollicit the most
indulgent Civil Magistracy of this
King-

Kingdom to the Perfecution of any
other, much lefs of,

My *Lord*,

Your Lordfhip's

London May
25. 1730.

Moft Obedient and

Humble Servant,

Tho. Woolfton.

A

SECOND PART

OF THE

DEFENCE, &c.

T's Time now to publiſh
another *Part* of my *De-*
fence, which, in my former, I gave my *Readers*
ſome Reaſon to expect
from me. If I ſhould
keep Silence much long-
er, my *Adverſaries* will be ready to charge
me with Cowardice, or Inſufficiency; and
ſay, that I'm either abſolutely confuted by
the *Writers* againſt me, or ſo terrified by
the Civil Magiſtrate's Authority, that I
either can't, or dare not, engage afreſh in
the ſame Cauſe. And I muſt confeſs, that

B   if

if I was not convinced of the Goodnefs of my Caufe, which is no other than God's, and of my Ability to defend it, I fhould chufe to hold my Peace, and be glad that it has fared no worfe with me.

One Reafon indeed why I have been fo long ere I publifh'd *this*, is pure Refpect to the Civil Powers, whom I am oblig'd, as a Chriftian, to honour and reverence, fo far as may be, without Difobedience to God. Had I haftily, and as foon almoft as *Sentence* was pafs'd on me, publifh'd *this*, fome might have interpreted it, as an Act of Defiance and Contempt of the Civil Authority, (for there are not wanting thofe who will put the worft Conftruction they can on my Conduct;) therefore I forbore for a while: And now that I appear again from the *Prefs*, it is not without profeffing a profound Veneration for our Civil Magiftracy, who, I am fure, will never think the worfe of a Man for vindicating his own Innocency, or for writing in a Caufe that, in his Confcience, he is perfuaded is moft juft and good.

Another Reafon why I committed this no fooner to the Prefs, was to wait the Publication of the *Bifhop* of *St. David's* his *Second Volume*, which he promifed us laft Winter. I was almoft of Opinion, that,

that, in my former *Defence*, I gave the *Bishop* such Intimations of my sincere Belief of Christianity, notwithstanding my *Discourses* on *Miracles*, and of the Falseness of his repeated Charge against me for Infidelity, that I question'd whether he would write again in the same Strain. If the *Bishop* is convinced of this his grand Mistake about me, then the very Foundation of his past and future Work is shaken, and I shall hear no more of him. But whether he is certainly convinc'd of his Mistake or not, I am concern'd to go on with these *Defences* of my self, and to vindicate the Goodness and Usefulness of the Design of my *Discourses* on *Miracles*, against what the *Bishops* of *London* and *St. David's*, and other *Adversaries* have written to the contrary.

But, before I enter upon such a *Defence* of my self and my *Discourses*, I must make, what is proper here, a short Preface. It is well known, that I am for Liberty of Debate, and against all Persecution or Force, or Impositions on the Consciences of Mankind. But for all that, there are some *Rules* in Controversy that we polemical *Writers* should observe, and be oblig'd to; or, instead of discovering and illustrating the Truth we pretend to

B 2   search

ſearch for, we ſhall but the more darken, obſtruct and perplex it. As,

Firſt, We ſhould endeavour to write as plainly and intelligibly as we can, and never amuſe our *Readers* with Expreſſions void of Senſe, or with falſe Reaſoning againſt our *Adverſaries,* where we want what's good and ſolid. This *Rule* none can except againſt: Whether I am an Obſerver of this *Rule,* my Readers are to be Judges. As I am to anſwer it to God and a good Conſcience, I endeavour to obſerve it; but much queſtion, whether ſome of my *Adverſaries* can ſay ſo too, or they would never vent ſuch dark, impertinent and unintelligible Stuff, if it was not, becauſe they are at a Loſs for what's clear and ſhining. There's no End of giving Inſtances out of their Writings to this Purpoſe. I ſhall only mention one, that's repeated amongſt them, and that is, of their pretended Diſtinction between Popiſh *Perſecution* and Proteſtant *Proſecution* for Opinions, wherewith they have amuſed weak and injudicious Heads. The Wiſe, I am ſure, can diſcern no more Difference here, than between a *Rope* and a *Halter* to hang an innocent Man, in which Caſe too there is a *nominal* Diſtinction without a *real* Difference.

Second

Secondly, We should be open and sincere in our Opinions, and not profess with our Mouths to believe, what we disown in our Hearts; nor, like *Watermen*, that look one way and row another, should we pretend to have one Design in View, when we are pursuing the quite contrary. This is a reasonable *Rule*, and ought to be observ'd, or we shall confound the Understandings of our *Readers*, who will soon lose Sight of our Arguments, if they apprehend not their Aim and Drift. This *Rule*, my Adversaries will say, is levell'd at my self, than whom no body has more dissembled and prevaricated in his Opinions. Have not you, will they say to me, frequently declared, that your Design in your *Discourses* is to make way for the Proof of the Truth of Christianity, and of the Messiahship of the Holy *Jesus*, when you mean and intend the Subveron of both? And is not here grand Hypocrisy, and a Transgression of this Rule ? Yes, if I intend the Subversion of Christ's Religion and Messiahship, here is grand Hypocrisy, and a Transgression of this *Rule* ; and I can't think of such a Piece of Prevarication without Horror. The Bishop of *St. David's*, (1) and Mr. *Stack-*

---

(1) *Vindication in Preface,* p. ix, x.

house, (2) in particular, have animadverted upon me for such Hypocrify; and if I was guilty of it, in much gentler Terms than I deferv'd. This Hypocrify, which they falfely charge me with, is as heinous a Sin as I can think of; it is as bad as wilful *Perjury*, as bad as a *Clergyman*'s taking the Abjuration Oath, with his Heart full of Zeal and Affection for the Pretender, and worfe than his giving his folemn Affent and Confent to Articles of Religion he believes little or nothing of. I fhould hardly have mention'd this *Rule* to be obferv'd in Controverfy, if I had been guilty of the Breach of it. It is fomewhat excufable in *Infidels* a little to difguife their real Sentiments, for fear of the Danger they may incur by an open Profeffion of them: But fuch a grofs and foul Mask of Hypocrify, as fome think I have here put on, is intolerable, and muft be hateful to *Infidels* as well as *Chriftians*, being obftructive to Truth, which, in all Inquirers after her, loves Sincerity and Simplicity. No doubt, but my *Adverfaries*, fome of them, will ftill think me a Tranfgreffor of this *Rule*; but my prefent and following *Defences* will abfolutely clear me. And if none of my *Adverfaries* are more guilty

(2) *Fair State of the Controverfy*, p. 293, 294.

of

of the Transgression of it than my self,
we are all entirely innocent.

Thirdly, In Controversy we should avoid
all wilful Misrepresentation of the Sense
of our *Adversaries,* and of the *Authors*
we pretend to cite. Mistakes and Mis-
apprehensions of one another will sometimes unavoidably happen, and are then
as innocent things as involuntary Errors.
But wilful Perversion and Falsification of
another Author's Words, to the Service of
our selves, or to the Prejudice of our *Adversaries,* is most blameable, and of that
ill Consequence to the Search after Truth,
that it will keep us always at a Distance
from her. This then is another good
Rule to be observed in Controversy, which
some may wonder I have mention'd, because of that Misrepresentation and Falsification of Authorities I am charg'd with.
And I must confess, my *Adversaries* have
here made an hideous Outcry against me;
which if I can't acquit my self of, I am
the foulest Controvertist that ever appear'd
in Print. The Bishop of *St. David's* (3)
calls my *Falsification* of Authorities, an
Immorality, and speculative *Forgery* ; but
if I was so guilty as he would have me
thought, he speaks too favourably of it.

(3) *In his Preface,* p. xi.

He

He should have deem'd it as great a Crime
as practical *Forgery* by the Law; and all
Philosophers and Lovers of Truth should
wish it might be likewise punish'd.

But, good Christian Reader, don't too
hastily pass thy Judgment on me. Sus-
pend awhile; it may be, that I may un-
expectedly vindicate my self. The Matter as yet is under Debate, whether my
Adversaries or I are the grand Misrepre-
senters and Falsifiers of Authorities. One
would think, that my Adversaries, who
were bent on the Accusation of me for the
foresaid Crime, should have kept themselves
clear of it: But the *Bishop* of *St. David*'s
(4) is such a resolute *Misrepresenter*, that
he could not find in his Heart faithfully to
transcribe the *Three Heads* of my *Discourses*; but by a Suppression of some Words,
and the Change of others, has given them
an odious and invidious Turn to my Disadvantage: And he has studied so hard
to pervert the Sense of the Fathers against
me, and so tortured his Brain to make
me a Misrepresenter of them, that I should
not wonder, if he had labour'd under a
Pain in his Head ever since, and is unable to write more. Tho' my Word should
not be taken for all this at present; yet

(4) *Vindication*, p. 2.

in

in the Sequel of thefe *Defences*, it will be made manifeft.

It is a great Temptation to our *Bifhops* falfely to accufe and mifreprefent their Adverfaries; becaufe they know their Writings don't equally fpread and go together among all their Readers. A *Bifhop's* Writing going more by itfelf amongft the *Clergy*, and other Friends to his Side of the Queftion, he is tempted to mifreprefent his Adverfaries, knowing his prejudiced Readers will take his Report of them, and credit it. For this Reafon, and no other, did the *Bifhop* of *Litchfield* (5) falfely charge the *Author* of the *Grounds* with odious Affertions, to which there is nothing akin in the Places feemingly referr'd to, nor in all that Author's Work.

However, the *Rule* in Controverfy before laid down is a good, ufeful and neceffary one. I pray God we may all be religious and confcientious Obfervers of it, or we fhall retard the Difcovery of Truth, and render our Attainment of it difficult, if not impoffible.

Fourthly, We fhould think our felves oblig'd to fet our Names to our Writings in Controverfy, efpecially where it is fuch a *warm* one as is ours at prefent. The

(5) *Defence of Chriftianity*, p. 295. 310.

C   Obfer-

Obfervation of this *Rule* would not only
prevent much of the Violation of the *two*
former; but would hinder abundance of
the Dirt of Scandal, Lies and Defamations,
that we too often throw at each other.
For what Reafon fome of the *Writers* (6)
againft me have induftrioufly conceal'd
their Names, I know full well. They perhaps would have it thought Modefty, and
that they are not ambitious of the publick
Praifes they may deferve for their learned
and elaborate Performances. And poffibly it may be Modefty in fome Theological Authors to conceal themfelves: But
where Men have the Impudence to defame, it's in vain to pretend to the Cloak
of Modefty to cover themfelves under.
Wherefore then do they fometimes who
write on the eftablifh'd Side of the Queftion, on which Honour and Preferment
goes, thus conceal themfelves? Why, that
they might belie and flander their Adverfaries the more fecurely, without being
expoftulated with for their Impudence. It's
to no Purpofe, they know, to upbraid an
anonymous Author with his Scandal, becaufe he can't be put to the Blufh for it.

---

(6) *Some Obfervations of a Layman.*
Letter to his Coufin T. Woolfton.
Or, Juft Chaftifement no Perfecution.
Scripture-Hiftory, &c.
2. Tom *of* Bedlam's
3. *For God or the Devil:*
4. *A Defence of the*

And

And a wise Man will not lose his Labour
to expose and confute a libellous Writing,
unless he knew whom to charge with the
Guilt of it. It is my Resolution to take
no Notice of any nameless Authors against
me, because I, being as it were blindfold-
ed, engage them at a Disadvantage, whilst
they have a full View of me. For this
Reason the *Tryal of the Witnesses* was
pass'd by, or I should have been tempted
to have made some Remarks on it. Let
such *Authors* come forth into the Light,
and it may be, they'll meet with the same
Favour I have done the *Bishop* of *St. David's*. In the mean time, I declare my
Abhorrence of Authors their Concealment
of their Names, and I hope all ingenuous
Writers in Controversy will do so too; tho'
for no other Reason, than to prevent Mis-
representations, Defamations, and personal
Reflections, which nameless Authors are
too often guilty of.

Fifthly, and *lastly*, Others make it a
common *Rule* to be observ'd in Controversy, that the *Disputants* should consider each other's Arguments impartially,
without the Byass of Prejudice and Interest. And a very good *Rule* this is, if
Men would but put it into Practice. But
I shall long despair of such Impartiality
in Controversy. Such is the Power of

Preju-

Prejudice and Interest, that they will influence Men to believe against the most
apparent Reason and Truth. Even Prejudice will much darken the Eyes of Mens
Underſtandings, but Intereſt will put them
quite out. O what a horrible Obſtacle
to the free Enquiry after Truth, is Intereſt! Againſt Demonſtration itſelf will Men
contend for Intereſt. Intereſt, upon Occaſion, will induce them to deſert the beſt
Opinions, and keep them tight to the
worſt. This Experience proves true, and
the various Faces of the Church, and
Changes of the *Clergy* (all for Intereſt) is
a Witneſs of it. God forbid that I ſhould
judge uncharitably of the Corruption of
human Nature under the Power of Intereſt; but I believe, that was our *Legiſla-*
ture to do, what they never will, that is,
ſet up the Figure of a *Calf* in our Churches, there would be no want of Prieſts to
worſhip him, if they were well paid for
it; nor of Academical *Students* to prove
his divine Power and Godſhip, if the Road
to Preferment lay that Way. For this
Reaſon, among many others, I am for the
Abolition of an hired and eſtabliſh'd Prieſthood, that this grand Bar of Intereſt may
be removed out of our Way to Truth.
And the *Biſhop* of *London*, that excellent
Prelate, as *Biſhop Smalbroke* calls him (for
ſo

so do we, like other Creatures, knab one another where it itches) should by rights be of my Mind, saying, (7) "Where there " is an Unwillingness to part with worldly " Interests, there must of Course be a *De-* " *sire* that the Christian Religion should " not be true; and a *Willingness* to fa- " vour and embrace any Argument that " is brought against it, and to cherish any " Doubts and Scruples that shall be rais'd " concerning it."   So feelingly does this *Bishop* speak of the Power of Interest, by which, as I would conceive, he honestly hints to the Inhabitants of *London* and *Westminster*, that the *Bishop* of their Dio-cese, and the *Parson* of their Parish, are most unfit Guides in Religion, because of the worldly Interests they may have to deceive them, and keep them in Igno-rance and Error.

Thus by way of Preface having spoken to the foregoing *Rules* to be observed in this Controversy, I come to a close *De-fence* of myself against the Charge of In-fidelity, and to vindicate the Usefulness of my *Discourses on Miracles* for the Proof of the Truth of Christianity, and of the Messiahship of the Holy *Jesus*, against all my Adversaries.   And the Method I

(7) *In his* First Pastoral Letter, p. 5.

shall

shall take to this Purpose, is this fol-lowing.

I. To show the Weakness, Childishness, and Insufficiency of the Arguments of my *Adversaries*, for the *Letter* of the Stories of *Jesus*'s Miracles; and further to prove both *ludicrously* and *seriously* the Absurdities, Incredibilities, and Improbabilities, that their literal Stories labour under.

II. To prove, that whether there be any Sense, Truth and Fact, or not, in the Letter of *Jesus*'s Miracles; yet they are Typical Things, and ought to be allegorically interpreted, and will receive a mysterious and more wonderful Accomplishment, after the manner, and to the same Purpose, that the Fathers and I do apply them, being no other (whether actually wrought or not) than Figures, Signs and Emblems of his future and mysterious Operations.

III. To show that the mysterious and future Accomplishment of these supposed Works and Miracles of *Jesus* alone can and will be the Proof of his Messiahship.

If I perform well upon these Heads, which are deserving of my *Reader*'s Review, because of their Pertinency to the Cause in Hand, I shall not only vindicate

myself

myfelf from the Charge of Infidelity, but juftify the Goodnefs and Ufefulnefs of my *Difcourfes*, in order to the Demonftration of *Jefus*'s Meffiahfhip. And in the midft of my handling of them, without going out of my Way, I fhall, as Occafion offers itfelf, take Notice of particular Mifreprefentations of the Fathers, and falfe Citations out of them, that my Adverfaries charge me with: And Bifhop *Smalbroke* and others had beft to look to it, or their Accufations againft me will recoil and return home to them. Then

I. I fhould fhow the Weaknefs, Childifhnefs and Infufficiency of the Arguments of my *Adverfaries* for the *Letter* of *Jefus*'s Miracles; and further argue both *ludicroufly* and *ferioufly* the Abfurdities, Incredibilities and Improbabilities, that their literal Stories labour under.

I fhould, I fay, firft treat on this Head, which naturally precedes the two following; but in as much as to handle it to Perfection, I fhould write as I did before, and fhall run in Danger of Profecution for Blafphemy and Infidelity; I muft of Neceffity wave and poftpone it, unlefs I could more than difpatch it in the Compafs of this *Part* of my *Defence*.

I have

I have heretofore made folemn Profeffions of my Belief of Chriftianity, and moft ferioufly declared in the plaineft Terms, that my Defign was not to do Service to Infidelity, but to make way for the Proof of Chrift's Religion and Meffiahfhip ; but my Word was not taken, being look'd upon as a Diffembler, an Hypocrite, and Prevaricator, for all that. And fhould I now ever fo gravely repeat the like Affeverations of the Integrity and Sincerity of my Heart, that my Objections againft the Letter of *Jefus*'s Miracles are none againft his Religion, but only intended to turn Mens Heads to the myftical Interpretations of them ; I queftion much whether I fhould be believed, and whether *Bifhop Smalbroke* (8) would not fay again, *that this is too thin a Difguife of what feems to be my great and worfe Defign.* What then in Prudence muft I do in this Cafe ? Why, I muft let *This Head,* which reafonably fhould precede, reft for a while ; and by treating on the *Second,* tho' out of Place, I muft firft effectually convince my Adverfaries, that I am no *Infidel* of wicked Defigns to fubvert Chriftianity, but only the *Miniftry of the Letter* ; and then, I conceive, I may fafely refume the Con

fideration

fideration of this *Firſt Head*, and without the Imputations of Infidelity and Blaſphemy, write as *merrily* or *gravely* as I pleaſe againſt the Letter.

Should any ſay, that this pretended Reaſon for waving this *Firſt Head* for the preſent, is nothing but Cowardice and Inability to write more on it, I can't help it. *Ictus Piſcator ſapit;* I have already ſuffer'd much for the ludicrous Treatment of the *Letter*, and it is Wiſdom to keep, if I can, out of the like Danger; neither will I do any thing, that in Conſcience I can forbear, to incur the Diſpleaſure of the Civil Magiſtrate. But however, if the *Biſhop* of *London* would enſure me againſt, what the *Biſhop* of *St. David*'s calls, the (9) *Nominal* Perſecutions of *Proteſtants*, which I am more afraid of, than of the *real* Perſecutions of *Papiſts*, I will ſoon enter upon this Head; otherwiſe for Self-Preſervation againſt the *nominal* Sufferings of Fines and Impriſonment, *&c.* I will forbear, promiſing my Readers, that in due Time, and on a more proper Occaſion, I will reſume the *merry Subject* of the *Letter*, and handle it to their entire Satisfaction.

And when I reſume *this Head*, I will begin where I before left off in my *Diſcourſes*

(9) *In his Dedication to the Queen.*

D

on

on *Miracles*; that is, with the Refurrection
of *Jefus*, which tho' I believe to have
been a miraculous Fact, that happen'd,
yet it was by no means timed and circumftanced, fo as eafily and readily to conciliate the Belief of Pofterity. God has
given to Man Reafon to judge of the Credibility of Events, and the Certainty of
Miracles: And if the Reafon of every Man
does not difapprove of the Management
of that Event, (fuppofing it has no figurative Meaning in it) I am much miftaken, when we come to ftate a Cafe, how
fuch a Miracle ought to be wrought and
conducted, to get and preferve the Credit of it.

Thus having told my Readers, why I
poftpone my *Firft Head*, I now enter upon the *Second*, which is

II. To fhew, that whether there be any
Senfe, Truth and Fact, or not, in the literal Stories of *Jefus's* Miracles, yet they
are all certainly typical Facts, and ought
to be allegorically interpreted, and will
receive a myfterious and more wonderful
Accomplifhment after the Manner, and
to the fame Purpofe, that the Fathers and
I do apply them, being no other (whether
actually wrought or not) than Figures,
Signs and Emblems of his future and myfterious Operations.

If

If the Authority of the Fathers would be admitted of, as decisive on *this Head*, there would soon be an End of all Controversy upon it. Give me Leave to recite some of their Testimonies to this Purpose, which I have heretofore urg'd in my *Discourses*. *Origen* says (10) That *Jesus*'s Works were *Symbols* of other Things to be done by his Power. St. *Hilary* (11) says, That *Jesus*'s Actions bore a Resemblance of what he would do hereafter. St. *Augustin* (12) says, That the Facts of *Jesus* are Signs of somewhat else to be done by him. And *Eusebius Gallicanus* (13) says, That our Saviour manifestly shews, that his Miracles are of a spiritual Signification, or in the Work of them he would not have done somewhat or other, that seems to want Sense and Reason. These few, out of a Multitude of Citations from the Fathers that might be produced, are sufficient to the Proof of the present Proposition, if their Authority might deter-

---

(10) Siquidem Symbola quædam erant, quæ tunc gerebantur, eorum quæ Jesu virtute semper perficiuntur. *In Matt.* C. xv.

(11) Peragunt Formam futuri Gesta præsentia. *In Matt.* C. xxi.

(12) Quæ a Jesu facta alicujus significantia erant. *In Serm.* lxxvii.

(13) Ipse Salvator noster apertissimè ostendit, quòd ejus miracula aliquid significent, dum ea faciendo aliquid agit, quod ratione carere videatur. *In Hom. quarta post Dominic. quartam.*

mine

mine our Dispute. And most pertinent
Citations they are too, tho' *Bishop Smalbroke* (14) says, *that even the Passages cited
by me from the Fathers, that are not falsified,
are impertinent* ; which is such an extravagant Stretch against the most glaring Truth,
that (to use the Bishop's (15) own Words
against himself) *it betrays a Mind lost to all
Sense of Modesty and Religion,* or he could
not have utter'd it.

And not only the Miracles of *Jesus* were
Signs and Figures of future Events; but,
according to *Origen,* (16) *every thing else
that he did:* From whence we may gather what was *Origen*'s Meaning, when
he said (17) *Christ*'s *first* Advent in the Flesh
is all Type and Shadow of his *second,* spiritual, and glorious Coming; which being
an *Opinion* that our *Clergy* are Strangers to,
I desire them to consider of it, and whether there is any Possibility of Truth in
it, because it is contrary to modern Conceptions about *Christ*'s *second* Advent.

(14) *In his Preface,* p. xi.
(15) *Ibid.* p. x.
(16) Similitudo erat & Typus futurorum unumquodque,
quod Jesus faciebat in Corpore. *In Isai.* C. vi.
(17) Adventus Christi unus quidem in Humilitate completus est, alius verò speratur in Gloria: Et hic primus Adventus in Carne, mystico quodam Sermone, in Scripturis sanctis
umbra ejus appellatur. *In Jesu Nave,* C. viii.

Nay

Nay further, according to the Fáthers, (18) the very Life and Miniſtry of *John the Baptiſt*, ſo far as it is recorded by the *Evangeliſts*, is Type and Figure of another's Miniſtry before Chriſt's ſpiritual Advent; and I am almoſt, if not altogether of the ſame Mind with them. It is beſide my preſent Buſineſs, to inſert here many of their Teſtimonies to this Purpoſe: But if the *Biſhop* of *St. David*'s would ſpare a little Time, which can't be better employ'd, and make a Collection of the Opinions of the Fathers about the *Baptiſt*'s Miniſtry, and print it, I dare ſay he'll thereupon preſent the learned World with the moſt ſurprizing Curioſity they ever were entertain'd with. Tho' it is improper for me to do ſuch a Work; yet I will here tell my *Readers* what will be the true Meaning of *John*'s *Preaching Repentance, for the Kingdom of Heaven is at Hand,* when his Miniſtry revives, *viz.* " It will
" be an Exhortation to Miniſters of the
" Letter, μετανοειν, to reconſider the Mat-
" ter and Error of their literal Expoſiti-
" ons, and to betake themſelves to ſpiri-
" tual and allegorical Interpretations of
" the Scriptures, in which allegorical and
" ſpiritual Senſes of them conſiſts the

(18) Pertingit ad uſque ſecundum & diviniorem Chriſti Adventum Johannis Teſtimonium. *Origen. in Lucam. Tom.* V.

" *King-*

" *Kingdom of Heaven.*" This I assert upon the Authority of *Origen,* (19) and if
the *Clergy* please to consult St. *Austin* and
others, they'll find them of the same Mind.
But, this by the by, having no more to
say to the Typicalness of *John*'s Ministry,
than whenever his foresaid mystical Preaching of Repentance shall revive, it can hardly be to a more viperous Generation of
Ecclesiastical *Scribes* and *Pharisees,* than are
the *Ministers* of the *Letter* at this present.

But against all these, and Ten Thousand more Testimonies of the Fathers for
the allegorical Interpretation of the Writings of the *Evangelists,* and of *Jesus's*
Miracles in particular, the *Bishop* of *St.
David*'s says, the Fathers are not of good
Authority in this Case, but, for all them,
who were Men of whimsical and volatile
Fancies, we ought to adhere to the *Letter* of the Story of *Christ*'s Life and Miracles. This the *Bishop* asserts roundly and
frequently in express or implicit Terms, as
his Readers may observe ; and I dare say,
the *Bishop* himself will not here charge me
with a Misrepresentation of his Opinion,

---

(19) Appropinquat enim Regnum Cœlorum, ut Scribæ
qui in simplici Littera acquiescunt, resipiscentes ab ejusmodi
Intellectu, erudiantur spirituali Doctrina, quæ est per Jesum
Christum, vivum Verbum, quæ vocatur Regnum Cœlorum.
In Matt. C. xiii.

tho'

tho', to spare Time and Paper, I quote not his own Words and large Paffages.

What Reafon does the *Bifhop* give, why the Authority of the Fathers for the allegorical Interpretation of the Evangelical Writings, and of *Jefus*'s Miracles, in particular, is not to be allow'd of? None at all. Does he quote fo much as a Canon of the Church, or a Vote in Convocation, or an Act of Parliament, or the confentient Opinion of all Proteftant *Writers* (which are the extrafcriptural Standards of modern Orthodoxy) for his Opinion? No. Does he then reject the Authority of the Fathers in all other Cafes, as well as in *this* before us? Nor this neither. He allows their Authority, (20) as they were good Perfons and credible Witneffes, " In Teftimony of *Facts*; "And about the Obfervation of the Lord's Day ; " And concerning the three Orders of the *Clergy* ; " And about the Government of the Church by Bifhops ; " And about the Books received into the Canon of the Scripture ;" But as for allegorical Interpretations of the Scriptures, they are of *little,* and (elfewhere) of *no* Authority. Who can forbear fmiling, unlefs the *Bifhop* had better *evinced* the Reafon of this Difference in their Au-

(20) P. 123, 124.

thority ?

thority ? If he had rejected their Authority in all Cases, he would have judged more equally and impartially of it.

In my Opinion, and I appeal to my *Readers*, whether it ben't their Opinion, that the *Bishop* had been an ingenuous and plain Dealer, if he had exprefs'd himfelf about the Authority of the Fathers in this following Manner, faying, " That the " Authority of the Fathers is good in *such* " and *such* Cases as aforefaid; becaufe " their Authority is agreeable enough to " the prefent Doctrine, Practice and Dif-" cipline of the Church: But the Autho-" rity of the Fathers is not good for the " allegorical Interpretation of the *New* " *Testament*, becaufe it is difagreeable to " our Prejudices, and becaufe their allego-" rical Expofitions of fome Miracles, if " they fhould receive fuch a Senfe, will " bring Shame and Reproach to our Mi-" niftry. Neither is the Authority of the " Fathers for Toleration, and againft Per-" fecution, good; becaufe it is deftructive " of Ecclefiaftical Power. Nor is the co-" pious Authority of the Fathers againft " Preaching for Hire, good; becaufe it " is averfe to our Interefts. Where the " Authority of the Fathers is agreeable to " our Interefts, Power, and Prejudices, " there will we be for the Authority of
" the

" the Fathers: But where the Fathers
" are againſt us, there will we be againſt
" them ; and why ſhould we not ?" This
is the true Senſe of the *Biſhop*, tho' he
is ſo unhappy as to want the Talent clearly and plainly to expreſs his Mind.

But, like many others, who can't write
Coherence, nor conſiſtently with themſelves ; ſo the *Biſhop*, for all his ſaying
that the allegorical Interpretations of
Scripture by the Fathers are of little or
no Authority, yet almoſt, if not altogether, contradicts himſelf, and grants as
much as I deſire, ſaying (21) thus, " With
" relation to any Expoſitions of Scripture
" made by the Fathers in early Times,
" they muſt be allow'd to have had *ſome*
" Advantage in being near to the Foun-
" tain itſelf." I ask for nothing more from
the Biſhop. Why do I contend for the
Authority of the Fathers as Interpreters
and Expoſitors? Only becauſe they lived
nearer to the Days of *Chriſt* and his Apoſtles, whoſe Mind and Will conſequently
they muſt needs know better, than we at
this Diſtance: And becauſe (what the
Biſhop elſewhere grants) thoſe primitive
Ages, as well as the Apoſtolical one, were
in ſome meaſure inſpired, upon the cre-

(21) *P.* 124

E   dible

dible Teſtimonies of *Origen*, *Irenæus*, and *Euſebius*, whoſe Words I ſhall not ſtay here to produce.

Hence then, in the Authority of the Fathers, I ſhould think, there is Foundation enough to build allegorical Interpretations on, and particularly to prove the literal Stories of Chriſt's Miracles to be Emblems of future and myſterious Operations; but all this will not do to pacify and ſtop the Mouths of my Gainſayers. This Controverſy is *pro Aris & Focis*, for the A L L of the Clergy that is dear to them ; and therefore they will ſhuffle and trifle for and againſt any Argument, rather than yield. Tho' the *Biſhop* of *St. David*'s above ſpeaks favourably of *Expoſitions made by the Fathers in early Times*, and may grant that the Church, in her firſt Ages was inſpired, yet he will ſtill wrangle againſt allegorical Interpretations, eſpecially ſuch as I have made on ſome Miracles; as for Inſtance, " On *Jeſus*'s driving the Buyers and Sellers out of the Temple; " On his precipitating the Swine with the Devils into the Sea ; " On his healing the Woman of an Iſſue of Blood; and the Woman of a Spirit of Infirmity, *&c.* becauſe the Intereſts and Reputations of the *Clergy*, as *Miniſters* of the *Letter*, are touch'd to the quick by them. So true

is

is that Saying of the *Bishop* of *London*, which deserves to be repeated, That " where there is an Unwillingness to part " with Prejudices and worldly Interests, " there must of Course be a *Desire* that the " Christian Religion (*which consists in the* " *Ministry of the Spirit*) should not be true; " and a *Willingness* to favour and embrace " any Argument that is brought against it, " and to cherish any Doubts and Scruples " that shall be rais'd concerning it.

What must I do here then, since no Authority, no, not the most primitive, will suffice in this Case? Why, I have nothing left to do, but absolutely to demonstrate, and make the Matter as plain as a *Pike-Staff*, that the Miracles of *Jesus* will certainly receive such a mysterious Accomplishment, as the Fathers and I have before-hand interpreted them in. Upon such a Demonstration, if the Mouths of my Adversaries are not stopt, yet the Eyes of all impartial *Readers* will be open'd to behold what a Heap of Impertinence the *Bishop* of *St. David*'s and others, have hitherto urg'd against me.

Now to demonstrate absolutely, that the Stories of *Jesus*'s Miracles will receive such a mysterious Accomplishment, as I, by the Help of the Fathers, have understood them in, I must do these *two* things.

E 2 *First,*

First, fhow, that the Old Teftament is to be allegorically interpreted, and is already in Part, and will be entirely fulfilled by *Jefus*, the true *Meffiah*, in an allegorical Senfe.   And thence

Secondly, Infer by a natural, obvious, and neceffary Confequence, that, what we vulgarly call the New Teftament is to be allegorically interpreted alfo, even in the Manner as I have underftood fome Parts of it.

The *Bifhop* of *St. David*'s allows, that there is better Authority, tho' not fufficient, for the Interpretation of the *Old Teftament* allegorically; but fuppofing it was better than it is, yet there is no Confequence that the *New* fhould be alfo allegorically interpreted. Behold his Words, for fear of a Charge of Mifreprefentation (22). " But befides this ill-founded
" Imitation of St. *Paul* (in allegorical In-
" terpretations of the *Old* Teftament)
" will his myftical Expofitions of any Paf-
" fages of the Old Teftament fupport their
" Pretenfions (meaning the Fathers and
" mine) to interpret the *New* in a like
" myftical manner? No, it will not.——
" And therefore (*after a little more Rea-*
" *foning againft this Confequence, he con-*

(22) P. 108.

" *cludes,*

" *cludes, that*) this Practice of *Origen* and
" other Fathers, that were myftical Ex-
" pofitors of the *New Teſtament*, was ve-
" ry precarious, and without Authority.
From which Words of the *Biſhop*, it is
plain, that his Opinion is, that whatever
Authority there may be for the allegorical
Interpretation of the *Old* Teſtament, there
is no Confequence to be thence drawn,
that the *New* is to be interpreted in a
like myftical manner. But in Anfwer to
the *Biſhop*, and in Confutation of his wild
and inconſiderate Affertion, I chufe to
treat on the two foregoing Particulars;
and the

Firſt is to fhow, that the *Old* Teſtament
is to be allegorically interpreted, and is already in Part, and will be entirely fulfilled
by *Jeſus* in an allegorical Senfe.

That the *Old* Teſtament is to be allegorically interpreted, I have Authority,
even ancient Authority enough, if that
would be allow'd to be fufficient to prove
my Point. We have Apoſtolical Authority and Example for it. The Paffages in
the Epiftles of St. *Paul* and *Barnabas* to
this Purpofe are numerous, and fo well
known, that I need not recite all, or any
of them. And from the Paffages in
St. *Paul*, that might be here produced,
the Fathers afferted and concluded from
his

his Authority, that the whole *Old* Testament was to be allegorized. This I believe the *Bishop* will grant, and spare me the Pains of Citations out of them. And if the *Bishop*, and my other *Adversaries*, were of the same Mind with the Fathers, on St. *Paul*'s Expressions in relation to allegorical Interpretations of the *Old* Testament, my present Dispute with them would be half over. And what is the Reason that the *Bishop* and others will not give into the Opinion of the Fathers on the Apostolical Passages to this Purpose? Because of their Prejudices to the *Letter* of the *Old Testament*, otherwise they would urge St. *Paul*'s Authority for the *Spirit* of it, as much as the Fathers or I can do. But being, I say, prepossess'd of *literal* Interpretations, and not discerning any Force and Truth in *spiritual* ones, they will not allow the mystical Expositions of Scripture by *Origen* and other Fathers, tho' made in Imitation of St. *Paul*, to be of good Authority. And therefore I must demonstrate to Sense and Reason, or Primitive and Apostolical Authority will stand me in no stead.

Again, If Authority for allegorical Interpretations of the *Old* Testament would avail any thing, there is ancienter, and I had like to have said *better*, Authority for them,

them, than *that* of the Fathers and Apoftles, *viz.* the Authority of the more ancient *Jews*. The Bifhop of *St. David's* (23)
fays, " The Chriftian Fathers (and why
" did he not fay the *Apoftles* too?) derived
this allegorical Practice from the Jewifh
" Interpreters." He owns (24) " that
" *Philo Judæus* was a great myftical Wri-
" ter, as his Works which are extant teftify;
and (25) confeffes that " there is Rea-
" fon to believe, that this myftical Way
" of expounding Scripture was of great-
" er Antiquity than *Philo* himfelf, even
" amongft the *Effens* and *Therapeuts*,
" whom *Philo* writes of, and who had
" amongft them feveral ancient Books of
" their Predeceffors or Founders, full of
" allegorical Interpretations." Thus far
the *Bifhop* fays well and truly. And what
Obfervation fhould he, as a Lover of Antiquity, have made hereupon? Should he
not have faid, *Id verius, quod prius*; the
older any Doctrine was, the more likely
to be true, in as much as Truth precedes
Error?

But could not the Bifhop have carry'd
his Story of the allegorical Interpretation
of the *Old Teftament* much higher? Yes,

(23) P. 93.
(94) P. 94.
(25) Ibid.

he

he might, and have told us what I do him
now, that the LXX Interpreters were *Allegorifts*, as appears from the Tranflation
itfelf, and from the Opinion of the ancient Jews and Fathers of the Church concerning them. And what's more ftill, he
might, as a Chriftian, upon the Authority of St. *Hilary* (26) have derived the allegorical Art of Interpretation from *Mofes*
himfelf, who received it from God, and
inftructed the *Seventy Elders* in it, from
whom it continued thro' all Ages of the
Jewifh and Chriftian Churches, without
Interruption, excepting that Oppofition
which the later *Caraites* of the Jews, and
Minifters of the *Letter* among Chriftians,
have made to it. If this be true, as I
firmly believe it, then the allegorical Method of Interpretation is of original and
divine Right. And it is reafonable to think
accordingly, that it is of *Mofaic* and *divine*
Extraction, or the Apoftles *Paul* and *Barnabas*, and the Fathers afterwards, had
never been permitted of God to countenance a Practice, in Imitation of the *Jews*,
if it was of a bafe, or of any other than
divine Original. The Confequence is, that

(26) Nam idem Mofes quamvis Veteris Teftamenti verba
in literis condidiffet, tamen feparatim quædam ex occultis
Legis fecretiora myfteria feptuaginta fenioribus, qui Doctores
deinceps manerent, intimaverat. *In Pfal. ii. Sect. i.*

we;

we at this Day ought to be allegorical
Interpreters of the *Old Testament*, or we
set ourselves against all Antiquity, and
oppose a Tradition that's like a Command, derived from *Moses* and God himself.

And what can the *Bishop* of St. *David's*
say to this Consequence ? Why, he'll tell
us, tho' the allegorical Method of Interpretation be as ancient as the *Therapeuts*
and some of their Predecessors, yet, whatever the *Jews* and Fathers may say of
its Antiquity, it came not from God and
Moses, or he would subscribe to it ; but
took its Rise, some Ages after the Giving
of the Law of *Moses*, tho' he knows not
how nor when. And I am willing the
Bishop should please himself with such an
Answer and Opinion, till I have absolutely demonstrated the Certainty of the allegorical Method, and thence made it manifest, that it is of Mosaick and divine
Original.

As to that other Account (27) of the
Original of mystical Interpretation of Scripture, or at least of the greater Progress
and Improvement of it, which the *Bishop*
out of *Porphyry* gives, by saying the Fathers
learned it of the gentile Philosophers, it

is the moſt ſenſeleſs and *unſcholarlike* Opinion that a Chriſtian can hold, and I was ſurpriſed to ſee it come from him. It is true that St. *Clement* of *Alexandria, Origen*, and others, were very converſant in the Writings of the *Greek* Philoſophers : And wherefore were they ſo? Was it to learn myſtical Theology of them? No, but, as St. *Jerom* (28) ſays, to confirm the Doctrines of our Religion, and to confute the *Gentiles* out of their own Books. For it was aſſerted by the Fathers, and confeſs'd by the *Gentile* Philoſophers, that the Mythology of the *Greeks*, the hieroglyphical Learning of the *Egyptians* and the Oneirocritiſm of the *Chaldæans*, was all borrowed from the *Hebrews*, and had their Riſe from the myſtical and allegorical Interpretation of the Scriptures, as ſhall be made manifeſt, if the *Biſhop* and I go on in this Controverſy : And *therefore* the Fathers ſtudied the Writings of the *Greeks*, and made the foreſaid Uſe of them in the Converſion of the *Gentiles ;* which the *Biſhop* can't but know, if he remembers at all, what he has read in St. *Clement* of *Alexandria*, and other Fathers. But this, by the by,

---

(28) *Origenes* decem ſcripſit Stromateas, omnia noſtræ religionis dogmata de *Platone, Ariſtotele, Numenio, Cornutoque* confirmans. *In Epiſt. ad Magnum.*

with a Hint to the *Bishop* to consider, whether he, who holds here with *Porphyry*, or I who hold with the Fathers, writes the most like an *Infidel.* So much then to the Accounts, which the *Bishop* of St. *David's* has given, of the Origine of the mystical Interpretation of Scripture.

The *Bishop* of *Litchfield,* who is to be looked on as a Writer in this Controversy, has a large *Chapter* against the allegorical Way of Interpretation. I shall comprise his Opinion in a few Words out of him. He says, (29) *he is not concerned to vindicate the Antiquity, ascribed by* Philo, *to the allegoric Way of writing, much less the Abuse it was carry'd to in After-Ages ; no, nor to defend, at all, this Manner of writing.* And as to St. *Paul*'s allegorizing the Scriptures, he says, (30) *It seems to be in compliance with the Demand of the Jewish Christians, who were affected with allegoric Interpretations, that St.* Paul *(who appears to have been no Fool) above all the other Apostles used that Way, which he was brought into against his own good liking.* And in another Place he says, (31) *The Laws and Facts recorded by* Moses, *are commonly interpreted to natural, moral, theo-*

(29) *Defence of Christianity,* p. 345.
(30) P. 347, 353, 358.
(31) P. 341.

F 2

logical

logical and even anagogick Senses, which no one supposed to have been ever in Moses's *Thoughts, or to be other than the Exercise of a subtle Wit, for the Instruction and Entertainment of the Hearers.* Whether this *Bishop* had his Wits about him, when he said, *No one supposed the anagogick Senses of the Law to have been ever in* Moses's *Thoughts,* I can't tell ; but if he had rubb'd up his Memory a little, he might have consider'd, what he says in another Place, (32) that the Anagogical was the accustomed Way of the whole Nation of the *Jews* from Moses's Time ; and he might have known what St. *Hilary,* whom I cited before, says, that *Moses* taught the Children of *Israel* the anagogical and allegorical Way ; and whatever he may think, *Origen* says, (33) that *Moses* by the Acuteness of his Understanding, penetrated into the mystical and anagogical Meaning of his own Law. And tho' this *Bishop* says above, that he is not concern'd to vindicate the Antiquity of the allegorick Way of writing ; yet I am oblig'd to vindicate its Antiquity and Truth, or I can't write a good *Defence of*

(32) P. 344.
(33) Perspicuum est Mosem mentis acie Legis Veritatem Historiarumque apud Scripturam Allegorias juxta Anagogen vidisse *In Johan. Tom.* VI.

Christianity, which should now bring me (to what I have undertaken) to make an absolute Demonstration of the Certainty of the allegorical Method of Interpretation, and of *Jesus*'s Messiahship upon it.

But before I enter upon a close Proof of this grand Undertaking, I must beg leave to tell my Readers a Story, which tho' it will for while defer my undertaken Demonstration, yet it is properly introductory to it. I had not long drawn up my foregoing Thoughts, (against the two Bishops, of *Litchfield* and St. *David*'s) of the Jewish and Christian Antiquity of the allegorical Method of Interpretation of Scripture, before I imparted them to my old Friend the *Jewish Rabbi*, who is a Cabalist and Allegorist, and desired his Sentiments upon them. Whereupon he was so kind as to send me the following Letter, with a pertinent Objection in it, against the Messiahship of the *Jesus* of our *Ministers* of the *Letter*; with a pertinent, I say, and lucky Objection, which paves the Way for my Demonstration of the Certainty of the allegorical Way of Interpretation, and of the Messiaship of the *Jesus* of us *Ministers* of the *Spirit*; and if I can but prevail upon the two forenamed *Bishops*, to give me their Assistance in answering the said Objection, by humouring

my

my Rabbi in it; we shall go a better Step, than has been hitherto taken, for the Conversion of the *Jews:* And this is Encouragement enough to such hearty Friends to Christianity as we are, to set about so great and glorious a Work. The Letter is as follows.

S I R,

AFTER condoling with you for the extraordinary Penalty that was laid on you for my Invective against *Jesus's* Miracle of *turning Water into Wine*, which, in my Opinion, you should not have been so heavily charg'd with, because it was purely *Cabalistical*, and contains in it nothing better or worse than the Conceptions that we *Jews* entertain of *Jesus* and his Miracles; I here send you my Thoughts on the short Account you have given of the Antiquity of the allegorical Method of the Interpretation of Scripture.

You and the Fathers of your Church are certainly in the right on't, to make it as old as *Moses*, agreeably to the Opinion, that we cabalistical *Jews* (34) at this Day entertain of it. If it was of

(34) Asseverant Judæi, deum Mosi primùm Legem scriptam tradidisse, atque hanc postea in longo illo Dierum 40 spatio, quo in monte apud se agebat Moses, exposuisse, ita ut singulorum præceptorum genuinum Sensum, Causas, & Fines tum Rationem quoque eadem adimplendi illi accurate declararet. *Apud Wagens. Tel. ignea.* p. 580.

later

later Date and original, your Adversaries
are oblig'd to assign the Time *when*, and
the Occasion *how*, such a surprising and
extraordinary Method of Interpretation
was introduced into the Jewish Nation.
If our Ancestors in the Days of God's
inspired Prophet, *Moses*, heard of none
but literal Senses of the Law, and if
neither he nor God himself ever intended
they should run into the allegorical Strain,
I ask when and what was *that Incident*
which turn'd the Heads of our ancient
Nation so religiously and devoutly to it?
I can easily conceive how it came to pass,
that the Sect of the *Caraites* amongst us
Jews, who now adhere to the Letter,
deserted mystical Interpretations; and
why your *Ministers* of the *Letter* have
forsaken them; and that was because they
don't relish nor apprehend those divine
Mysteries, which *your* and *our* ancient
Allegorists so much talk'd of, as veil'd and
latent under the Law of *Moses*. But if
this be a good Reason, why they have
forsaken the allegorical Method, it is a
much better Reason, why our Ancestors,
of themselves should never have taken
it up. And therefore it is plain to me,
that God and *Moses* upon the Institution
of the Law, at the same Time imparted
the allegorical Method; or it could never
after-

afterwards, *by chance*, have enter'd into the Heads of Men, who have hitherto dif-cern'd fo little Ufe and Fruits of it.

The Reafon why God by *Mofes* com-municated to the *Ifraelites*, and by his Providence fince has kept up the allego-rical Way of Interpretation of the Scrip-tures, was to prepare the World for the Reception of the *Meffiah*, who was to be the Accomplifher of them in an allego-rical Senfe ; and our Anceftors accordingly fo much excercifed their Thoughts in divine and myftical Contemplations on the Law ; becaufe, they fancied, they could thereby, as through *a Glafs darkly*, attain to fome glimmering Forefight of the Kingdom of the *Meffiah* : For you muft know, that our old Cabalifts (35) held (what your *Jefus* undertook to fulfil) that all Things that were written in the Law and the Prophets, were, *to a Tittle*, Type and Prophecy of the *Meffiah*, who would be fo far the clear Fulfiller and Illuftrater of them, as that Men would then fee God *Face to Face* : And, to be particular, they expected, in the firft Place, that the *Meffiah* would work the Redemp-tion of his Church after the fame manner, and by the like Signs and Wonders that

(35) See *Bafnage*'s Hiftory of the *Jews*, p. 189.

Mofes

Moses wrought the Deliverance of the *Israelites* out of *Egypt.*

Agreeable to these our old Opinions of the Scripture, and to our Expectations of a *Messiah*, did the Fathers of your Church endeavour to prove *Jesus*'s Messiahship, by an allegorical Explication and Application of the Law and the Prophets to him: But in as much as they labour'd in vain, proving little or nothing, this Way, to the Satisfaction of our old *Jews*; and in as much as your Priesthood have altogether given over this Way of Proof; we persist in our Disbelief of *Jesus*'s Messiahship, and expect another for the foresaid grand Purposes. Give me Leave here to make an Objection, founded on the concurrent and consentient Opinions of *your* Fathers and *our* Ancestors, against the Messiahship of *Jesus*, which if your Priests can answer, agreeably to their united Opinions, they will not only make a Convert of me, but open a Door for the Conversion of our whole Nation.

" It is agreed between us Jews, and
" you Christians (excepting two or three
" modern Commentators) that the Words
" of *Deuteronomy*, xviii. 18. *I will raise*
" *them up a Prophet from among their Bre-*
" *thren like unto thee*, are a Prophecy of the
" Messiah. From which Prophecy our

G   Ance-

" Anceſtors (36) look'd upon *Moſes* as a
" Type of the Meſſiah, *in all Things*, and
" expected that the *Meſſiah* at his coming
" would by way of Antitype, imitate and
" reſemble *Moſes* in all the Hiſtory of his
" Life, juſt as Face anſwereth to Face in
" a Glaſs, or as a Subſtance agrees to its
" Shadow.   And I am well aſſured that
" the Fathers of your Church accordingly
" held and believed, what they endea-
" voured to prove, that there was an ex-
" act Similitude between *Jeſus* in the
" Chriſtian Church, and *Moſes* in the
" Jewiſh.   Now if your Prieſthood can
" perfect that Proof, and ſhow me, either
" in a literal or allegorical Senſe, an ex-
" act Reſemblance, Correſpondence, and
" Likeneſs between them, I muſt of Ne-
" ceſſity turn Chriſtian.   It may be per-
" haps a Work of too large an Extent for
" them to ſhew this Agreement between
" *Jeſus* and *Moſes* in all and every Parti-
" cular; I will be content therefore, if they
" can ſhew me a Similitude between them
" in a ſmall Part of *Moſes*'s Life; as for
" Inſtance, in the Hiſtory of *Moſes*'s de-
" livering the *Iſraelites* out of *Egypt*.   It

(36) Doctioribus inter Judæos notiſſimum eſt, quod Mo-
ſes qui primus fuit Salvator Iſraelis, etiam in omni Vita &
Operibus ſuis fuerit Typus & Figura ultimi Redemptoris.
Chriſtiani Meyer de Gen. Chriſti, *p.* 145.

" was

" was moſt expreſſly the Opinion of our
" Anceſtors, that the Meſſiah would de-
" liver his People from Bondage, and, if
" I forget not, from *Roman* Bondage, after
" the Manner, and by the like Wonders,
" that *Moſes* delivered his People from
" *Egyptian.* *Jerom,* (37) a Father of your
" Church has recorded *this* as the uni-
" verſal Opinion of our Anceſtors, and
" and therefore you have the leſs Rea-
" ſon to queſtion it. And agreeably to
" this Opinion of our Anceſtors, the Fa-
" thers of your Church aſſerted, that *Chriſt*
" was ſuch a *Meſſiah,* and did deliver
" his Church from *Roman* Servitude,
" after the ſame Manner (in a Figure)
" that *Moſes* delivered his *Iſraelites* out of
" *Egypt.* Nay, your Apoſtle *Paul* (38)
" ſeems to aſſert it, ſaying, *Brethren, I*
" *would not, that ye ſhould be ignorant,*
" *how that all our Fathers were under the*
" *Cloud, and all paſſed through the Sea,*
" *aud were all baptized unto Moſes in the*
" *Cloud and in the Sea.* Now theſe things
" *were our Examples or Types.* In which

(37) Judæi veteres expectabant ſimilem Ægyptiacæ Liberationem, ut ſcilicet Pharoah & omnis ejus Exercitus qui
per 430 Annos Populum Dei captivu'm tenuit, in mari ru-
bro ſubmerſus eſt; ſic etiam Romani qui eodem Annorum
numero Judæos poſſeſſuri, ultione Domini deleantur. *In*
Joelis C. iii.

(38) 1 Cor. *C.* x, 1, 2, 6.

" Words

" Words *Paul* apparently alludes to, and
" confirms the Opinion of our Ancestors,
" which he had imbibed before his Con-
" version; and intimates that *Jesus*, whom
" he took for the *Messiah*, was working a
" Redemption of his Church after the
" Manner of the Deliverance of the *Israe-*
" *lites* out of *Egypt.* And so did your
" Fathers understand these Words of
" *Paul,* and accordingly many of them
" labour'd to shew the Similitude between
" the *Israelitish* and *Christian* Redemption,
" in order to the Conversion of the *Jews.*
" But they, it seems, labour'd in vain,
" shewing no tolerable nor visible Like-
" ness of this sort between *Jesus* and
" *Moses*; and therefore our Nation to this
" Day continues in Disbelief of *Jesus*'s
" Messiahship. However, we have not
" so pertinaciously rejected *Jesus*'s Messi-
" ahship, as not to give you Leave to
" resume the old Argument of it, from
" his Likeness to *Moses* in all things. If
" your *Priests* can now show a Likeness
" between them; if they can at this Day
" prove that *Jesus* wrought the like Mi-
" racles and Wonders (tho' in a figura-
" tive and allegorical Sense) for the Re-
" demption of his Church from *Roman*
" Servitude, as *Moses* did for the Delive-
" rance of *Israelites* out of *Egypt*, we
                                    " will

" will grant him to be the *Messiah*, and
" will believe in him. But as we despair
" of such a Proof, so we reasonably persist
" in our Disbelief of his Messiahship.
" Your *Divines* indeed, because of the
" foresaid Prophecy in *Deuteronomy*, do
" talk of a Likeness between *Moses* and
" *Jesus*; but it is not at all agreeable to
" the Sentiments of *your* Fathers, or the
" Expectations of *our* Ancestors concern-
" ing the *Messiah*'s Similitude to *Moses*.
" They tell us, that *Jesus* and *Moses* were
" alike, because both wrought Miracles;
" but this will not do, till they prove a
" Likeness between their Miracles, as to
" Number, Nature, Use and Circum-
" stance. The Miracles that the *Messiah*
" is to work, and which are to prove his
" Messiahship, must be of a similar Na-
" ture, and to the like Purpose that *Moses*'s
" were in *Egypt*, as *our* Ancestors assert-
" ed, and *your* Fathers granted: But since
" no such Similitude is shown to be be-
" tween them, we disown *Jesus*'s Messi-
" ahship, and appeal to the Reason and
" Understanding of all indifferent Judges
" in the Controversy, whether we are not
" in the right on't for so doing.

Thus, Sir, for the Use of your *Clergy*,
have I form'd an Objection against *Jesus*'s
Messiahship, an Objection that is founded

on the concurrent Opinions of *our* Ancestors and of *your* Fathers: And I shall with some Longings and Impatience wait till I hear what they have to say to it. The Objection, in my Opinion, absolutely destroys *Jesus*'s Pretences to the Messiahship, unless his *Priests*, by way of Answer to it, can prove the foresaid Similitude between him and *Moses*; between the Miracles of the One and the Miracles of the Other; between the Deliverance of the *Jewish* and the Redemption of the *Christian* Church, out of an *Egypt*.

I am thinking what your *Clergy* can say to the Objection. Will they deny, that it was the Opinion of both *your* Fathers and of *our* Ancestors, that there ought to be such a Similitude between the *Messiah* and *Moses*, as is before describ'd? That they can't do, because of the innumerable Testimonies to be produced out of them to confirm it. Will they then say, that it was a false and eroneous Opinion, which both ancient Jews and Fathers entertain'd concerning the *Messiah*? This surely they will not do; because of the Consequence, which charges the Apostle *Paul* himself (in the above-cited Place) and the primitive Christians, with the grossest Error and Mistake concerning

cerning *Jesus* and his Messiahship; **and**
yet I can't think they will ever give into
the joint Opinion aforesaid of both *Jews*
and Fathers; because of the Impossibility
of proving *Jesus* to be like *Moses in all
Things*, according to the literal Sense of
the Law, which they adhere to; and because of the Improbability of doing it, in
an allegorical Sense, after the Way of their
Fathers, or, in all this Time surely, the
Matter must have been made out, to the
Satisfaction and Conversion of our Nation.

I long, I tell you, to hear what your
Christian *Priesthood* will say to the Objection, which surely they will not let slip,
without their Remarks and Observations
upon it, any more than my Objections
against the literal Story of some of *Jesus*'s
Miracles. And this is your and my Comfort, that if you publish this present Objection against *Jesus*'s Messiahship, the
Clergy can't account it a ludicrous, profane, and blasphemous one (as they did
my others) and so bring you again under Prosecution for it : No, it is a plain,
serious, and reasonable Objection, founded on ancient Jewish and Ecclesiastical
Authority; and a pertinent, solid, and
rational Answer is expected to it.

Now the Controversy about *Jesus*'s
Messiahship is thus far revived and com-
menced,

menced, let us, in God's Name, go on with it, till we come to a final Determination, either in the Demonftration, or Confutation of it. Your *Clergy*, can't, I think, for Shame, any more interrupt the free Courfe of the Controverfy, which will make us Jews fecretly infult and triumph over them; and not only confirm us in our Unbelief of *Jefus's* Meffiahfhip, but will occafion others to defert their Faith in him.

It's a ftrange thing to confider how your Priefthood have, in thefe latter Ages, managed the Controverfy between Jews and Chriftians, all by themfelves, furioufly difputing againft Adverfaries, whom they will not allow with Impunity to fpeak in their own Caufe: So do they make God, who is to decide the Controverfy, like an unjuft and partial Judge, that will hear only the Pleadings and Evidence on one Side of the Queftion.

But your *Clergy* will fay, that in their Writings againft the Jews, they make Objections for us as well as Anfwers for themfelves, and that's fufficient. Not fo, fay I, unlefs their Objections were as good and ftrong as we can make for our felves. But however, if your *Divines* fo pleafe, I will thus agree the Matter with them, *viz.* That they alone fhall make

Obje-

Objections for us, if they'll let us alone to make Answers for them, which is most just and equal; and then the World shall behold the most pleasant and comical *Farce* of a Controversy, they ever were entertain'd with.

I remember, that in my Letter, you published, against *Jesus's* Resurrection, I promised the Controversy between the *Jews* and *Christians*, by my Consent, should turn on that Miracle. Your *Clergy*, one or other of them, have answer'd that *Letter*: and so might expect to hear of my Conversion, if I had nothing to reply to them. My Reply you durst not publish, for fear of worldly Tribulation, and so I am free from that Promise. But now that you have fortunately given me an Occasion to make the more proper and substantial Objection against *Jesus's* Messiahship, herein contain'd, I hope it will be freely and fully debated and consider'd to the Determination of the Controversy between us. So wishing you Health and Happiness, I am *Yours*,

N. N.

So ends the Letter of my good old Friend, the Jewish *Rabbi*, which was a most seasonable and acceptable Present, in as much as the Objection, contain'd in

H

it,

it, will open a fair Way for me to prove, that the Stories of *Jesus*'s Miracles, as recorded in the Evangelists, are and ought to be allegorically understood, and will certainly receive such a mystical Accomplishment, as I, by the Help of the Fathers, have conceived of them. The *Bishop* of *St. David*'s, and my other Adversaries, may not, in all Probability, be aware of this Use to be made of the foresaid Objection; and I don't expect that on a sudden they should; but if they'll favour me with, what otherwise I'll endeavour to force them to, their Opinion and Debates about the foresaid Objection against *Jesus*'s Messiahship, they shall soon discern this Use and Consequence of it, that *Jesus*'s Miracles are not *literally* but *allegorically* to be understood, and will accordingly receive an Accomplishment.

I trust then, that the *Bishop* of *St. David*'s, who is principally concern'd, will, without more Importunity, favour me with his Opinion on the foregoing *Jewish* Objection, which may be done in a small Compass of Paper, either in *Print*, or in an *Epistle*.

I expect he should tell me plainly and expresly, whether it was really the joint Opinion of the ancient *Jews* and Fathers of the Church, as is asserted in the Objection,

jection, that the *Meſſiah* was to be a Prophet like *Moſes* in all things, in the whole
Hiſtory of his Life, and particularly with
regard to the miraculous Deliverance of
the *Iſraelites* out of *Egypt*. If the *Biſhop*
ſhould, what I humbly conceive he will
not, deny that it was the joint Opinion
of both *Jews* and Fathers, as is before
repreſented in the Objection, and ſhould
pretend to urge Reaſons and Authorities,
which he will hardly find, why ſuch a
Likeneſs and Agreement between the
Meſſiah and *Moſes* ought not to be look'd
for; then my *Rabbi* and I will confirm
the joint Opinion aforeſaid, with Citations, almoſt innumerable out of the *Jews*
and Fathers, till the *Biſhop* ſhall yield to
the Number and Clearneſs of them.

If the *Biſhop* ſhould own, what I am
almoſt perſuaded he will, that it was the
joint Opinion of Fathers and *Jews*, that
there ought to be ſuch a Similitude and
Harmony between the *Meſſiah* and *Moſes*,
as is repreſented above; but ſhould ſay,
that it was an erroneous and falſe Opinion, which the old Cabaliſtical *Jews*, by
chance, and unfortunately took up; and
which the Fathers, even the Apoſtle himſelf, unwarily and unhappily run into,
complying with an Opinion of the *Jews*
about the *Meſſiah*, without Conſideration

of

of the Weaknefs of it ; then I, with a little of my *Rabbi*'s Help, will further prove the Truth and Certainty of the faid Opinion, and demonftrate, that He can be no true Meffiah, who in the Hiftory of himfelf and of his Church does not exactly, *to a tittle*, correfpond to the Hiftory of *Mofes* and of his People.

But if the *Bifhop* fhould, what I am willing to hope he will, ingenuoufly confefs, there ought to be fuch an Agreement and Likenefs between *Mofes* and the *Meffiah* as is fignified in the Objection, then he and I will go heartily to Work, and for the Honour of *Jefus*, whom we believe to be the *Meffiah*, will abfolutely demonftrate the Similitude, there is between him and *Mofes* *in all Things*. And this, by the by, in the Opinion of our Fathers, is the *ONLY* Way to prove *Jefus*'s Meffiahfhip, *viz.* by his Refemblance to *Mofes*, and by his Accomplifhment of the Mofaick Types and Prophecy concerning him, who, upon his own Word, came to fulfil the Law and the Prophets *to a Tittle*.

If the *Bifhop* and I fhould be fo fortunate, and I truft in God we fhall, as to prove a moft apparent and manifeft Likenefs between *Jefus* and *Mofes*, even fuch a Likenefs as my *Rabbi* above demands, then

then shall we stop his Mouth, and soon pave a certain Way (which will be vast Honour to the *Bishop*) for the Conversion of the *Jews*.

I don't despair of the *Bishop*'s joint Labours and Endeavours with mine to so great and good a Work (for I can't think in my Heart, that he'll otherwise wrangle about the Objection above) so (if the *Bishop* pleases) we'll begin this Work with a Demonstration of the Likeness there is between the Redemption of the *Christian* Church, and the Deliverance of the *Israelitish* out of *Egypt*. Not only St. *Augustin* (39) hints that they who would show a Likeness between *Jesus* and *Moses*, ought to begin here; but thereby we shall humour my *Rabbi* in his Objection, who calls for (upon the concurrent Testimonies of *Jews* and Fathers) a Proof of such a Likeness between the Redemptions of the two Churches, or he shall think it reasonable still to persist in his Disbelief of *Jesus*'s Messiahship.

And if the *Bishop* and I should be so happy as to shew in an apparent Manner, this Similitude between the Redemption of the Jewish and Christian Church out

---

(39) Eloquar Propositiones sive Ænigmata ab Initio, id est, ex quo Populi Congregatio adducta est ex Ægypto. *In Ps.* lxxvii. *Sect.* 4.

of

of *Egypt*, then meeting with Succeſs in our Studies, will we proceed further, and illuſtrate other Prophecies of ſucceeding Times of the Church; for I will not part with the *Biſhop*, till he is able to travel by himſelf, in his Contemplations on the Law and the Prophets, and to behold, what with an ordinary *Teleſcope* at the Eyes of his Underſtanding he may diſcern, and ſhow to his Epiſcopal Brethren, *Chriſt* ſpiritually ſitting and coming on the Clouds of the *Letter* to the ſame Purpoſes that the old Jews, Fathers and Apoſtles ſay he is to come, *viz.* To open and illuſtrate the Parables and Ænigma's of the Scriptures, to reſtore Prophecy, to ſhew us God Face to Face; and to raiſe All from a ſpiritual Death to Life again. And bleſſed are all thoſe, who love and deſire ſuch his Appearance.

In my *Third Diſcourſe* on *Miracles*, I happen'd to ſpeak of *Chriſt's* ſecond and ſpiritual Advent on the Clouds of the Law and Prophets; and to ſay " that the " common Notion of his Coming on aeri- " al Clouds for the Reſurrection of dead " Bodies, *&c.* is the moſt ſenſeleſs and " unphiloſophical, that ever was taught " to Mankind;" which gave Offence to my *Biſhop*, who animadverted upon me for it; but if he ever get Sight, which I

don't

don't queſtion, of *Chriſt*'s Coming on the
metaphorical Clouds of Prophecy, he'll not
only be of my Mind here, but will be ſen-
ſible with me, that all or moſt of our ſy-
ſtematical Divinity, that is built on the
Letter of the Scriptures, is falſe and
groundleſs; and of that ill Tendency to
the Corruption of Mens Morals, that it is
not ſo much a Wonder, that wiſe, good,
and thinking *Gentlemen* are betaking themſelves to Natural Religion, as it is, that
there are any Belivers of Chriſtianity, upon the *Literal Scheme*, left among us. If
it had not been *Force*, more than *Reaſon*,
that has hitherto kept Mankind in their
Chriſtian Faith; or if Liberty had been
indulg'd them to conſider the Abſurdities
of the *Letter* of the Scriptures, they would
have run ere now, by Shoals, into Infidelity: But the allegorical Interpretation
(which the Cabaliſtical *Jews* (40) ſay, will
convert *Atheiſts*) will reduce Mankind to
the Belief of the inſpired Authority of the
Scriptures, by ſhewing them the perfect
Reaſon, the divine *Wiſdom*, and reſplen-
dent *Truth* of them; otherwiſe call'd the
Meſſiah, the χρισμα, the Spirit, or the
Chriſt of them, than *whom*, or than *which*
nothing can be more deſired by Philoſo-

(40) See *Baſnage*'s Hiſtory of the *Jews*, p. 189.

phers,

phers, to come for the spiritual Renova-
tion, Restoration, Resurrection and Illumination of Man; *consequently* and implicitly for the Work of those mystical Miracles, of which those wrought by *Christ*
in the Flesh are but Types and Figures.
Whether the *Bishop* of *St. David*'s be already apprised of this Consequence, I
can't tell; but if he rub his Intellects but
a little, he must needs apprehend the
Consequence of the foresaid spiritual Advent of *Christ thus* far " That Ministers
of the Letter then are certainly to be
turn'd out of the Church: " That the
Woman of the Church then will be cured of her Infirmity at the Spirit of Prophesy: " That the Eyes of Mankind, like
the blind Man's, will be then open'd to
see, what he has hitherto been dark about,
the Mystery of the Providence of God in
all Ages. And so of the mystical Accomplishment of the other Miracles, with a
little Application of Thought, may he
discern the Consequence. And when he
does so, then he will see too, what sort
of a Christian I am, whom our *Ecclesiasticks* have falsely accused, and unjustly
persecuted for Impiety, Profaneness, Blasphemy and Infidelity, only because I have
written against the *Letter* of *Jesus*'s Miracles, in order to turn Mens Heads to
the

the Confideration of their myftical Accomplifhment at *Chrift*'s fecond fpiritual and glorious Advent on the Clouds of the Law and the Prophets.

I have indeed written againft the *literal* Stories of *Jefus*'s Miracles, which I ftill naufeate and abominate the Confinement of Mens Thoughts to it; but if our *Clergy* would but a little bear with me, they fhall fee, I *alone* do Honour to their literal Stories, by making them beautiful Emblems of future and more wonderful Operations. I have indeed call'd *Jefus* an Impoftor, Juggler, Fortune-teller (and what not?) by way of Objection againft the *Letter* of his Miracles; but I *alone* fhall do him Honour, in thofe very Miracles, which he wrought in the Flefh, by proving him to be the Wifdom, as well as Power of God, and that *God was in him of a Truth*, and endued him with a divine Prefcience of Futurities, or he could not then have wrought fuch curious and admirable Models and Prefigurations of his myfterious Works at his *fecond* Advent.

Whether the *Bifhop* of *St. David*'s, and others, can as yet certainly difcern the forefaid Confequence of Chrift's myftical Accomplifhment of his Miracles upon his fpiritual Advent, I can't guefs; but if they'll favour me with their Opinion on

I

my

my *Rabbi*'s Objection above, which will lead us to the allegorical Interpretation of the Law, they shall soon clearly see it.

And now I would have the *Bishop* of *St. David*'s to compare *this Part* of my *Defence* with the *Third Chapter* of his *Vindication*, which treats *on the Practice of the Fathers in interpreting the Scriptures in a mystical and allegorical Method*, and consider whether He or I write the most like a Christian of an orthodox and primitive Faith and Practice. The *Bishop* says (41) " That it is certain, that without such " Assistance (*of the Spirit*) as St. *Paul* en-" joy'd, the mystical Expositions of the " Scripture by *Origen* and other Fathers, " tho' made in Imitation of St. *Paul*, have " no such Authority as that of St. *Paul* " stampt on them." What, in the Name of Wonder, does the *Bishop* here mean? Tho' St. *Paul* has not allegoriz'd the whole Law, but only some few Parts; yet he expressly says, often enough, that the whole is a *Figure* and *Shadow* of Things to come under *Christ*; and our Saviour himself, as the Fathers understood him, intimates often, that all Things that were written in the Law and the Prophets, are Types and Prophecy of him, and that he

(41) P. 108.

came

came to fulfil them *to a Tittle*. Is not
here Authority enough for the Fathers to
allegorize the whole Law and the Prophets, in order to fhew the Agreement
between the Type and Antitype; between
the Shadow and the Subftance; between
the Figure and the Thing figured; and
between the Prophecy and its Accomplifhment. And whether the Fathers, in their
allegorical Expofitions, rightly or not, hit
off the Senfe of the Prophecy; (for it muft
be confefs'd they varioufly allegorized *this*
and *that* Paffage of Scripture) yet it was
their and *our* Duty and Office, from the
Words of *Chrift*, and the Practice of the
Apoftle, to keep on in the allegorical Method, till an Harmony between the Prophecy and its Accomplifhment was made
moft clear.

The *Bifhop* fays in this his *Third Chapter*
of his *Vindication*, " That the Fathers
" and I have abufively cited this Paffage
" of St. *Paul*, *The Letter killeth, but the*
" *Spirit giveth Life*, in Juftification of our
" myftical Expofitions;" whereupon the
Bifhop gave us a large Explication out of
his own Head, on that whole Verfe; which
(becaufe of the Shallownefs of my own
Pate, or the Confufion of the Bifhop's)
I don't underftand, and much queftion,
whether the *Bifhop* underftands himfelf.

How-

However, I will here paraphraftically give my *Readers* the eafy, plain, and intelligible Senfe of the Fathers and my felf on that whole Verfe (42) thus, *Who hath made us able Minifters of the New Teftament, not of the Letter* [that is, not of the literal Senfe of the Law and the Prophets, which is the *Old* Teftament] *but of the Spirit ,* [that is, of the fpiritual Senfe of the Law and the Prophets, which is the *New* Teftament] *for* [as the Teftimony of *Jefus,* according to St. *John,* is the Spirit of Prophecy, fo] *the Letter* [that is, the literal Senfe of the Law and Prophets] *killeth* [that is, nulls the Teftimony of *Jefus* which is in them] *but the Spirit* [that is, the fpiritual Senfe of the Law and Prophets] *giveth Life* [to their prophetical Teftimony.] This is moft certainly the Senfe of the Fathers on this Text; and I believe the *Bifhop* will not gainfay it, tho' he may diflike it. Hence the Fathers, when they fpoke *properly* and not *vulgarly,* call'd the fpiritual Senfe of the Law and the Prophets, the (43) *New Teftament,* and afferted that there was or would be fuch an Agreement between the *Old* and *New* Teftament; that is, between the

(42) 2 *Cor.* iii. 6.
(43) Et non Litera Legis, fed ejus Spiritus, hoc eft, Novitas Teftamenti. *Tertull. contra Marcion.* Lib. V. C. 11.

Tefta-

Teſtament of the *Letter*, and the Teſtament of the *Spirit* of the Scriptures, as
that there would not be (44) one Tittle
in the *one*, that would not be conſonantly
fulfilled in the *other;* and ſo far as I already apprehend this Harmony between
theſe two Teſtaments, of the *Letter*, and
of the *Spirit*, I muſt needs ſay with *Origen* (45) that it's *pleaſant and raviſhing to
behold and contemplate it*, and hope in a
ſhort time to make the Biſhop of St. *David*'s a Partaker of the ſame Pleaſure. The
ſame right Notion had the Fathers of the
Goſpel of *Chriſt*, which they have of the
New Teſtament. *Vulgarly* ſpeaking, the
Writings of the Evangeliſts, and of the
Apoſtles, were call'd the *Goſpel* of *Chriſt:*
But properly ſpeaking, Chriſt's *ſpiritual
Accompliſhment* of the Law was the *Goſpel:*
Hence is the Meaning of their frequent
ſaying, " That under the Law the Goſ-
pel was vail'd, and under the Goſpel the
Law was reveal'd." Hence they ſaid,
" That thoſe Men had nothing of the
Goſpel, who underſtood not the Spirit of
the *Law*." Hence they ſaid, " The Goſ-

---

(44) Veteris Teſtamenti ad Novum tanta Congruentia, ut
Apex nullus, qui non conſonet, relinquetur. *Sti. Auguſtini de
Utilit. Credendi*, Sect. 9.

(45) Jucundum eſt iſtum Conſenſum intelligere circa con-
venientia duorum Teſtamentorum. *In Matt. Tract. 6.*

pel was hid to thofe, who had the Veil
of the *Letter* upon their Hearts in reading of the Old Teftament." Hence it
was too, that they faid, " That the Gofpel was but *in Part*, and that too in a
very *little Part*, reveal'd at *Chrift*'s firft
Coming; the full Revelation of it being
referv'd for his fecond and more glorious
Advent, which the World is now in great
Want of, for the curing of their fpiritual
Blindnefs, *Deafnefs*, and *Lamenefs*; that
is, for the Correction of their grofs Ignorance and Errors in Religion; for the
Healing of their Divifions; for the Manifeftation of Truth; for the Converfion of
Jews and *Gentiles*; and for the Reformation of the Manners of Mankind.

Dear *Jefu*, to what a fad Purpofe have
our Hired Priefthood and *Minifters* of the
Letter, of all Denominations, hitherto
ftudied and preach'd, even till they have
loft the true, primitive, and Apoftolical
Notion of " the *Gofpel*; " of *Revelation*;
and " of the *New Teftament* !

The Bifhop of *London* has of late publifh'd two *Paftoral Letters* on the Certainty, Neceffity, and Ufe of Revelation,
againft *Infidels*, particularly againft my
felf, whom he (God help his Underftanding!) takes for a Favourer of Infidelity :
And to do the *Man* Juftice, I believe he's
fincere,

fincere, and laments at his Heart the Un-belief of this Age: But however, when the true *Gospel*, otherwise call'd the *Revelation* of the Law and the Prophets, or the *New Teftament* (which will be fatal to the Miniftry of the Letter, and an hired Priefthood) fhall be republifhed, re-ftored, and repreach'd, I dare fay, with-out Cenforioufnefs, or pretending to a prophetick Spirit, that He, of all the In-habitants of *London* and *Weftminfter*, will be the greateft Enemy to it; and for no other Reafon than his own, " becaufe of " his Unwillingnefs to part with his " worldly Interefts, which will induce " him to embrace any Arguments againft " it, and to cherifh any Doubts and Scru-" ples concerning it.

Whether the Bifhop of St. *David*'s in-tends to proceed in this Controverfy againft me, as he has begun, I know not. He promifed us his *Second Volume* laft Winter, but has adjourn'd the Publica-tion of it to the next, and I am apt to think he'll defer it to *latter Lammas* : For being, I fuppofe, fenfible, that his *Firft Volume* is built on the falfe Bottom of my fuppofed Infidelity, he'll hardly trouble the World with another of that kind. But however, I'll not releafe him out of the Controverfy. I fhall infift upon his

letting

letting me know his Opinion on my *Rab-bi's* Objection againſt *Jeſus's* Meſſiahſhip, herein contain'd, which if he'll favour me with, I'll forgive him all the Virulence, and paſs by all the Impertinence (to ſay no worſe) of his *Vindication:* Otherwiſe I ſhall be tempted to do an unpleaſant Work to myſelf, as well as an ungrateful one to him; that is, further to expoſtulate with him for his falſe Accuſations, Miſ-repreſentations, and other ill Uſage of me.

When I review my *Diſcourſes* on *Mi-racles,* and conſider not only their viſible Tendency to the Proof of *Jeſus's* Meſſi-ahſhip, but my ſolemn Declarations of the Belief of Chriſtianity; I wonder that ſuch a Number of Writers againſt me ſhould all of them (excepting Mr. *Lau-rence* (46) whom I here thank and praiſe for his Ingenuity) take me for an Infidel. I don't indeed much wonder, that the inferior Tribe of *Levi* (ſuch is their egre-gious Ignorance!) ſhould take me for one; but that ſuch preſumed great *Scholars,* as are the Biſhops of *London* and St. *David's,* ſhould ſo miſtake me, is aſtoniſhing. And I am not as yet fully ſatisfied, whether it be their *Ignorance* or their *Malice,* thus

(46) *In his Expoſtulatory Letter to Mr.* Woolſton.

to

to accufe me of Infidelity: If it was really *Ignorance* in them, they'll foon be convinced of their Error; and then, like good Chriftians, they'll make me Satifaction for the Injuries done me. But if it was *Malice*, and in Revenge on me for writing fo much againft an *Hired-Priefthood*, then they'll go on, and *die hard*, without any Remorfe for the Troubles, Sufferings and Expences they have put me to.

As I am really a Chriftian, and fhall, by God's Help, demonftrate the Meffiahfhip of *Jefus*, to which my *Difcourfes* on his *Miracles* were fubfervient; fo I will make bold to tell the *Bifhops* concern'd, that I am as certainly perfecuted, as ever any Chriftian was fince the Days of the Apoftles: And they will do well to confider, whether they have not everlaftingly difgraced themfelves, and done fome Difhonour to the beft Civil Adminiftration, that ever Nation was blefs'd with, by engaging them in the Perfecution of the moft fincere Advocate for the Truth of Chriftianity, that ever fet Pen to Paper.

I am fo far from being an Infidel, that, notwithftanding my *Difcourfes* on *Miracles*, I am an implicit Believer, and moft devout Admirer of Doctrines, Hiftorical Facts, and Traditions of the primitive

K   Church,

Church, adhering to many Notions of the Fathers, besides their allegorical Scheme (as will be seen in the Sequel of this Controversy) which the *Divines* of these last Ages have rejected, as so many Weaknesses and Mistakes in them. And when I come more fully to open my Mind, it will be well if the *Clergy* don't change their *Note* about me; and instead of accusing me of Infidelity, ridicule me for too much Credulity, and even Superstition; or I would not espouse *such* and *such* Doctrines and Traditions, which all learned and Protestant *Criticks* have discarded. Some of these old Notions I'll keep to myself, for fear of being over-much laught at by the *Clergy* for them, but others upon Occasion I will divulge; and don't care if I tell my *Readers* here one of them, thus:

" The Fathers intimate that *Ministers*
" of the *Letter* are Worshippers of the
" Apocalyptical *Beast*, or *Anti-Christ*;
" and that *that Beast* of a God, old *Baal*,
" was a Type of *Anti Christ*." This their Opinion I found hard to digest; but if there be any Truth in it, it can't be unlawful to jest a little with his Priests, or to ridicule their nonsensical, foolish and absurd Doctrines, founded on the *Letter*.

But

But let my Theological Notions and Speculations be of what kind foever; what Harm can my Arguings for them do to the Community? None at all. If they are not of God, they will come to nought fooner and better than by a Perfecution of me for them. But if they are of God, they will ftand and prevail againft all Oppofition of the *Clergy,* who will lofe their Reputation, if they take any other Meafures, than what Reafon and Religion do allow of, to fupprefs them.

My earneft Requeft then to the *Clergy* is, that under the Debate I am like to have with them, they would be pleafed to keep their Temper; or wife and impartial By-ftanders will fay, that it's more for their Interefts than the Truth, that they are zealous and furious.

I am not afraid of another Profecution at Law, becaufe I already have, or foon fhall cut off all Pretences to it, by clearing myfelf of all Sufpicions of Infidelity; but, for all that, I am more apprehenfive of the Rage and Indignation of the *Clergy,* than if I had been a downright *Atheift.* No *Atheift* or *Deift* is or can be of that dangerous Confequence to the modern Priefthood, as the Chriftian Allegorift. Againft the Growth of Deifm and Atheifm, the *Clergy* may be able for fome

time

time to maintain their Ground; but upon the Revival of the *Miniſtry* of the *Spirit* of the Law and the Prophets, they
can't ſtand long. And if I ſhould demon-
ſtrate, what I have undertaken, the Certainty of the allegorical Scheme, and *Jeſus*'s Meſſiahſhip upon it; tho' *Jews* and
Infidels then will be ready to rejoice, yet
Miniſters of the Letter, notwithſtanding
their pretended Love to, and Faith in
Jeſus, will be enraged; and it will be
well, if I don't feel the Weight of their
Diſpleaſure and Reſentment. If that fooliſh old *Dotard*, Mr. *Ayſcough* (47) the
Rector of St. *Olave*'s, *Southwark*, could
find in his Heart to inſtigate the Mob to
*drag me through the Streets, and throw me
into ſome Repoſitory of Filth and Naſtineſs,*
what may I not dread from young hot-
headed *Prieſts*, upon the Performance of
what is here undertaken? But I hope our
pious and good *Biſhops*, notwithſtanding
the Danger of their *Thouſands* a Year,
will be my Safeguard.

After all, it is a ſad and melancholick
Conſideration, that the Underſtandings of
Mankind, eſpecially of the Wiſe, Thinking and Philoſophical Part of them, ſhould
be enſlaved to the Intereſts of Eccleſiaſti-

---

(47) *In his* Lent Sermon *at St.* Saviour's, Anno 1729.

cal

cal *Clodpates,* who for the fake of *Mammon* more than *Truth,* are furious and turbulent; otherwife any Opinions in Religion might be profefs'd, confiftently with the Peace of the Publick; and any Speculations publifh'd without Animofities and Moleftations.

What Courfe can be taken with the *Clergy,* to perfuade them to Patience and Forbearance, whilft I prove them to be the moft ftupid Sect of Philofophers, who have amongft them the feweft Rudiments of true Philofphy, and even of the Gofpel, of any Sect the World ever knew? It's faid, there is nothing fo abfurd, which fome of the old Philophers have not held; but there is nothing, for Abfurdity, equal to this Belief, that the *Bible,* for its literal Story, is the Word of God, and given by Infpiration of him.

The *Bifhop* of *St. David*'s complains (48) of my unmannerly Behaviour towards my Ecclefiaftical Superiors; and I muft confefs, I am no body at that low and *Right Reverend* Bow, that he is fam'd for, or I might have put in for a *Bifhoprick* before now: But if our *Bifhops* and *Clergy* will be pleafed to keep their Temper, till I get to the End of this Controverfy, I'll

(48) *In his Preface,* p. xvii.

pass such Compliments upon them for their good Humour and Learning too, if they deserve it, as they hardly ever met with.

To conclude, I have written as plainly and intelligibly as I can, in this *Part* of my *Defence*. If any one shall complain of Obscurity any where, I will, upon Intimation, endeavour to illustrate it. I have, in some Places, asserted Things upon the Authority of the Fathers, without producing their Testimonies, in Proof of them; but if any question, whether their Testimonies can be here or there urg'd, they shall, upon a proper Occasion, have Satisfaction given them. The Reason why I have sometimes omitted the Testimonies of the Fathers, where they might be look'd for, is because I study Brevity, intending never to publish at once a larger *Volume* than this present. And no body need question my Testimonies to be ready at Hand; because I have neither the Courage nor Confidence (like many others) to vent any new Doctrines out of my own Head. My Talent is only to illustrate what the Fathers have asserted; and tho' some would account me a Falsifier and Misrepresenter of primitive Authorities, my honest Endeavours shall be to turn the Hearts of our *Clergy*, who are like Children in Understanding, to the Fathers.

Fathers. I shall end all *seriously, gravely, calmly* and *sedately*, with the same Words that I began my *First Discourse* on *Miracles* with, saying, " If ever there was a " useful Controversy started or revived in " this Age of the Church, it is this about " the Messiahship of the Holy *Jesus*, " which the *Discourse of the Grounds*, &c. " has of late rais'd. I believe this Con- " troversy will end in the absolute De- " monstration of *Jesus's* Messiahship from " Prophecy, which is the only Way to " prove him to be the Messiah, that great " Prophet expected by the *Jews*, and pro- " mised under the old Testament." And whether Bishop *Smalbroke* or Mr. *Stackhouse* will believe me, or not, I do now solemnly declare, that what I have written in my *Discourses*, or shall write in these *Defences*, is with a View to, what I am persuaded I shall effect, the absolute Demonstration of the Messiahship of the Holy *Jesus*, to whom be Glory for ever and ever. *Amen.*

F I N I S.

BOOKS written by Mr. WOOLSTON,
and sold by him next Door to the Star
in Aldermanbury, *and by the Booksellers
of* London *and* Westminster.